COWA!

Paifu Goes on an Errand

FRIGHT 1

BIRDSTUDIO

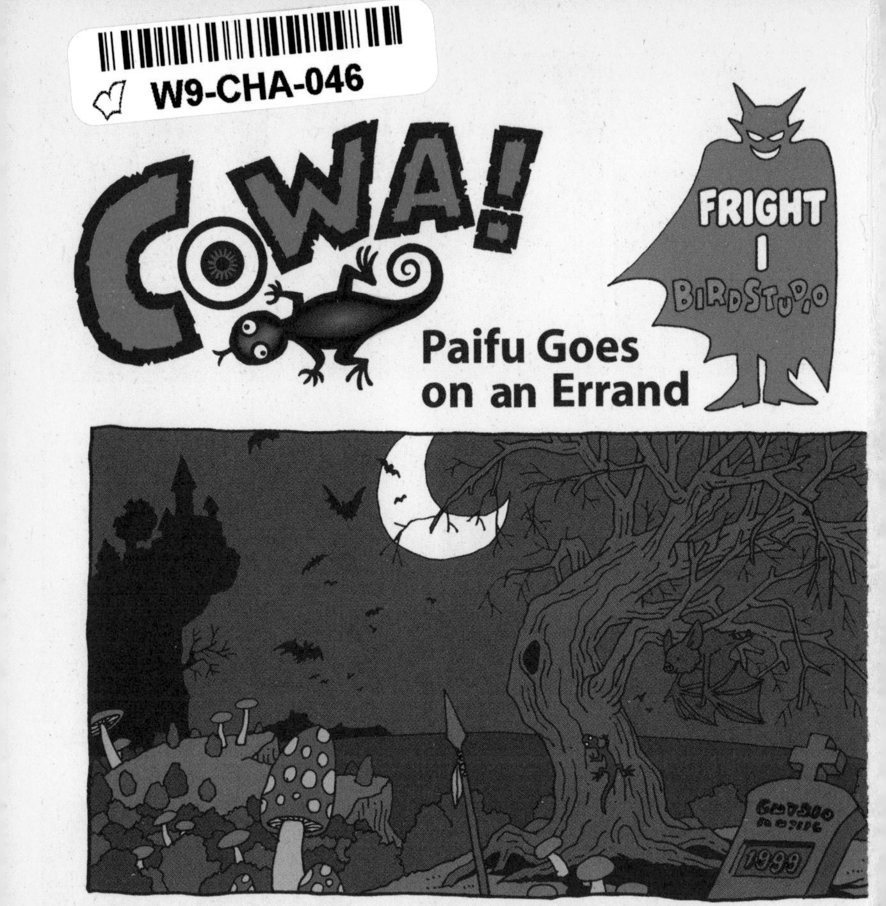

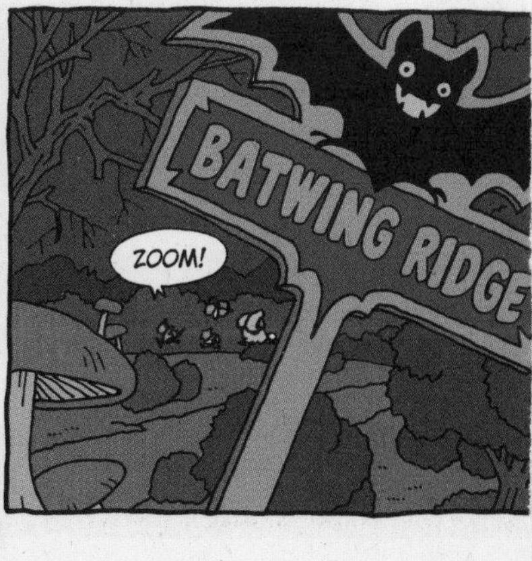
BATWING RIDGE
ZOOM!

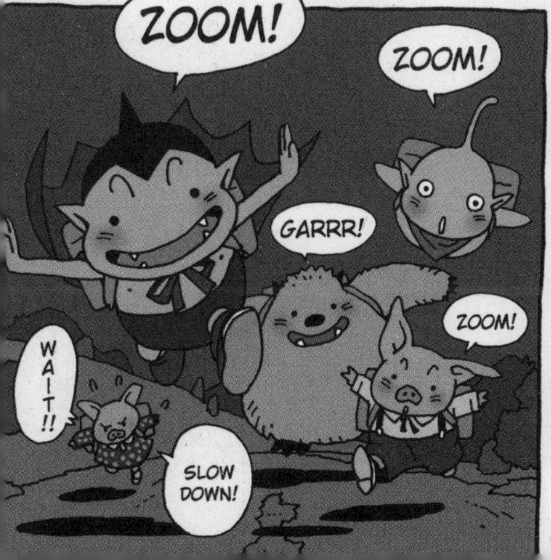
ZOOM!
ZOOM!
GARRR!
ZOOM!
WAIT!!
SLOW DOWN!

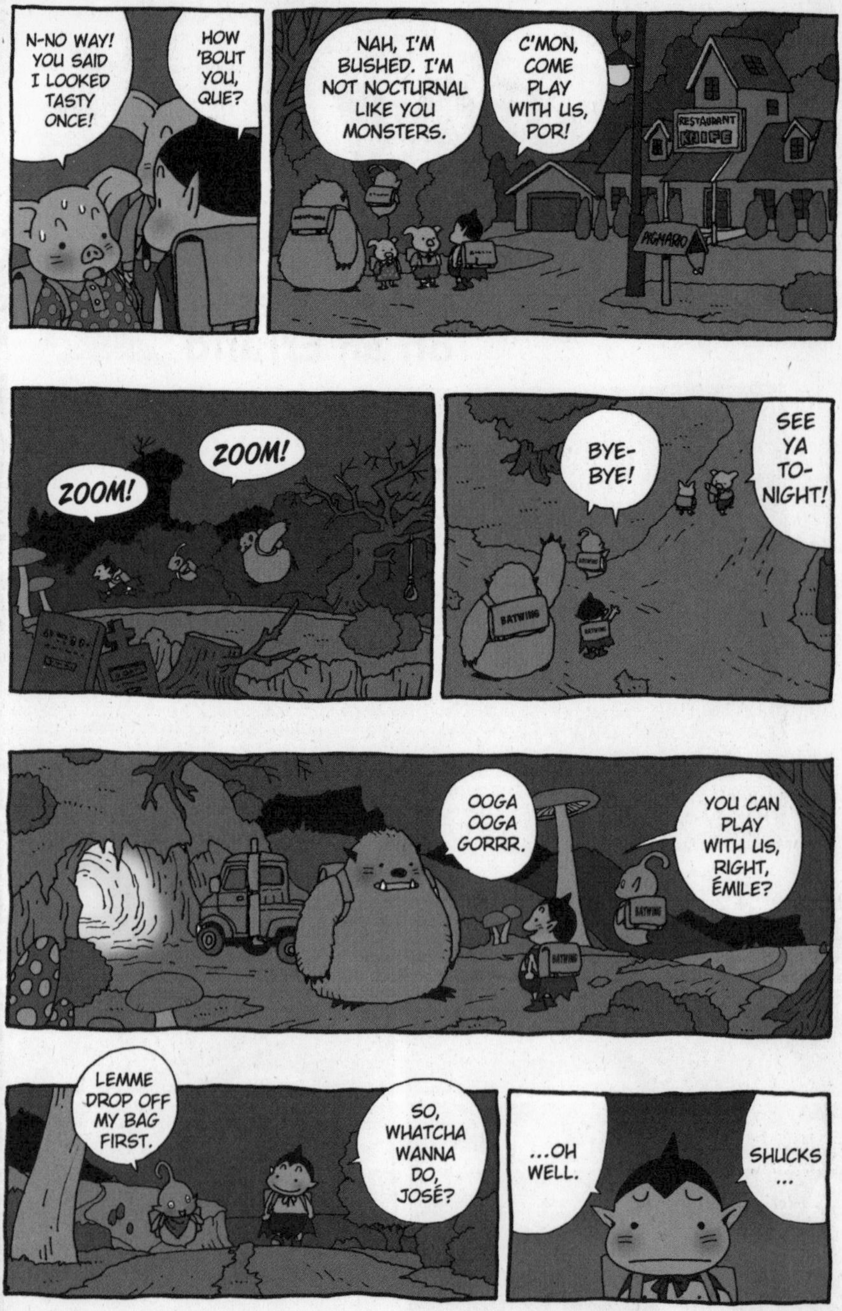
RESTAURANT KNIFE
PIGMARIO
C'MON, COME PLAY WITH US, POR!
NAH, I'M BUSHED. I'M NOT NOCTURNAL LIKE YOU MONSTERS.
HOW 'BOUT YOU, QUE?
N-NO WAY! YOU SAID I LOOKED TASTY ONCE!
SEE YA TO-NIGHT!
BYE-BYE!
BATWING
ZOOM!
ZOOM!
YOU CAN PLAY WITH US, RIGHT, ÉMILE?
OOGA OOGA GORRR.
SHUCKS ...
...OH WELL.
SO, WHATCHA WANNA DO, JOSÉ?
LEMME DROP OFF MY BAG FIRST.

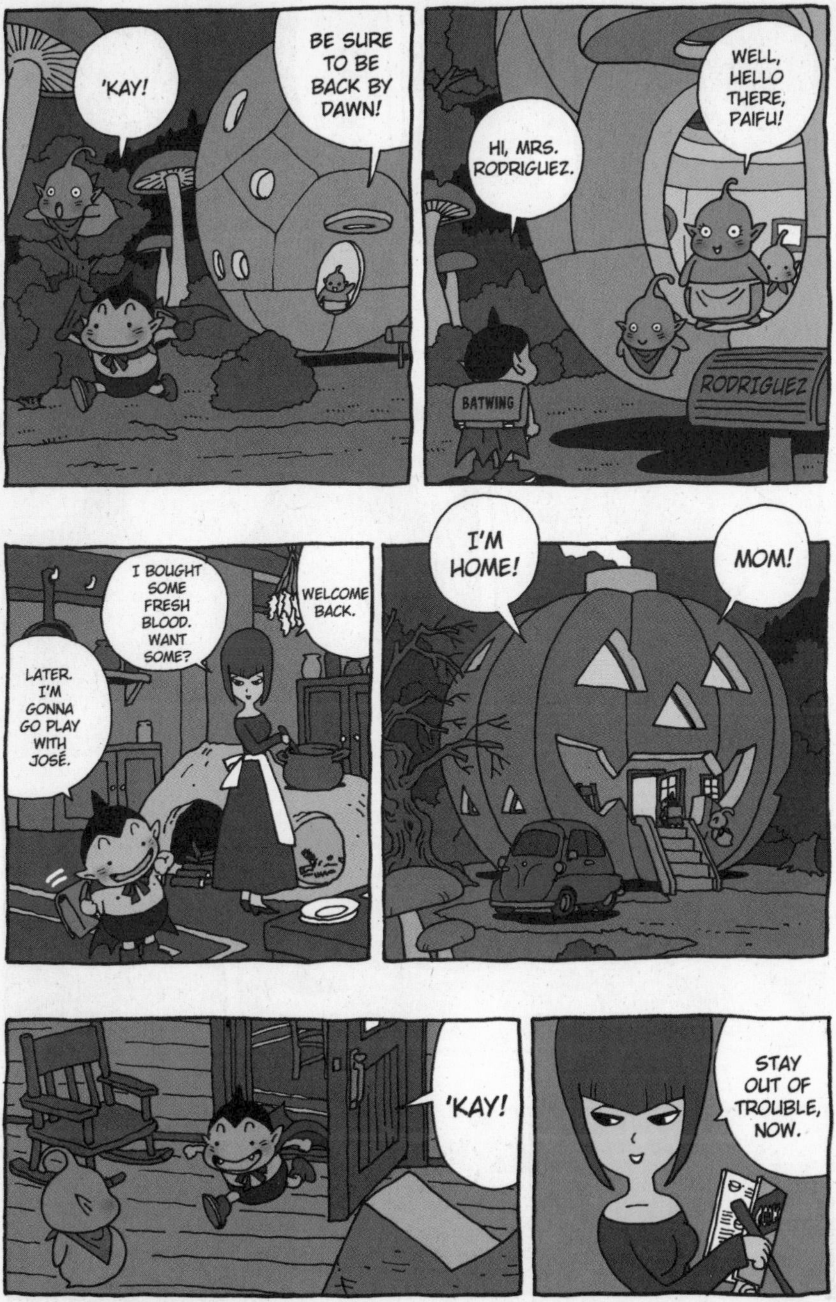
WELL, HELLO THERE, PAIFU!
HI, MRS. RODRIGUEZ.
RODRIGUEZ
BATWING
BE SURE TO BE BACK BY DAWN!
'KAY!
MOM!
I'M HOME!
WELCOME BACK.
I BOUGHT SOME FRESH BLOOD. WANT SOME?
LATER. I'M GONNA GO PLAY WITH JOSÉ.
STAY OUT OF TROUBLE, NOW.
'KAY!

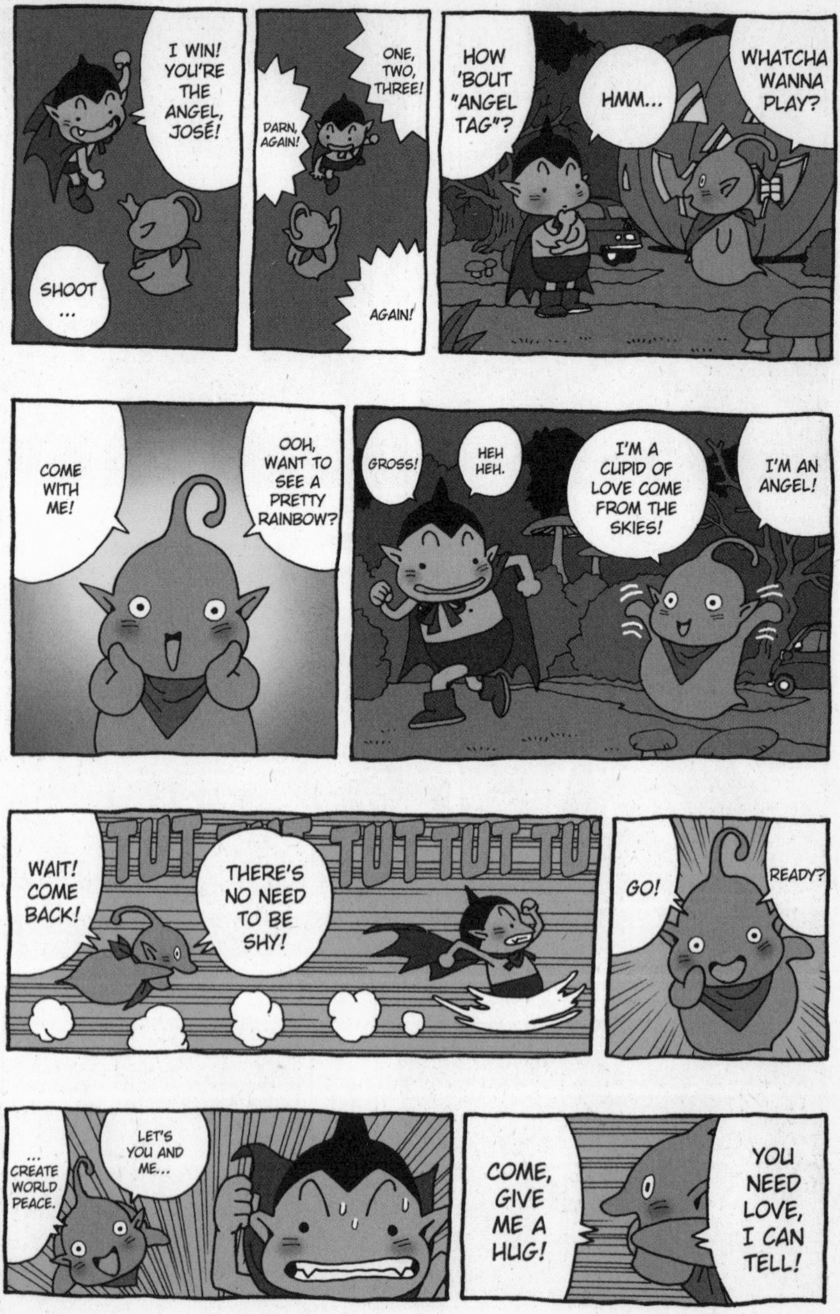
WHATCHA WANNA PLAY?
HMM...
HOW 'BOUT "ANGEL TAG"?
ONE, TWO, THREE!
DARN, AGAIN!
AGAIN!
I WIN! YOU'RE THE ANGEL, JOSÉ!
SHOOT ...
I'M AN ANGEL!
I'M A CUPID OF LOVE COME FROM THE SKIES!
HEH HEH.
GROSS!
OOH, WANT TO SEE A PRETTY RAINBOW?
COME WITH ME!
READY?
GO!
TUT TUT TUT TUT
THERE'S NO NEED TO BE SHY!
WAIT! COME BACK!
YOU NEED LOVE, I CAN TELL!
COME, GIVE ME A HUG!
LET'S YOU AND ME...
... CREATE WORLD PEACE.

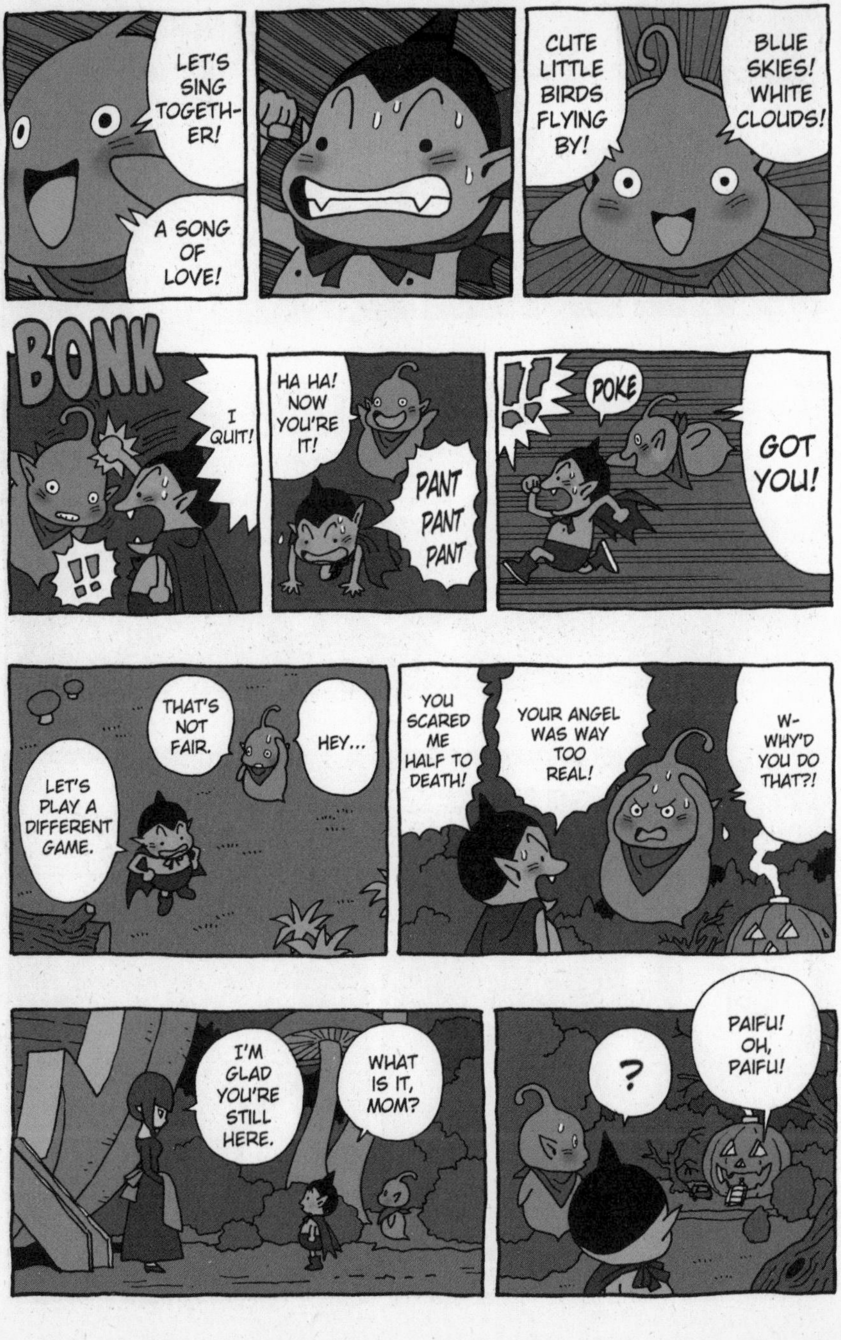
BLUE SKIES! WHITE CLOUDS!
CUTE LITTLE BIRDS FLYING BY!
LET'S SING TOGETH-ER!
A SONG OF LOVE!
GOT YOU!
POKE
!!
HA HA! NOW YOU'RE IT!
PANT PANT PANT
BONK
I QUIT!
!!
W- WHY'D YOU DO THAT?!
YOUR ANGEL WAS WAY TOO REAL!
YOU SCARED ME HALF TO DEATH!
HEY...
THAT'S NOT FAIR.
LET'S PLAY A DIFFERENT GAME.
PAIFU! OH, PAIFU!
?
WHAT IS IT, MOM?
I'M GLAD YOU'RE STILL HERE.

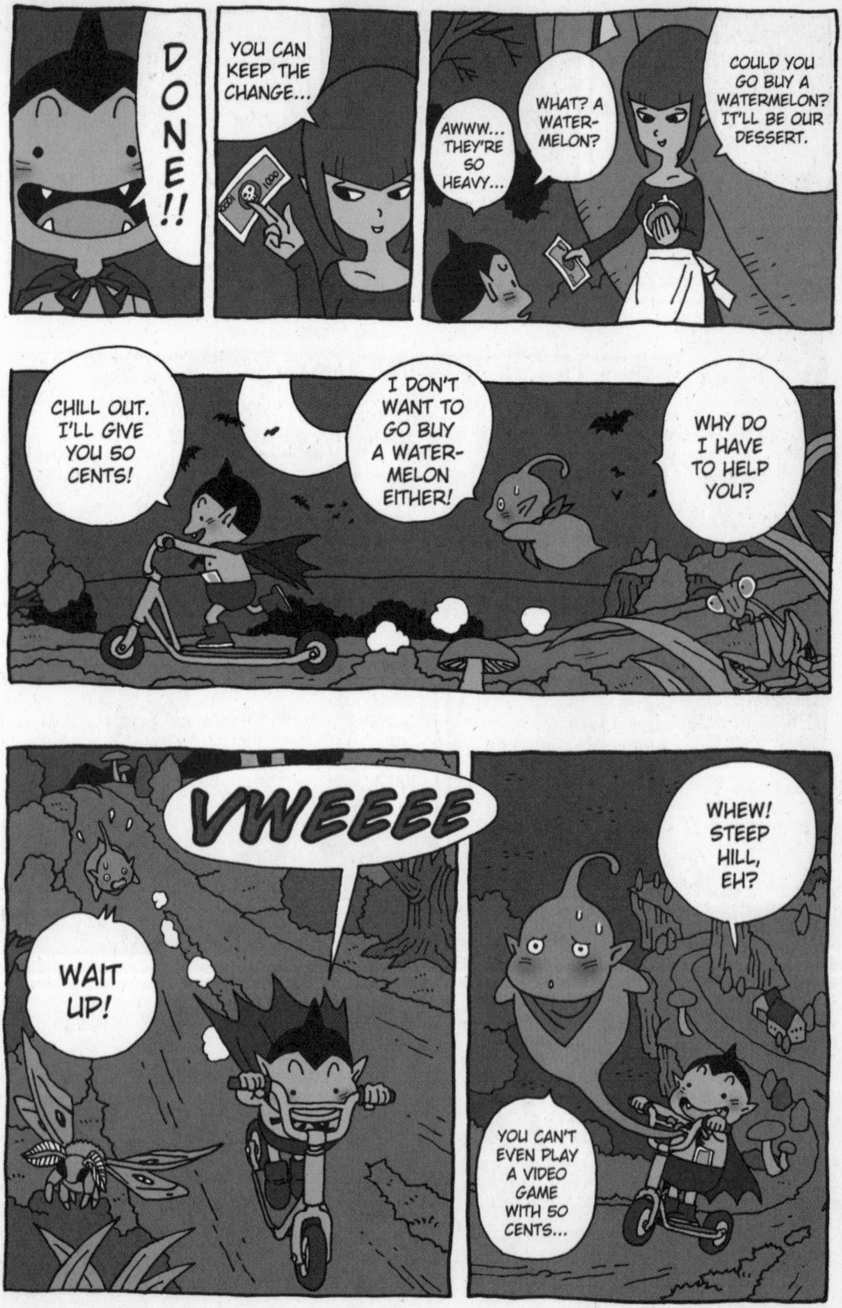
COULD YOU GO BUY A WATERMELON? IT'LL BE OUR DESSERT.
WHAT? A WATER-MELON?
AWWW... THEY'RE SO HEAVY...
YOU CAN KEEP THE CHANGE...
DONE!!
WHY DO I HAVE TO HELP YOU?
I DON'T WANT TO GO BUY A WATER-MELON EITHER!
CHILL OUT. I'LL GIVE YOU 50 CENTS!
WHEW! STEEP HILL, EH?
YOU CAN'T EVEN PLAY A VIDEO GAME WITH 50 CENTS...
VWEEEE
WAIT UP!

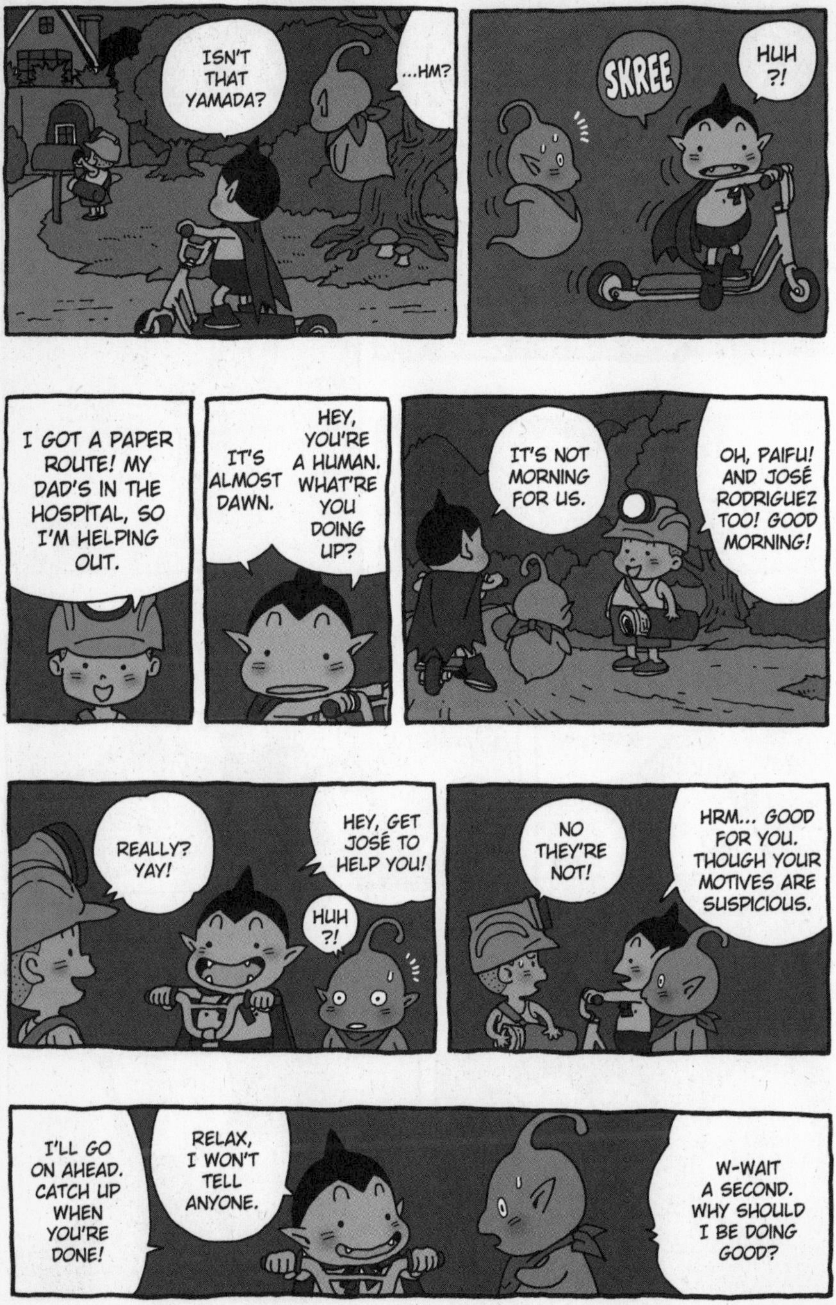
HUH ?!
SKREE
...HM?
ISN'T THAT YAMADA?
OH, PAIFU! AND JOSÉ RODRIGUEZ TOO! GOOD MORNING!
IT'S NOT MORNING FOR US.
HEY, YOU'RE A HUMAN. WHAT'RE YOU DOING UP?
IT'S ALMOST DAWN.
I GOT A PAPER ROUTE! MY DAD'S IN THE HOSPITAL, SO I'M HELPING OUT.
HRM... GOOD FOR YOU. THOUGH YOUR MOTIVES ARE SUSPICIOUS.
NO THEY'RE NOT!
HEY, GET JOSÉ TO HELP YOU!
REALLY? YAY!
HUH ?!
W-WAIT A SECOND. WHY SHOULD I BE DOING GOOD?
RELAX, I WON'T TELL ANYONE.
I'LL GO ON AHEAD. CATCH UP WHEN YOU'RE DONE!

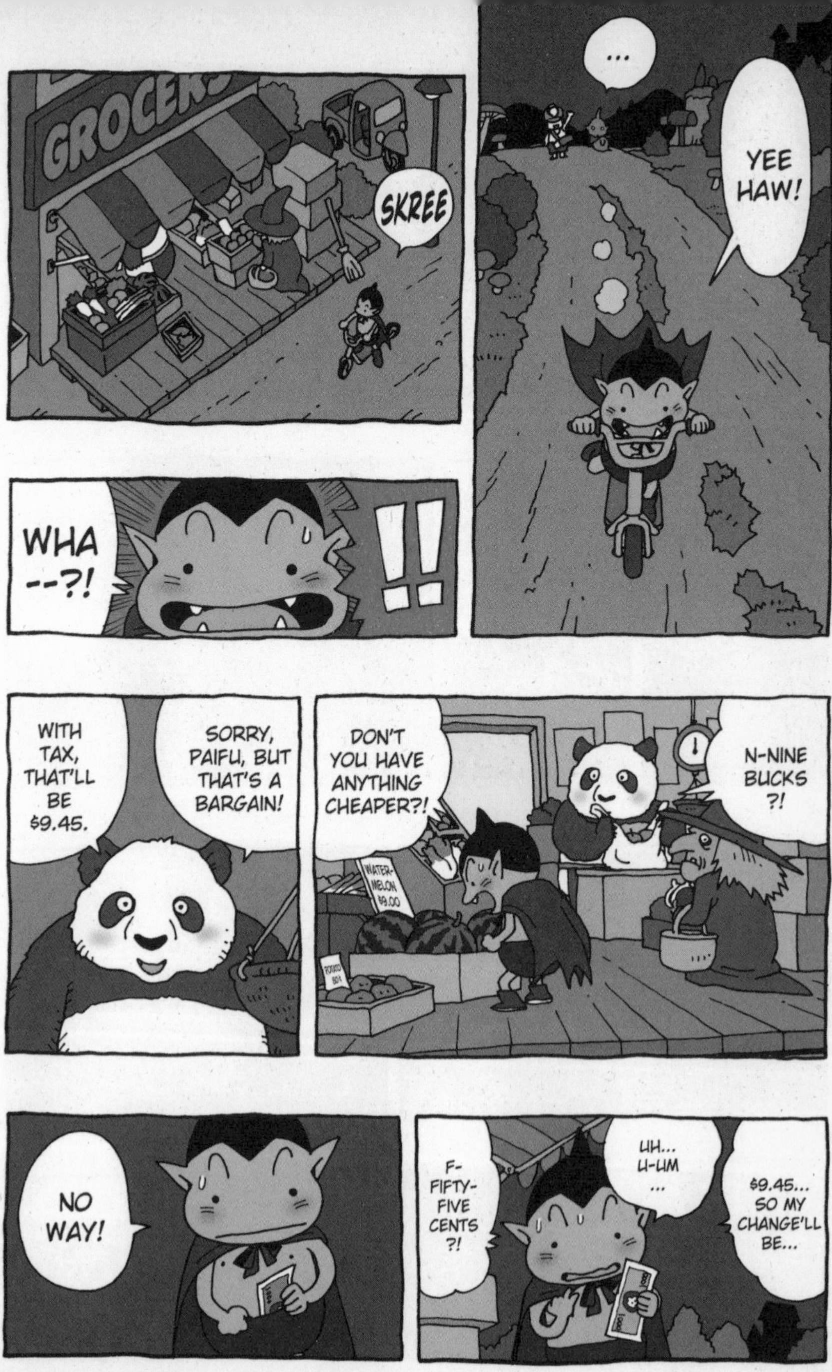
...
YEE HAW!
SKREE
WHA --?!
!!
N-NINE BUCKS ?!
DON'T YOU HAVE ANYTHING CHEAPER?!
WATER-MELON $9.00
SORRY, PAIFU, BUT THAT'S A BARGAIN!
WITH TAX, THAT'LL BE $9.45.
$9.45... SO MY CHANGE'LL BE...
UH... U-UM ...
F-FIFTY-FIVE CENTS ?!
NO WAY!

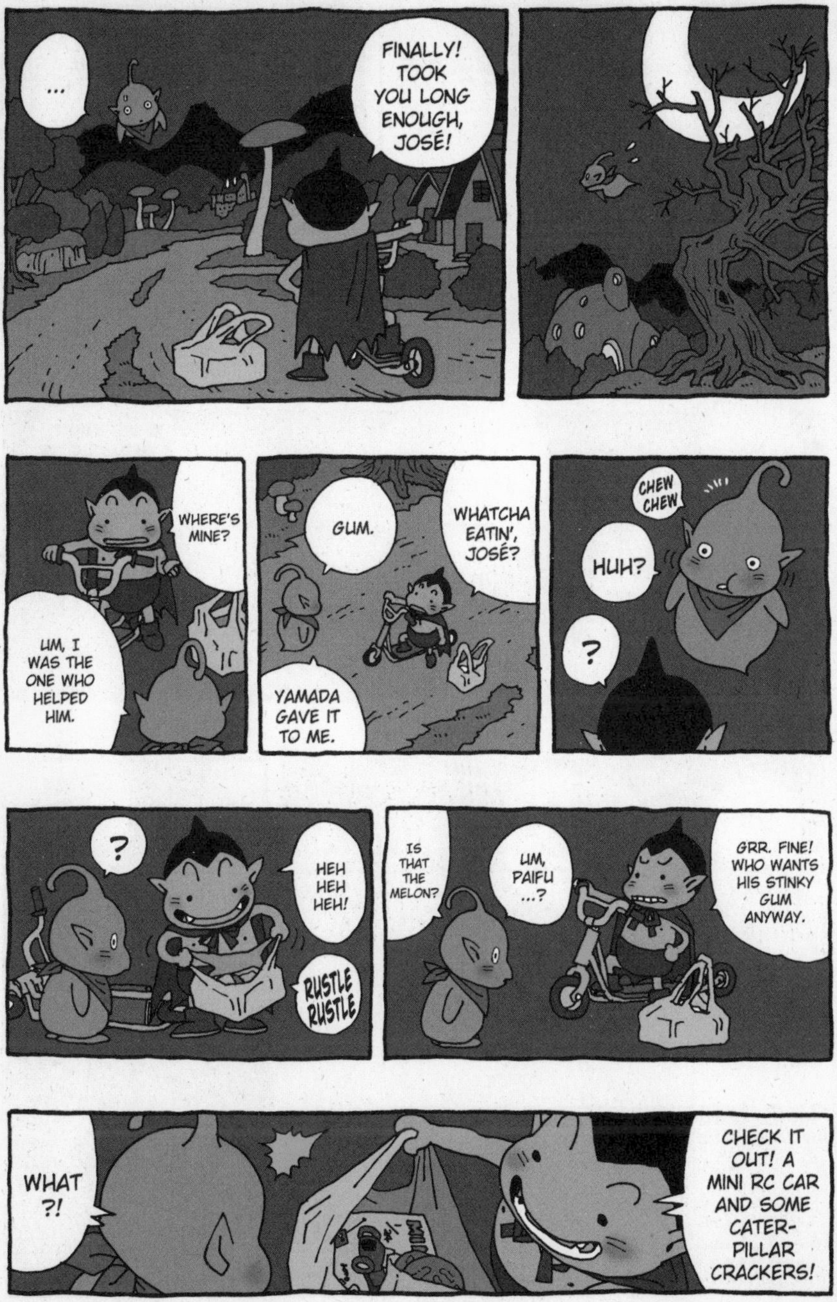
FINALLY! TOOK YOU LONG ENOUGH, JOSÉ!
...
CHEW CHEW
HUH?
?
WHATCHA EATIN', JOSÉ?
GUM.
YAMADA GAVE IT TO ME.
WHERE'S MINE?
UM, I WAS THE ONE WHO HELPED HIM.
GRR. FINE! WHO WANTS HIS STINKY GUM ANYWAY.
UM, PAIFU ...?
IS THAT THE MELON?
HEH HEH HEH!
?
RUSTLE RUSTLE
CHECK IT OUT! A MINI RC CAR AND SOME CATER-PILLAR CRACKERS!
WHAT ?!

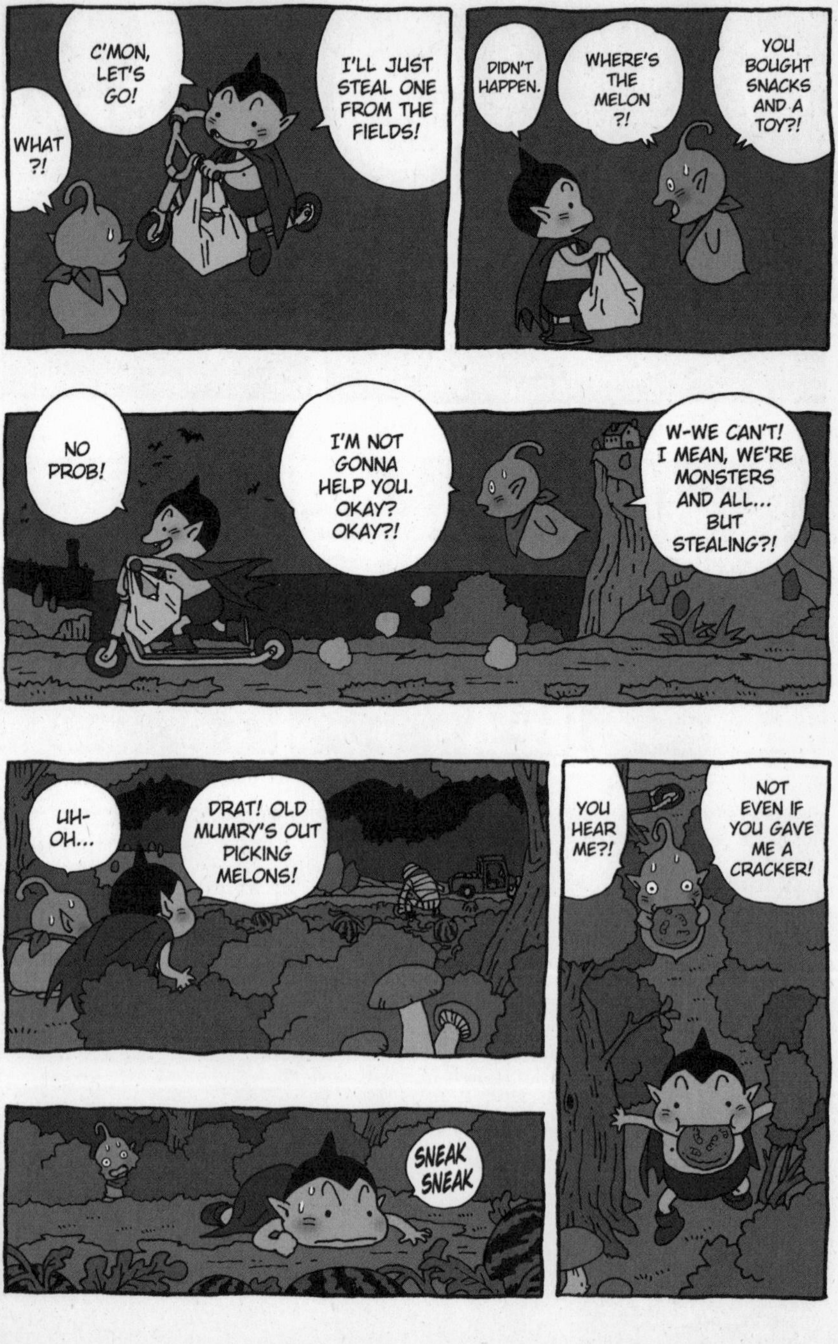
YOU BOUGHT SNACKS AND A TOY?!
WHERE'S THE MELON?!
DIDN'T HAPPEN.
I'LL JUST STEAL ONE FROM THE FIELDS!
C'MON, LET'S GO!
WHAT?!
W-WE CAN'T! I MEAN, WE'RE MONSTERS AND ALL... BUT STEALING?!
I'M NOT GONNA HELP YOU. OKAY? OKAY?!
NO PROB!
NOT EVEN IF YOU GAVE ME A CRACKER!
YOU HEAR ME?!
DRAT! OLD MUMRY'S OUT PICKING MELONS!
UH-OH...
SNEAK SNEAK

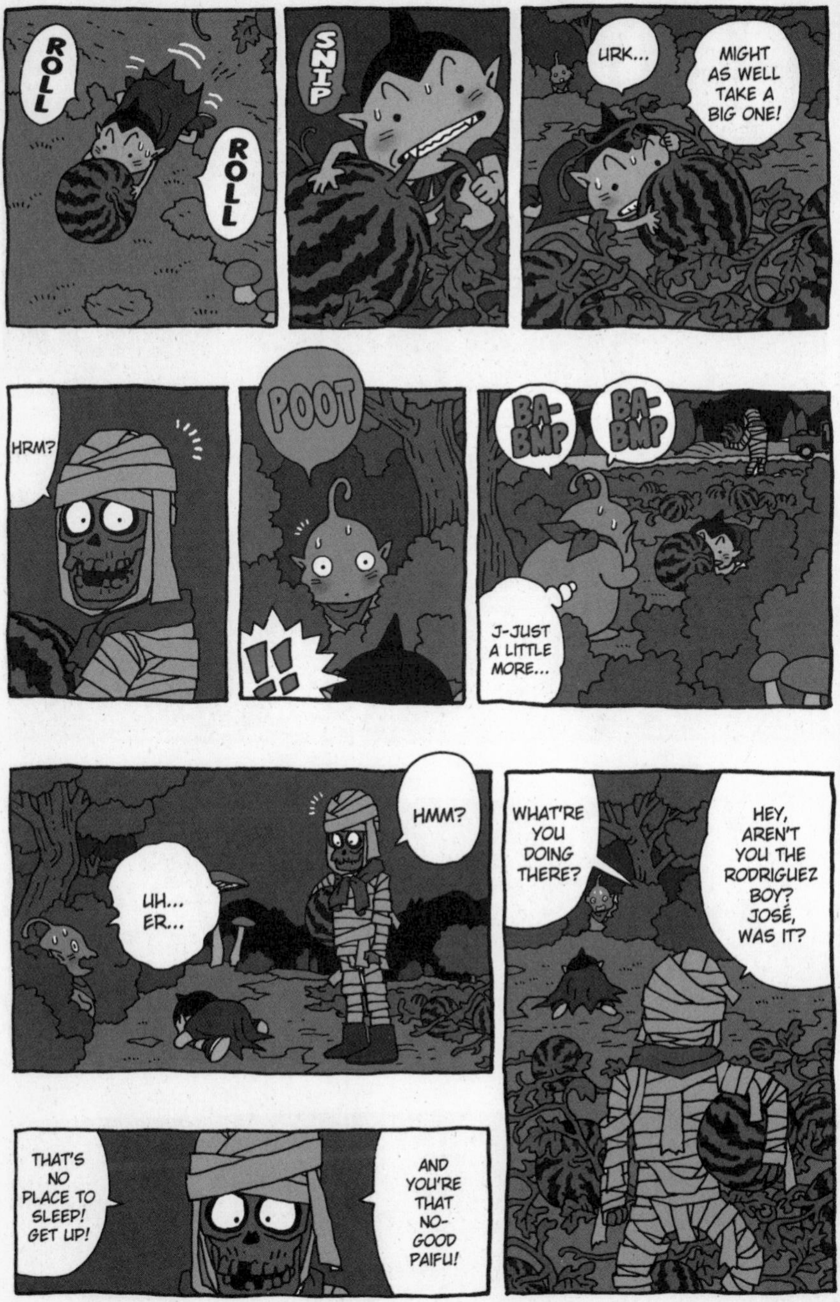
URK...
MIGHT AS WELL TAKE A BIG ONE!
SNIP
ROLL
ROLL
BA-BMP
BA-BMP
J-JUST A LITTLE MORE...
POOT
!!
HRM?
HEY, AREN'T YOU THE RODRIGUEZ BOY? JOSÉ, WAS IT?
WHAT'RE YOU DOING THERE?
HMM?
UH... ER...
AND YOU'RE THAT NO-GOOD PAIFU!
THAT'S NO PLACE TO SLEEP! GET UP!

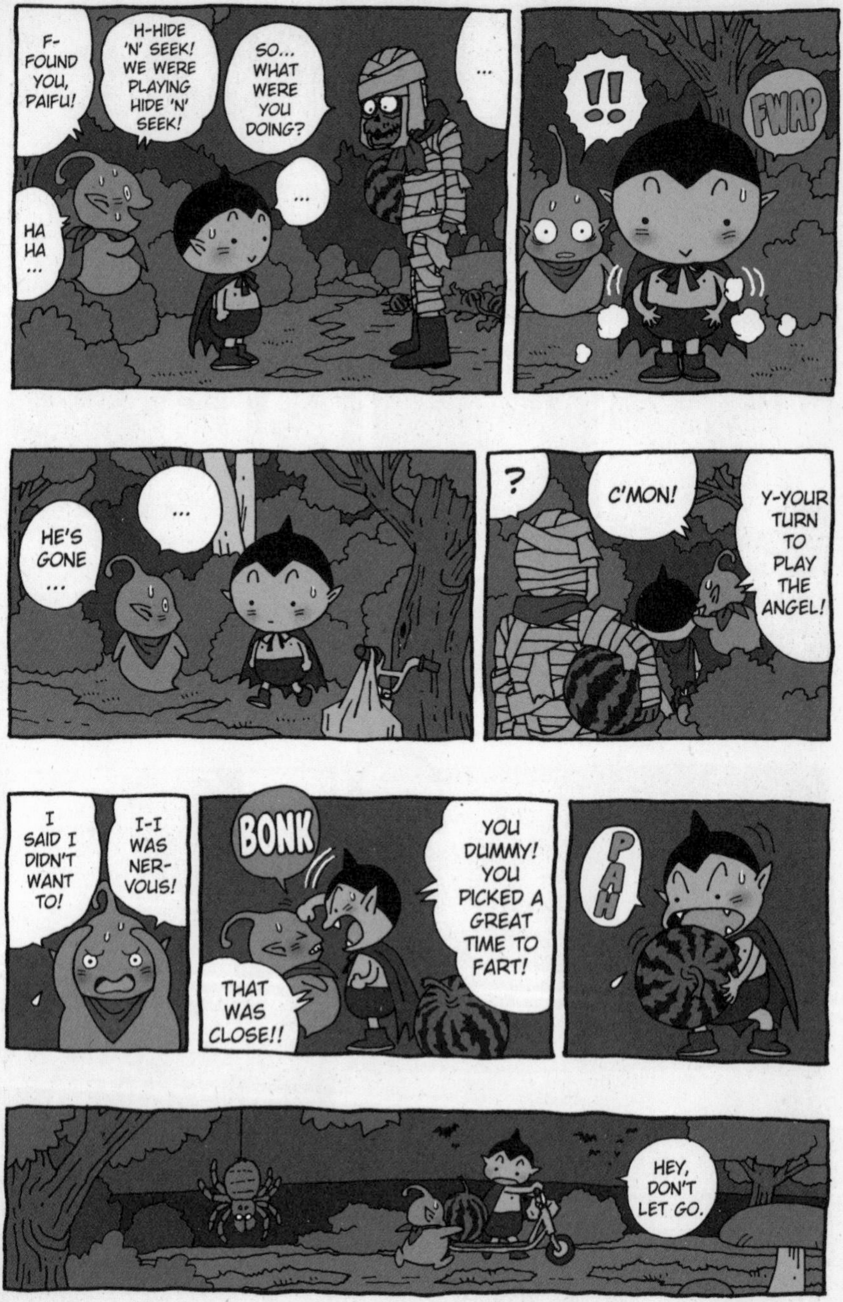
FWAP
!!
...
SO... WHAT WERE YOU DOING?
H-HIDE 'N' SEEK! WE WERE PLAYING HIDE 'N' SEEK!
F- FOUND YOU, PAIFU!
...
HA HA ...
Y-YOUR TURN TO PLAY THE ANGEL!
C'MON!
?
...
HE'S GONE ...
PAH
YOU DUMMY! YOU PICKED A GREAT TIME TO FART!
BONK
THAT WAS CLOSE!!
I-I WAS NER- VOUS!
I SAID I DIDN'T WANT TO!
HEY, DON'T LET GO.

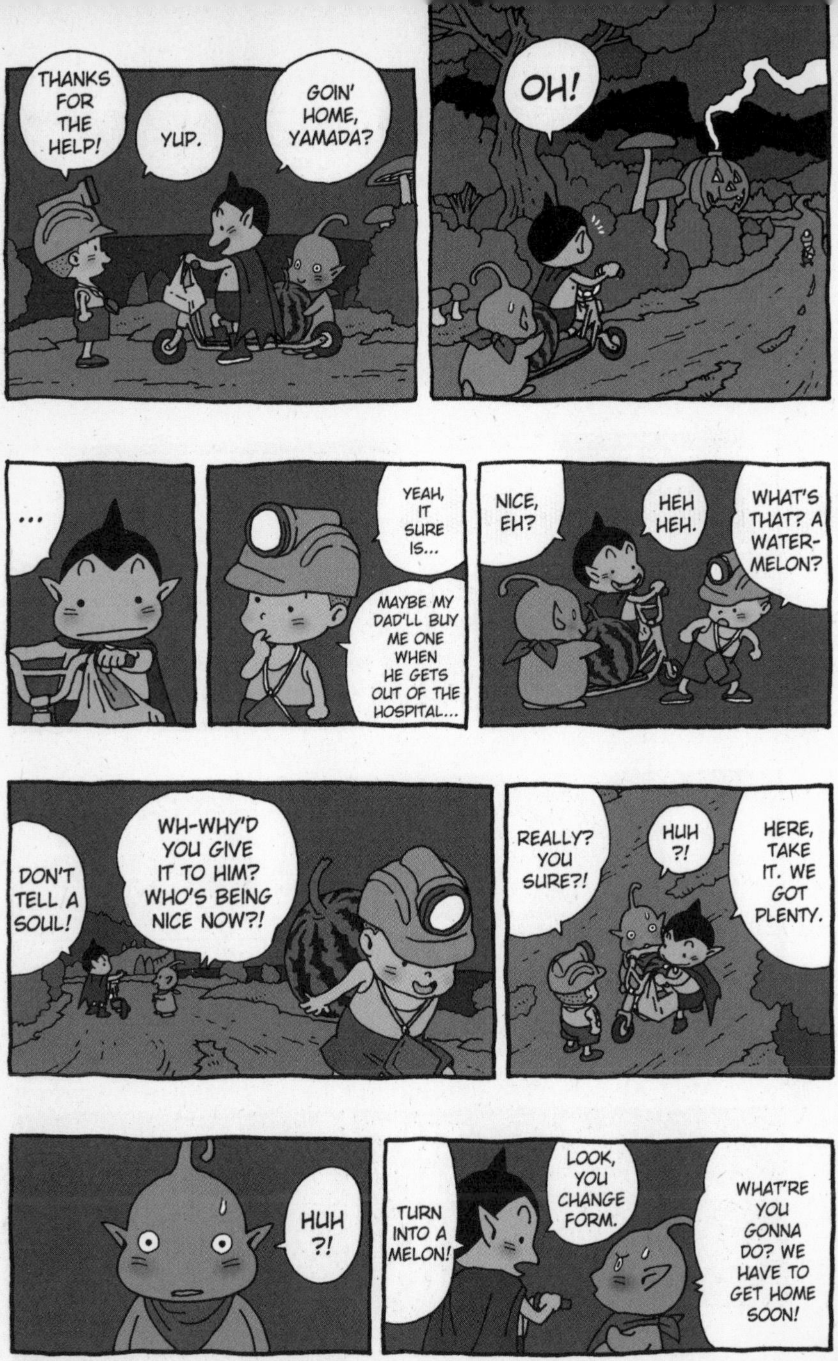
OH!
GOIN' HOME, YAMADA?
YUP.
THANKS FOR THE HELP!
WHAT'S THAT? A WATER-MELON?
HEH HEH.
NICE, EH?
YEAH, IT SURE IS...
MAYBE MY DAD'LL BUY ME ONE WHEN HE GETS OUT OF THE HOSPITAL...
...
HERE, TAKE IT. WE GOT PLENTY.
HUH ?!
REALLY? YOU SURE?!
WH-WHY'D YOU GIVE IT TO HIM? WHO'S BEING NICE NOW?!
DON'T TELL A SOUL!
WHAT'RE YOU GONNA DO? WE HAVE TO GET HOME SOON!
LOOK, YOU CHANGE FORM.
TURN INTO A MELON!
HUH ?!

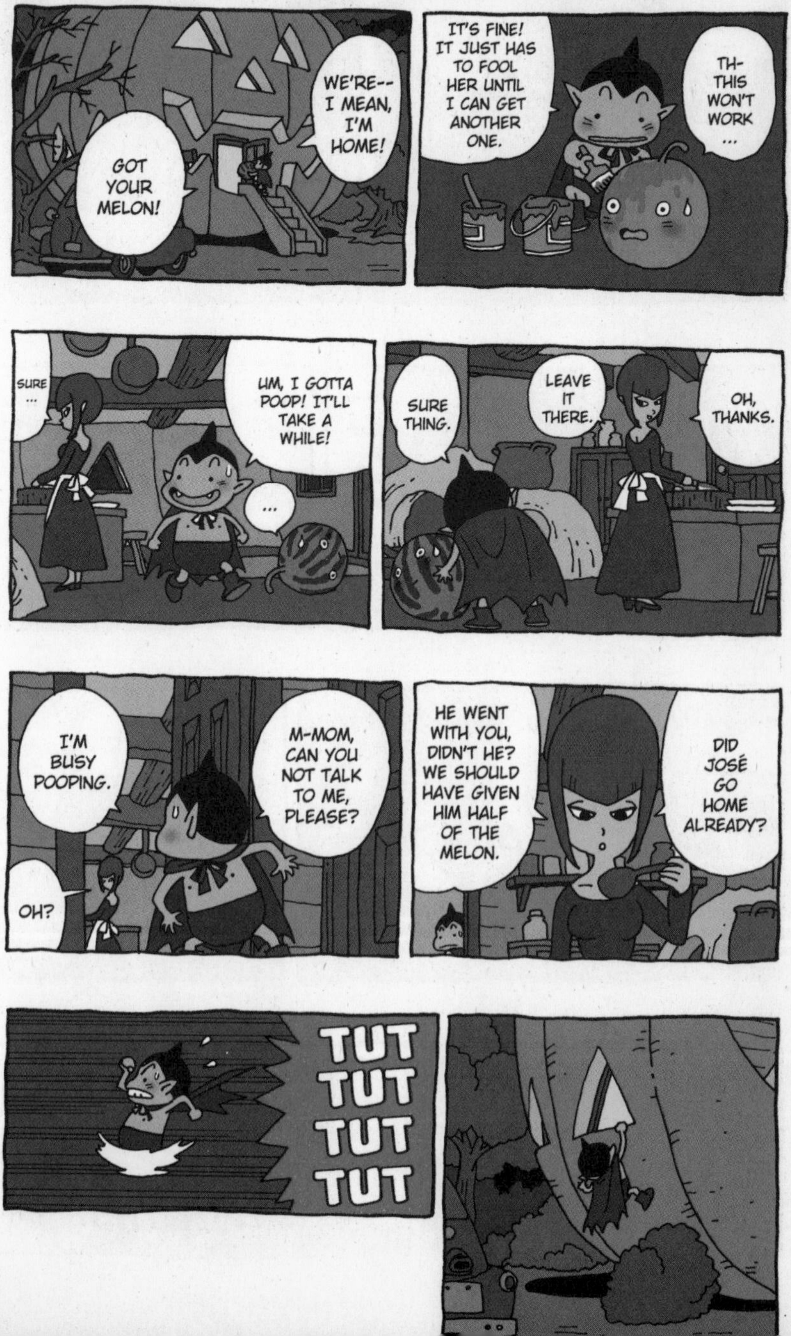
TH- THIS WON'T WORK ...
IT'S FINE! IT JUST HAS TO FOOL HER UNTIL I CAN GET ANOTHER ONE.
WE'RE-- I MEAN, I'M HOME!
GOT YOUR MELON!
OH, THANKS.
LEAVE IT THERE.
SURE THING.
UM, I GOTTA POOP! IT'LL TAKE A WHILE!
...
SURE ...
DID JOSÉ GO HOME ALREADY?
HE WENT WITH YOU, DIDN'T HE? WE SHOULD HAVE GIVEN HIM HALF OF THE MELON.
M-MOM, CAN YOU NOT TALK TO ME, PLEASE?
I'M BUSY POOPING.
OH?
TUT TUT TUT TUT

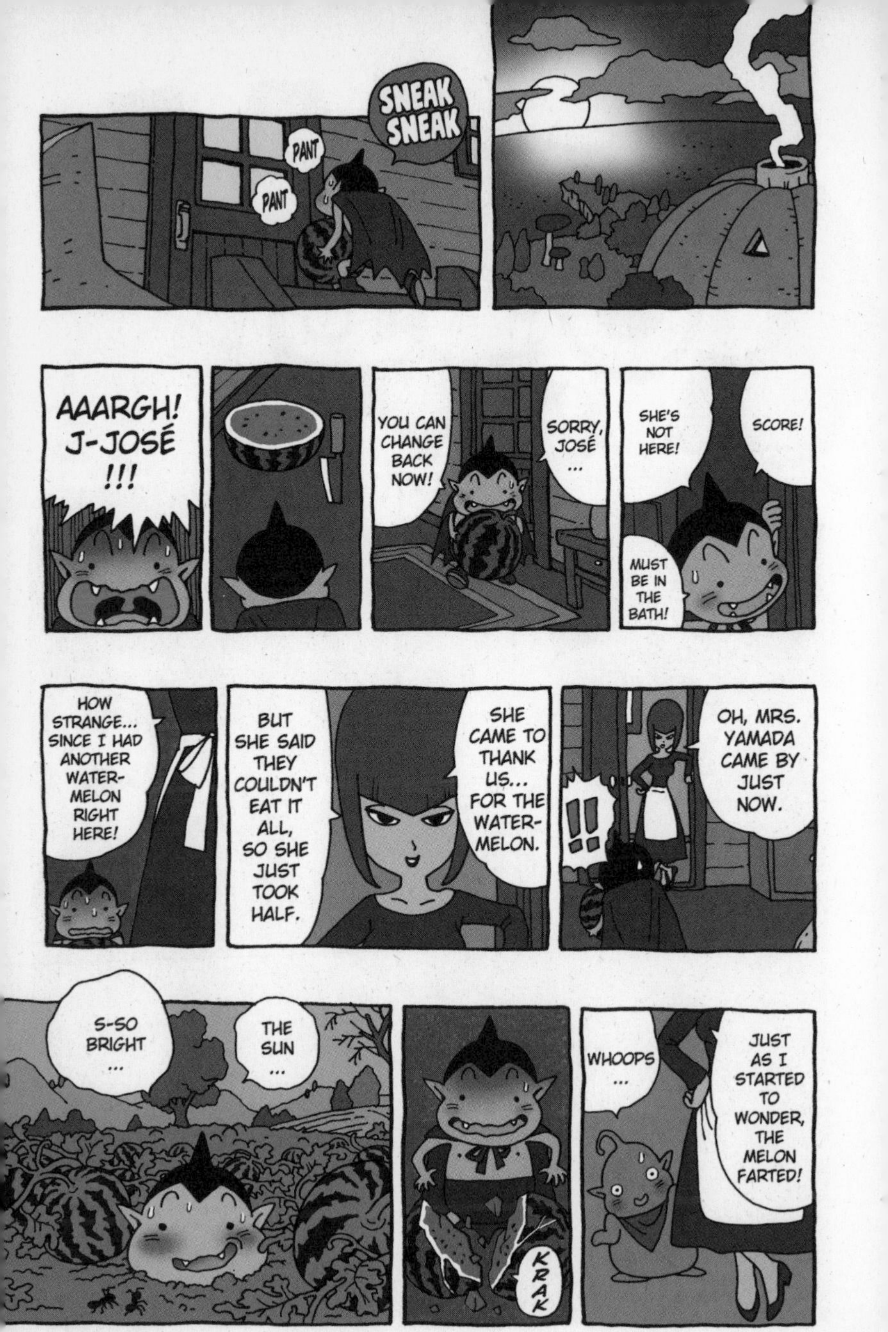
SNEAK SNEAK
PANT
PANT
SCORE!
SHE'S NOT HERE!
MUST BE IN THE BATH!
SORRY, JOSÉ ...
YOU CAN CHANGE BACK NOW!
AAARGH! J-JOSÉ !!!
OH, MRS. YAMADA CAME BY JUST NOW.
!!
SHE CAME TO THANK US... FOR THE WATER-MELON.
BUT SHE SAID THEY COULDN'T EAT IT ALL, SO SHE JUST TOOK HALF.
HOW STRANGE... SINCE I HAD ANOTHER WATER-MELON RIGHT HERE!
JUST AS I STARTED TO WONDER, THE MELON FARTED!
WHOOPS ...
KRAK
THE SUN ...
S-SO BRIGHT ...

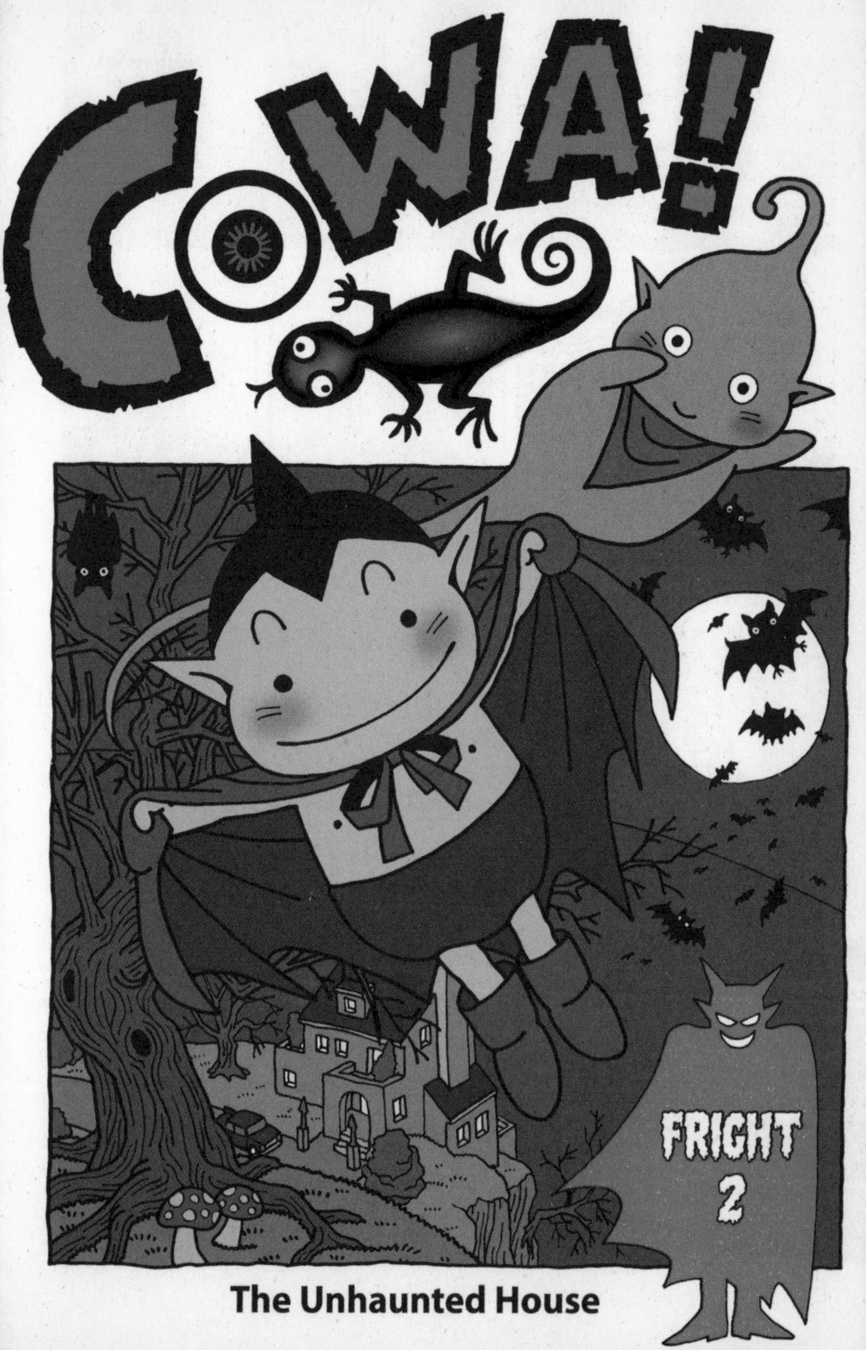
COWA!
FRIGHT 2
The Unhaunted House

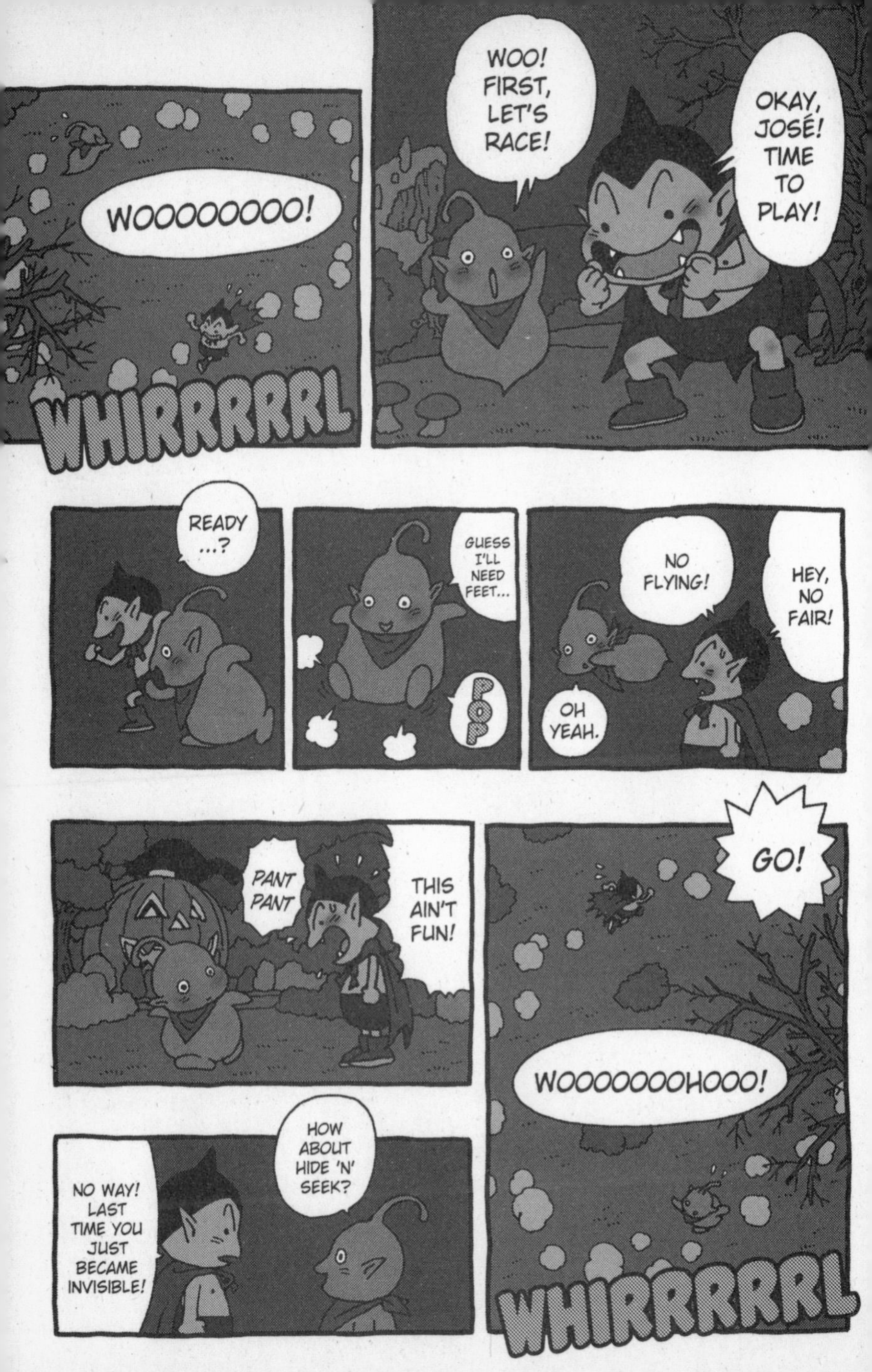
OKAY, JOSÉ! TIME TO PLAY!
WOO! FIRST, LET'S RACE!
WOOOOOOOO!
WHIRRRRRL
HEY, NO FAIR!
NO FLYING!
OH YEAH.
GUESS I'LL NEED FEET...
POP
READY ...?
GO!
WOOOOOOOHOOO!
WHIRRRRRL
THIS AIN'T FUN!
PANT PANT
HOW ABOUT HIDE 'N' SEEK?
NO WAY! LAST TIME YOU JUST BECAME INVISIBLE!

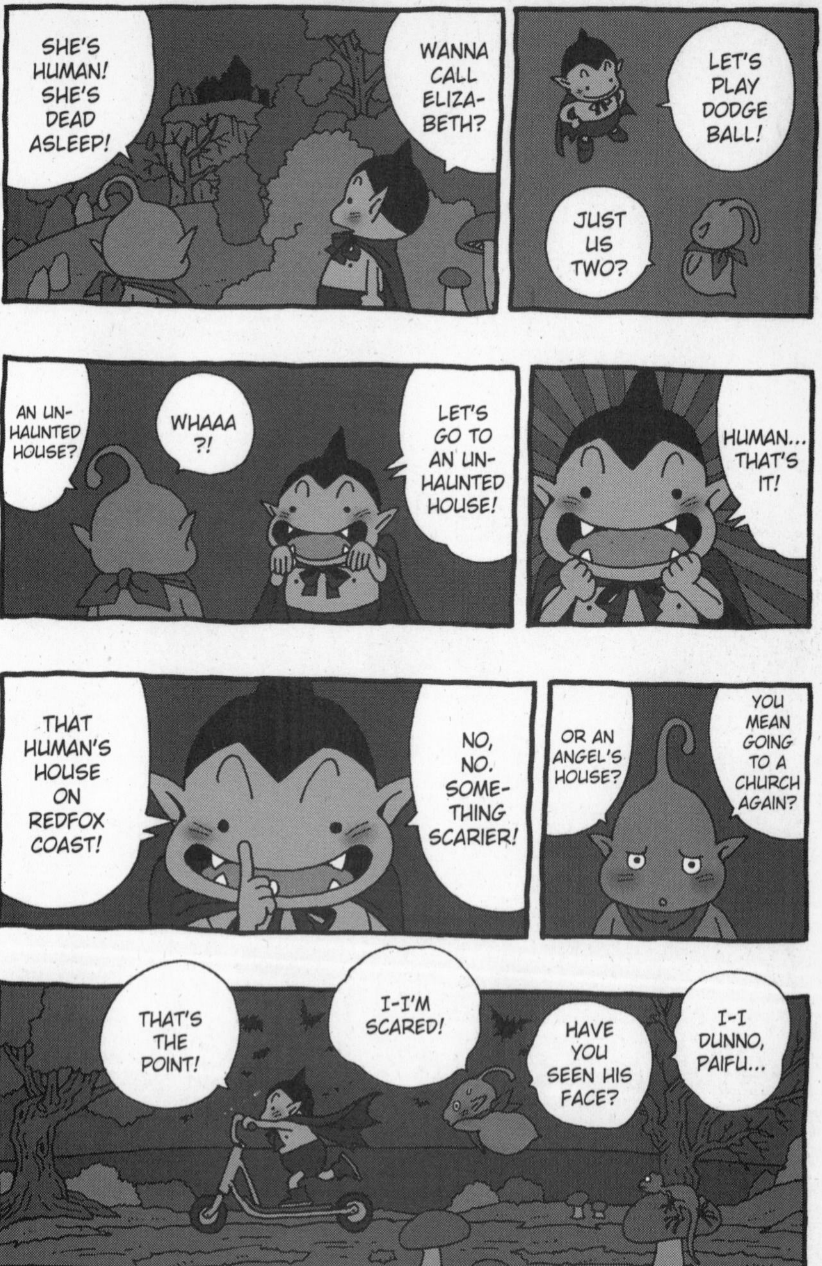
LET'S PLAY DODGE BALL!
JUST US TWO?
WANNA CALL ELIZA-BETH?
SHE'S HUMAN! SHE'S DEAD ASLEEP!
HUMAN... THAT'S IT!
LET'S GO TO AN UN-HAUNTED HOUSE!
WHAAA ?!
AN UN-HAUNTED HOUSE?
YOU MEAN GOING TO A CHURCH AGAIN?
OR AN ANGEL'S HOUSE?
NO, NO. SOME-THING SCARIER!
THAT HUMAN'S HOUSE ON REDFOX COAST!
I-I DUNNO, PAIFU...
HAVE YOU SEEN HIS FACE?
I-I'M SCARED!
THAT'S THE POINT!

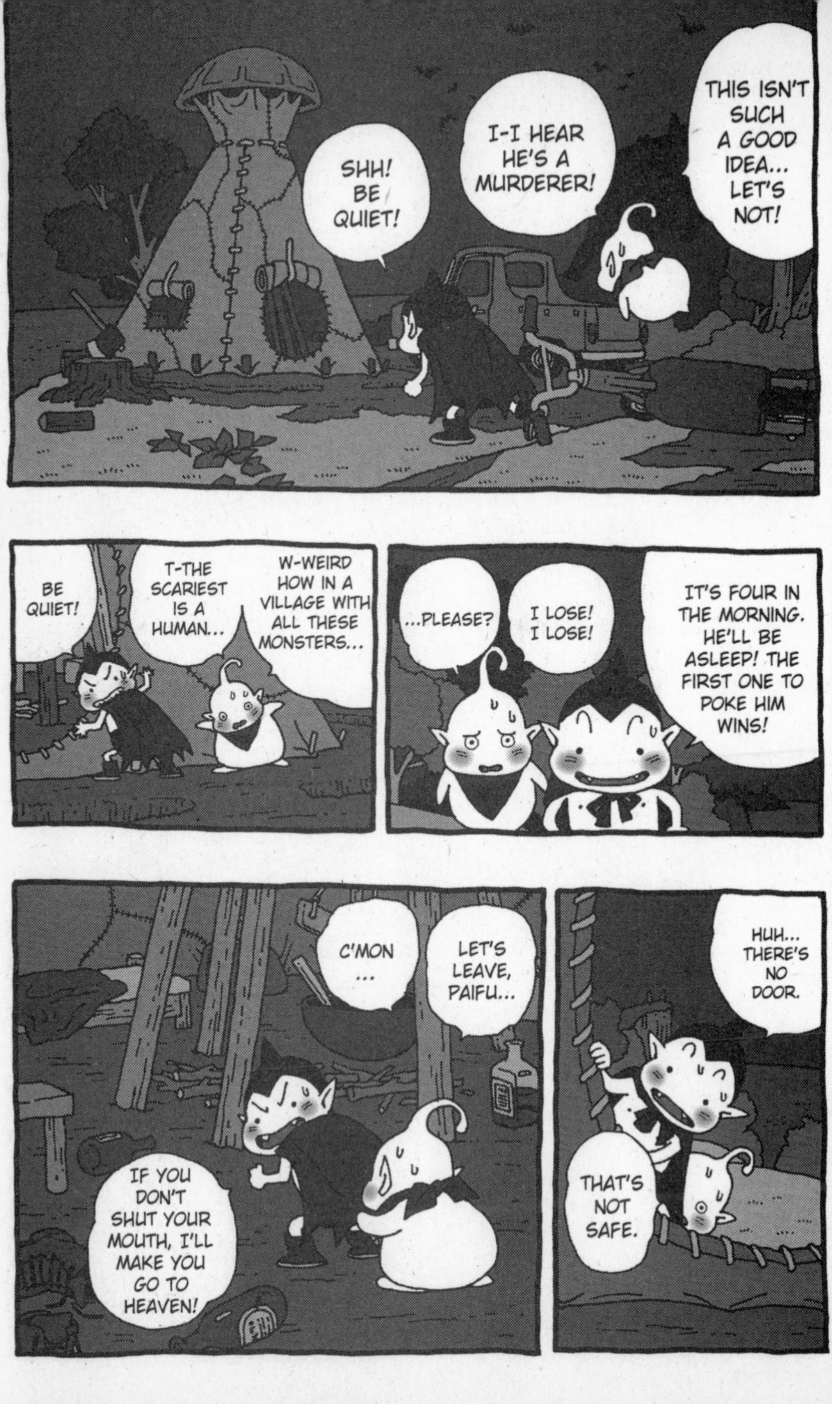
THIS ISN'T SUCH A GOOD IDEA... LET'S NOT!
I-I HEAR HE'S A MURDERER!
SHH! BE QUIET!
IT'S FOUR IN THE MORNING. HE'LL BE ASLEEP! THE FIRST ONE TO POKE HIM WINS!
I LOSE! I LOSE!
...PLEASE?
W-WEIRD HOW IN A VILLAGE WITH ALL THESE MONSTERS...
T-THE SCARIEST IS A HUMAN...
BE QUIET!
HUH... THERE'S NO DOOR.
THAT'S NOT SAFE.
LET'S LEAVE, PAIFU...
C'MON ...
IF YOU DON'T SHUT YOUR MOUTH, I'LL MAKE YOU GO TO HEAVEN!

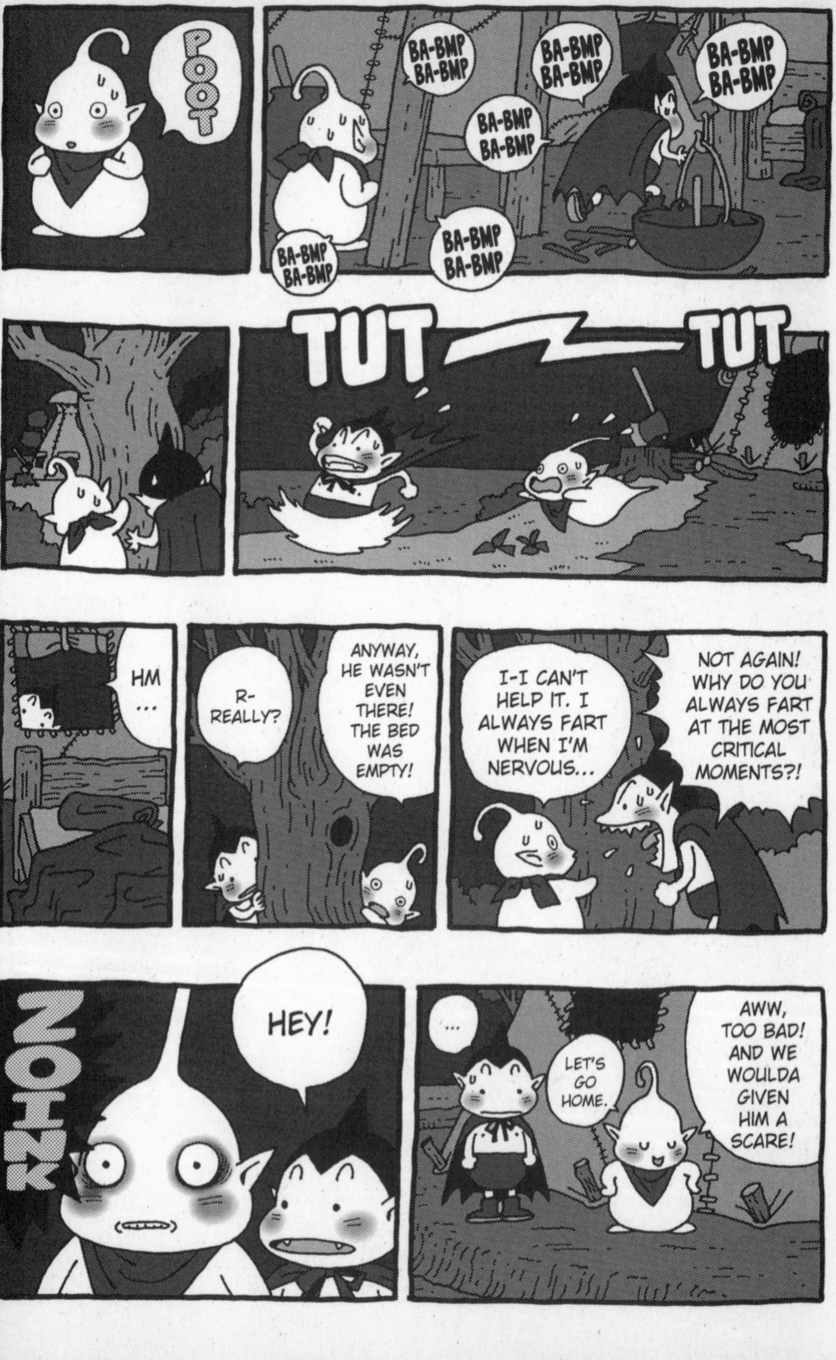
BA-BMP BA-BMP
BA-BMP BA-BMP
BA-BMP BA-BMP
BA-BMP BA-BMP
BA-BMP BA-BMP
BA-BMP BA-BMP
POOT
TUT TUT
NOT AGAIN! WHY DO YOU ALWAYS FART AT THE MOST CRITICAL MOMENTS?!
I-I CAN'T HELP IT. I ALWAYS FART WHEN I'M NERVOUS...
ANYWAY, HE WASN'T EVEN THERE! THE BED WAS EMPTY!
R- REALLY?
HM ...
AWW, TOO BAD! AND WE WOULDA GIVEN HIM A SCARE!
LET'S GO HOME.
...
HEY!
ZOINK

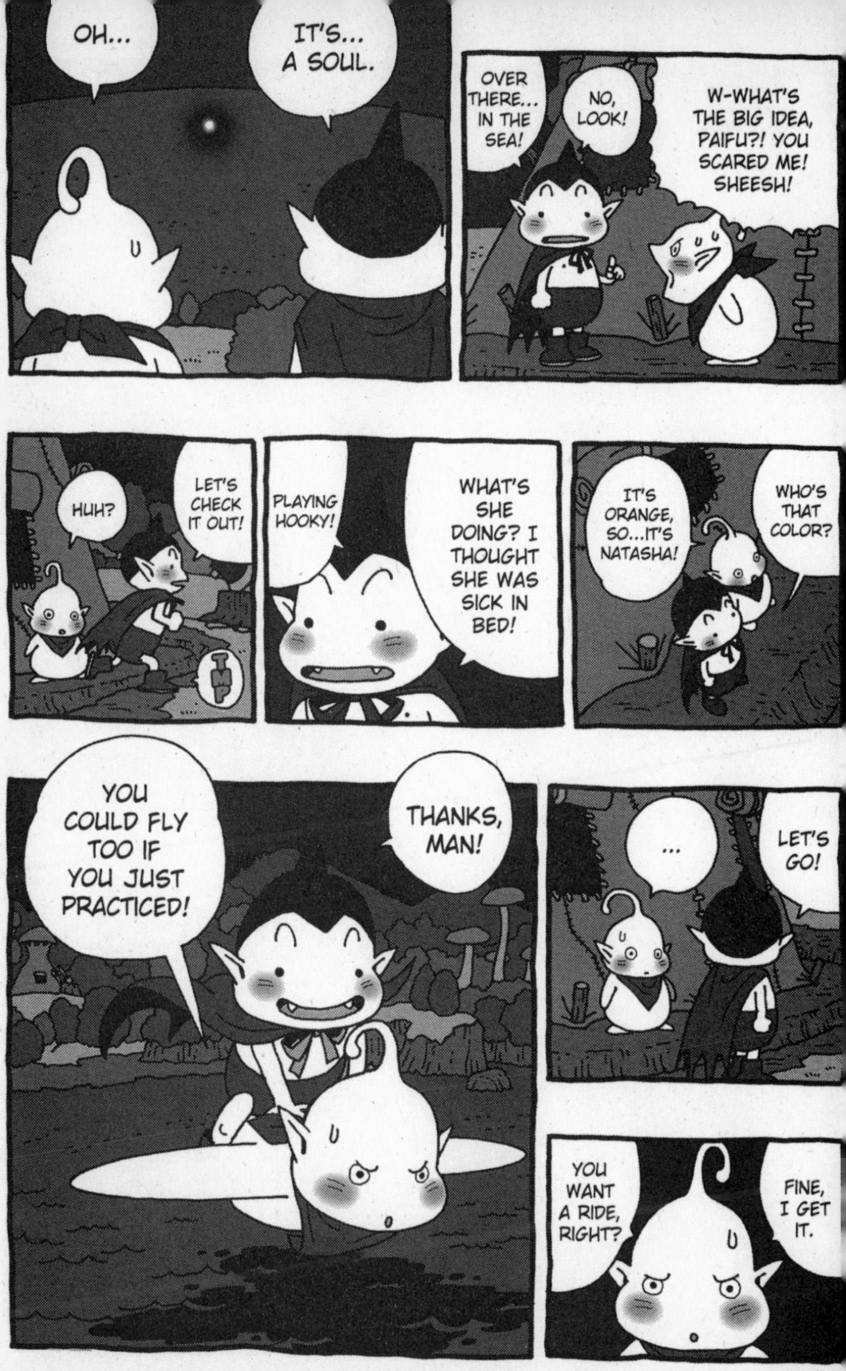

W-WHAT'S THE BIG IDEA, PAIFU?! YOU SCARED ME! SHEESH!
NO, LOOK!
OVER THERE... IN THE SEA!
IT'S... A SOUL.
OH...
WHO'S THAT COLOR?
IT'S ORANGE, SO...IT'S NATASHA!
WHAT'S SHE DOING? I THOUGHT SHE WAS SICK IN BED!
PLAYING HOOKY!
LET'S CHECK IT OUT!
HUH?
TMP
LET'S GO!
...
FINE, I GET IT.
YOU WANT A RIDE, RIGHT?
THANKS, MAN!
YOU COULD FLY TOO IF YOU JUST PRACTICED!

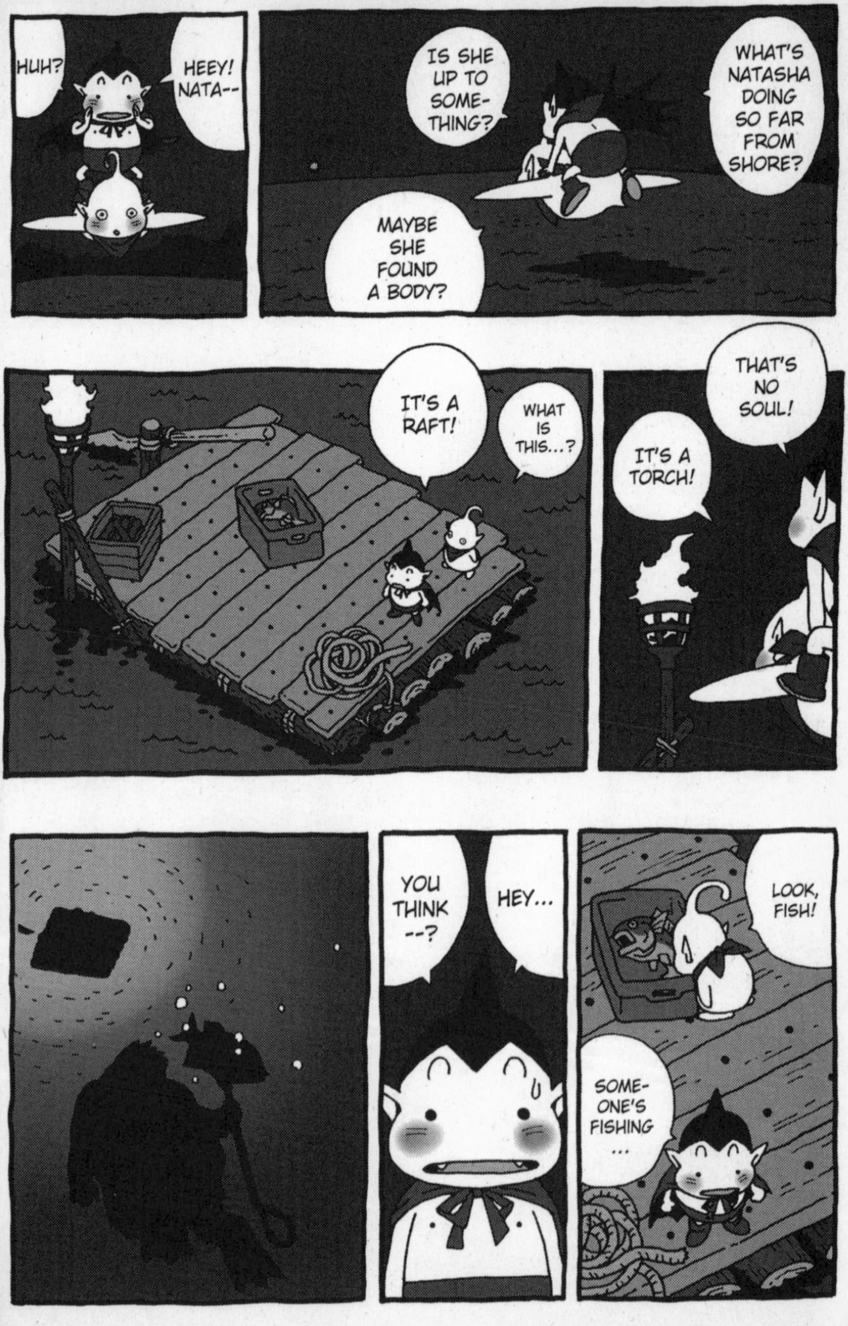
WHAT'S NATASHA DOING SO FAR FROM SHORE?
IS SHE UP TO SOME-THING?
MAYBE SHE FOUND A BODY?
HEEY! NATA--
HUH?
THAT'S NO SOUL!
IT'S A TORCH!
WHAT IS THIS...?
IT'S A RAFT!
LOOK, FISH!
SOME-ONE'S FISHING ...
HEY...
YOU THINK --?

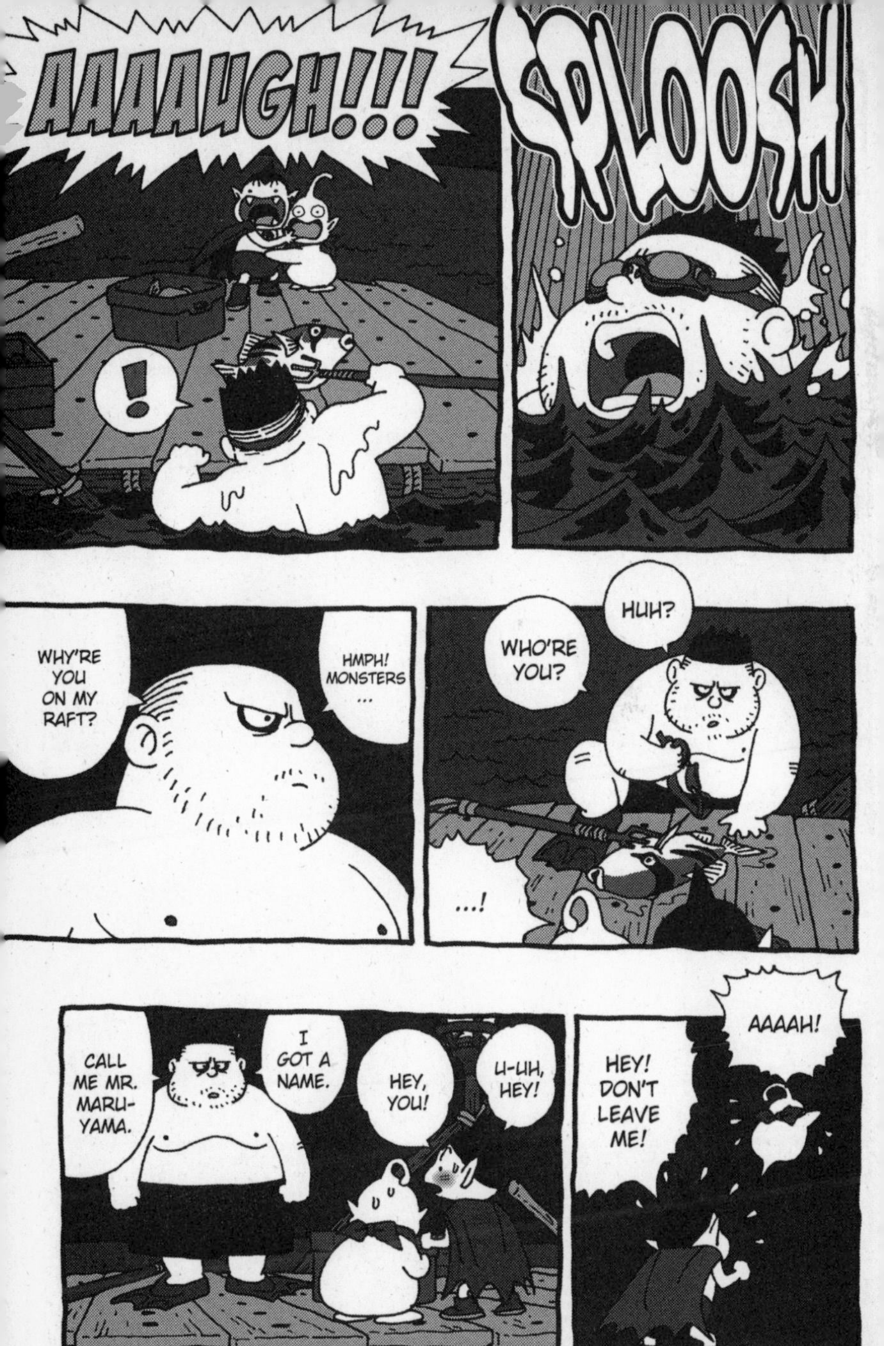
SPLOOSH
AAAAUGH!!!
!
HUH?
WHO'RE YOU?
...!
HMPH! MONSTERS ...
WHY'RE YOU ON MY RAFT?
AAAAH!
HEY! DON'T LEAVE ME!
U-UH, HEY!
HEY, YOU!
I GOT A NAME.
CALL ME MR. MARU-YAMA.

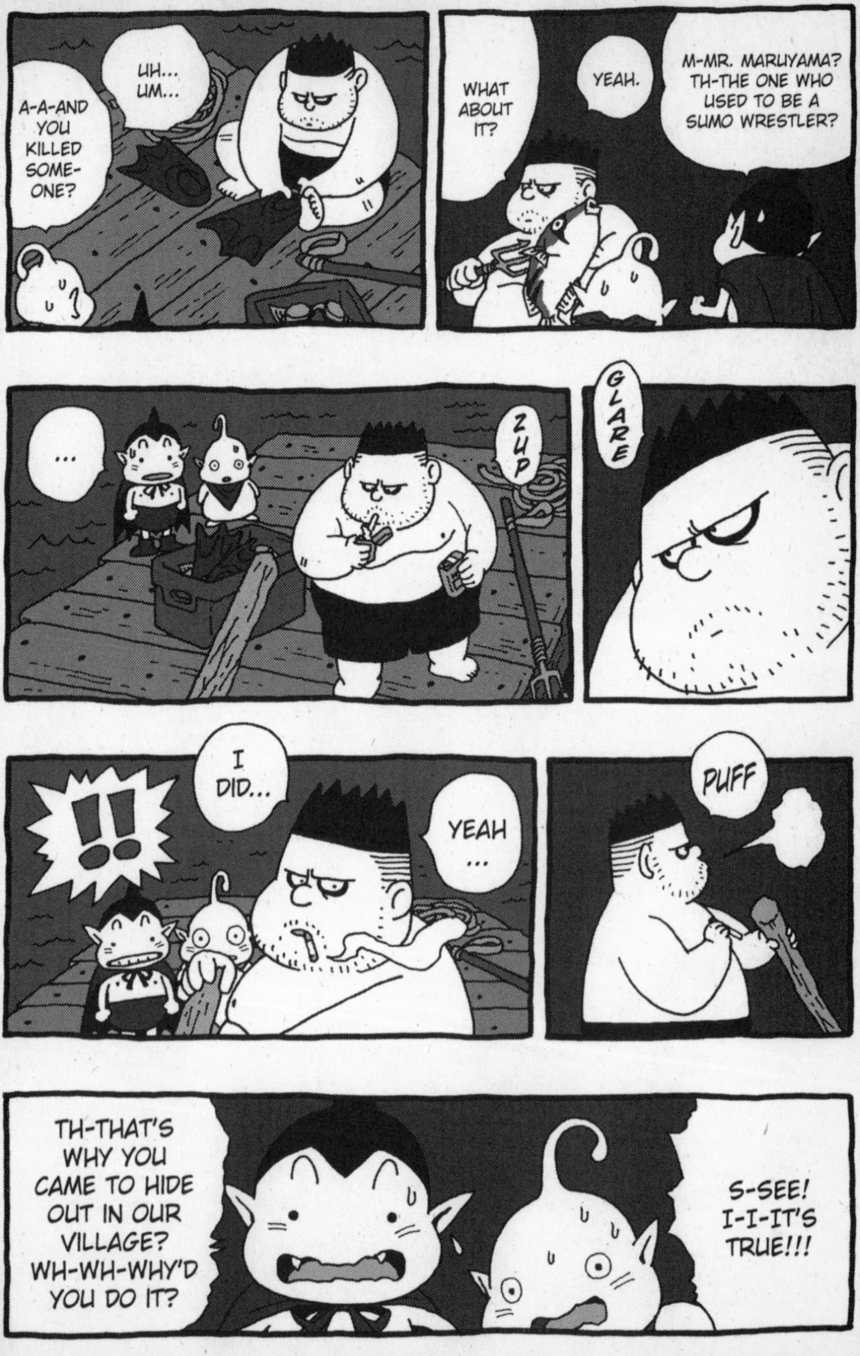
M-MR. MARUYAMA? TH-THE ONE WHO USED TO BE A SUMO WRESTLER?
YEAH.
WHAT ABOUT IT?
UH... UM...
A-A-AND YOU KILLED SOME-ONE?
GLARE
ZUP
...
PUFF
YEAH ...
I DID...
!!
S-SEE! I-I-IT'S TRUE!!!
TH-THAT'S WHY YOU CAME TO HIDE OUT IN OUR VILLAGE? WH-WH-WHY'D YOU DO IT?

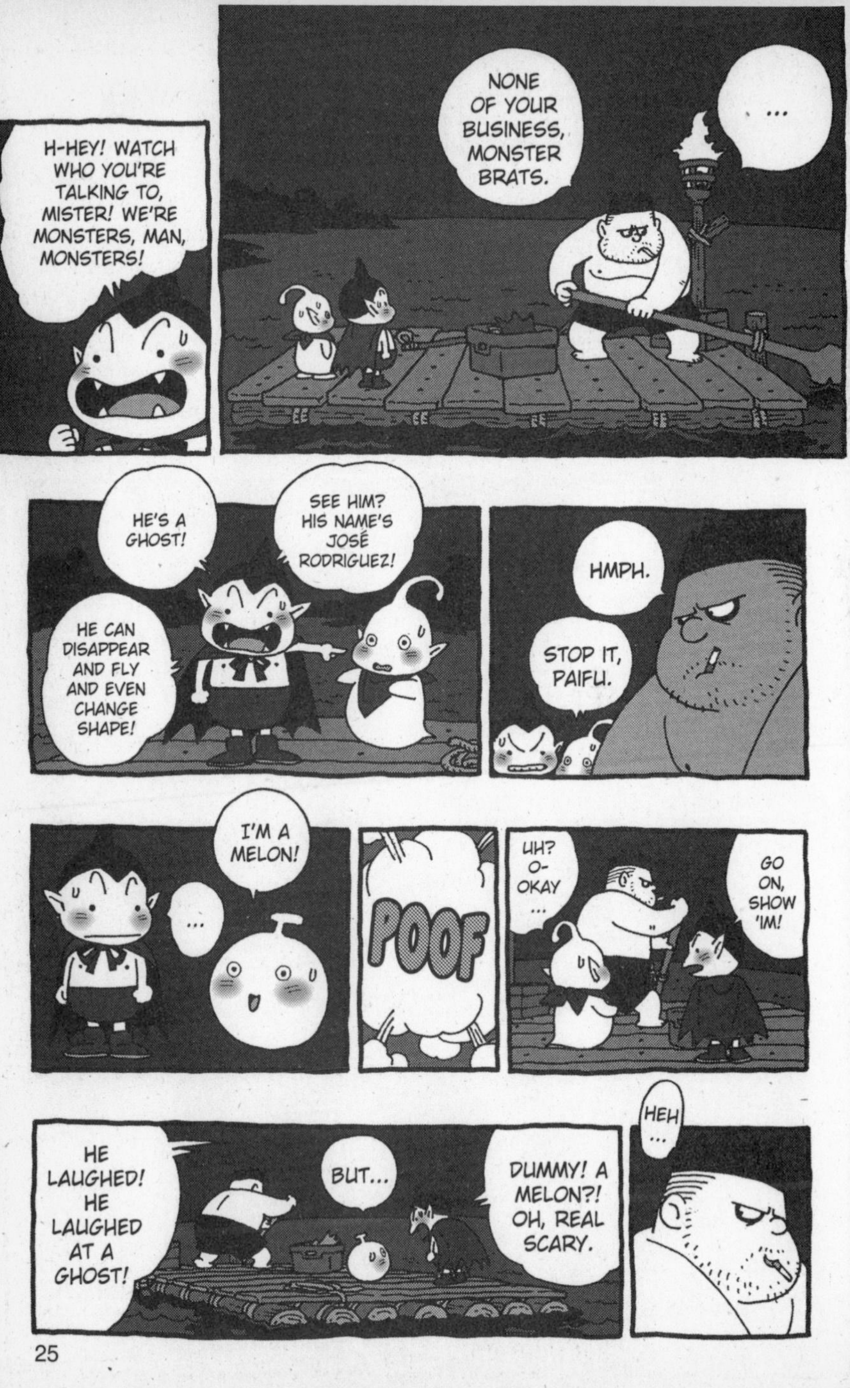
. ...
NONE OF YOUR BUSINESS, MONSTER BRATS.
H-HEY! WATCH WHO YOU'RE TALKING TO, MISTER! WE'RE MONSTERS, MAN, MONSTERS!
HMPH.
STOP IT, PAIFU.
SEE HIM? HIS NAME'S JOSÉ RODRIGUEZ!
HE'S A GHOST!
HE CAN DISAPPEAR AND FLY AND EVEN CHANGE SHAPE!
GO ON, SHOW 'IM!
UH? O-OKAY ...
POOF
I'M A MELON!
...
HEH ...
DUMMY! A MELON?! OH, REAL SCARY.
BUT...
HE LAUGHED! HE LAUGHED AT A GHOST!

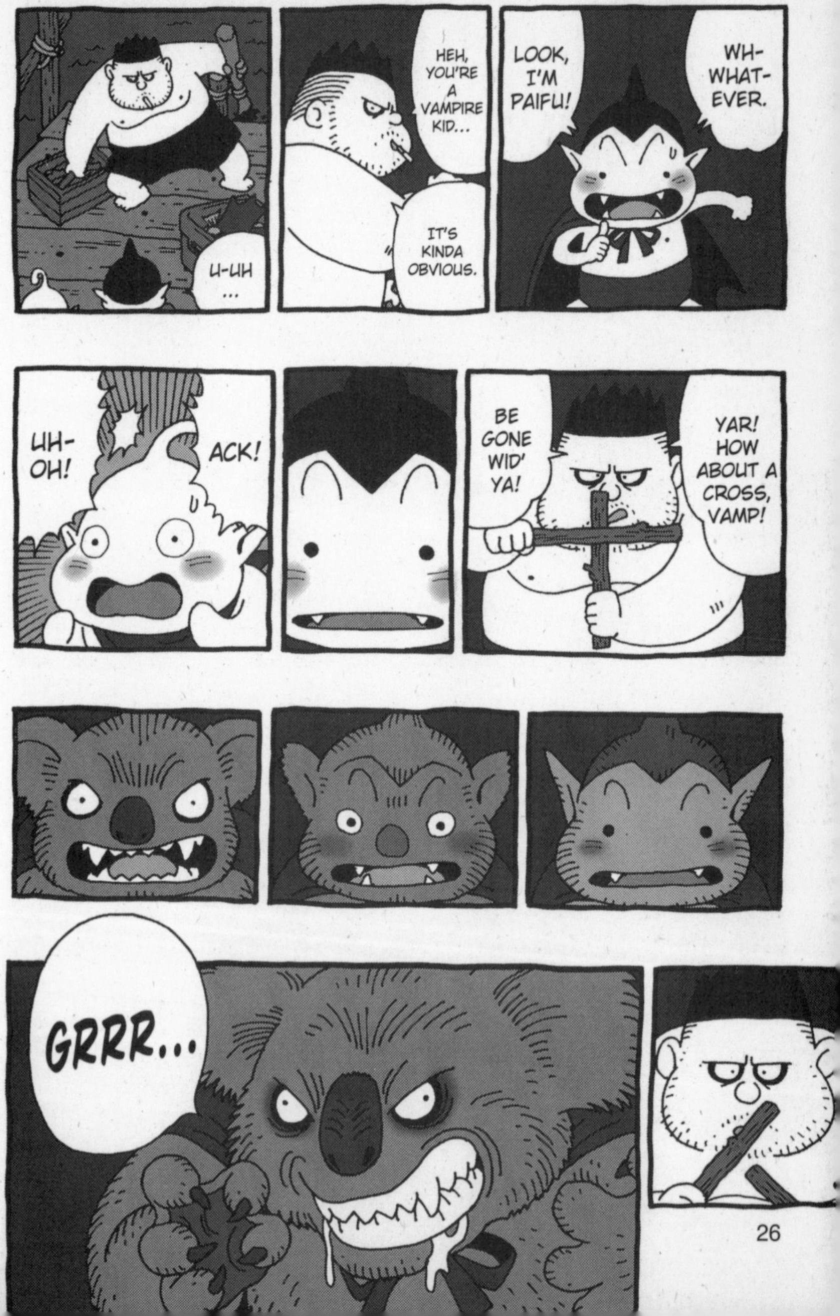

WH-WHAT-EVER.
LOOK, I'M PAIFU!
HEH, YOU'RE A VAMPIRE KID...
IT'S KINDA OBVIOUS.
U-UH ...
YAR! HOW ABOUT A CROSS, VAMP!
BE GONE WID' YA!
ACK!
UH-OH!
GRRR...

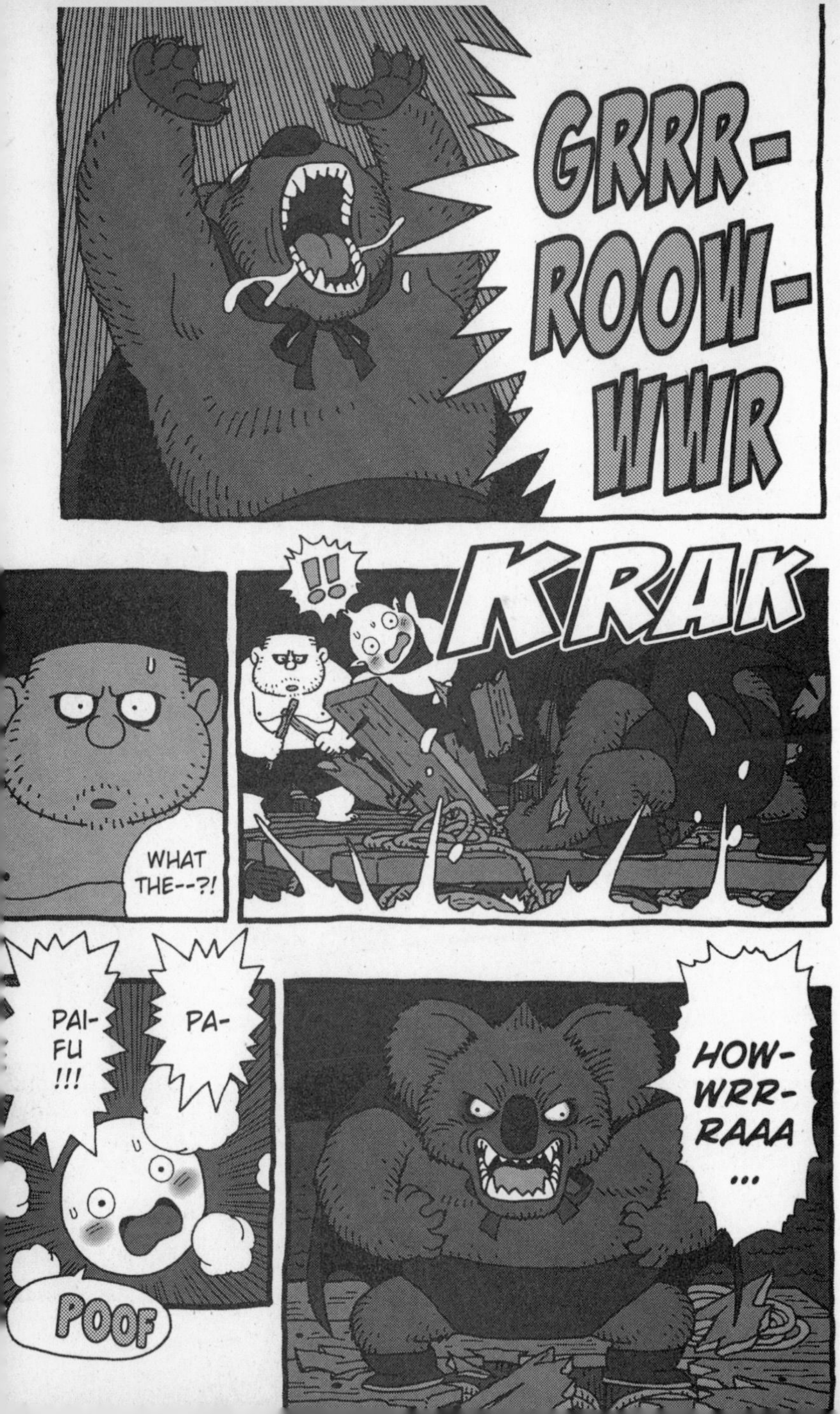
GRRR-ROOW-WWR
KRAK
!!
WHAT THE--?!
HOW-WRR-RAAA...
PA-
PAI-FU!!!
POOF

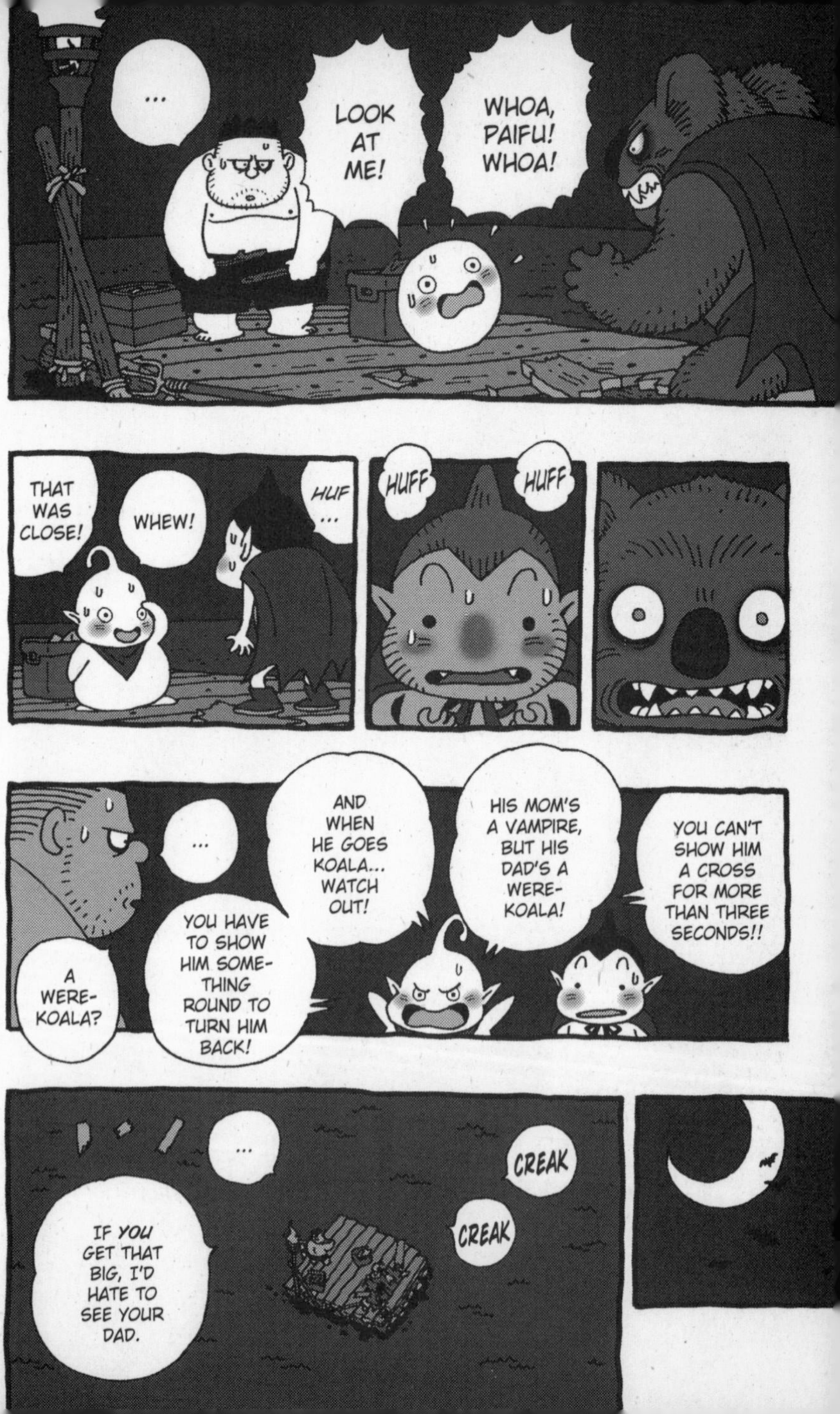
WHOA, PAIFU! WHOA!
LOOK AT ME!
...
HUFF
HUFF
HUF...
WHEW!
THAT WAS CLOSE!
YOU CAN'T SHOW HIM A CROSS FOR MORE THAN THREE SECONDS!!
HIS MOM'S A VAMPIRE, BUT HIS DAD'S A WERE-KOALA!
AND WHEN HE GOES KOALA... WATCH OUT!
YOU HAVE TO SHOW HIM SOMETHING ROUND TO TURN HIM BACK!
...
A WERE-KOALA?
CREAK
CREAK
...
IF *YOU* GET THAT BIG, I'D HATE TO SEE YOUR DAD.

READ THIS WAY

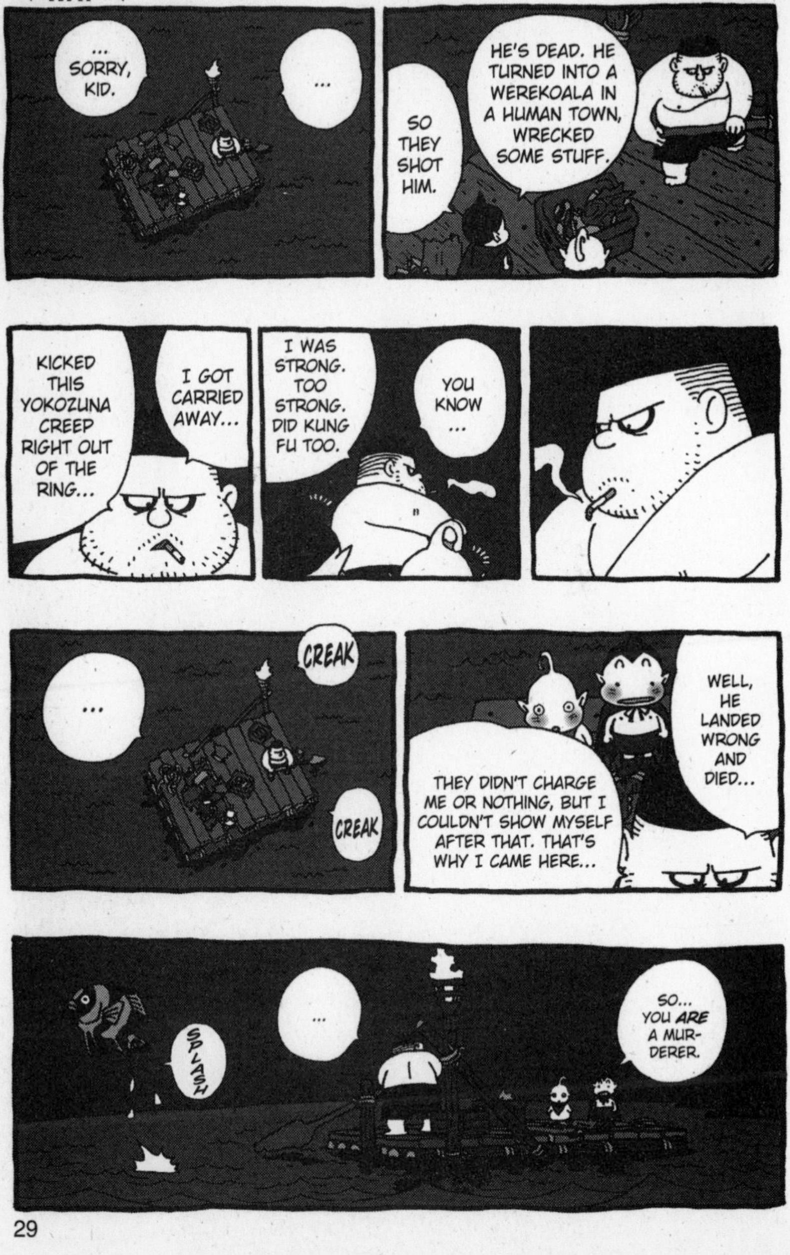
HE'S DEAD. HE TURNED INTO A WEREKOALA IN A HUMAN TOWN, WRECKED SOME STUFF.
SO THEY SHOT HIM.
...
... SORRY, KID.
YOU KNOW ...
I WAS STRONG. TOO STRONG. DID KUNG FU TOO.
I GOT CARRIED AWAY...
KICKED THIS YOKOZUNA CREEP RIGHT OUT OF THE RING...
WELL, HE LANDED WRONG AND DIED...
THEY DIDN'T CHARGE ME OR NOTHING, BUT I COULDN'T SHOW MYSELF AFTER THAT. THAT'S WHY I CAME HERE...
CREAK
...
CREAK
SO... YOU ***ARE*** A MURDERER.
...
SPLASH

COWA!

FRIGHT 3

Paifu and Arpon

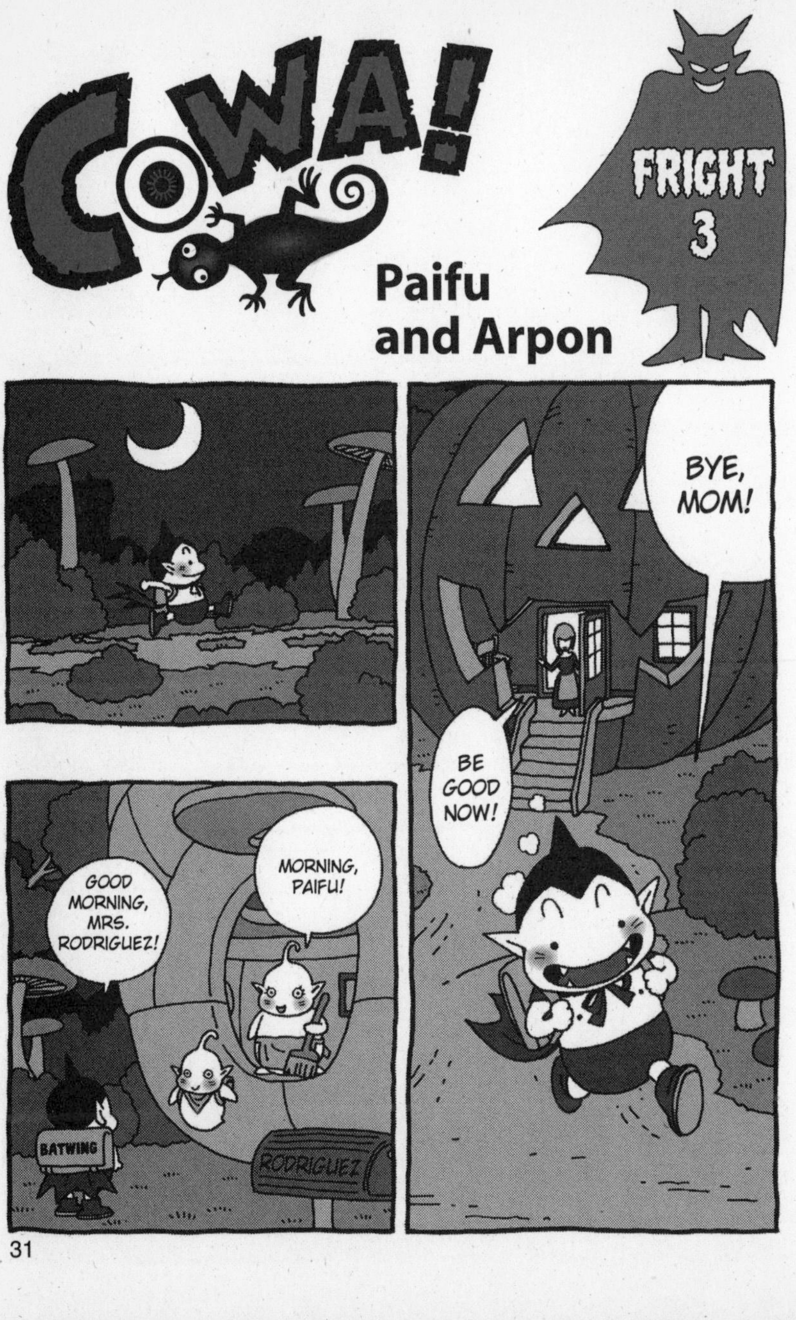

BYE, MOM!
BE GOOD NOW!
MORNING, PAIFU!
GOOD MORNING, MRS. RODRIGUEZ!
RODRIGUEZ
BATWING

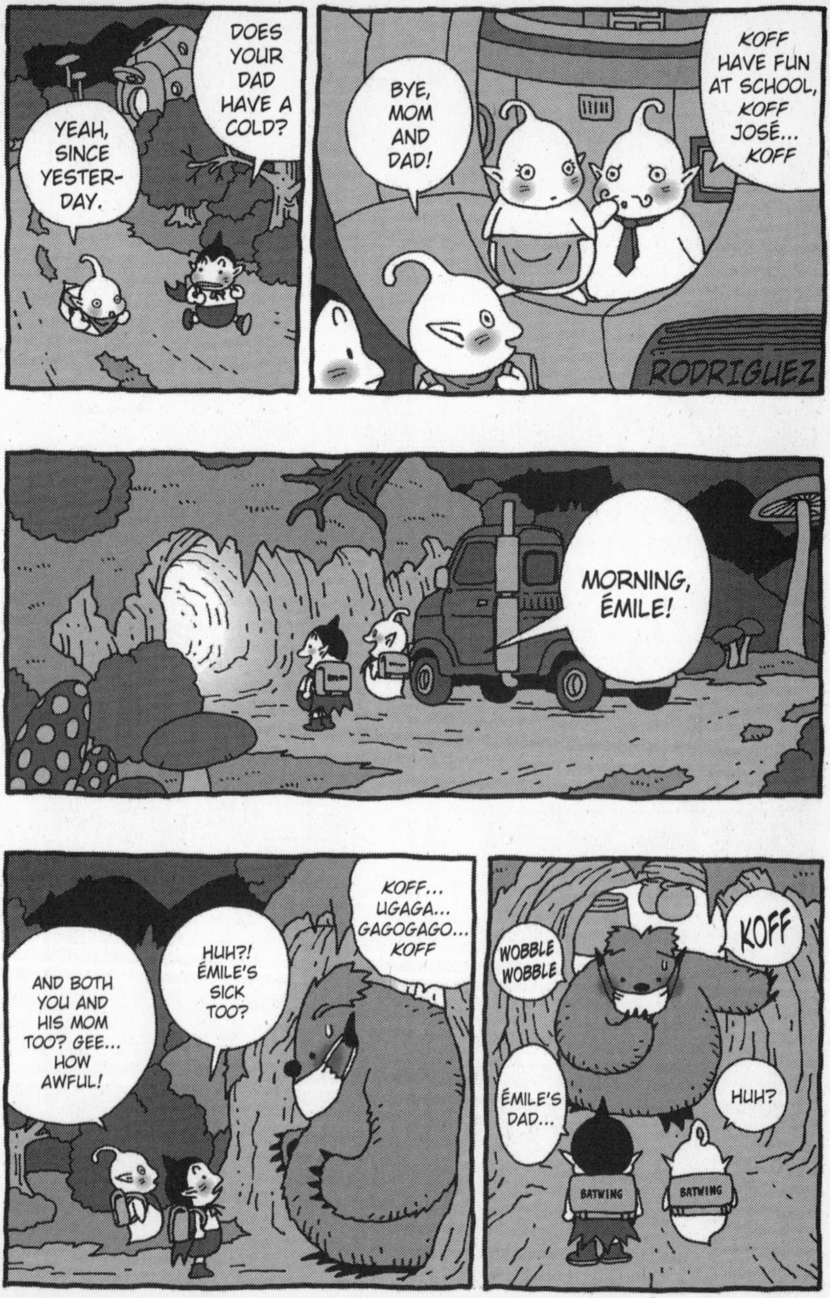
KOFF HAVE FUN AT SCHOOL, KOFF JOSÉ... KOFF
BYE, MOM AND DAD!
RODRIGUEZ
DOES YOUR DAD HAVE A COLD?
YEAH, SINCE YESTER-DAY.
MORNING, ÉMILE!
KOFF
WOBBLE WOBBLE
HUH?
ÉMILE'S DAD...
BATWING
BATWING
KOFF... UGAGA... GAGOGAGO... KOFF
HUH?! ÉMILE'S SICK TOO?
AND BOTH YOU AND HIS MOM TOO? GEE... HOW AWFUL!

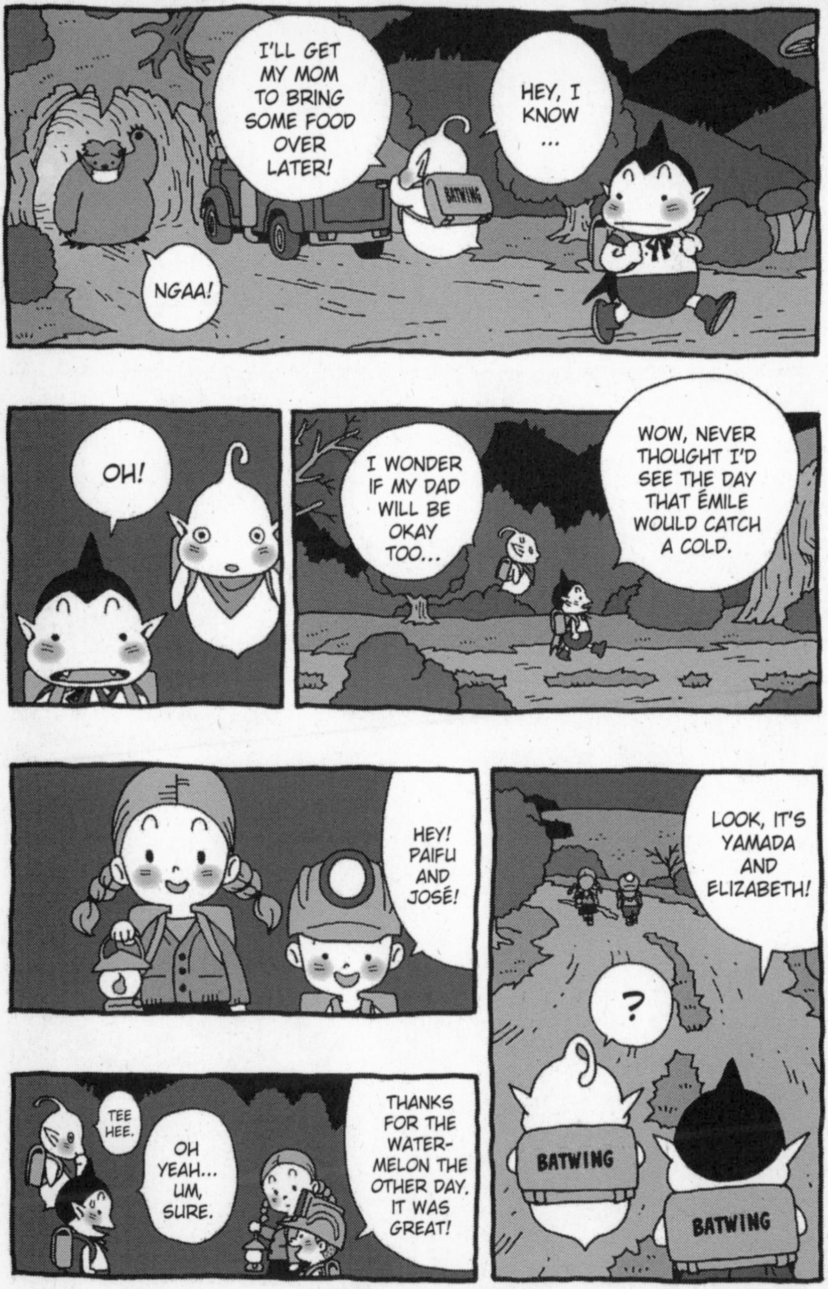
HEY, I KNOW ...
I'LL GET MY MOM TO BRING SOME FOOD OVER LATER!
BATWING
NGAA!
WOW, NEVER THOUGHT I'D SEE THE DAY THAT ÉMILE WOULD CATCH A COLD.
I WONDER IF MY DAD WILL BE OKAY TOO...
OH!
LOOK, IT'S YAMADA AND ELIZABETH!
?
BATWING
BATWING
HEY! PAIFU AND JOSÉ!
THANKS FOR THE WATER-MELON THE OTHER DAY. IT WAS GREAT!
OH YEAH... UM, SURE.
TEE HEE.

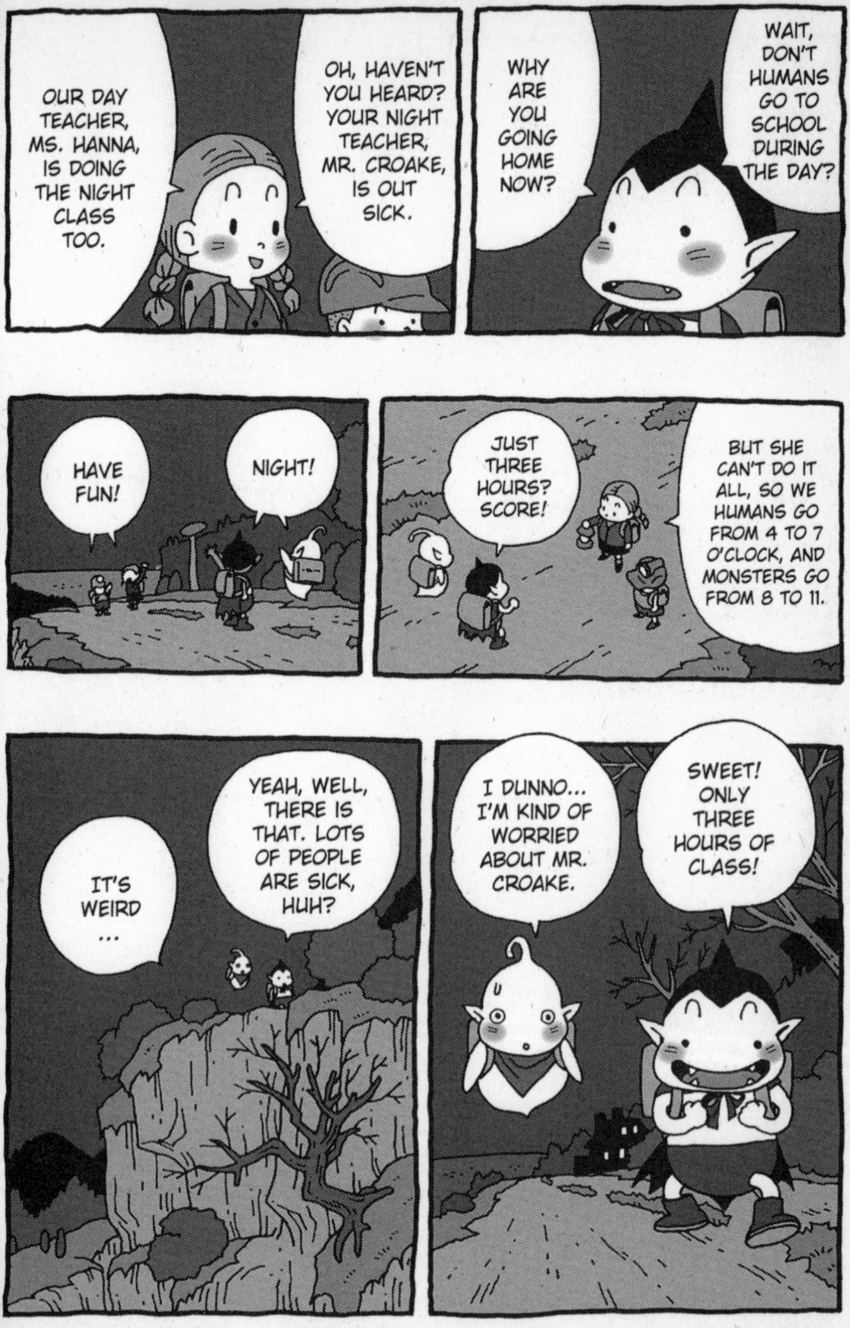
WAIT, DON'T HUMANS GO TO SCHOOL DURING THE DAY?
WHY ARE YOU GOING HOME NOW?
OH, HAVEN'T YOU HEARD? YOUR NIGHT TEACHER, MR. CROAKE, IS OUT SICK.
OUR DAY TEACHER, MS. HANNA, IS DOING THE NIGHT CLASS TOO.
BUT SHE CAN'T DO IT ALL, SO WE HUMANS GO FROM 4 TO 7 O'CLOCK, AND MONSTERS GO FROM 8 TO 11.
JUST THREE HOURS? SCORE!
NIGHT!
HAVE FUN!
SWEET! ONLY THREE HOURS OF CLASS!
I DUNNO... I'M KIND OF WORRIED ABOUT MR. CROAKE.
YEAH, WELL, THERE IS THAT. LOTS OF PEOPLE ARE SICK, HUH?
IT'S WEIRD...

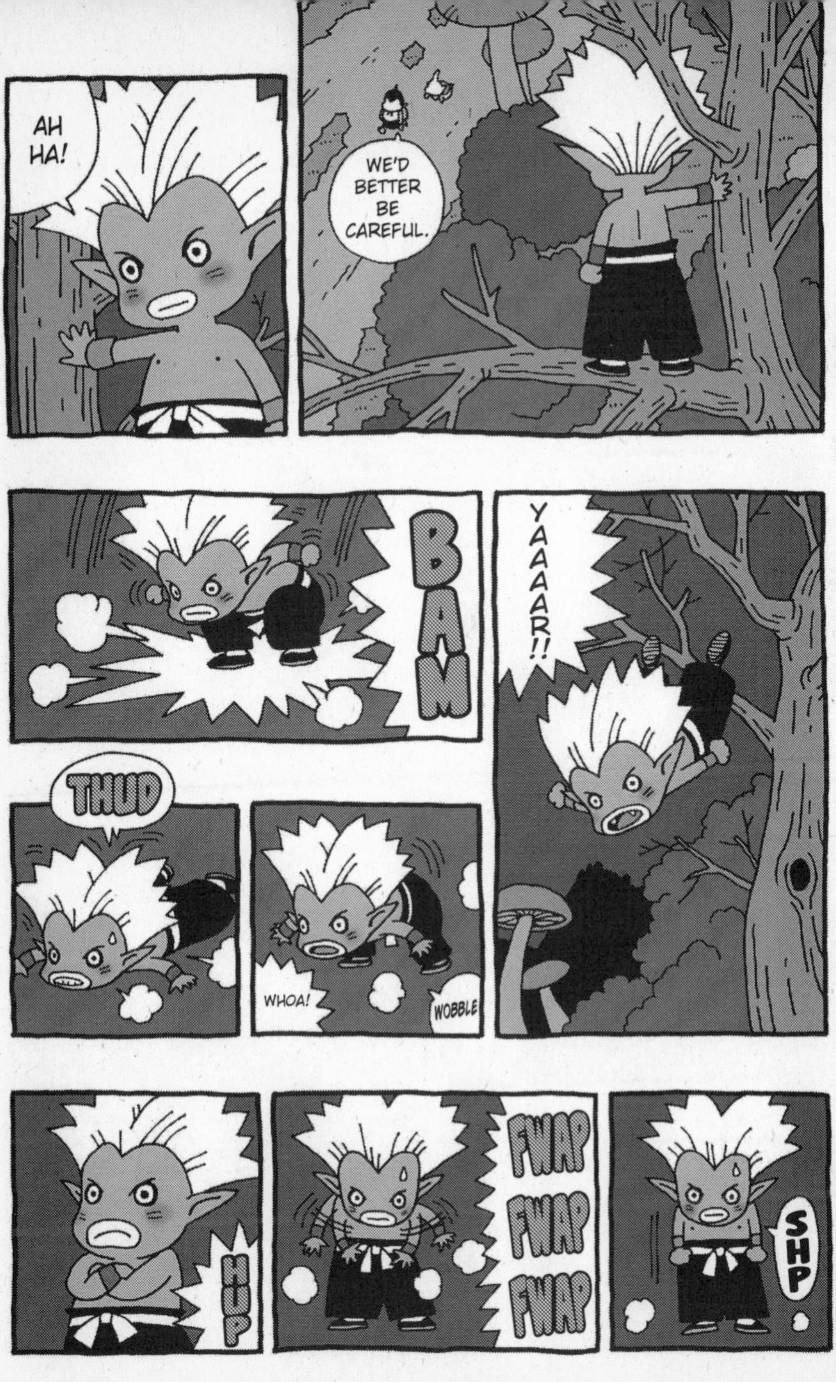
WE'D BETTER BE CAREFUL.
AH HA!
YAAAAAR!!
BAM
WHOA!
WOBBLE
THUD
SHP
FWAP
FWAP
FWAP
HUP

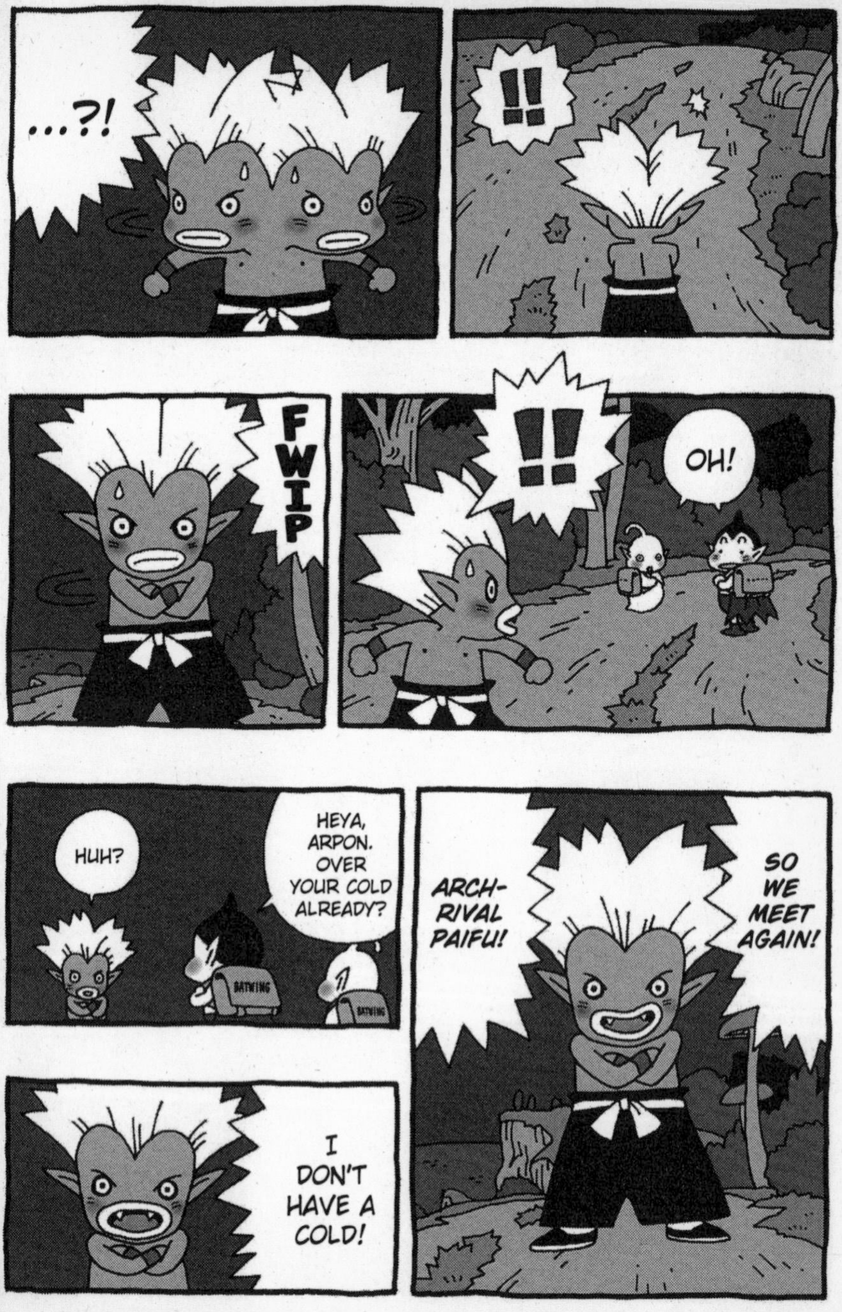
!!
...?!
!!
OH!
FWIP
SO WE MEET AGAIN!
ARCH-RIVAL PAIFU!
HEYA, ARPON. OVER YOUR COLD ALREADY?
HUH?
BATWING
BATWING
I DON'T HAVE A COLD!

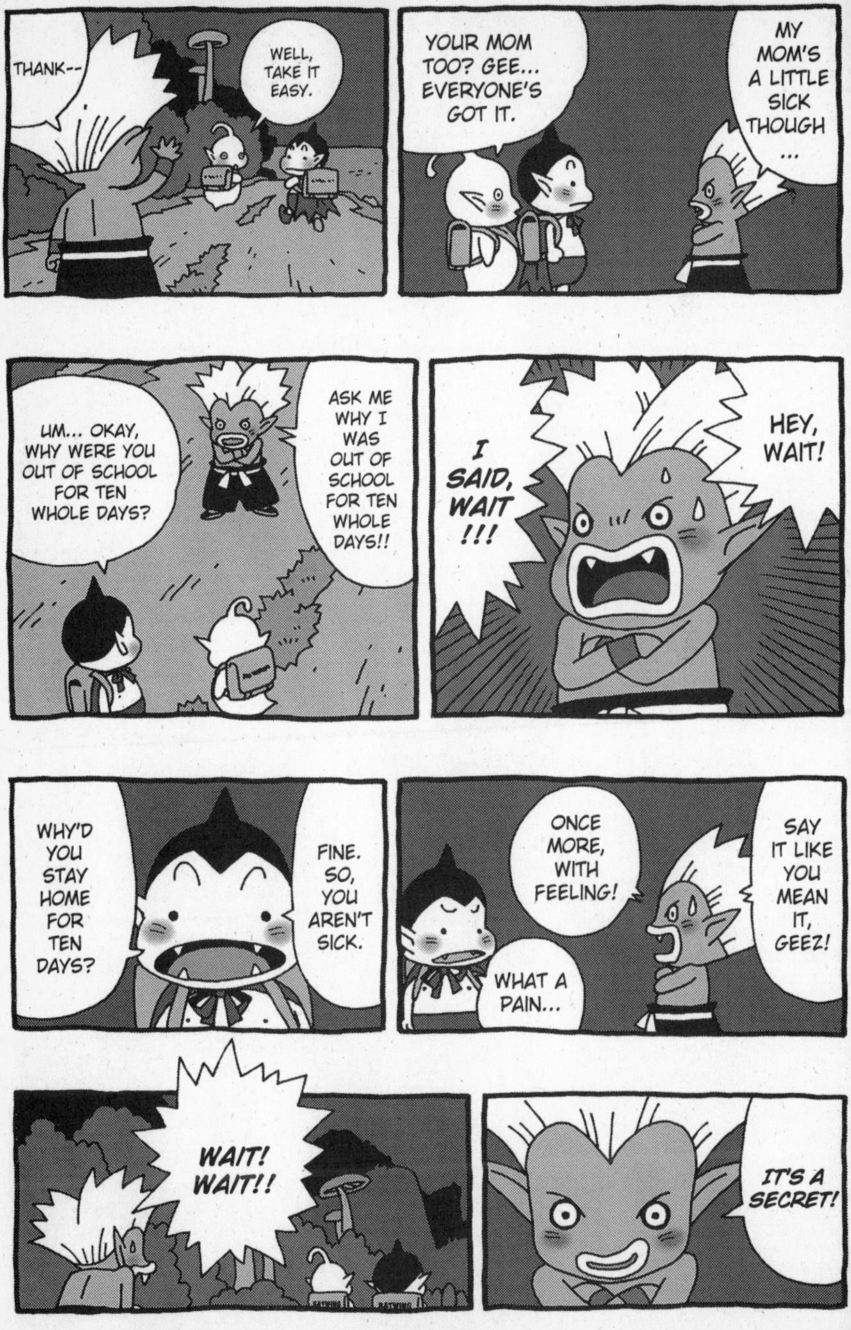
MY MOM'S A LITTLE SICK THOUGH...
YOUR MOM TOO? GEE... EVERYONE'S GOT IT.
WELL, TAKE IT EASY.
THANK--
HEY, WAIT!
I SAID, WAIT!!!
ASK ME WHY I WAS OUT OF SCHOOL FOR TEN WHOLE DAYS!!
UM... OKAY, WHY WERE YOU OUT OF SCHOOL FOR TEN WHOLE DAYS?
SAY IT LIKE YOU MEAN IT, GEEZ!
ONCE MORE, WITH FEELING!
WHAT A PAIN...
FINE. SO, YOU AREN'T SICK.
WHY'D YOU STAY HOME FOR TEN DAYS?
IT'S A SECRET!
WAIT! WAIT!!

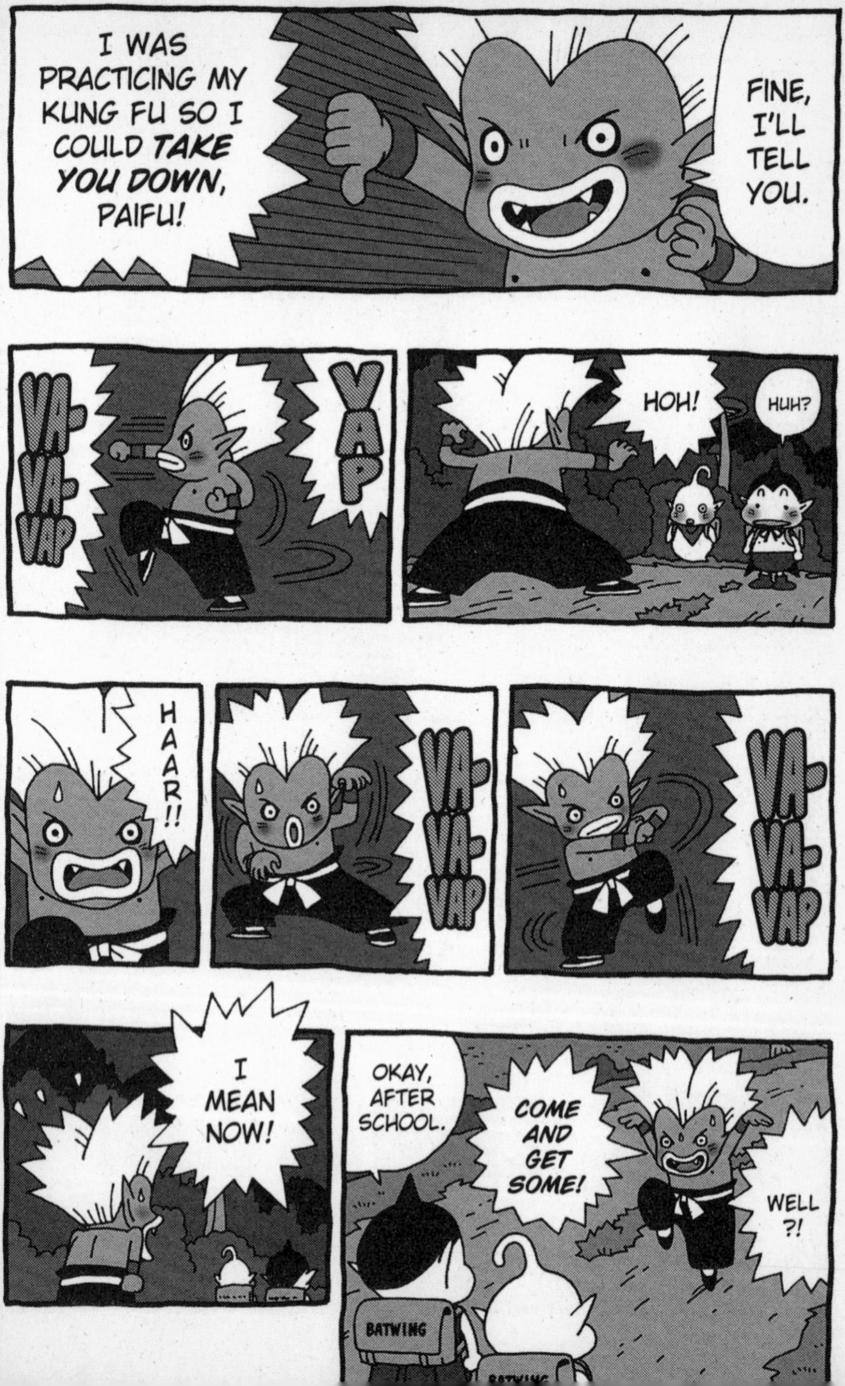
FINE, I'LL TELL YOU.
I WAS PRACTICING MY KUNG FU SO I COULD TAKE YOU DOWN, PAIFU!
HUH?
HOH!
VAP
VA VA VAP
VA VA VAP
VA VA VAP
HAAR!!
WELL ?!
COME AND GET SOME!
OKAY, AFTER SCHOOL.
BATWING
I MEAN NOW!

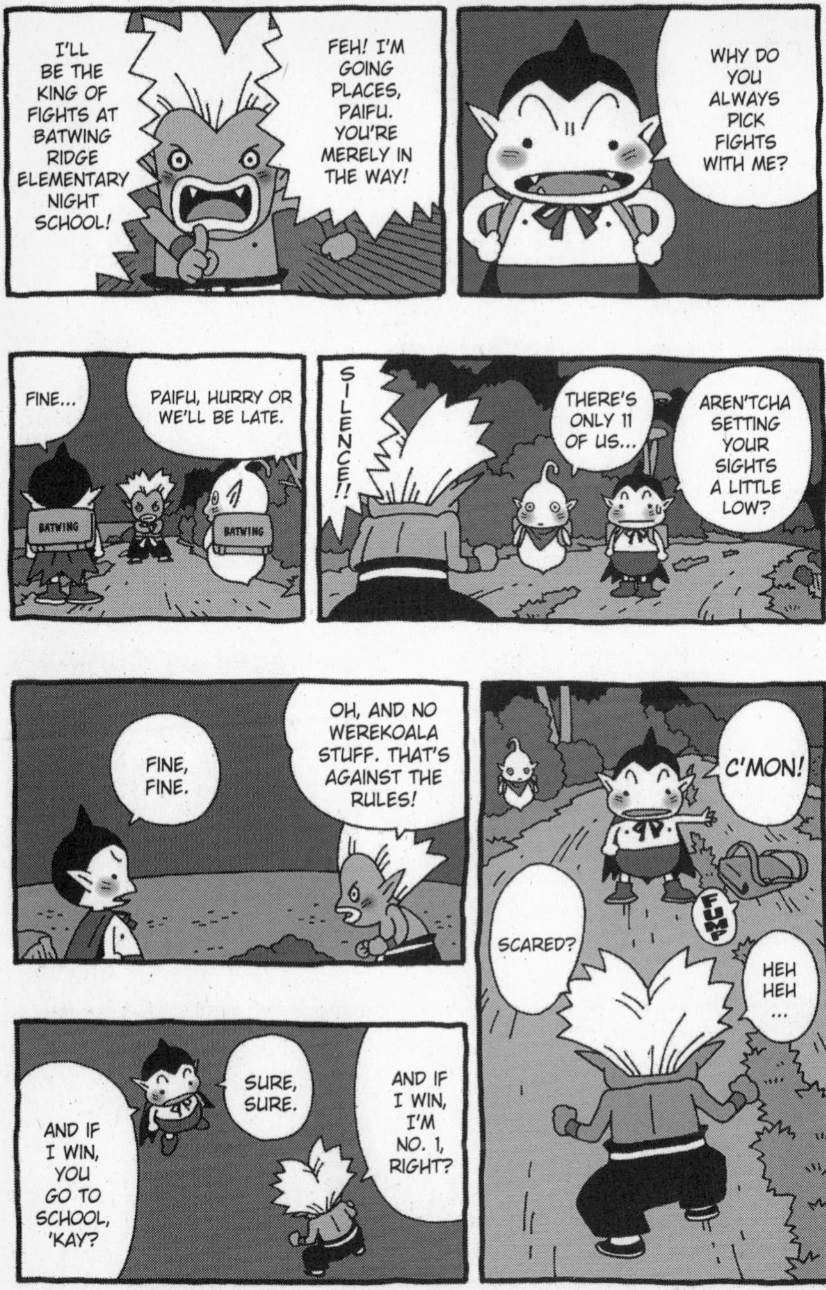
WHY DO YOU ALWAYS PICK FIGHTS WITH ME?
FEH! I'M GOING PLACES, PAIFU. YOU'RE MERELY IN THE WAY!
I'LL BE THE KING OF FIGHTS AT BATWING RIDGE ELEMENTARY NIGHT SCHOOL!
AREN'TCHA SETTING YOUR SIGHTS A LITTLE LOW?
THERE'S ONLY 11 OF US...
SILENCE!!
PAIFU, HURRY OR WE'LL BE LATE.
FINE...
BATWING
BATWING
C'MON!
FUMP
SCARED?
HEH HEH ...
OH, AND NO WEREKOALA STUFF. THAT'S AGAINST THE RULES!
FINE, FINE.
AND IF I WIN, I'M NO. 1, RIGHT?
SURE, SURE.
AND IF I WIN, YOU GO TO SCHOOL, 'KAY?

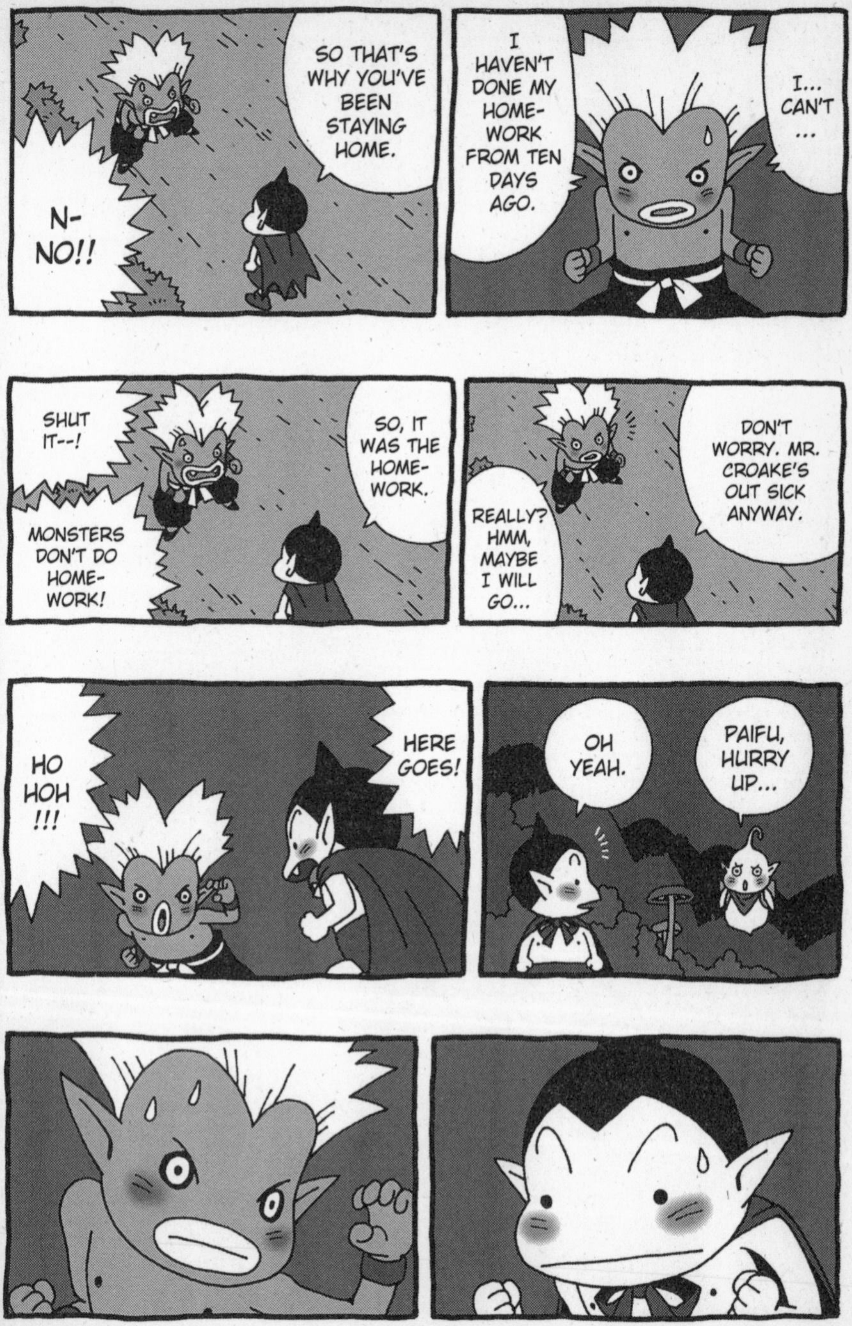
I... CAN'T ...
I HAVEN'T DONE MY HOMEWORK FROM TEN DAYS AGO.
SO THAT'S WHY YOU'VE BEEN STAYING HOME.
N-NO!!
DON'T WORRY. MR. CROAKE'S OUT SICK ANYWAY.
REALLY? HMM, MAYBE I WILL GO...
SO, IT WAS THE HOMEWORK.
SHUT IT--!
MONSTERS DON'T DO HOMEWORK!
PAIFU, HURRY UP...
OH YEAH.
HERE GOES!
HO HOH !!!

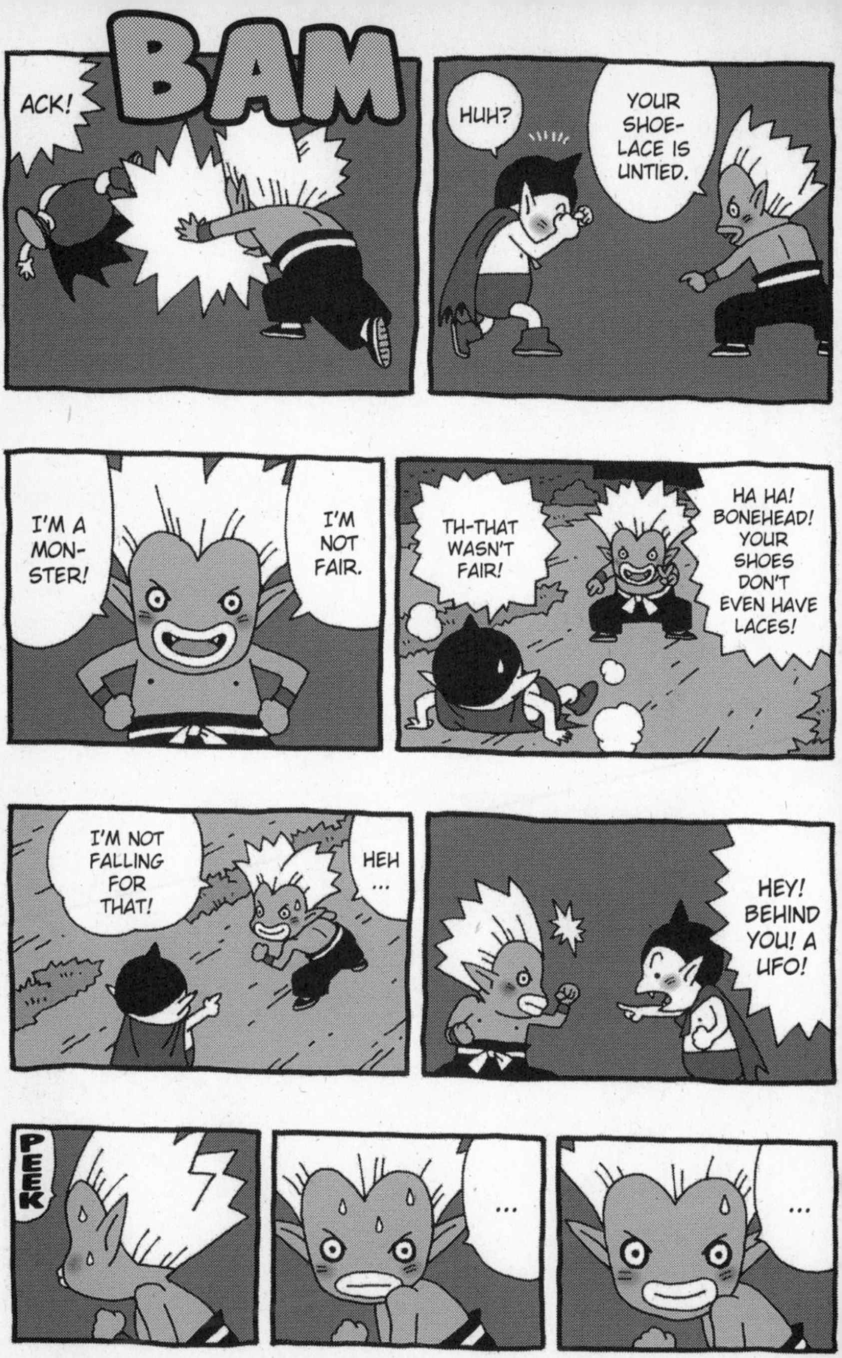
YOUR SHOE-LACE IS UNTIED.
HUH?
BAM
ACK!
HA HA! BONEHEAD! YOUR SHOES DON'T EVEN HAVE LACES!
TH-THAT WASN'T FAIR!
I'M NOT FAIR.
I'M A MON-STER!
HEY! BEHIND YOU! A UFO!
HEH ...
I'M NOT FALLING FOR THAT!
...
...
PEEK

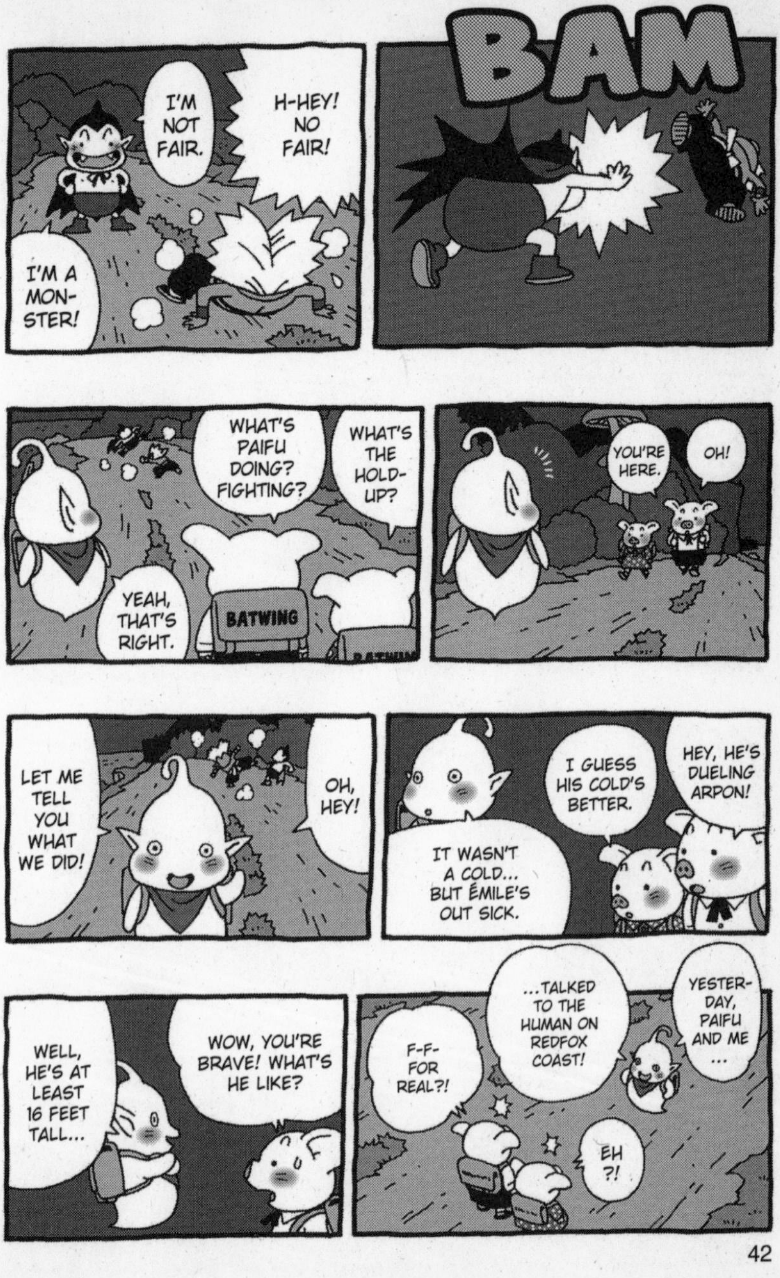
BAM
H-HEY! NO FAIR!
I'M NOT FAIR.
I'M A MON-STER!
OH!
YOU'RE HERE.
WHAT'S THE HOLD-UP?
WHAT'S PAIFU DOING? FIGHTING?
BATWING
YEAH, THAT'S RIGHT.
HEY, HE'S DUELING ARPON!
I GUESS HIS COLD'S BETTER.
IT WASN'T A COLD... BUT ÉMILE'S OUT SICK.
OH, HEY!
LET ME TELL YOU WHAT WE DID!
YESTER-DAY, PAIFU AND ME ...
...TALKED TO THE HUMAN ON REDFOX COAST!
F-F-FOR REAL?!
EH ?!
WOW, YOU'RE BRAVE! WHAT'S HE LIKE?
WELL, HE'S AT LEAST 16 FEET TALL...

READ THIS WAY

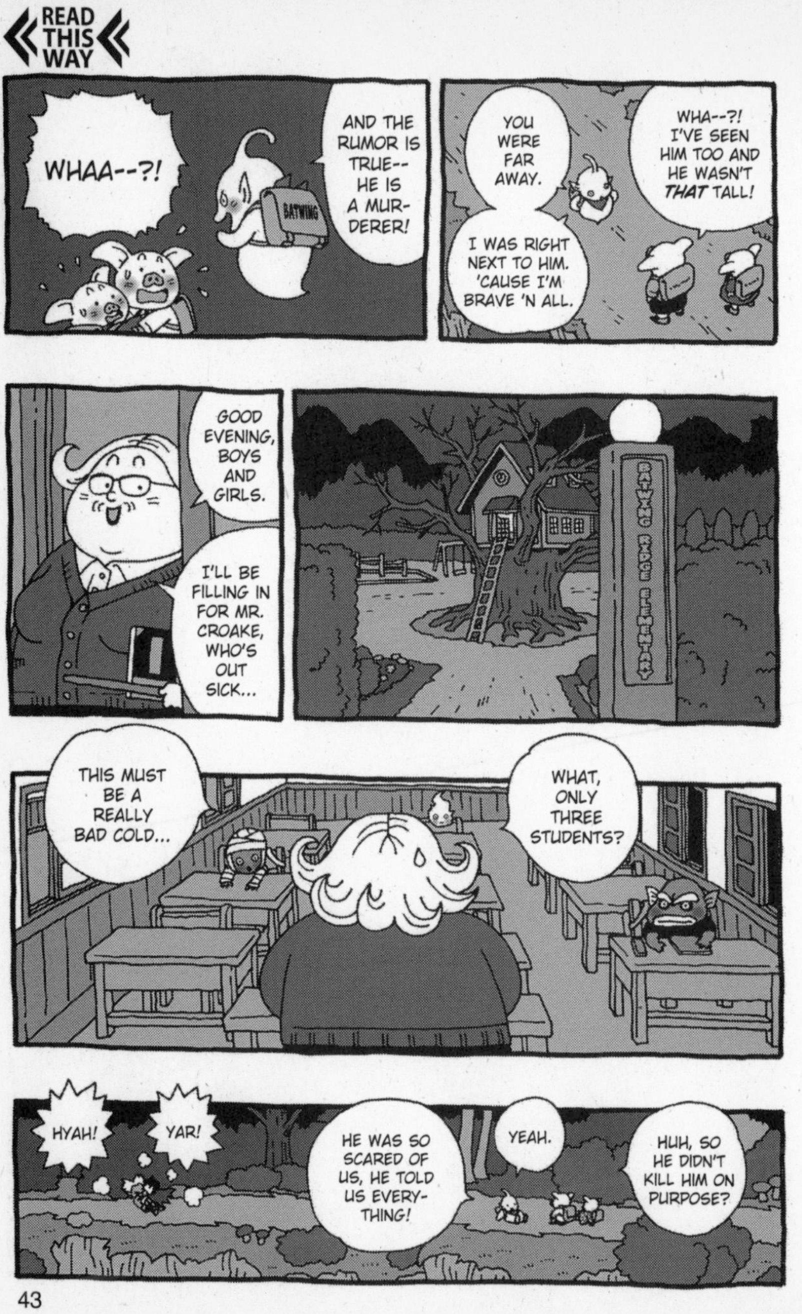

WHA--?! I'VE SEEN HIM TOO AND HE WASN'T *THAT* TALL!
YOU WERE FAR AWAY.
I WAS RIGHT NEXT TO HIM. 'CAUSE I'M BRAVE 'N ALL.
AND THE RUMOR IS TRUE-- HE IS A MURDERER!
BATWING
WHAA--?!
BATWING RIDGE ELEMENTARY
GOOD EVENING, BOYS AND GIRLS.
I'LL BE FILLING IN FOR MR. CROAKE, WHO'S OUT SICK...
WHAT, ONLY THREE STUDENTS?
THIS MUST BE A REALLY BAD COLD...
HUH, SO HE DIDN'T KILL HIM ON PURPOSE?
YEAH.
HE WAS SO SCARED OF US, HE TOLD US EVERY-THING!
YAR!
HYAH!

COWA!

FRIGHT 4

Monster Flu

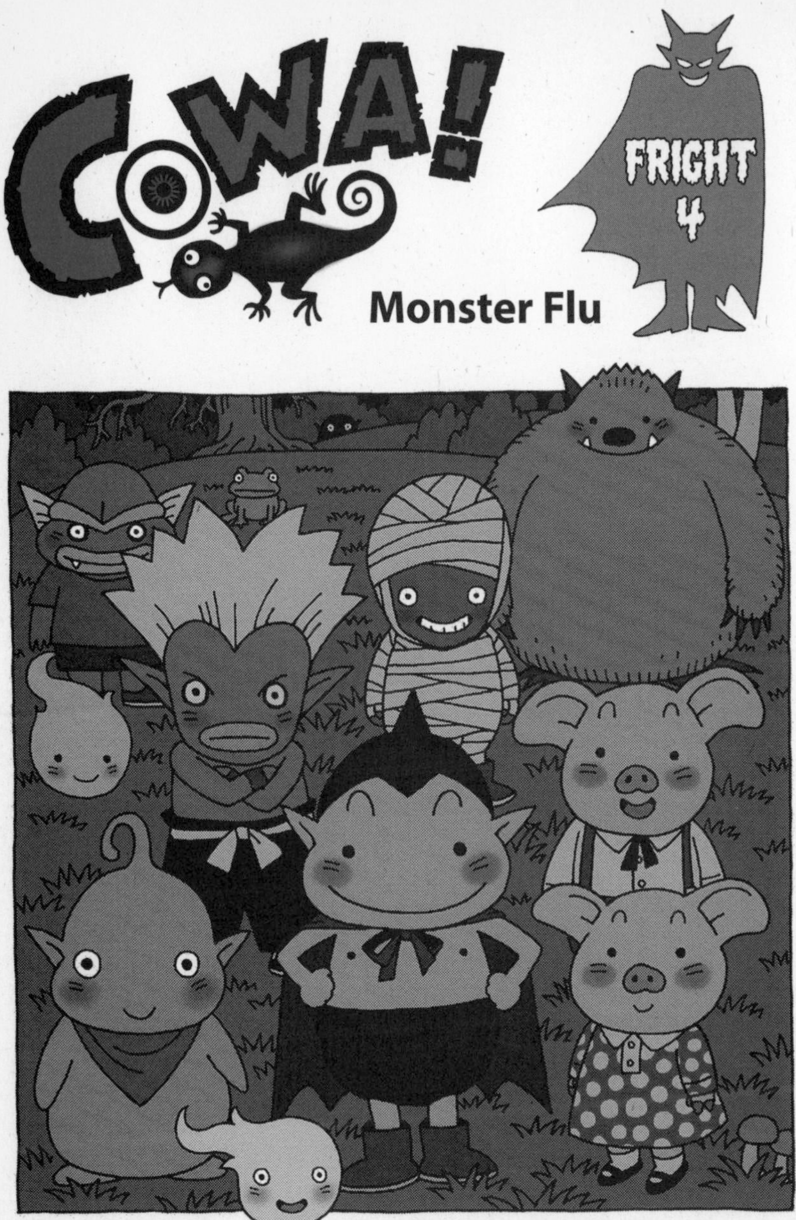

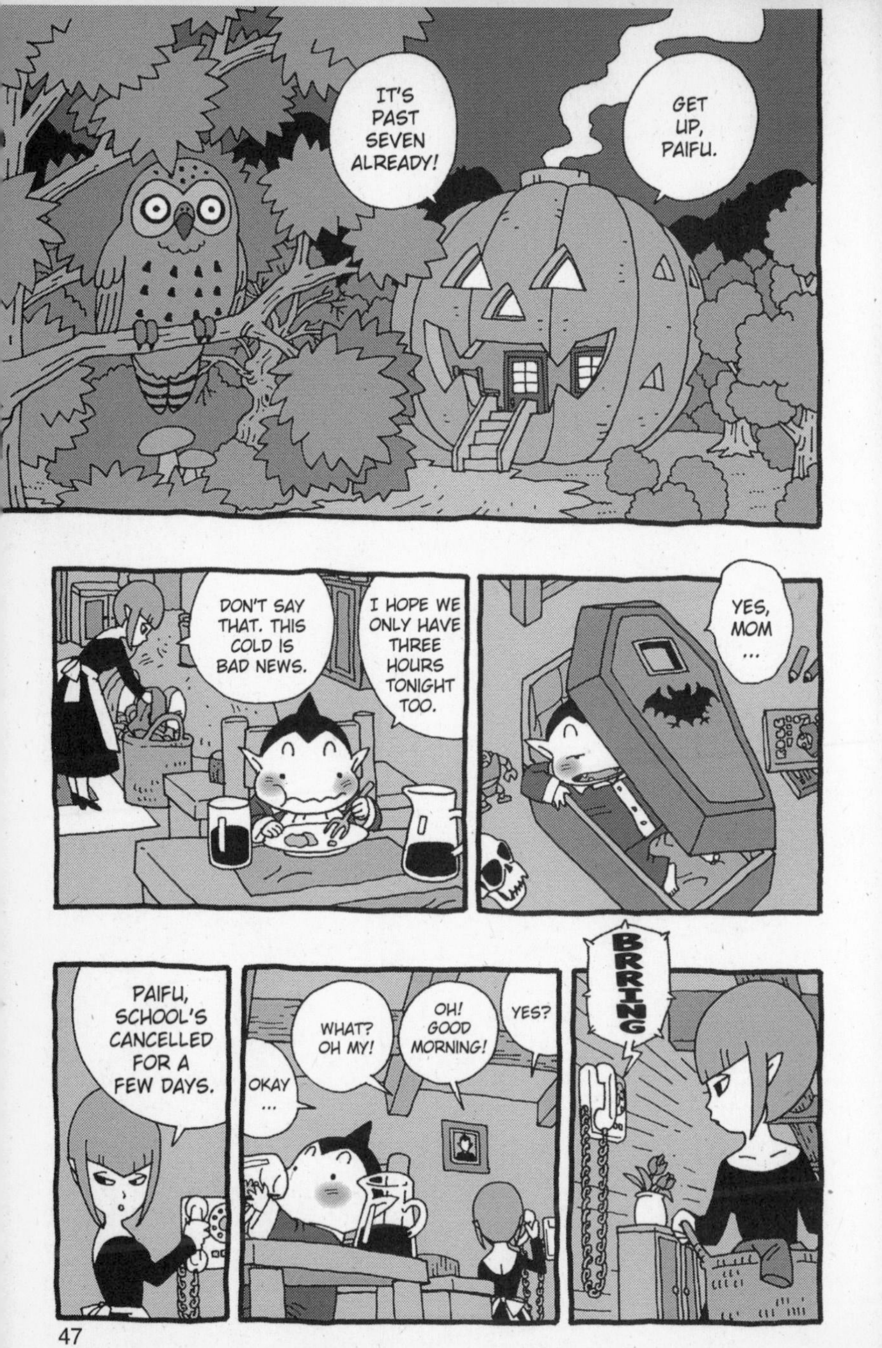
GET UP, PAIFU.
IT'S PAST SEVEN ALREADY!
YES, MOM ...
I HOPE WE ONLY HAVE THREE HOURS TONIGHT TOO.
DON'T SAY THAT. THIS COLD IS BAD NEWS.
BRRING
YES?
OH! GOOD MORNING!
WHAT? OH MY!
OKAY ...
PAIFU, SCHOOL'S CANCELLED FOR A FEW DAYS.

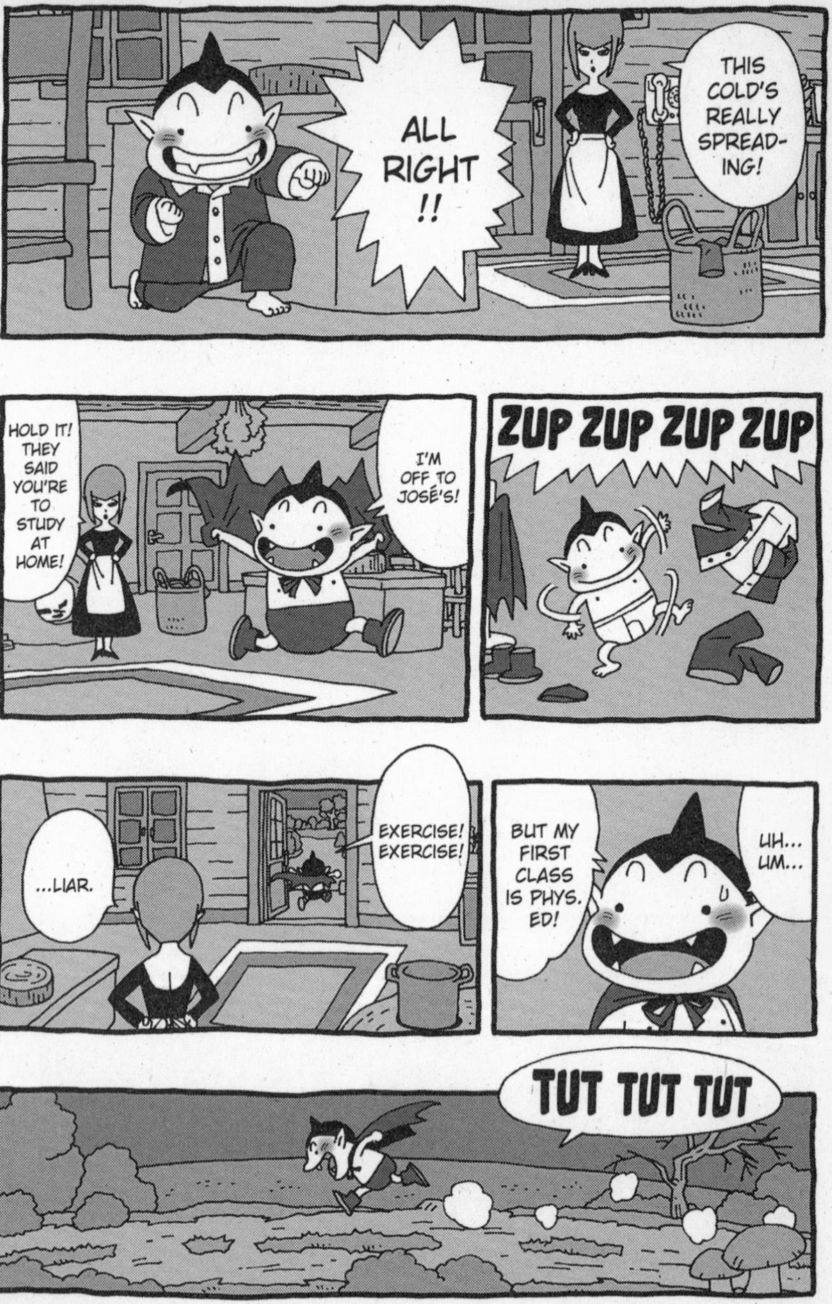
THIS COLD'S REALLY SPREAD-ING!
ALL RIGHT!!
ZUP ZUP ZUP ZUP
I'M OFF TO JOSÉ'S!
HOLD IT! THEY SAID YOU'RE TO STUDY AT HOME!
UH... UM...
BUT MY FIRST CLASS IS PHYS. ED!
EXERCISE! EXERCISE!
...LIAR.
TUT TUT TUT

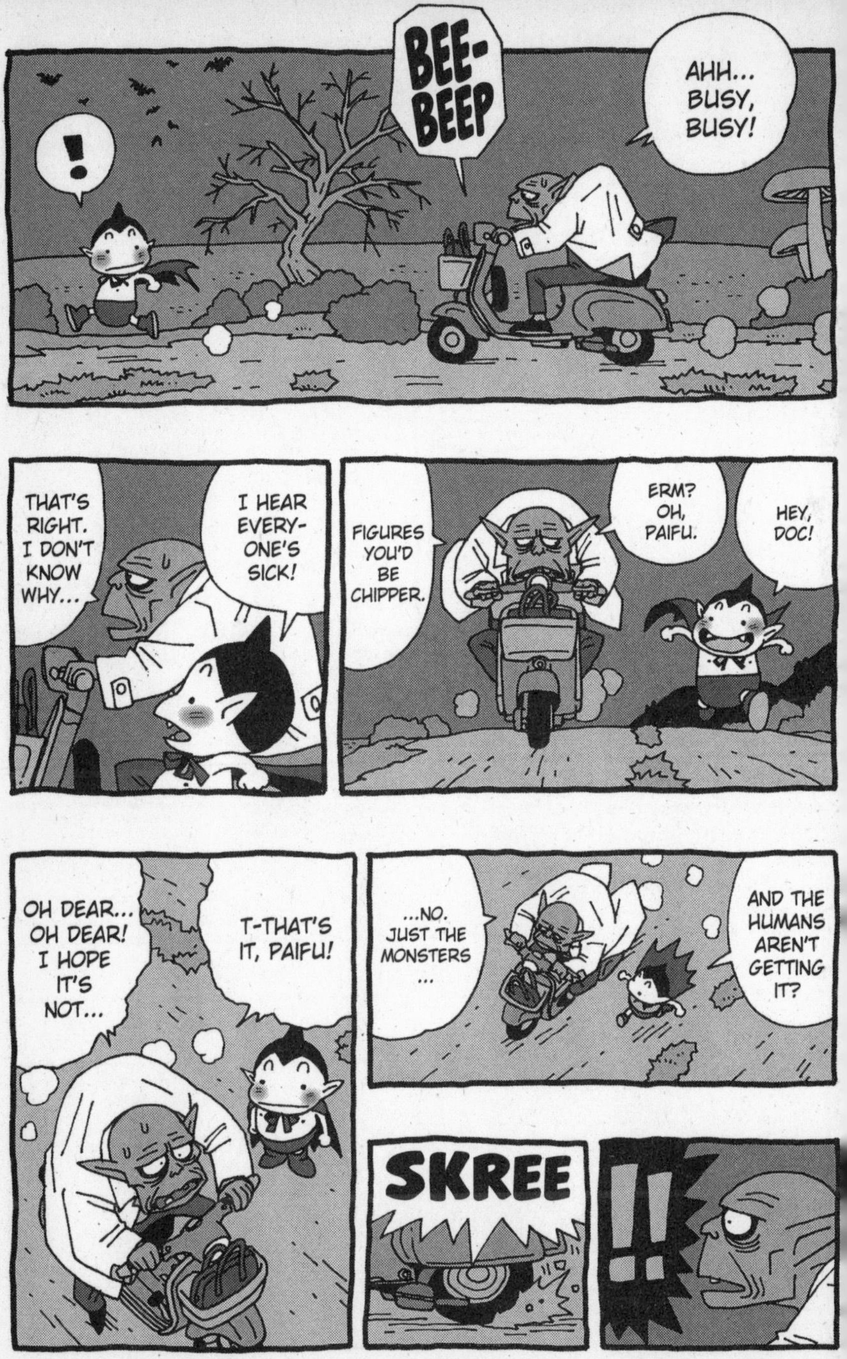
AHH... BUSY, BUSY!
BEE-BEEP
!
HEY, DOC!
ERM? OH, PAIFU.
FIGURES YOU'D BE CHIPPER.
I HEAR EVERY-ONE'S SICK!
THAT'S RIGHT. I DON'T KNOW WHY...
AND THE HUMANS AREN'T GETTING IT?
...NO. JUST THE MONSTERS ...
!!
SKREE
T-THAT'S IT, PAIFU!
OH DEAR... OH DEAR! I HOPE IT'S NOT...

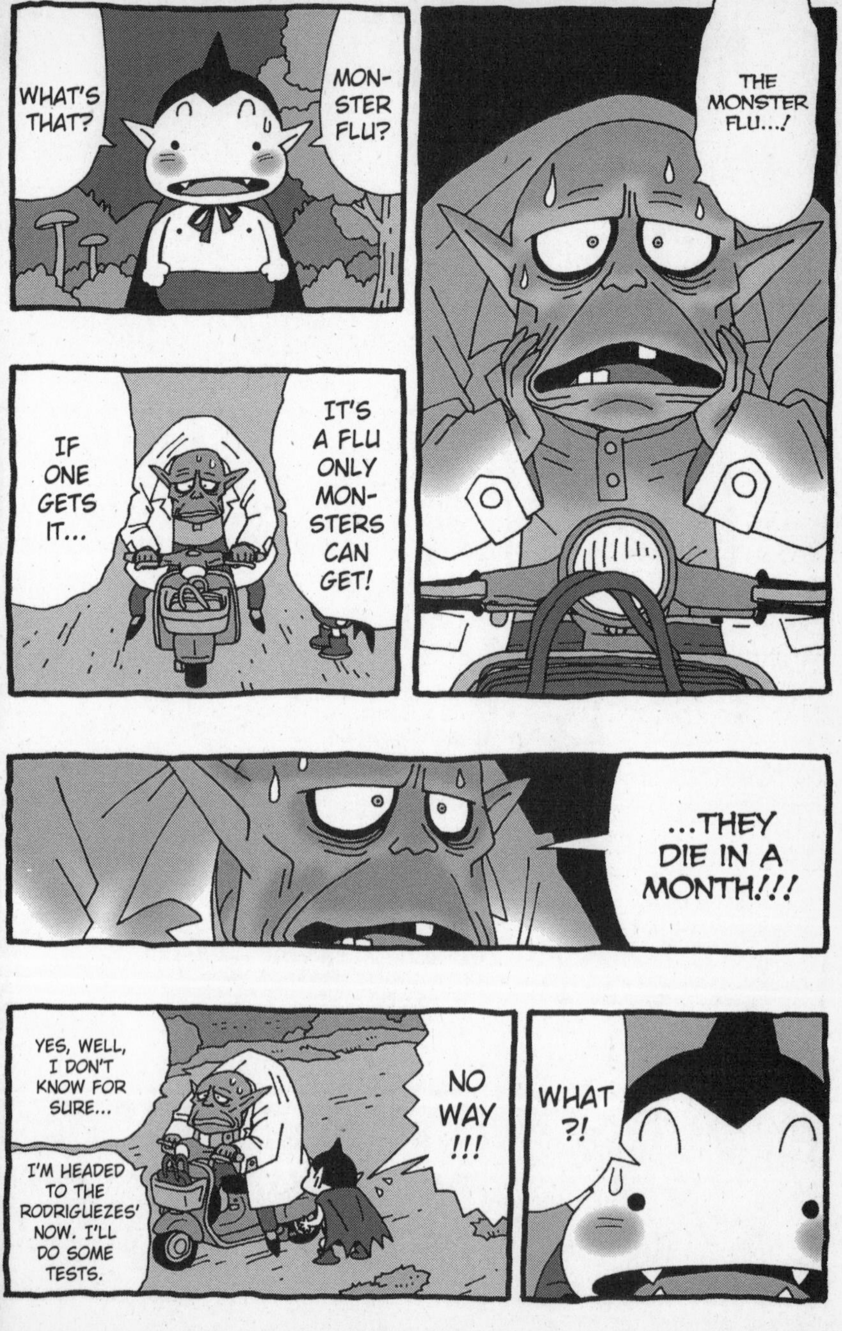
THE MONSTER FLU...!
MON-STER FLU?
WHAT'S THAT?
IT'S A FLU ONLY MON-STERS CAN GET!
IF ONE GETS IT...
...THEY DIE IN A MONTH!!!
WHAT ?!
NO WAY !!!
YES, WELL, I DON'T KNOW FOR SURE...
I'M HEADED TO THE RODRIGUEZES' NOW. I'LL DO SOME TESTS.

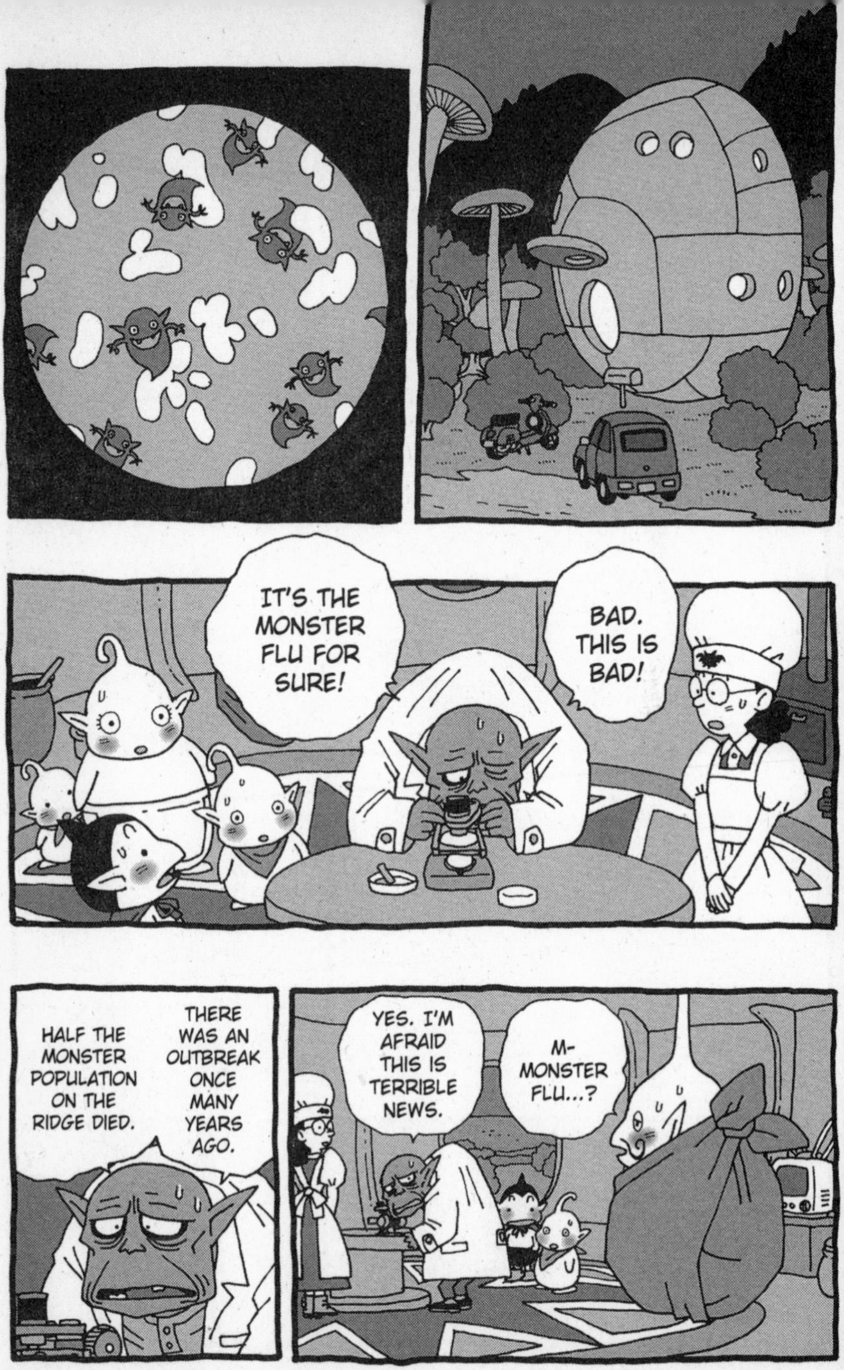
BAD. THIS IS BAD!
IT'S THE MONSTER FLU FOR SURE!
M- MONSTER FLU...?
YES. I'M AFRAID THIS IS TERRIBLE NEWS.
THERE WAS AN OUTBREAK ONCE MANY YEARS AGO.
HALF THE MONSTER POPULATION ON THE RIDGE DIED.

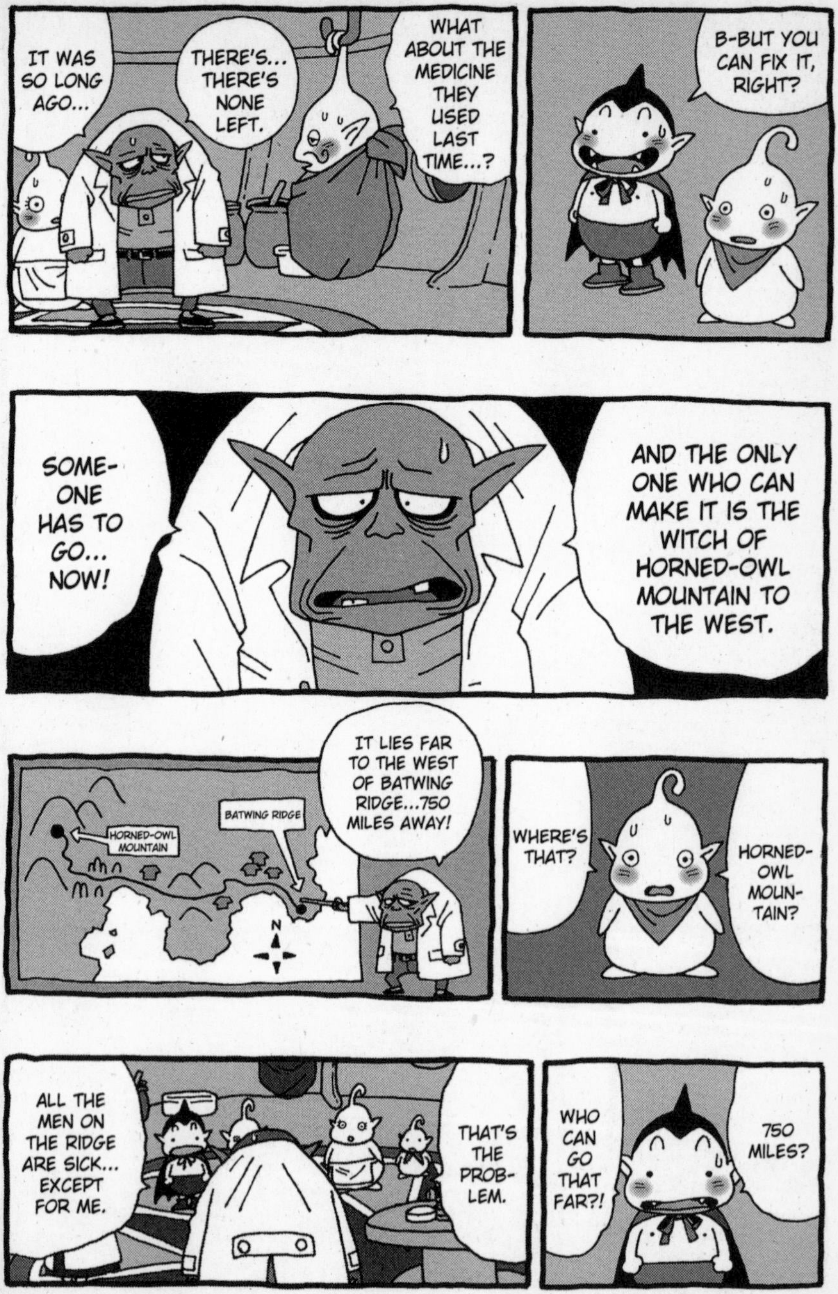
B-BUT YOU CAN FIX IT, RIGHT?
WHAT ABOUT THE MEDICINE THEY USED LAST TIME...?
THERE'S... THERE'S NONE LEFT.
IT WAS SO LONG AGO...
AND THE ONLY ONE WHO CAN MAKE IT IS THE WITCH OF HORNED-OWL MOUNTAIN TO THE WEST.
SOME-ONE HAS TO GO... NOW!
HORNED-OWL MOUN-TAIN?
WHERE'S THAT?
IT LIES FAR TO THE WEST OF BATWING RIDGE...750 MILES AWAY!
BATWING RIDGE
HORNED-OWL MOUNTAIN
N
750 MILES?
WHO CAN GO THAT FAR?!
THAT'S THE PROB-LEM.
ALL THE MEN ON THE RIDGE ARE SICK... EXCEPT FOR ME.

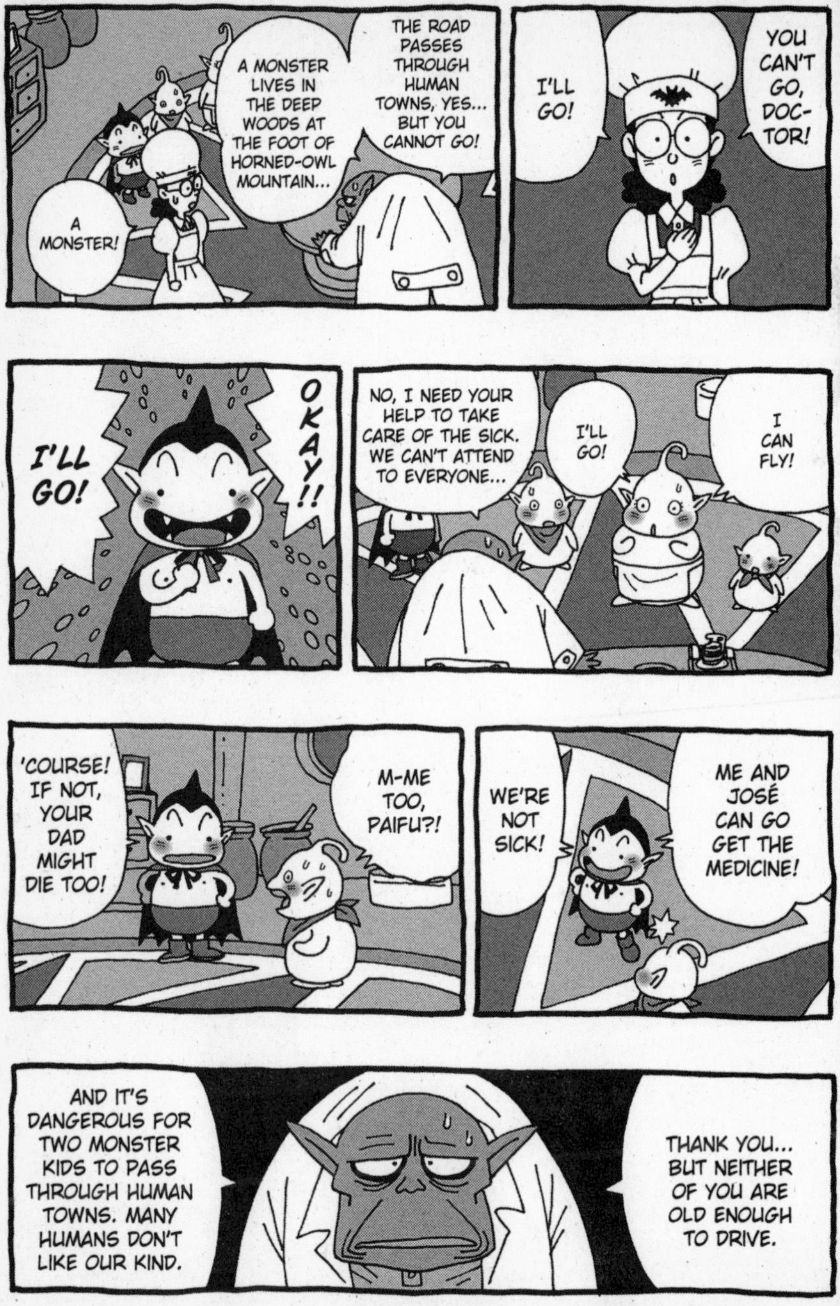
A MONSTER!
A MONSTER LIVES IN THE DEEP WOODS AT THE FOOT OF HORNED-OWL MOUNTAIN...
THE ROAD PASSES THROUGH HUMAN TOWNS, YES... BUT YOU CANNOT GO!
I'LL GO!
YOU CAN'T GO, DOC-TOR!
I'LL GO!
OKAY!!
NO, I NEED YOUR HELP TO TAKE CARE OF THE SICK. WE CAN'T ATTEND TO EVERYONE...
I'LL GO!
I CAN FLY!
M-ME TOO, PAIFU?!
'COURSE! IF NOT, YOUR DAD MIGHT DIE TOO!
WE'RE NOT SICK!
ME AND JOSÉ CAN GO GET THE MEDICINE!
THANK YOU... BUT NEITHER OF YOU ARE OLD ENOUGH TO DRIVE.
AND IT'S DANGEROUS FOR TWO MONSTER KIDS TO PASS THROUGH HUMAN TOWNS. MANY HUMANS DON'T LIKE OUR KIND.

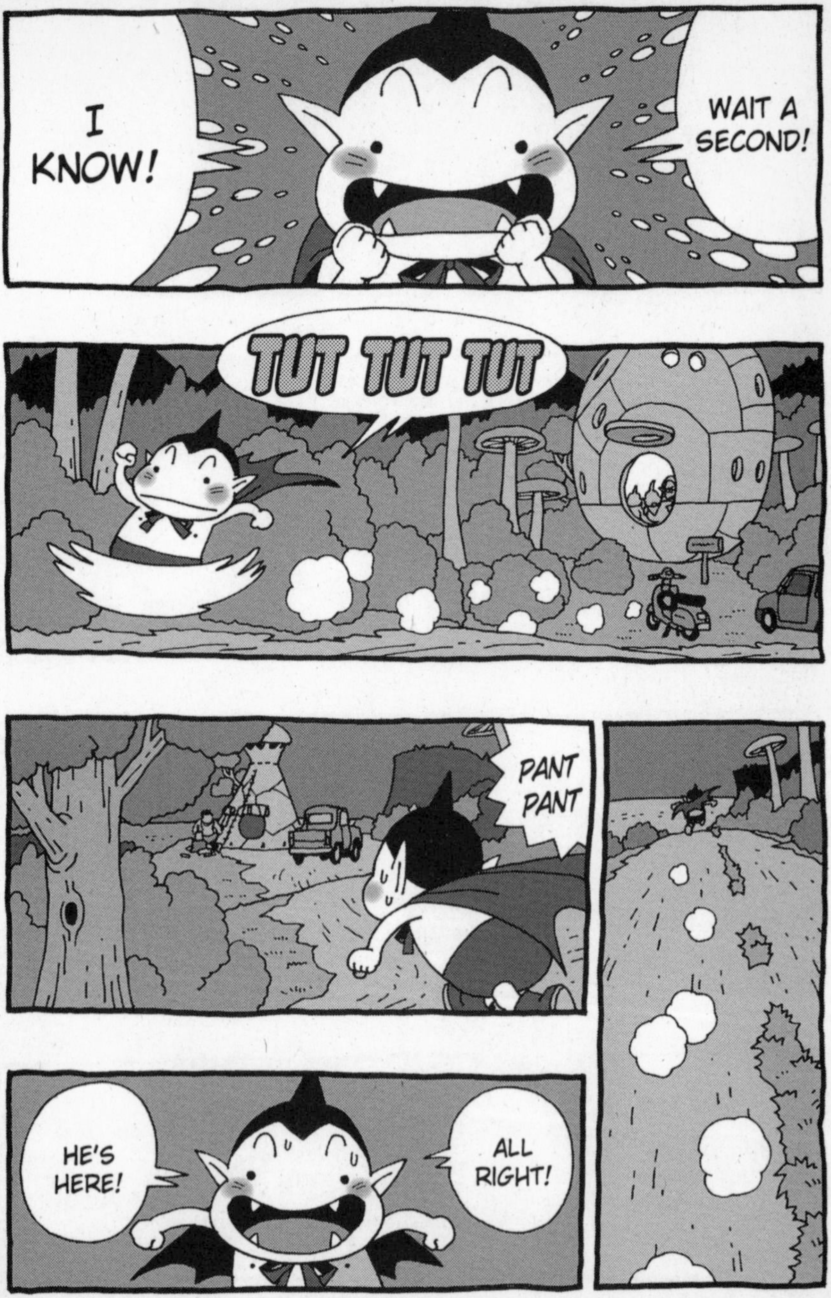
WAIT A SECOND!
I KNOW!
TUT TUT TUT
PANT PANT
ALL RIGHT!
HE'S HERE!

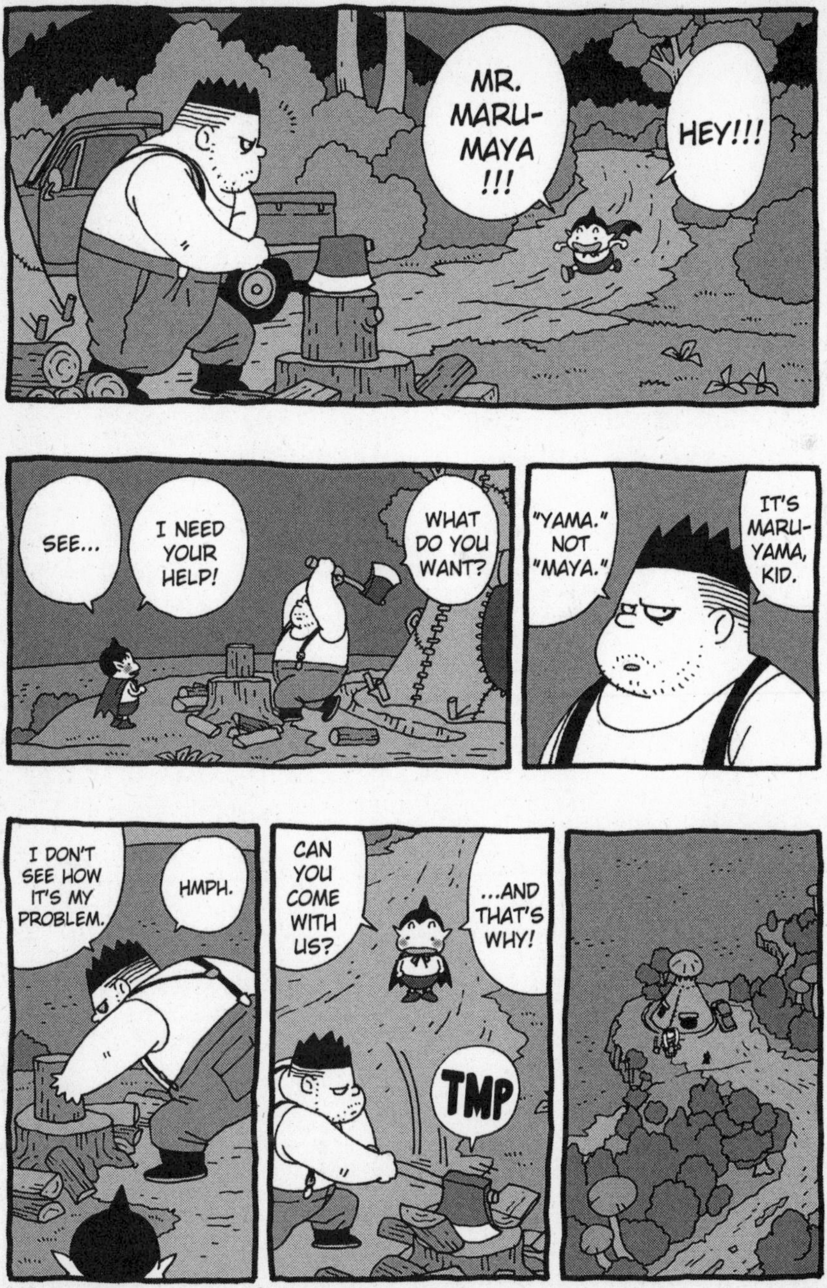
HEY!!!
MR. MARU-MAYA!!!
IT'S MARU-YAMA, KID.
"YAMA." NOT "MAYA."
WHAT DO YOU WANT?
I NEED YOUR HELP!
SEE...
...AND THAT'S WHY!
CAN YOU COME WITH US?
TMP
HMPH.
I DON'T SEE HOW IT'S MY PROBLEM.

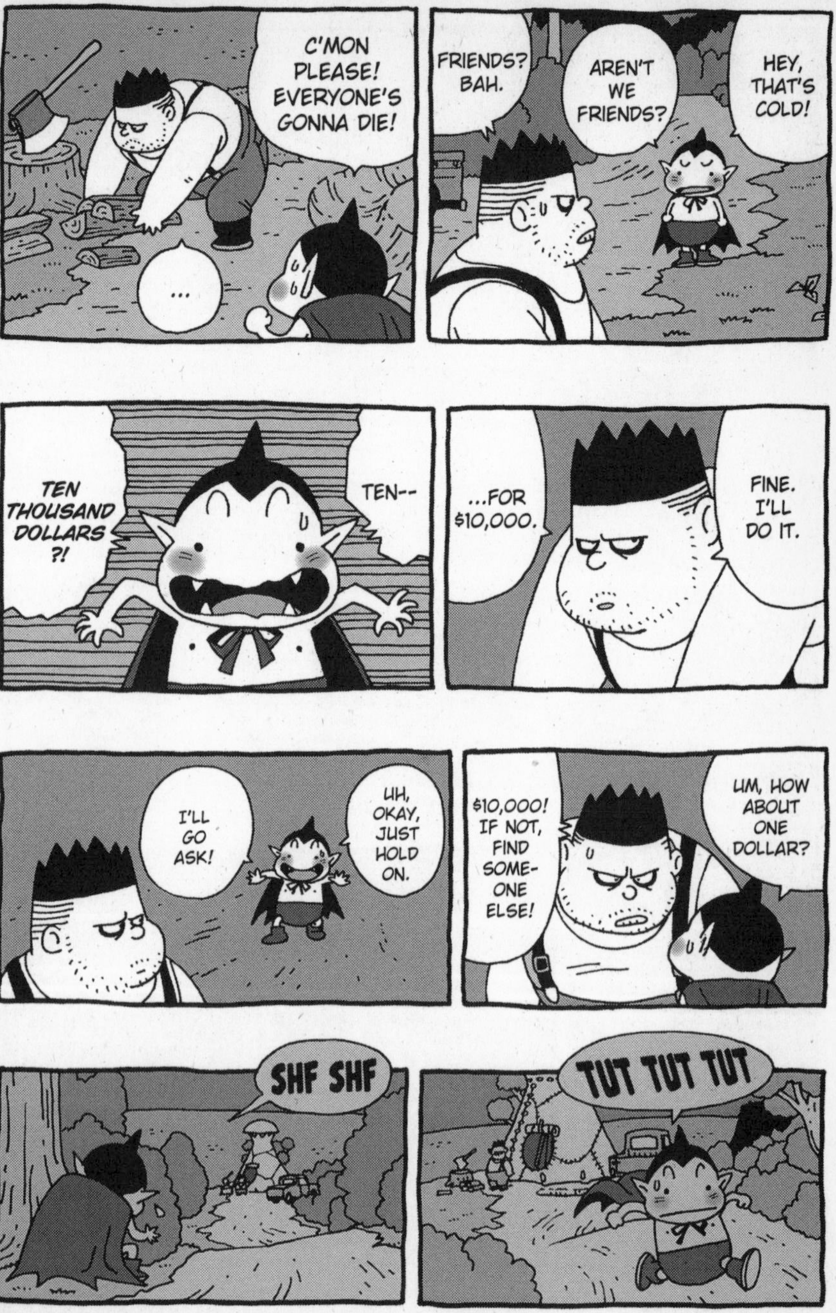
HEY, THAT'S COLD!
AREN'T WE FRIENDS?
FRIENDS? BAH.
C'MON PLEASE! EVERYONE'S GONNA DIE!
...
FINE. I'LL DO IT.
...FOR $10,000.
TEN--
TEN THOUSAND DOLLARS?!
UM, HOW ABOUT ONE DOLLAR?
$10,000! IF NOT, FIND SOME-ONE ELSE!
UH, OKAY, JUST HOLD ON.
I'LL GO ASK!
TUT TUT TUT
SHF SHF

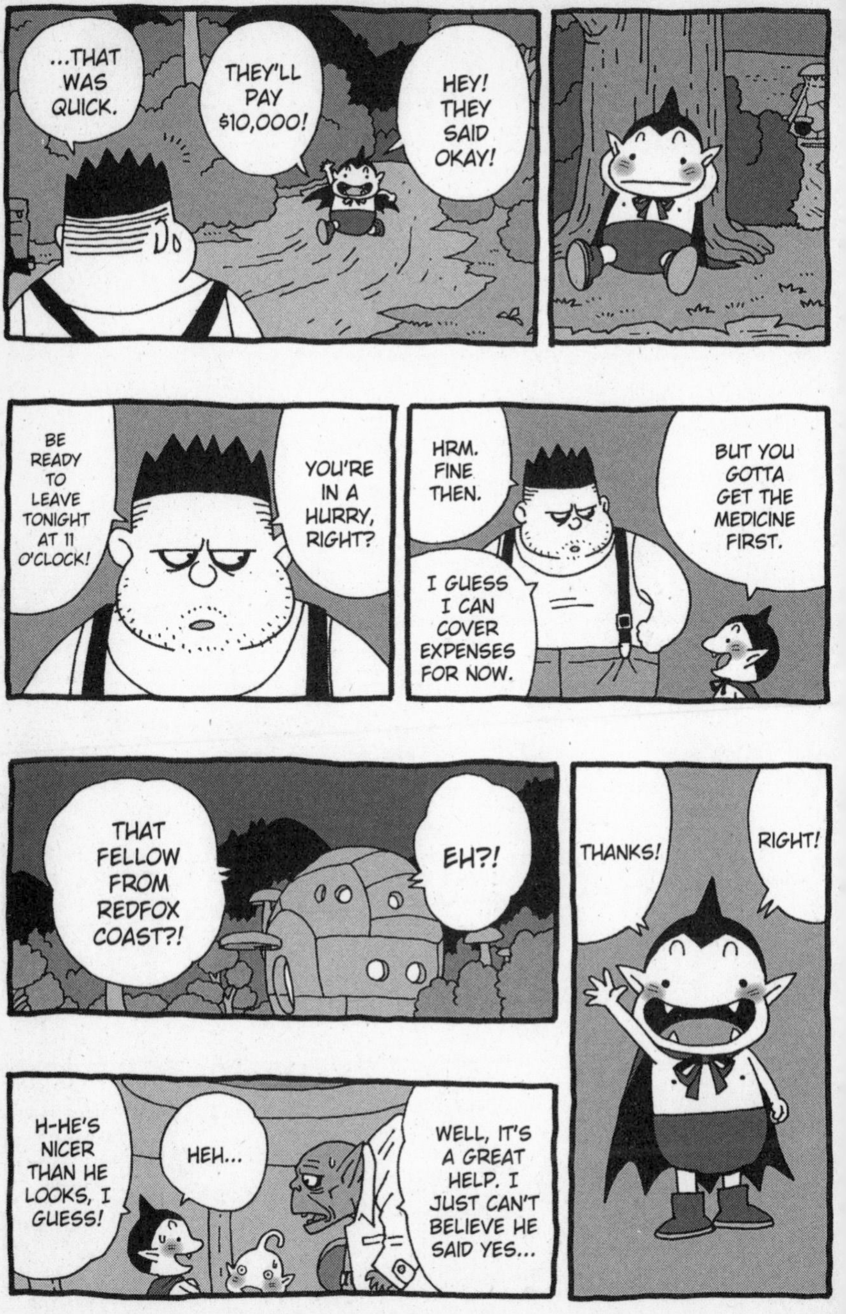
HEY! THEY SAID OKAY!
THEY'LL PAY $10,000!
...THAT WAS QUICK.
BUT YOU GOTTA GET THE MEDICINE FIRST.
HRM. FINE THEN.
I GUESS I CAN COVER EXPENSES FOR NOW.
YOU'RE IN A HURRY, RIGHT?
BE READY TO LEAVE TONIGHT AT 11 O'CLOCK!
RIGHT!
THANKS!
EH?!
THAT FELLOW FROM REDFOX COAST?!
WELL, IT'S A GREAT HELP. I JUST CAN'T BELIEVE HE SAID YES...
HEH...
H-HE'S NICER THAN HE LOOKS, I GUESS!

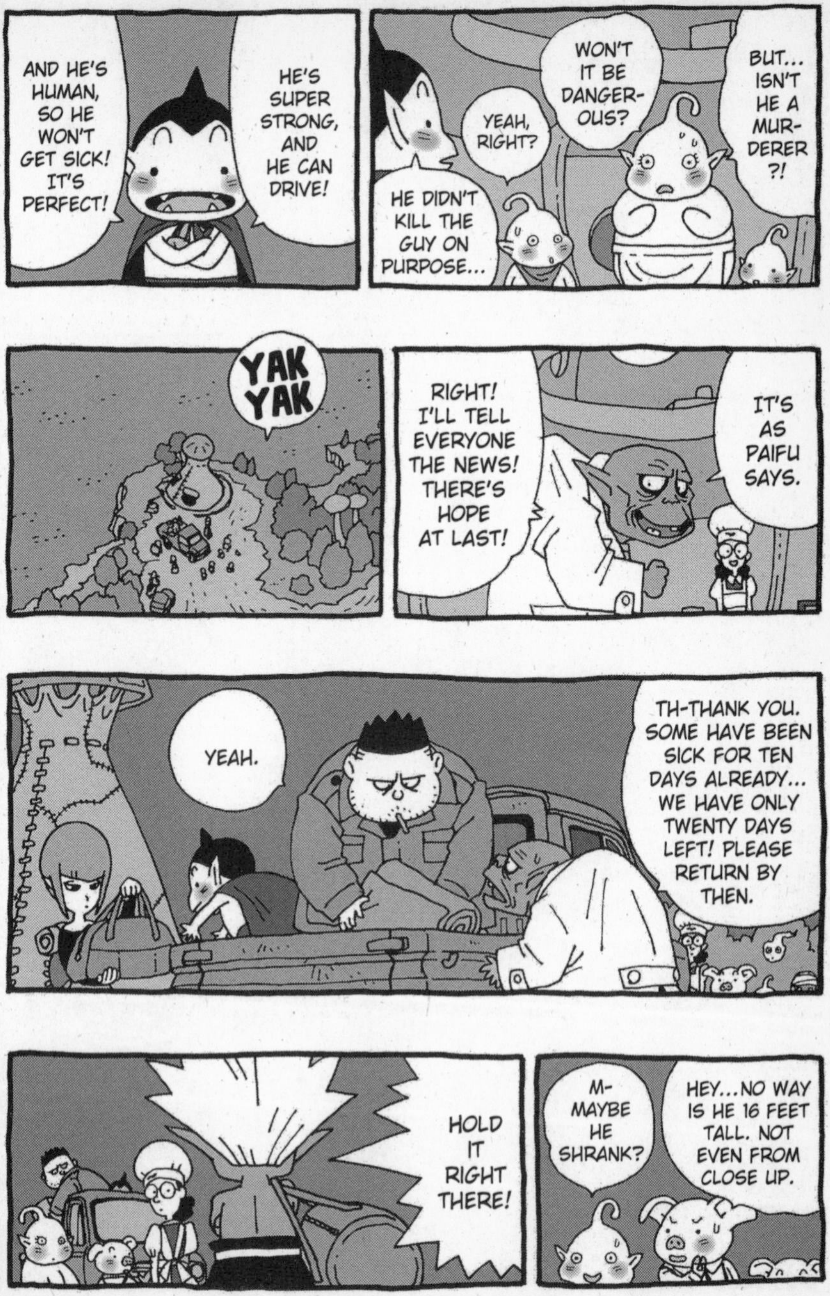
BUT... ISN'T HE A MURDERER?!
WON'T IT BE DANGEROUS?
YEAH, RIGHT?
HE DIDN'T KILL THE GUY ON PURPOSE...
HE'S SUPER STRONG, AND HE CAN DRIVE!
AND HE'S HUMAN, SO HE WON'T GET SICK! IT'S PERFECT!
IT'S AS PAIFU SAYS.
RIGHT! I'LL TELL EVERYONE THE NEWS! THERE'S HOPE AT LAST!
YAK YAK
TH-THANK YOU. SOME HAVE BEEN SICK FOR TEN DAYS ALREADY... WE HAVE ONLY TWENTY DAYS LEFT! PLEASE RETURN BY THEN.
YEAH.
HEY...NO WAY IS HE 16 FEET TALL. NOT EVEN FROM CLOSE UP.
M-MAYBE HE SHRANK?
HOLD IT RIGHT THERE!

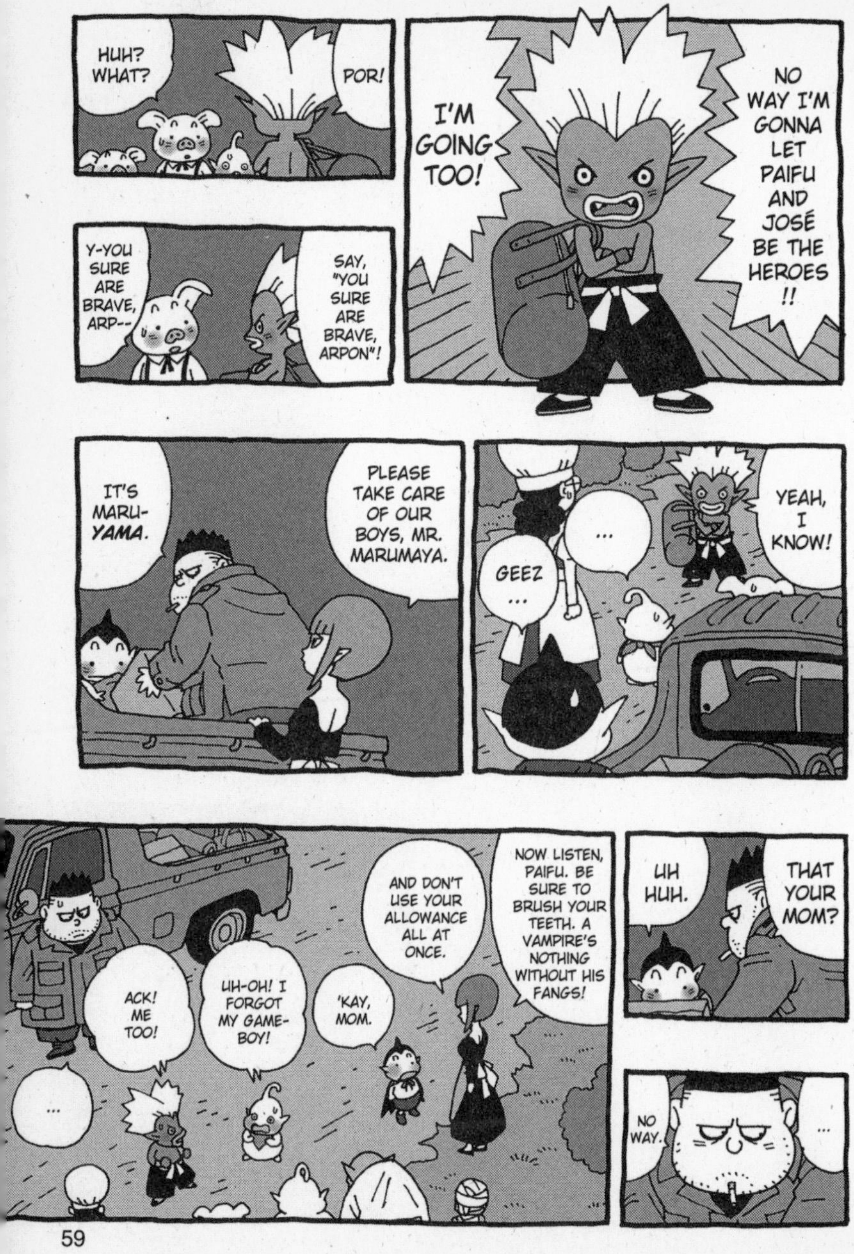
NO WAY I'M GONNA LET PAIFU AND JOSÉ BE THE HEROES!!
I'M GOING TOO!
POR!
HUH? WHAT?
SAY, "YOU SURE ARE BRAVE, ARPON"!
Y-YOU SURE ARE BRAVE, ARP--
YEAH, I KNOW!
...
GEEZ ...
PLEASE TAKE CARE OF OUR BOYS, MR. MARUMAYA.
IT'S MARU-*YAMA*.
THAT YOUR MOM?
UH HUH.
...
NO WAY.
NOW LISTEN, PAIFU. BE SURE TO BRUSH YOUR TEETH. A VAMPIRE'S NOTHING WITHOUT HIS FANGS!
AND DON'T USE YOUR ALLOWANCE ALL AT ONCE.
'KAY, MOM.
UH-OH! I FORGOT MY GAME-BOY!
ACK! ME TOO!
...

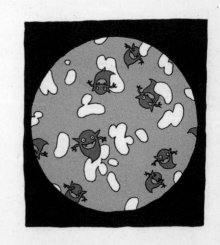

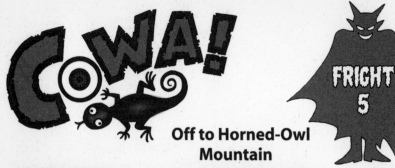

COWA!

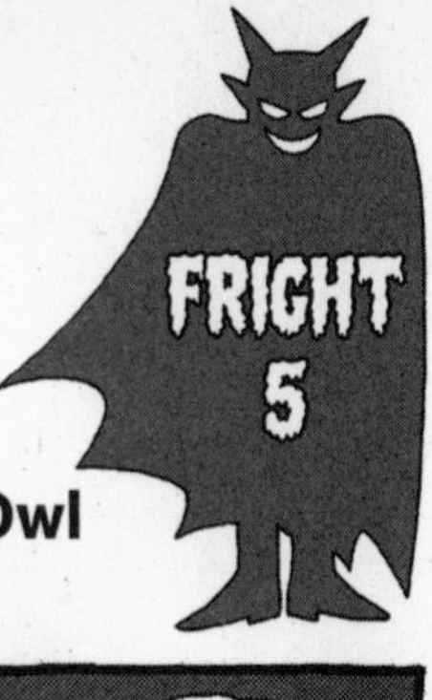
FRIGHT
5

Off to Horned-Owl Mountain

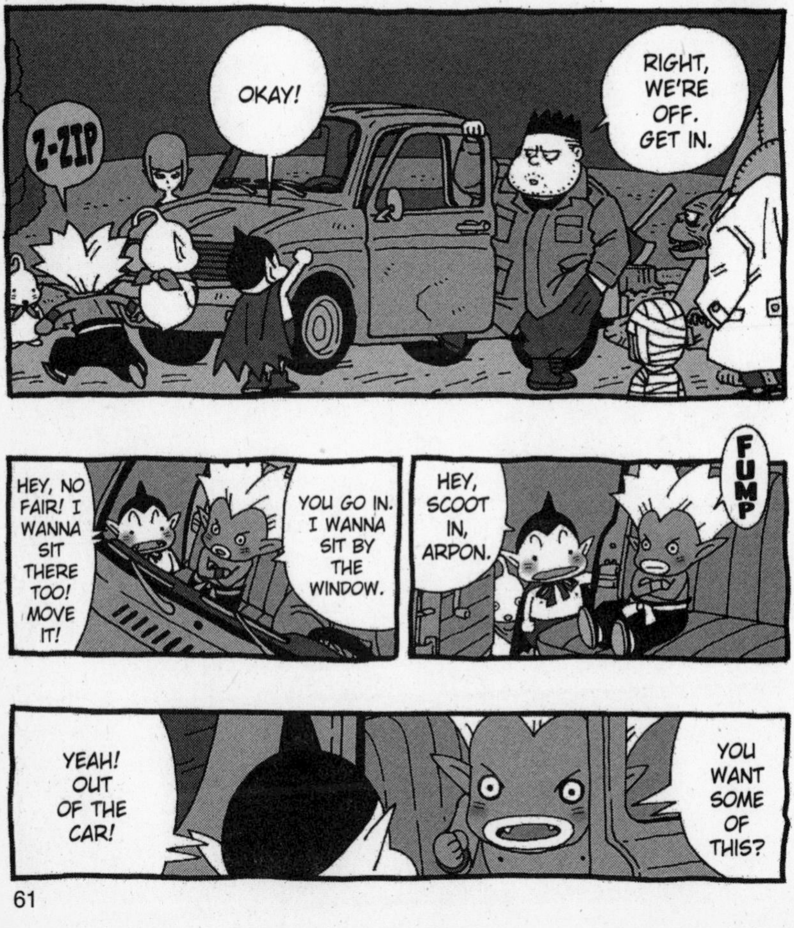
RIGHT, WE'RE OFF. GET IN.
OKAY!
Z-ZIP
FUMP
HEY, SCOOT IN, ARPON.
YOU GO IN. I WANNA SIT BY THE WINDOW.
HEY, NO FAIR! I WANNA SIT THERE TOO! MOVE IT!
YOU WANT SOME OF THIS?
YEAH! OUT OF THE CAR!

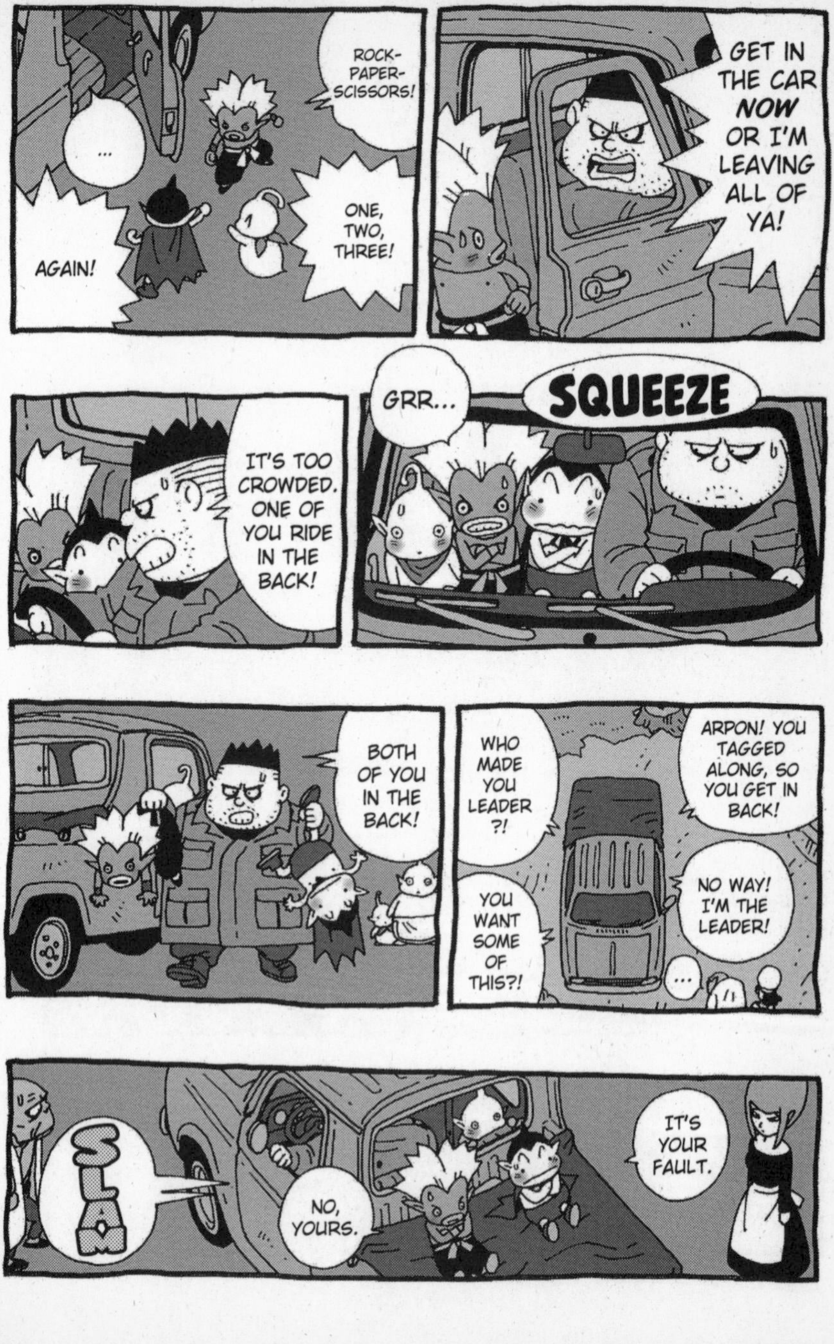
GET IN THE CAR NOW OR I'M LEAVING ALL OF YA!
ROCK-PAPER-SCISSORS!
...
ONE, TWO, THREE!
AGAIN!
SQUEEZE
GRR...
IT'S TOO CROWDED. ONE OF YOU RIDE IN THE BACK!
ARPON! YOU TAGGED ALONG, SO YOU GET IN BACK!
WHO MADE YOU LEADER ?!
NO WAY! I'M THE LEADER!
YOU WANT SOME OF THIS?!
...
BOTH OF YOU IN THE BACK!
IT'S YOUR FAULT.
NO, YOURS.
SLAM

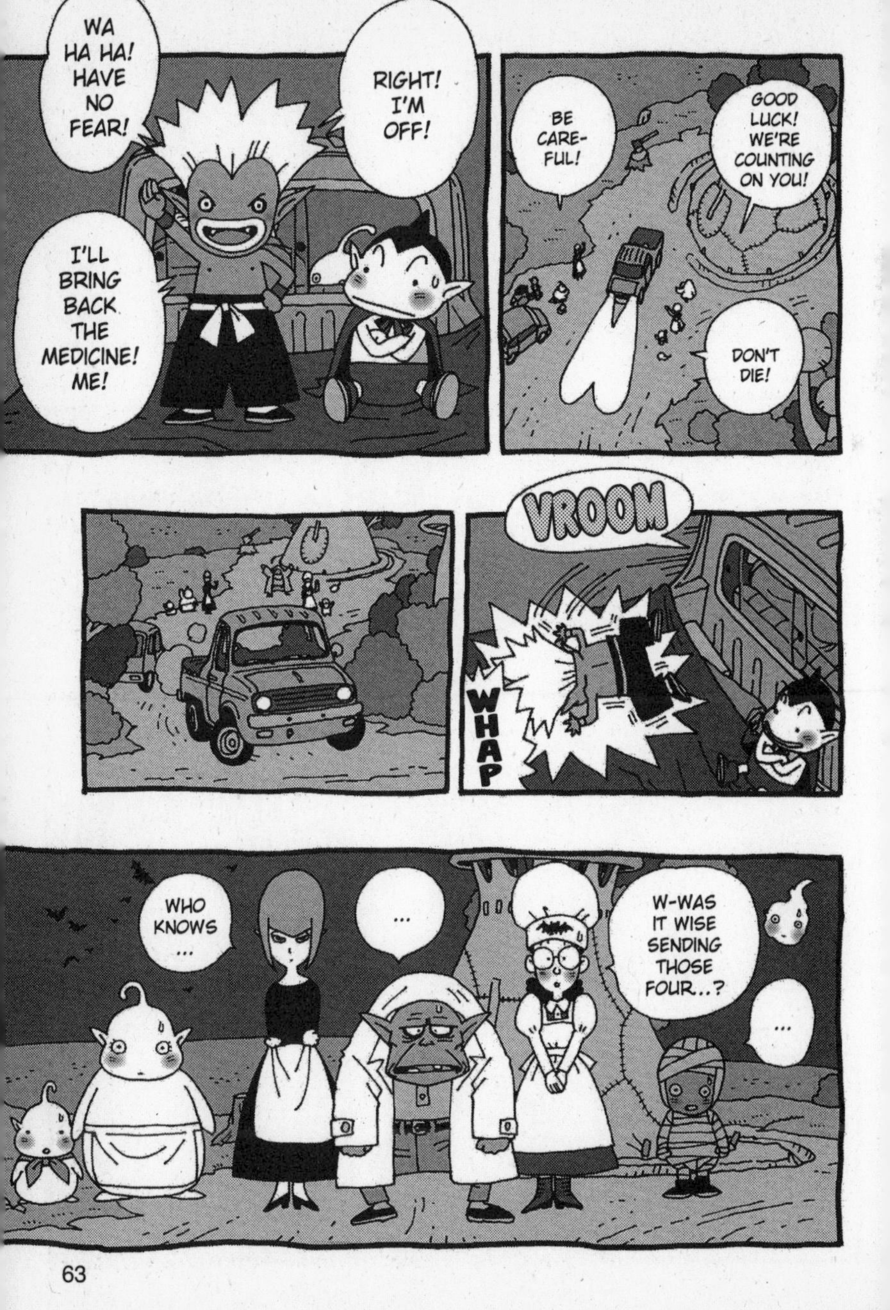
GOOD LUCK! WE'RE COUNTING ON YOU!
BE CARE-FUL!
DON'T DIE!
RIGHT! I'M OFF!
WA HA HA! HAVE NO FEAR!
I'LL BRING BACK THE MEDICINE! ME!
VROOM
WHAP
W-WAS IT WISE SENDING THOSE FOUR...?
...
...
WHO KNOWS...

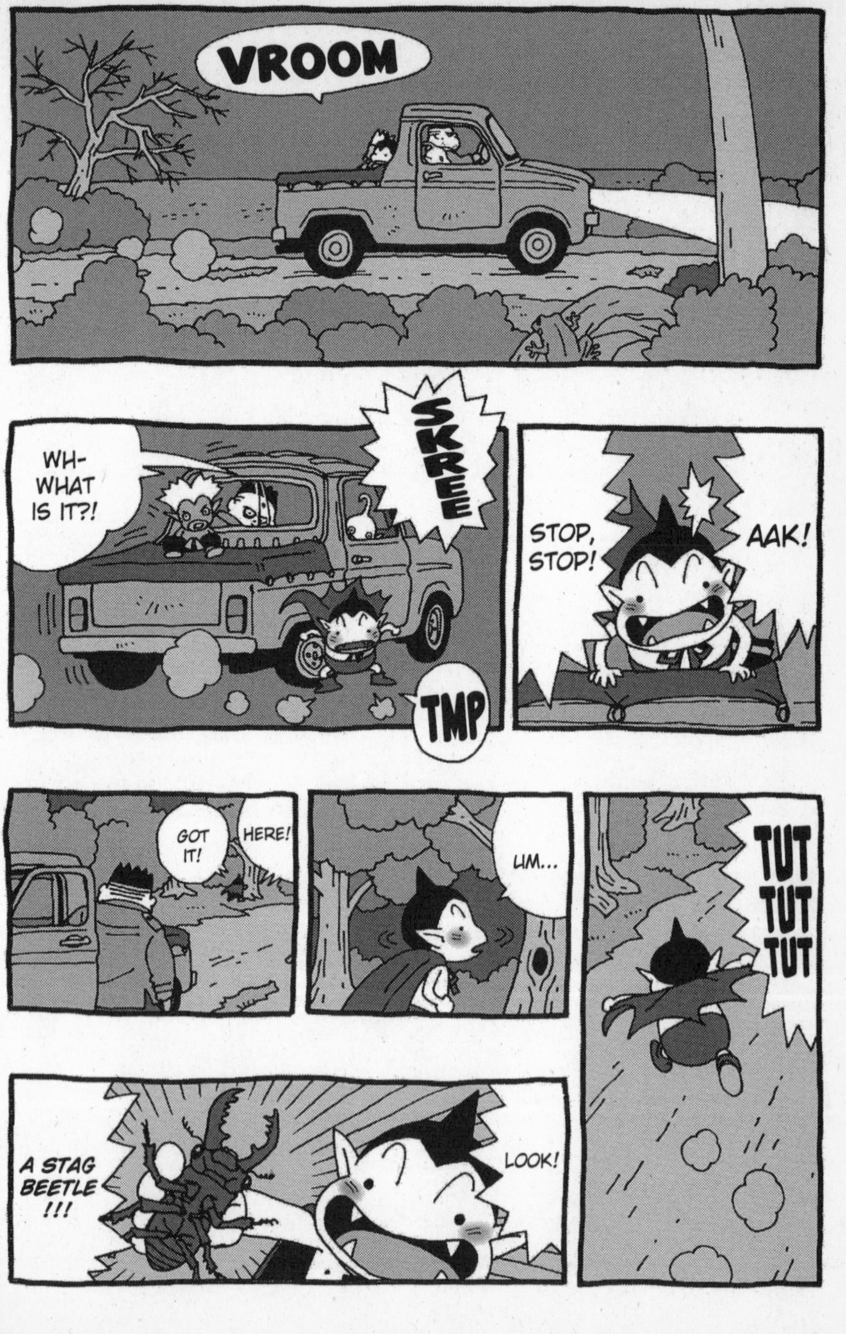
VROOM
AAK!
STOP, STOP!
SKREE
WH-WHAT IS IT?!
TMP
TUT TUT TUT
UM...
HERE!
GOT IT!
LOOK!
A STAG BEETLE!!!

READ THIS WAY

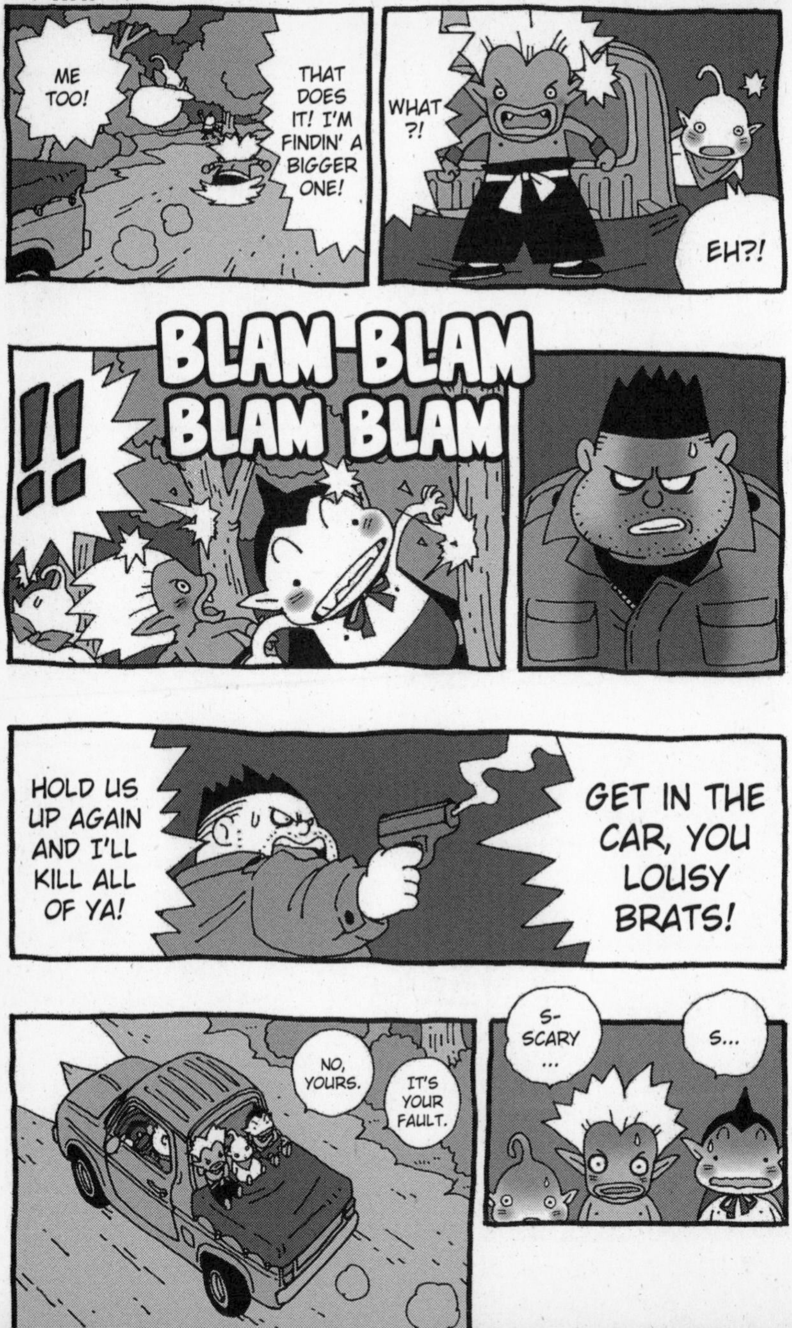

WHAT ?!
EH?!
THAT DOES IT! I'M FINDIN' A BIGGER ONE!
ME TOO!
BLAM BLAM BLAM BLAM
!!
GET IN THE CAR, YOU LOUSY BRATS!
HOLD US UP AGAIN AND I'LL KILL ALL OF YA!
S...
S- SCARY ...
IT'S YOUR FAULT.
NO, YOURS.

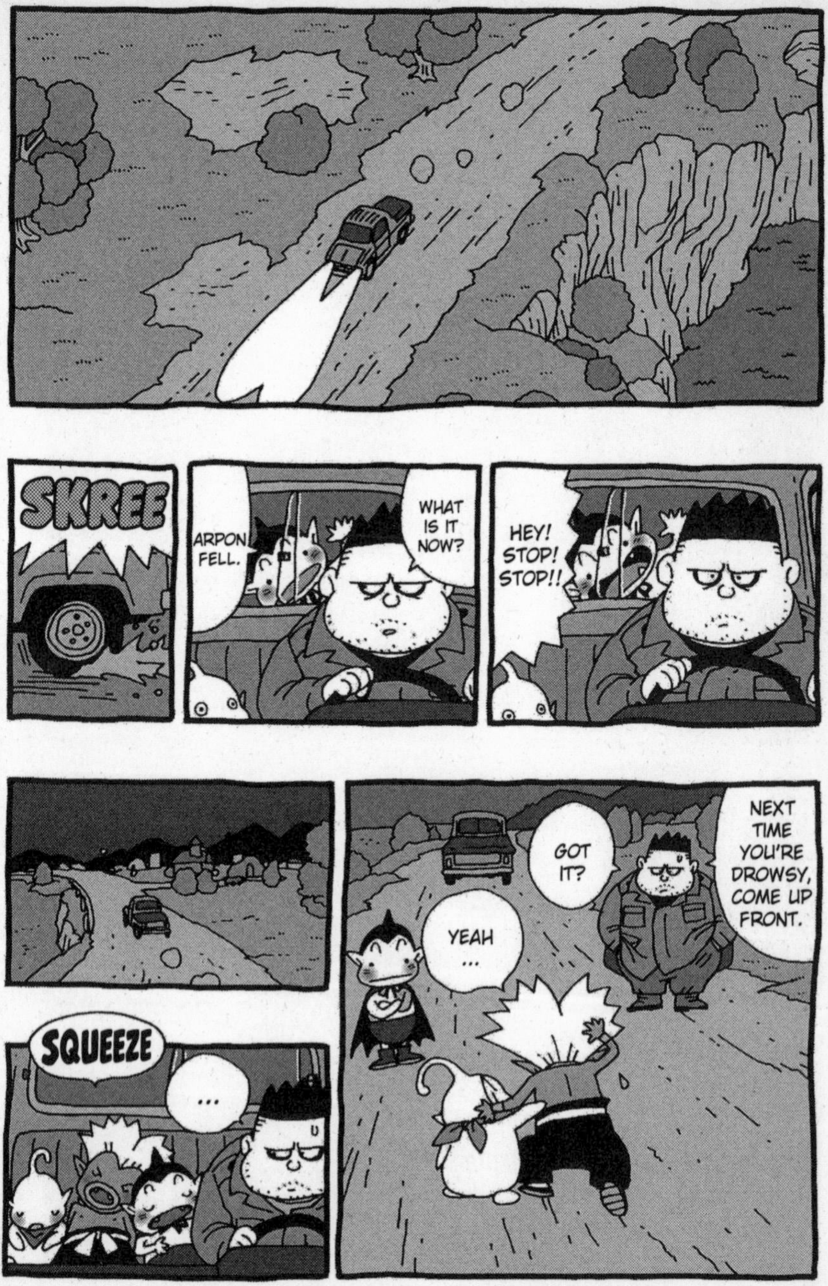
HEY! STOP! STOP!!
WHAT IS IT NOW?
ARPON FELL.
SKREE
NEXT TIME YOU'RE DROWSY, COME UP FRONT.
GOT IT?
YEAH ...
SQUEEZE
...

READ THIS WAY

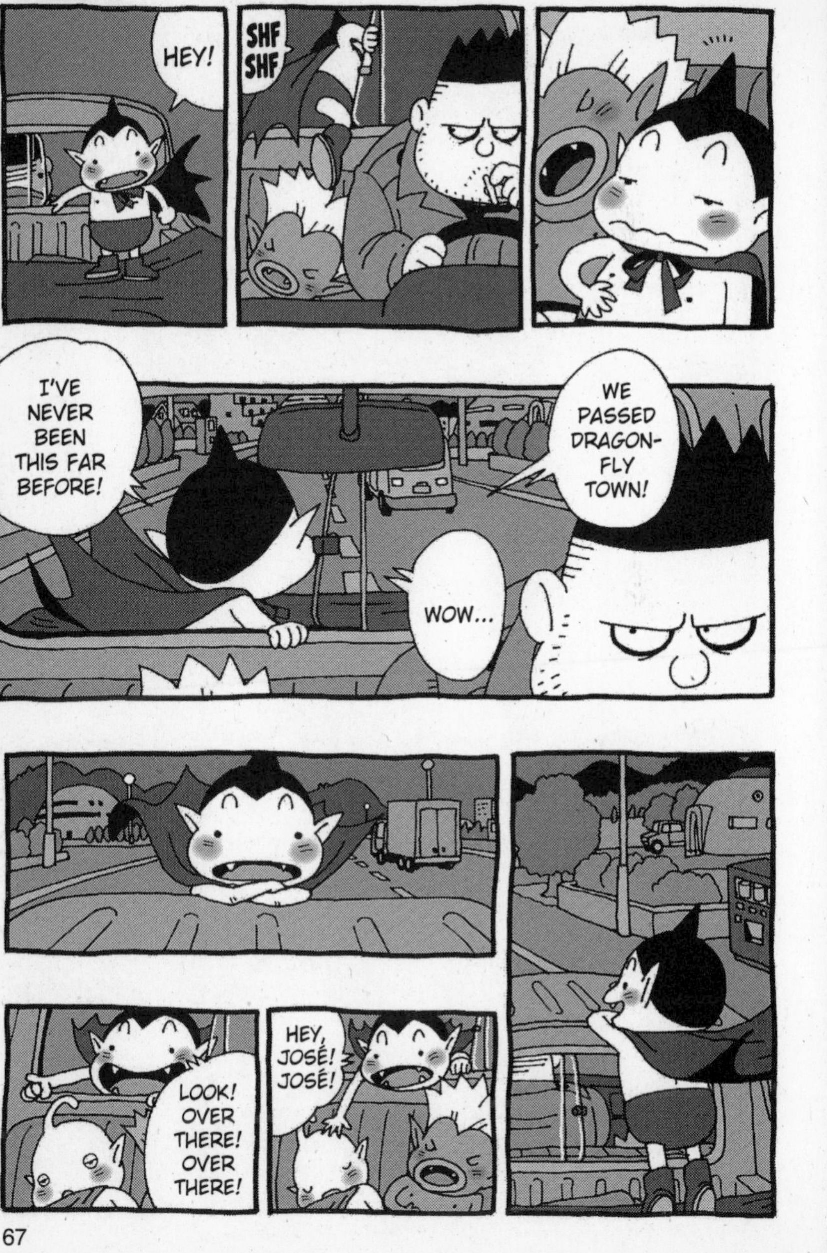
SHF SHF
HEY!
WE PASSED DRAGON-FLY TOWN!
WOW...
I'VE NEVER BEEN THIS FAR BEFORE!
HEY, JOSÉ! JOSÉ!
LOOK! OVER THERE! OVER THERE!

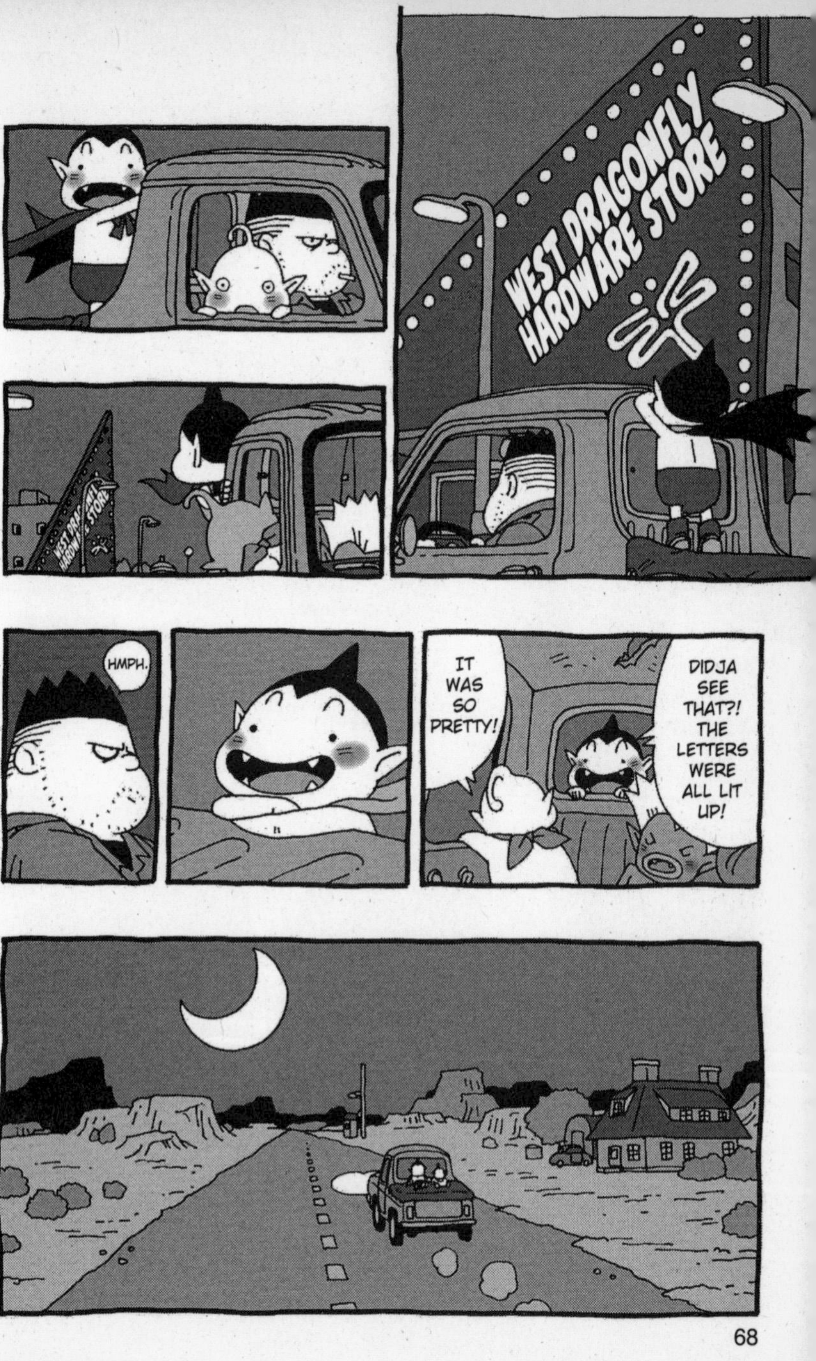
WEST DRAGONFLY HARDWARE STORE
DIDJA SEE THAT?! THE LETTERS WERE ALL LIT UP!
IT WAS SO PRETTY!
HMPH.

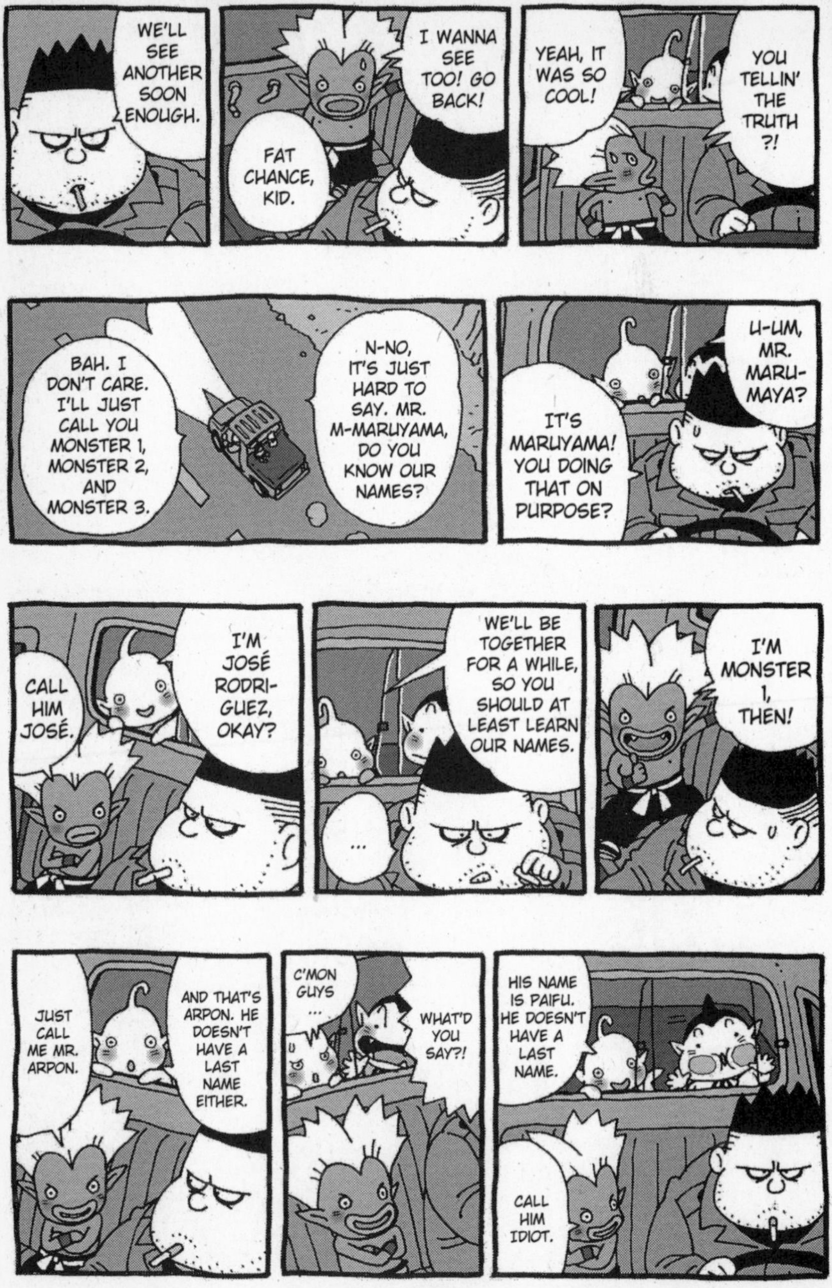
YOU TELLIN' THE TRUTH?!
YEAH, IT WAS SO COOL!
I WANNA SEE TOO! GO BACK!
FAT CHANCE, KID.
WE'LL SEE ANOTHER SOON ENOUGH.
U-UM, MR. MARU-MAYA?
IT'S MARUYAMA! YOU DOING THAT ON PURPOSE?
N-NO, IT'S JUST HARD TO SAY. MR. M-MARUYAMA, DO YOU KNOW OUR NAMES?
BAH. I DON'T CARE. I'LL JUST CALL YOU MONSTER 1, MONSTER 2, AND MONSTER 3.
I'M MONSTER 1, THEN!
WE'LL BE TOGETHER FOR A WHILE, SO YOU SHOULD AT LEAST LEARN OUR NAMES.
...
I'M JOSÉ RODRIGUEZ, OKAY?
CALL HIM JOSÉ.
HIS NAME IS PAIFU. HE DOESN'T HAVE A LAST NAME.
CALL HIM IDIOT.
WHAT'D YOU SAY?!
C'MON GUYS ...
AND THAT'S ARPON. HE DOESN'T HAVE A LAST NAME EITHER.
JUST CALL ME MR. ARPON.

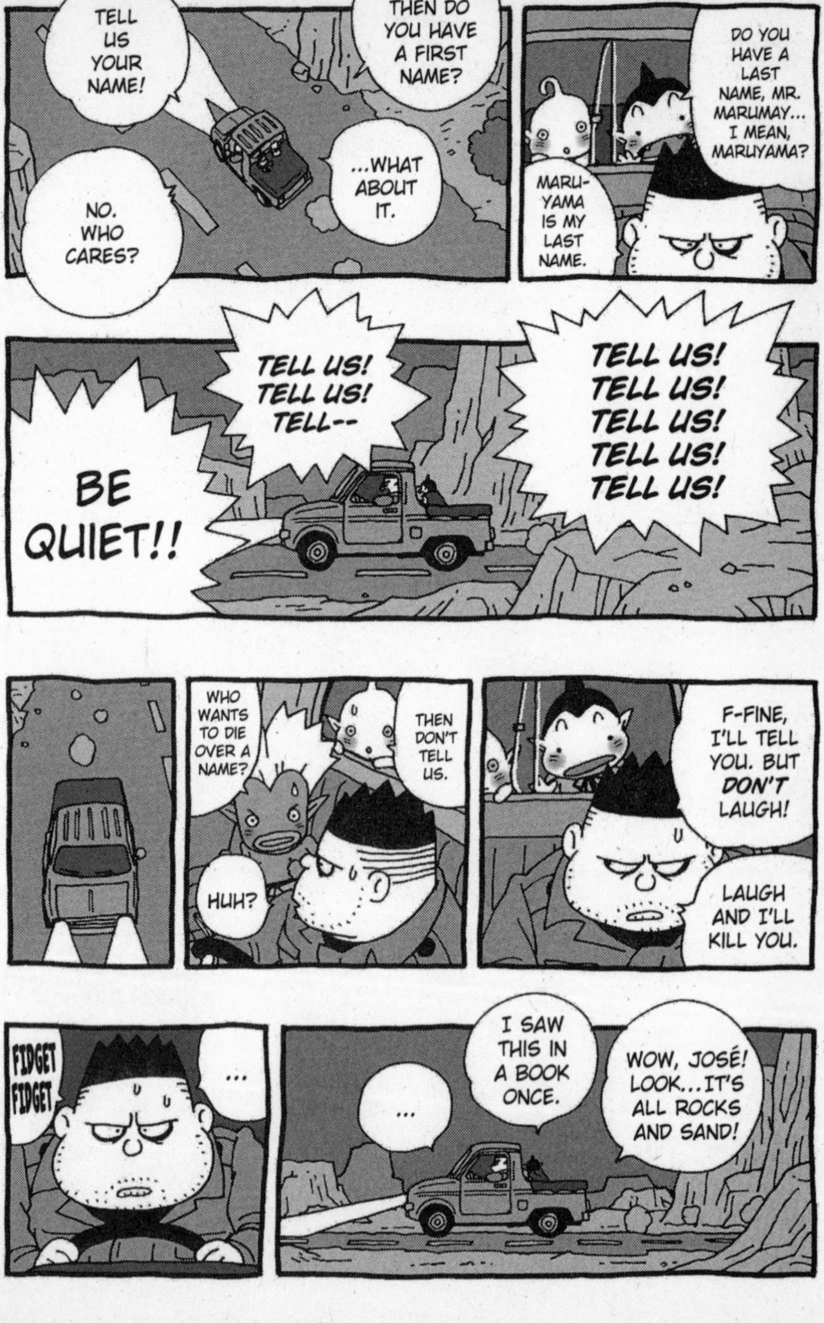

DO YOU HAVE A LAST NAME, MR. MARUMAY... I MEAN, MARUYAMA?
MARUYAMA IS MY LAST NAME.
WHAT?! THEN DO YOU HAVE A FIRST NAME?
...WHAT ABOUT IT.
TELL US YOUR NAME!
NO. WHO CARES?
TELL US! TELL US! TELL US! TELL US! TELL US!
TELL US! TELL US! TELL--
BE QUIET!!
F-FINE, I'LL TELL YOU. BUT *DON'T* LAUGH!
LAUGH AND I'LL KILL YOU.
THEN DON'T TELL US.
WHO WANTS TO DIE OVER A NAME?
HUH?
WOW, JOSÉ! LOOK...IT'S ALL ROCKS AND SAND!
I SAW THIS IN A BOOK ONCE.
...
...
FIDGET FIDGET

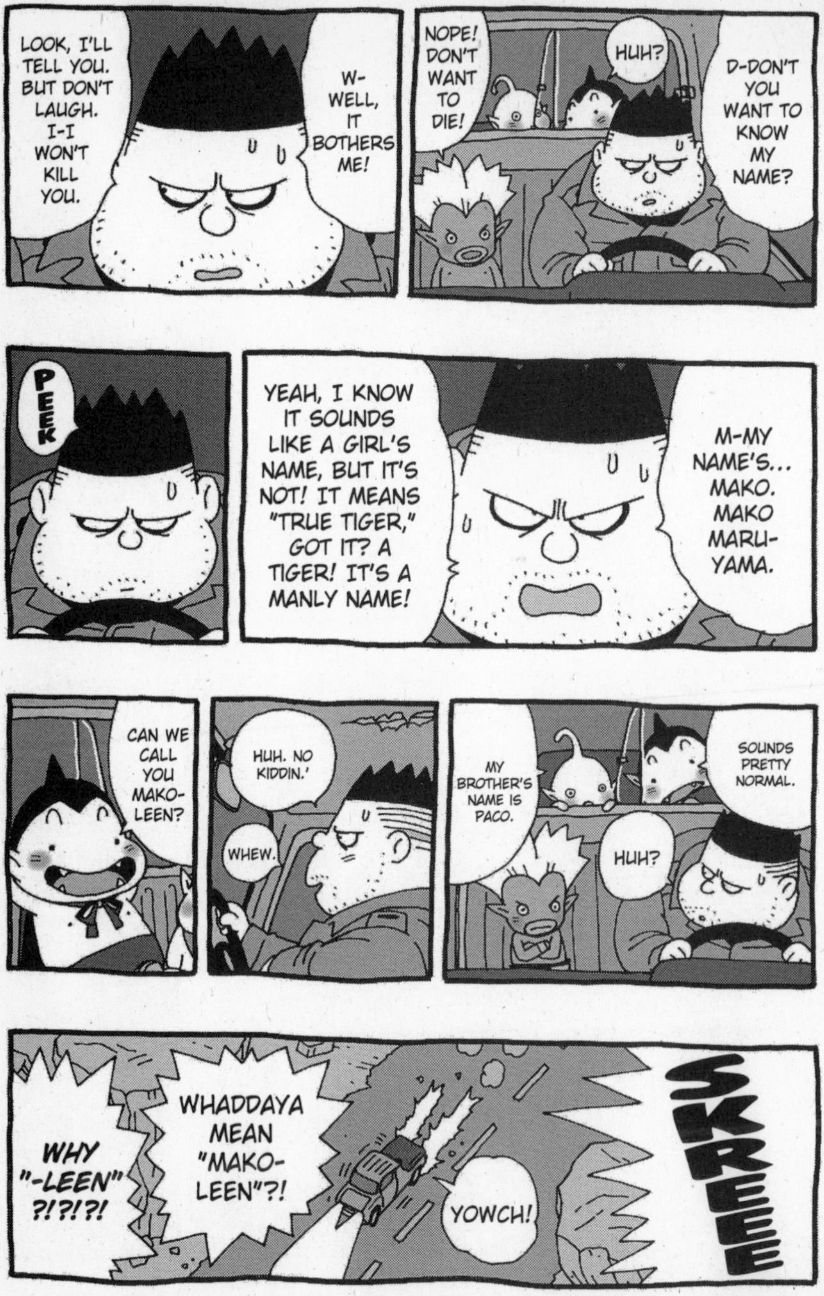
D-DON'T YOU WANT TO KNOW MY NAME?
HUH?
NOPE! DON'T WANT TO DIE!
W-WELL, IT BOTHERS ME!
LOOK, I'LL TELL YOU. BUT DON'T LAUGH. I-I WON'T KILL YOU.
M-MY NAME'S... MAKO. MAKO MARU-YAMA.
YEAH, I KNOW IT SOUNDS LIKE A GIRL'S NAME, BUT IT'S NOT! IT MEANS "TRUE TIGER," GOT IT? A TIGER! IT'S A MANLY NAME!
PEEK
SOUNDS PRETTY NORMAL.
HUH?
MY BROTHER'S NAME IS PACO.
HUH. NO KIDDIN.'
WHEW.
CAN WE CALL YOU MAKO-LEEN?
SKREEE
YOWCH!
WHADDAYA MEAN "MAKO-LEEN"?!
WHY "-LEEN"?!?!?!

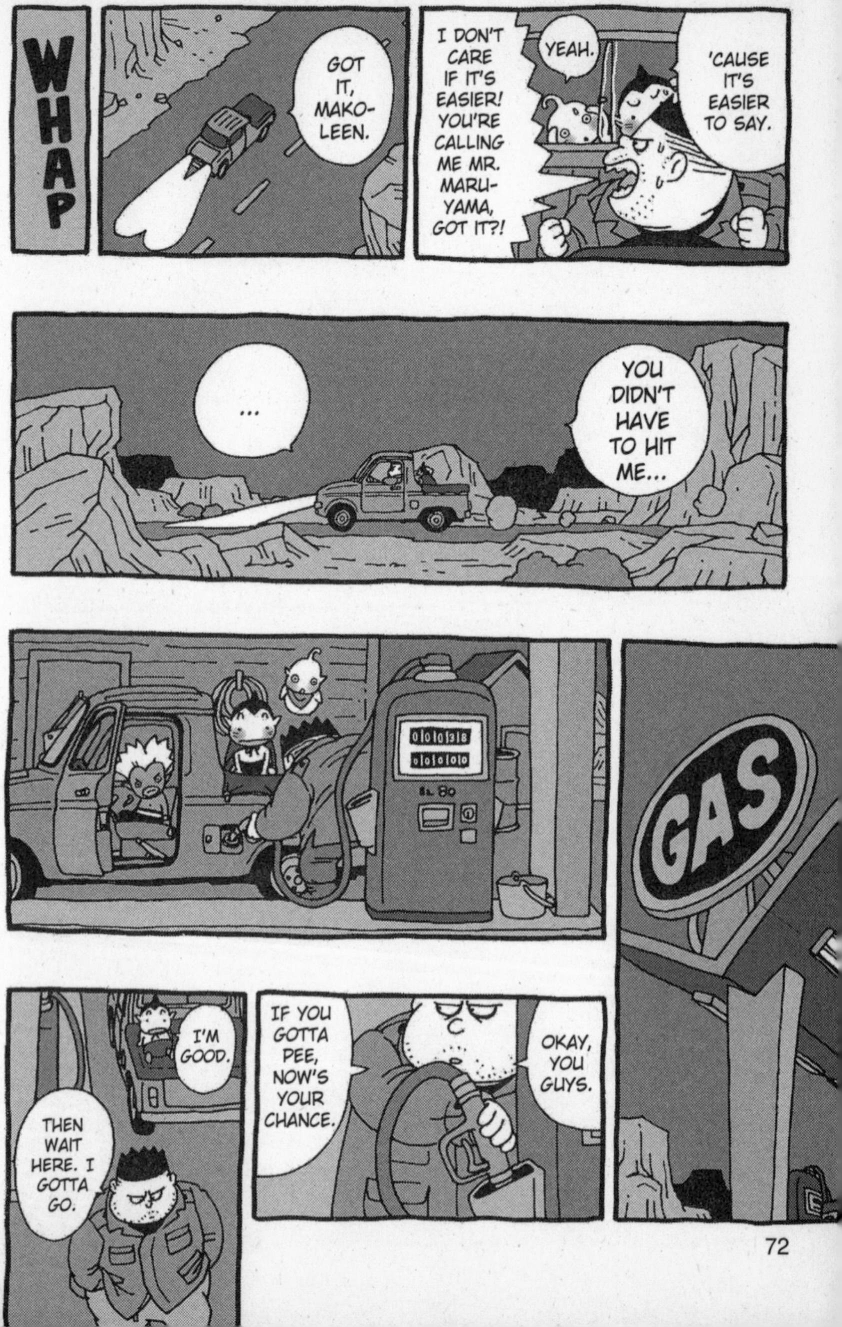
'CAUSE IT'S EASIER TO SAY.
YEAH.
I DON'T CARE IF IT'S EASIER! YOU'RE CALLING ME MR. MARUYAMA, GOT IT?!
GOT IT, MAKOLEEN.
WHAP
YOU DIDN'T HAVE TO HIT ME...
...
GAS
OKAY, YOU GUYS.
IF YOU GOTTA PEE, NOW'S YOUR CHANCE.
I'M GOOD.
THEN WAIT HERE. I GOTTA GO.

READ THIS WAY

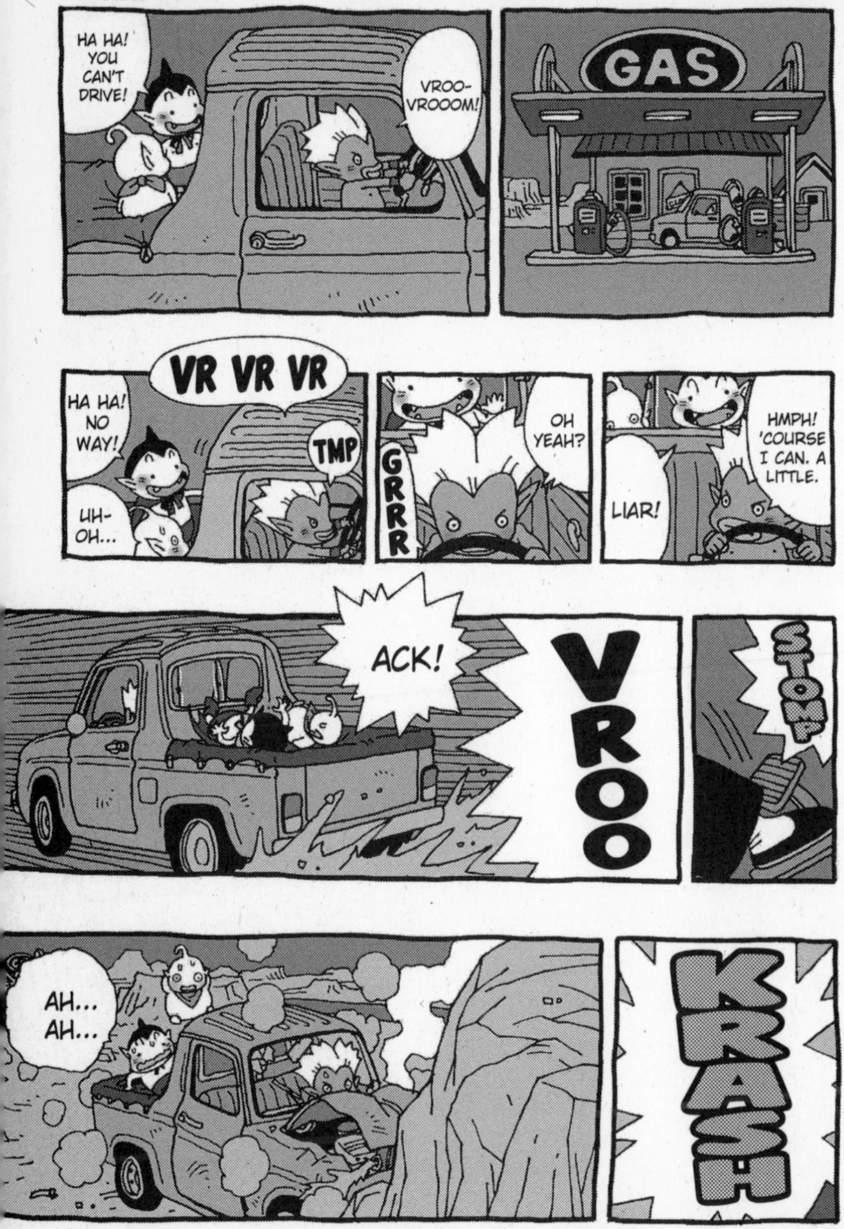
GAS
VROO- VROOOM!
HA HA! YOU CAN'T DRIVE!
HMPH! 'COURSE I CAN. A LITTLE.
LIAR!
OH YEAH?
GRRR
VR VR VR
TMP
HA HA! NO WAY!
UH- OH...
STOMP
VROO
ACK!
KRASH
AH... AH...

COWA!

FRIGHT 6

Mako "The Murderer" Maruyama

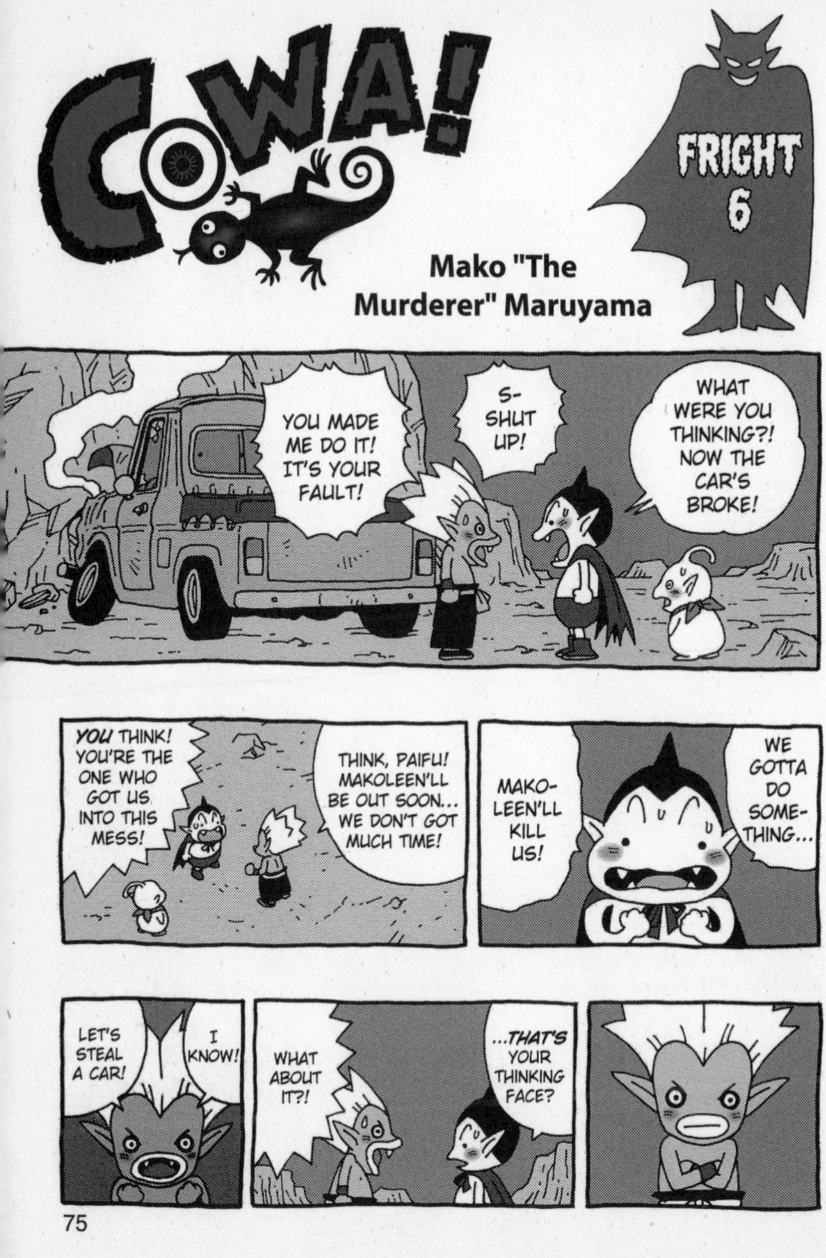
WHAT WERE YOU THINKING?! NOW THE CAR'S BROKE!
S-SHUT UP!
YOU MADE ME DO IT! IT'S YOUR FAULT!
WE GOTTA DO SOMETHING...
MAKOLEEN'LL KILL US!
THINK, PAIFU! MAKOLEEN'LL BE OUT SOON... WE DON'T GOT MUCH TIME!
YOU THINK! YOU'RE THE ONE WHO GOT US INTO THIS MESS!
...THAT'S YOUR THINKING FACE?
WHAT ABOUT IT?!
I KNOW!
LET'S STEAL A CAR!

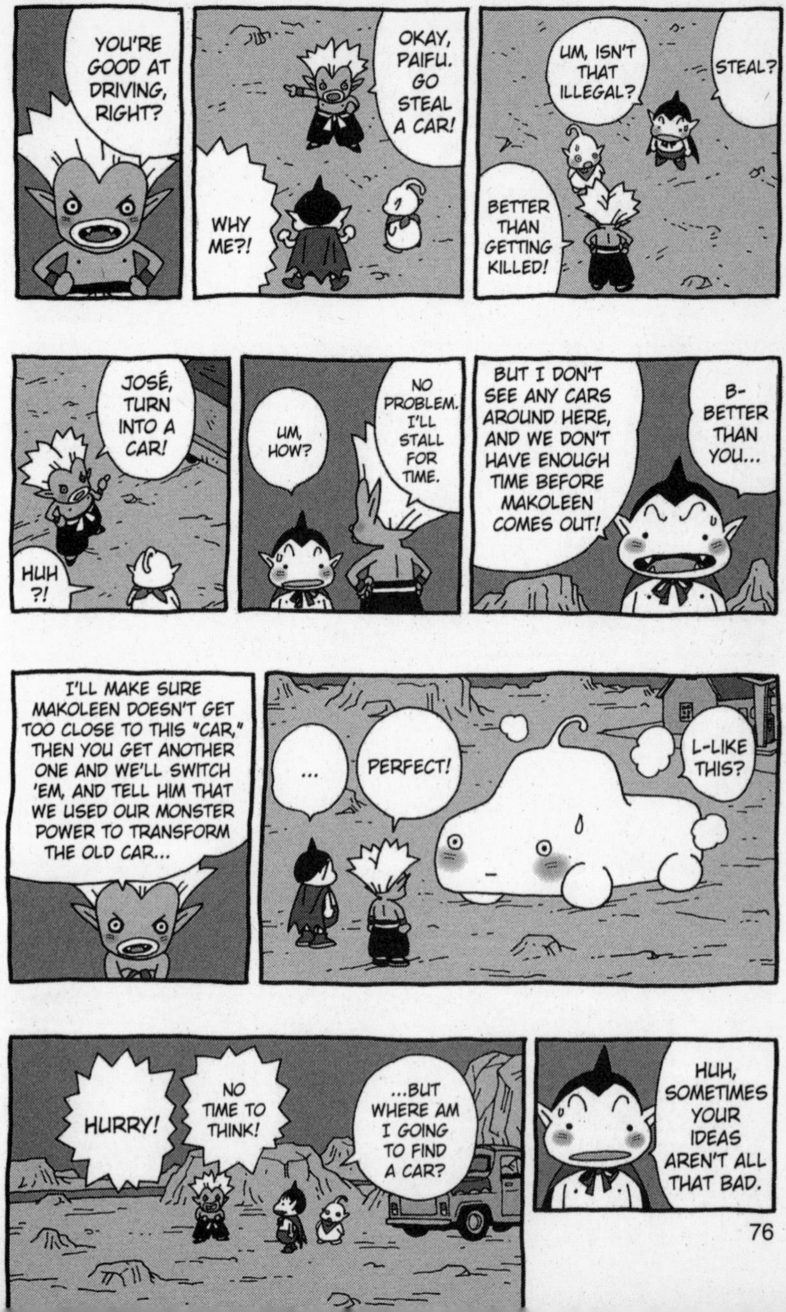
YOU'RE GOOD AT DRIVING, RIGHT?
OKAY, PAIFU. GO STEAL A CAR!
WHY ME?!
STEAL?
UM, ISN'T THAT ILLEGAL?
BETTER THAN GETTING KILLED!
JOSÉ, TURN INTO A CAR!
HUH ?!
NO PROBLEM. I'LL STALL FOR TIME.
UM, HOW?
BUT I DON'T SEE ANY CARS AROUND HERE, AND WE DON'T HAVE ENOUGH TIME BEFORE MAKOLEEN COMES OUT!
B- BETTER THAN YOU...
I'LL MAKE SURE MAKOLEEN DOESN'T GET TOO CLOSE TO THIS "CAR," THEN YOU GET ANOTHER ONE AND WE'LL SWITCH 'EM, AND TELL HIM THAT WE USED OUR MONSTER POWER TO TRANSFORM THE OLD CAR...
L-LIKE THIS?
PERFECT!
...
HURRY!
NO TIME TO THINK!
...BUT WHERE AM I GOING TO FIND A CAR?
HUH, SOMETIMES YOUR IDEAS AREN'T ALL THAT BAD.

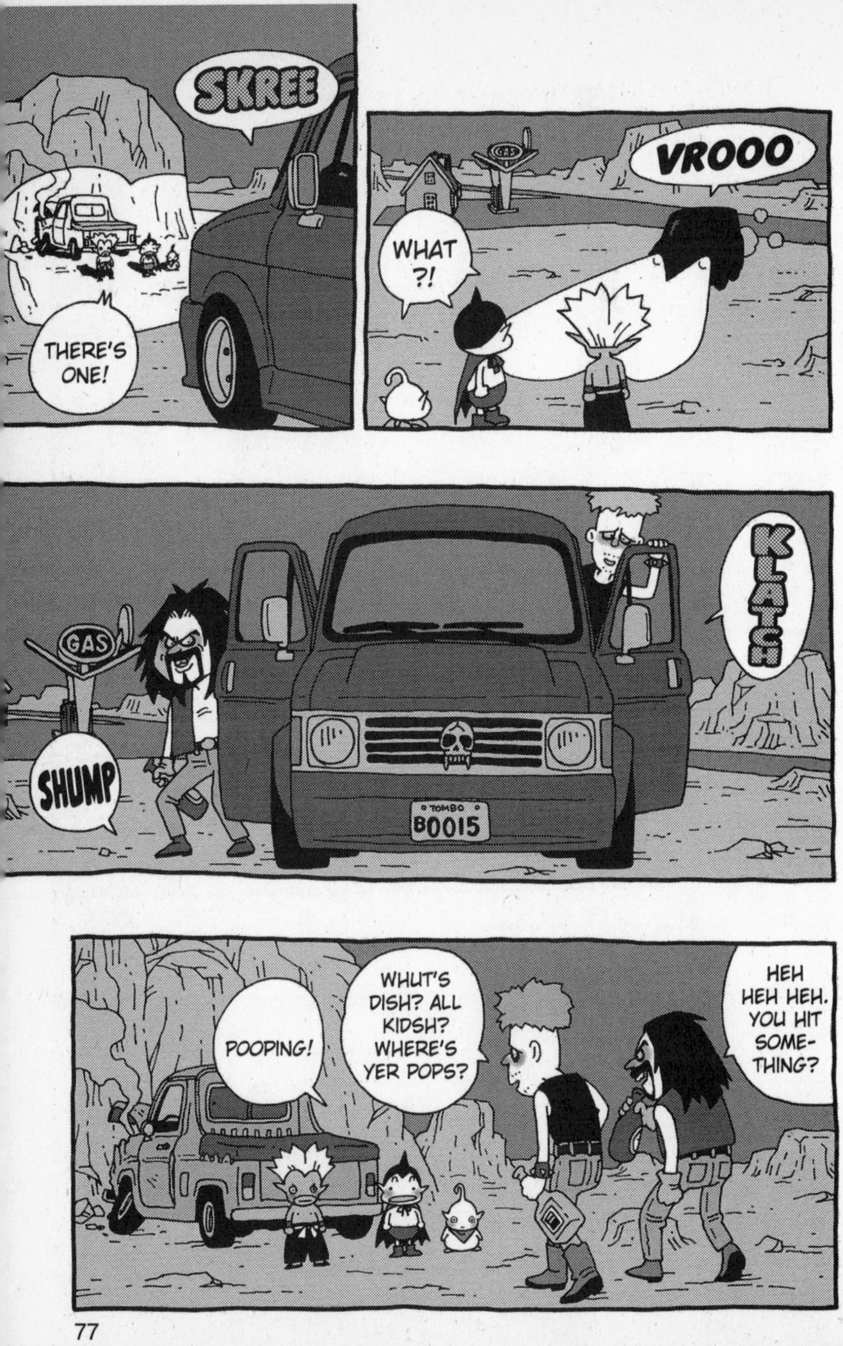
VROOO
WHAT ?!
SKREE
THERE'S ONE!
KLATCH
GAS
SHUMP
TOMBO
B0015
HEH HEH HEH. YOU HIT SOME-THING?
WHUT'S DISH? ALL KIDSH? WHERE'S YER POPS?
POOPING!

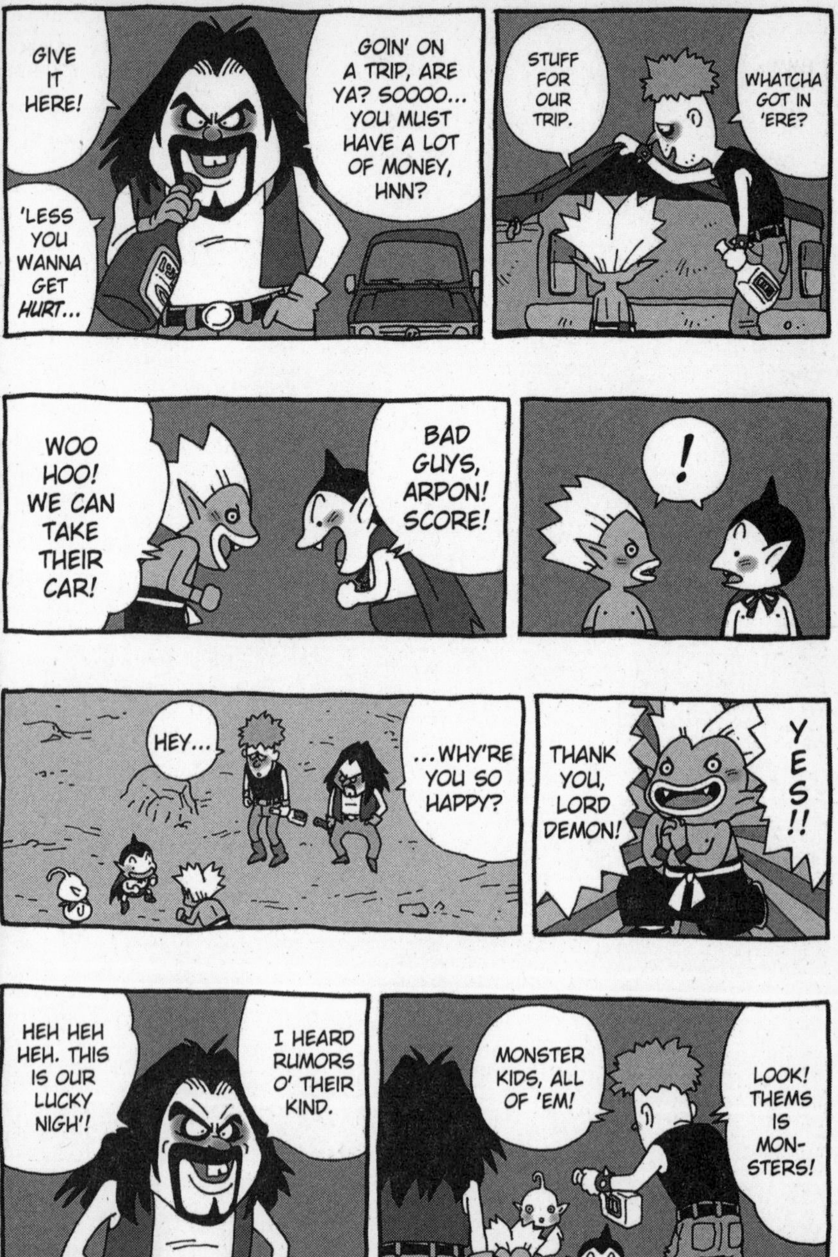
WHATCHA GOT IN 'ERE?
STUFF FOR OUR TRIP.
GOIN' ON A TRIP, ARE YA? SOOOO... YOU MUST HAVE A LOT OF MONEY, HNN?
GIVE IT HERE!
'LESS YOU WANNA GET *HURT*...
!
BAD GUYS, ARPON! SCORE!
WOO HOO! WE CAN TAKE THEIR CAR!
YES!!
THANK YOU, LORD DEMON!
HEY...
...WHY'RE YOU SO HAPPY?
LOOK! THEMS IS MON-STERS!
MONSTER KIDS, ALL OF 'EM!
I HEARD RUMORS O' THEIR KIND.
HEH HEH HEH. THIS IS OUR LUCKY NIGH'!

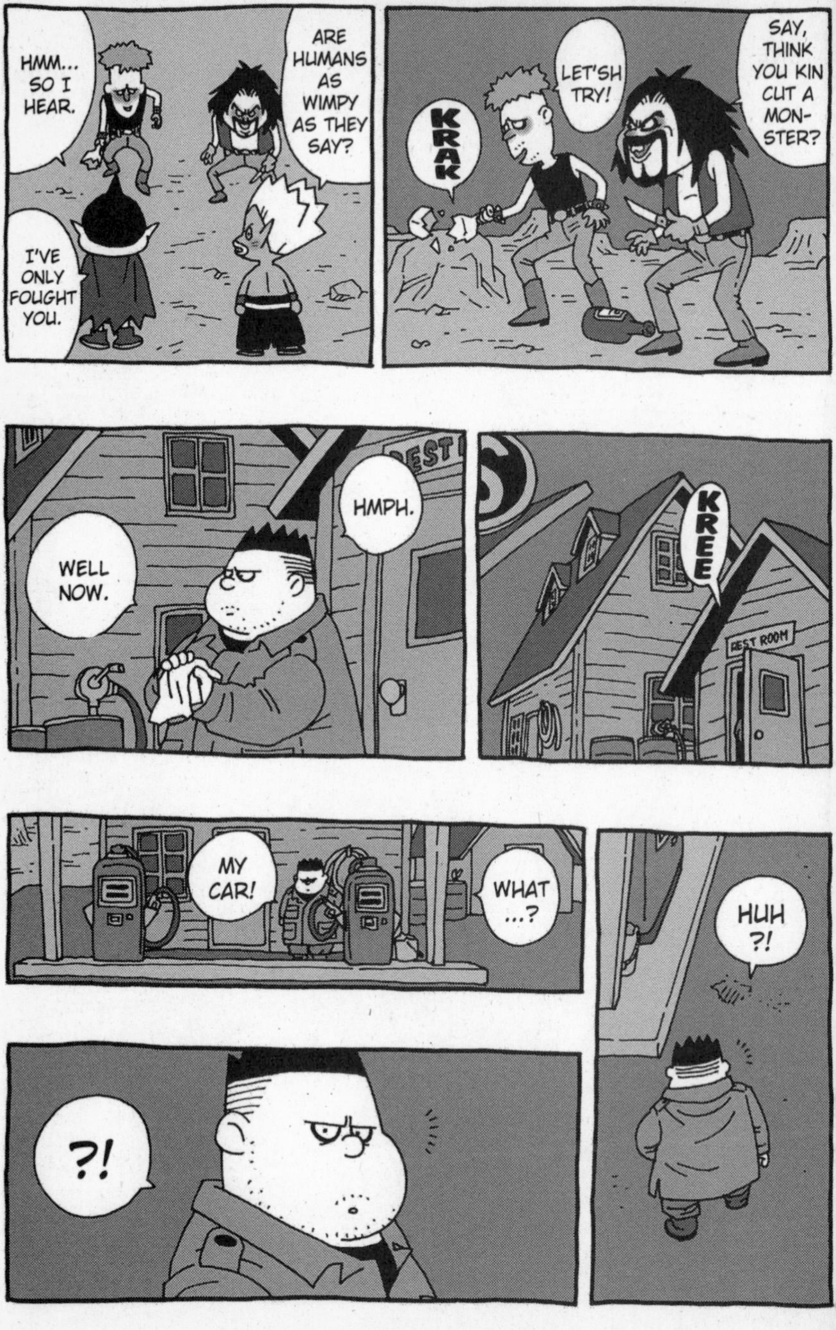
SAY, THINK YOU KIN CUT A MONSTER?
LET'SH TRY!
KRAK
ARE HUMANS AS WIMPY AS THEY SAY?
HMM... SO I HEAR.
I'VE ONLY FOUGHT YOU.
KREE
REST ROOM
HMPH.
WELL NOW.
HUH ?!
WHAT ...?
MY CAR!
?!

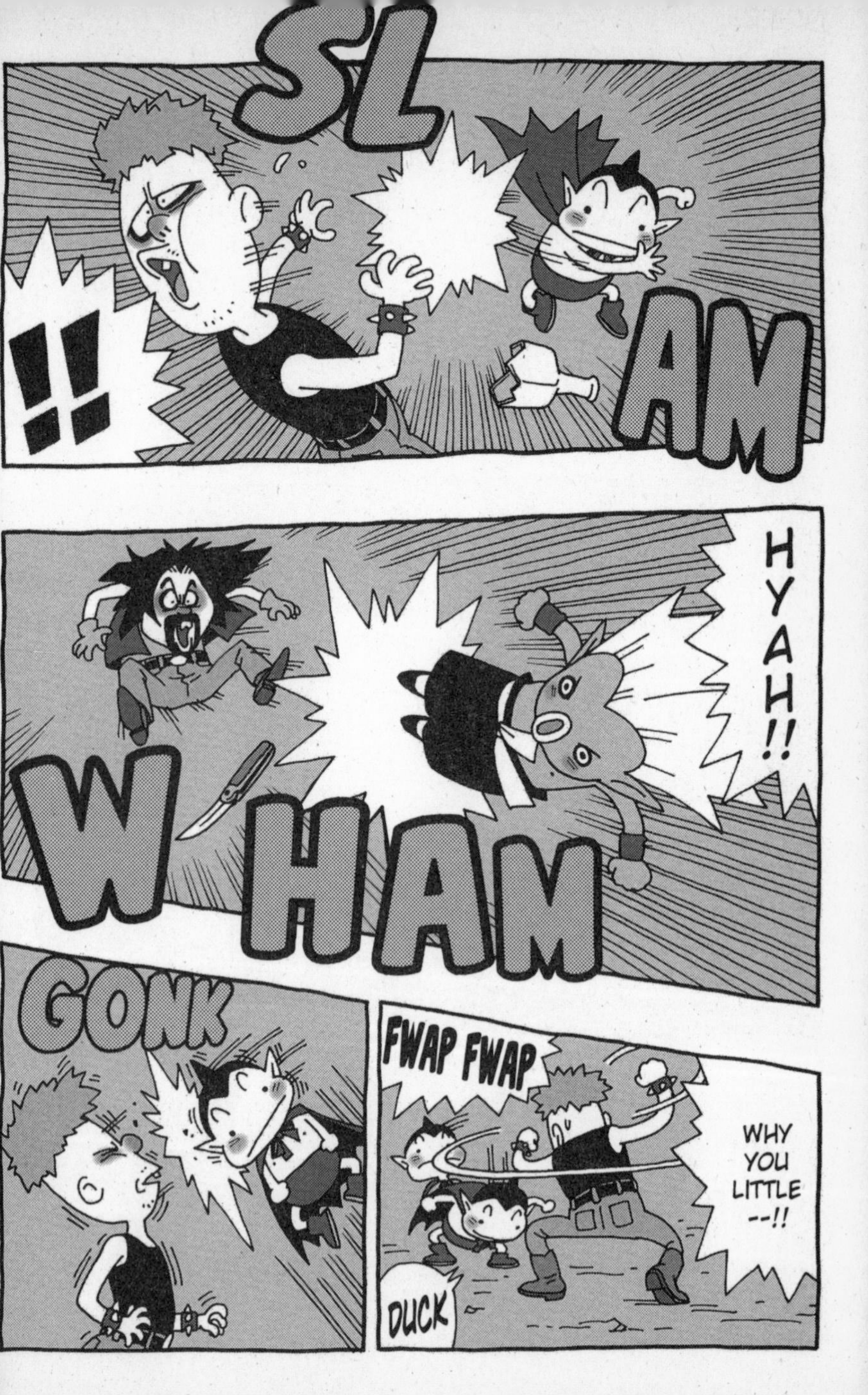
SL
AM
!!
HYAH!!
W HAM
FWAP FWAP
WHY YOU LITTLE --!!
DUCK
GONK

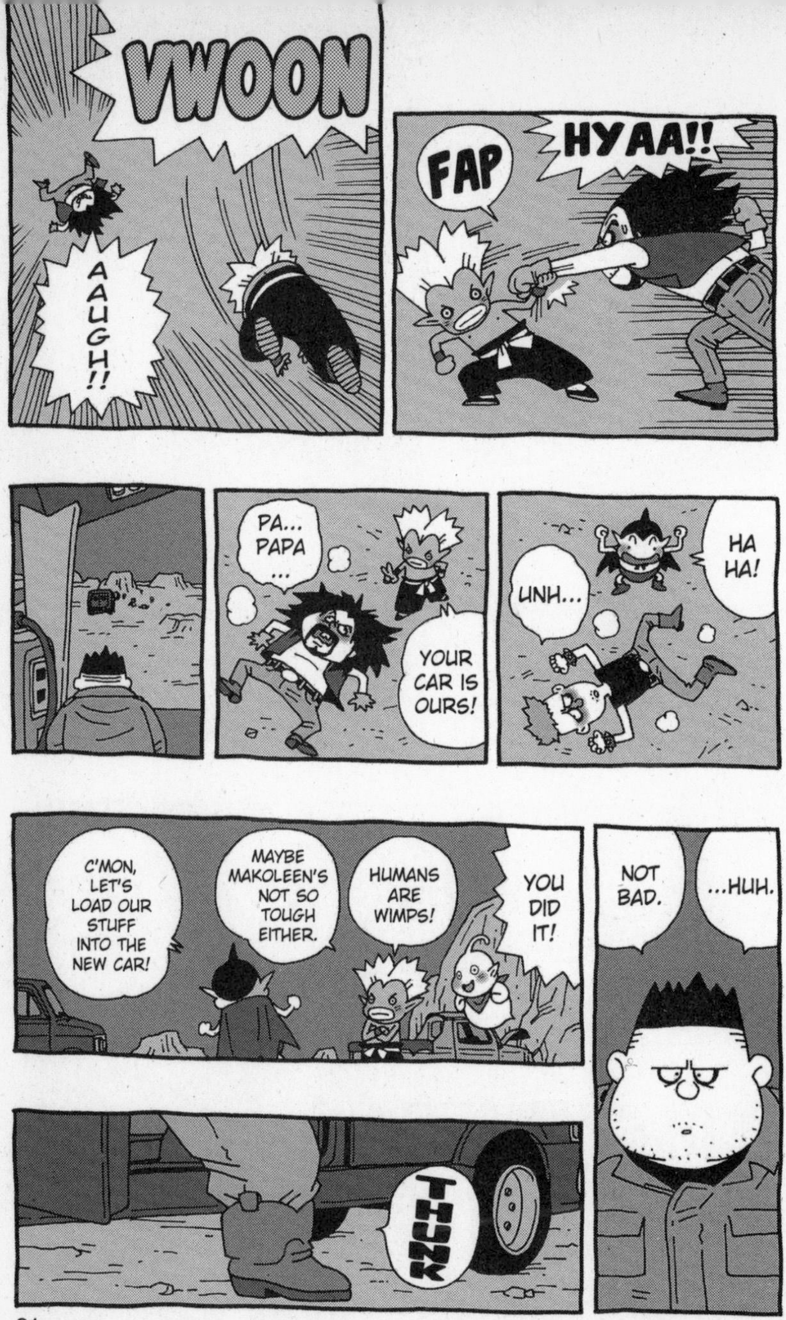
HYAA!!
FAP
VWOON
AAUGH!!
HA HA!
UNH...
PA... PAPA ...
YOUR CAR IS OURS!
...HUH.
NOT BAD.
YOU DID IT!
HUMANS ARE WIMPS!
MAYBE MAKOLEEN'S NOT SO TOUGH EITHER.
C'MON, LET'S LOAD OUR STUFF INTO THE NEW CAR!
THUNK

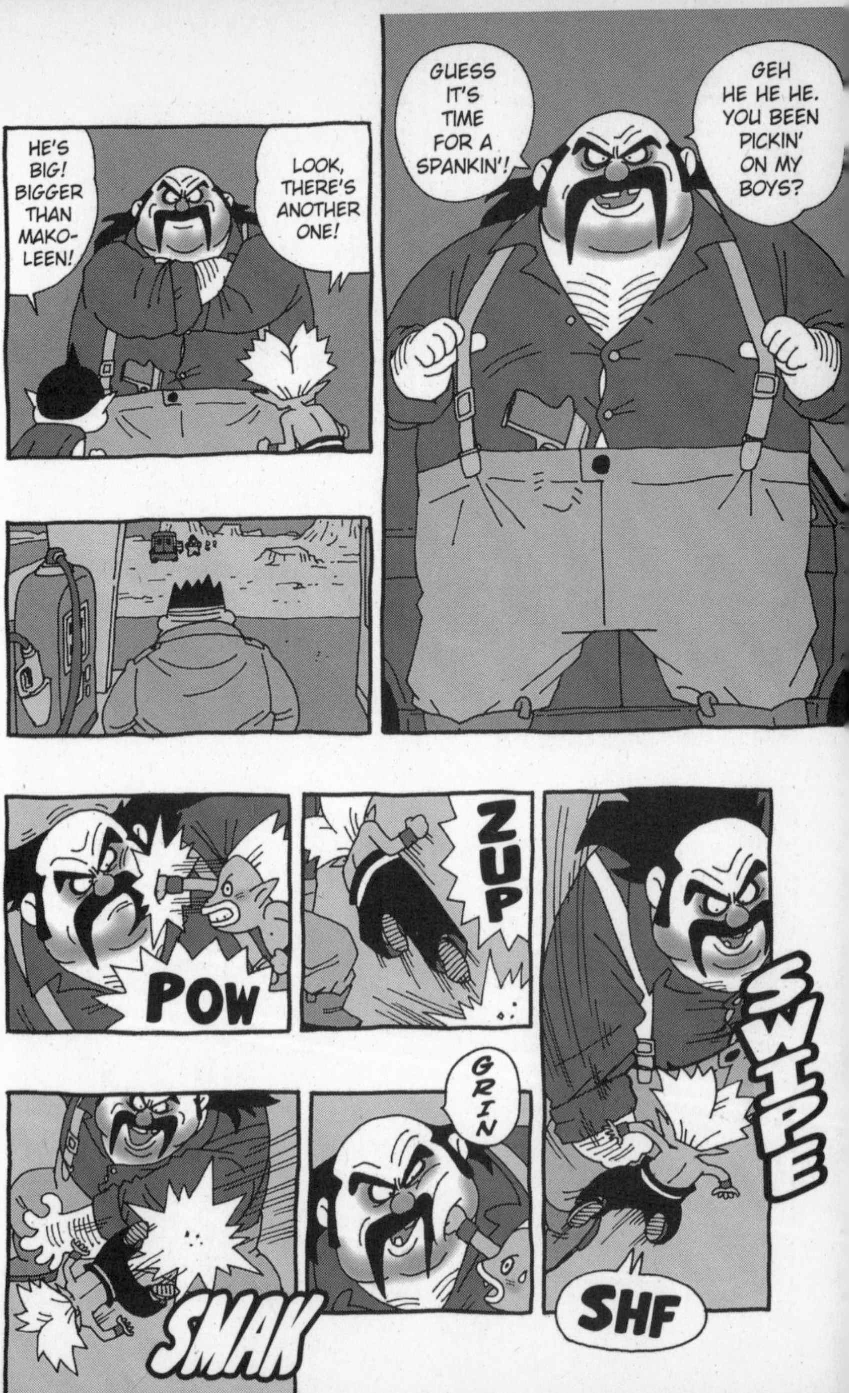
GEH HE HE HE. YOU BEEN PICKIN' ON MY BOYS?
GUESS IT'S TIME FOR A SPANKIN'!
LOOK, THERE'S ANOTHER ONE!
HE'S BIG! BIGGER THAN MAKO-LEEN!
SWIPE
SHF
ZUP
POW
GRIN
SMAK

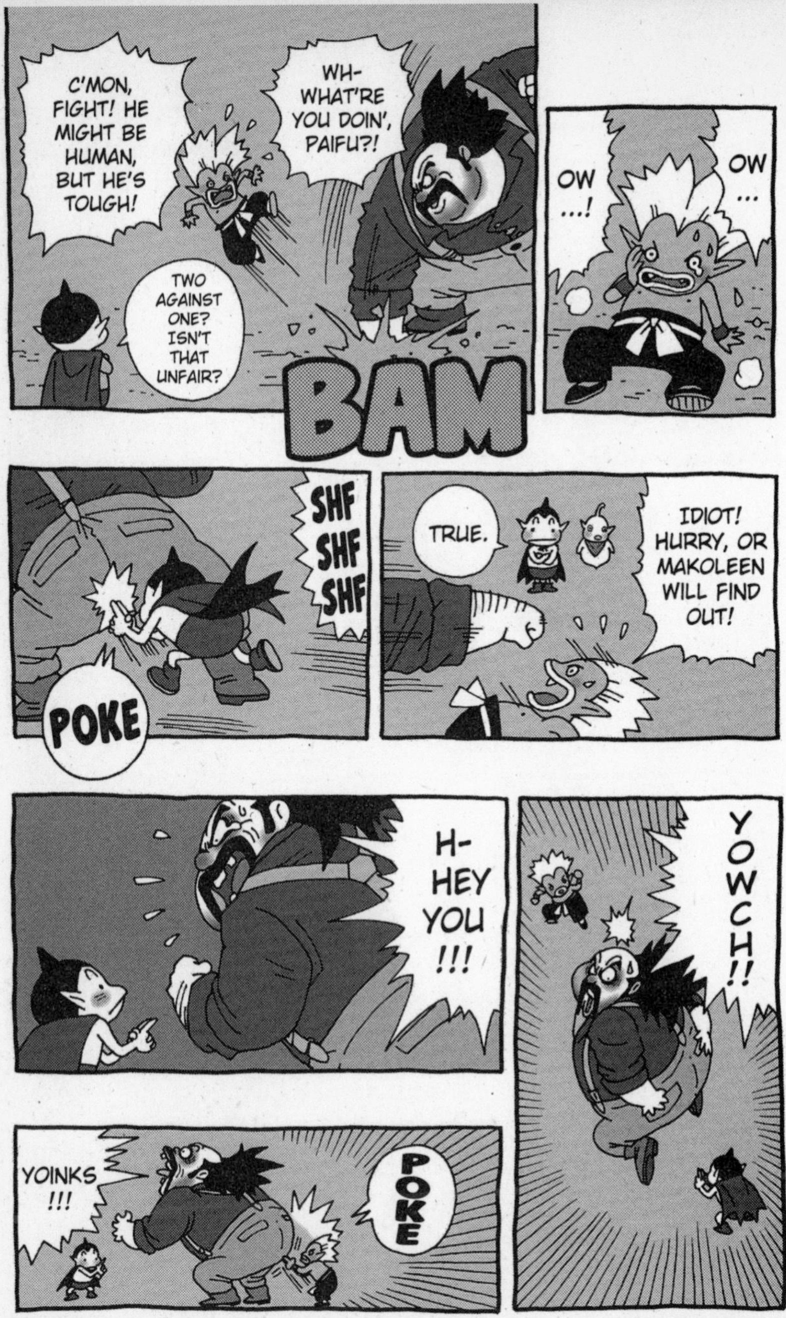

OW ...
OW ...!
WH- WHAT'RE YOU DOIN', PAIFU?!
C'MON, FIGHT! HE MIGHT BE HUMAN, BUT HE'S TOUGH!
TWO AGAINST ONE? ISN'T THAT UNFAIR?
BAM
IDIOT! HURRY, OR MAKOLEEN WILL FIND OUT!
TRUE.
SHF SHF SHF
POKE
YOWCH!!
H- HEY YOU!!!
POKE
YOINKS!!!

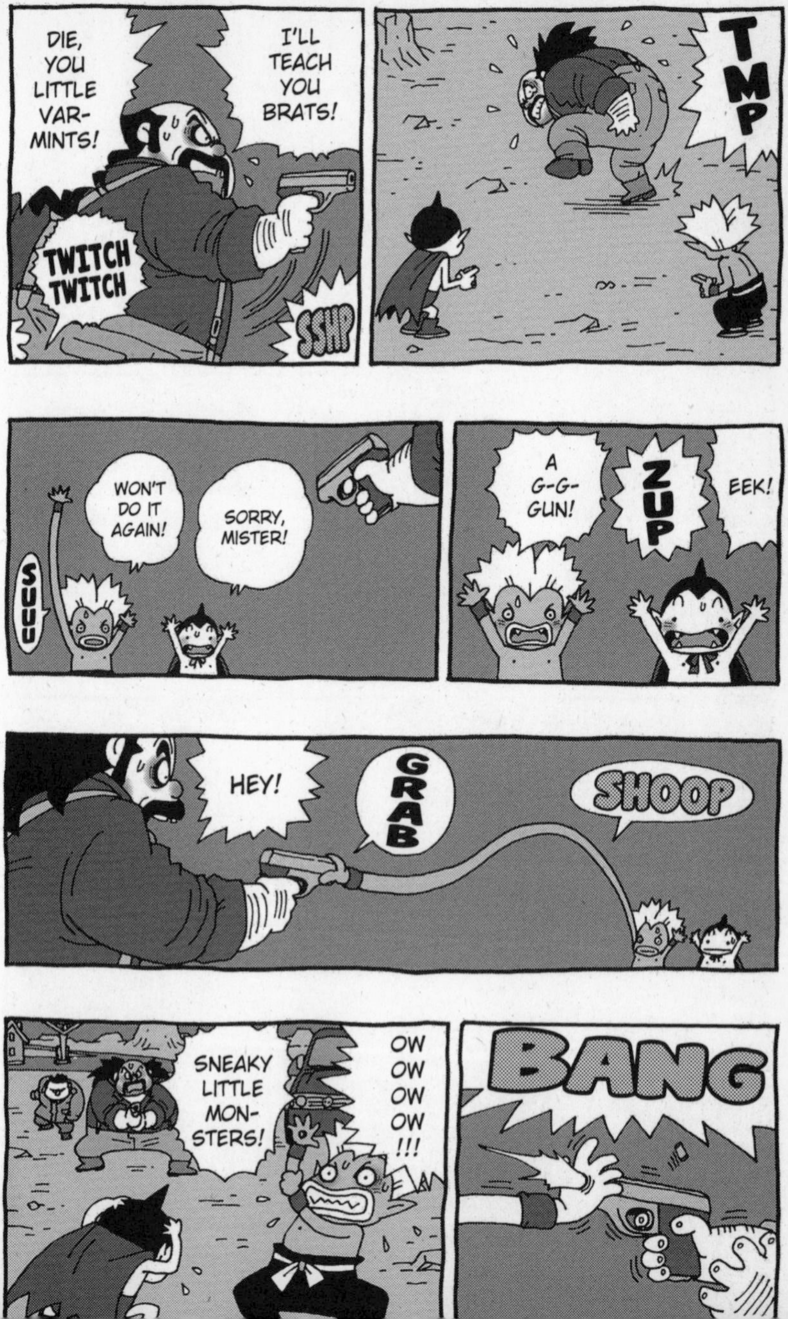
TMP
I'LL TEACH YOU BRATS!
DIE, YOU LITTLE VAR-MINTS!
TWITCH TWITCH
SSHP
EEK!
ZUP
A G-G-GUN!
SORRY, MISTER!
WON'T DO IT AGAIN!
SUUU
SHOOP
GRAB
HEY!
BANG
OW OW OW OW !!!
SNEAKY LITTLE MON-STERS!

READ THIS WAY

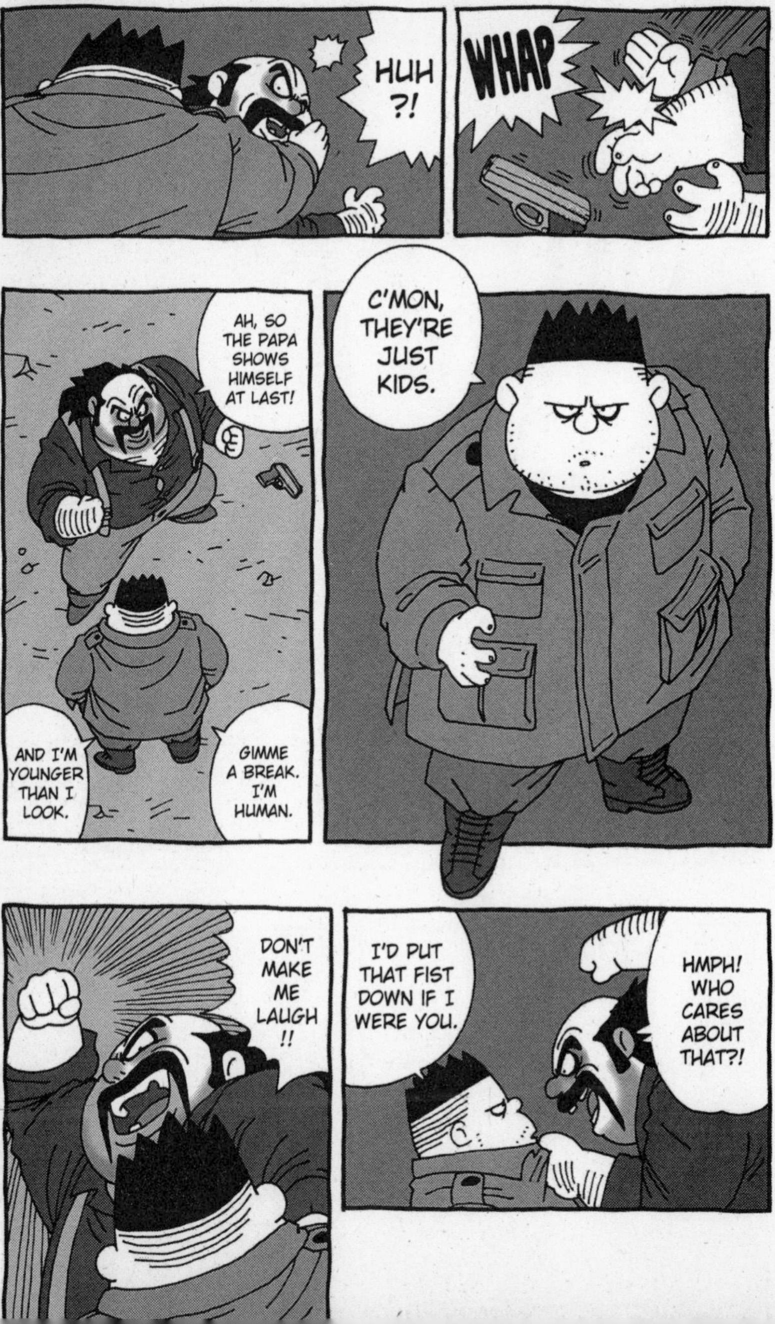
WHAP
HUH?!
C'MON, THEY'RE JUST KIDS.
AH, SO THE PAPA SHOWS HIMSELF AT LAST!
GIMME A BREAK. I'M HUMAN.
AND I'M YOUNGER THAN I LOOK.
HMPH! WHO CARES ABOUT THAT?!
I'D PUT THAT FIST DOWN IF I WERE YOU.
DON'T MAKE ME LAUGH!!

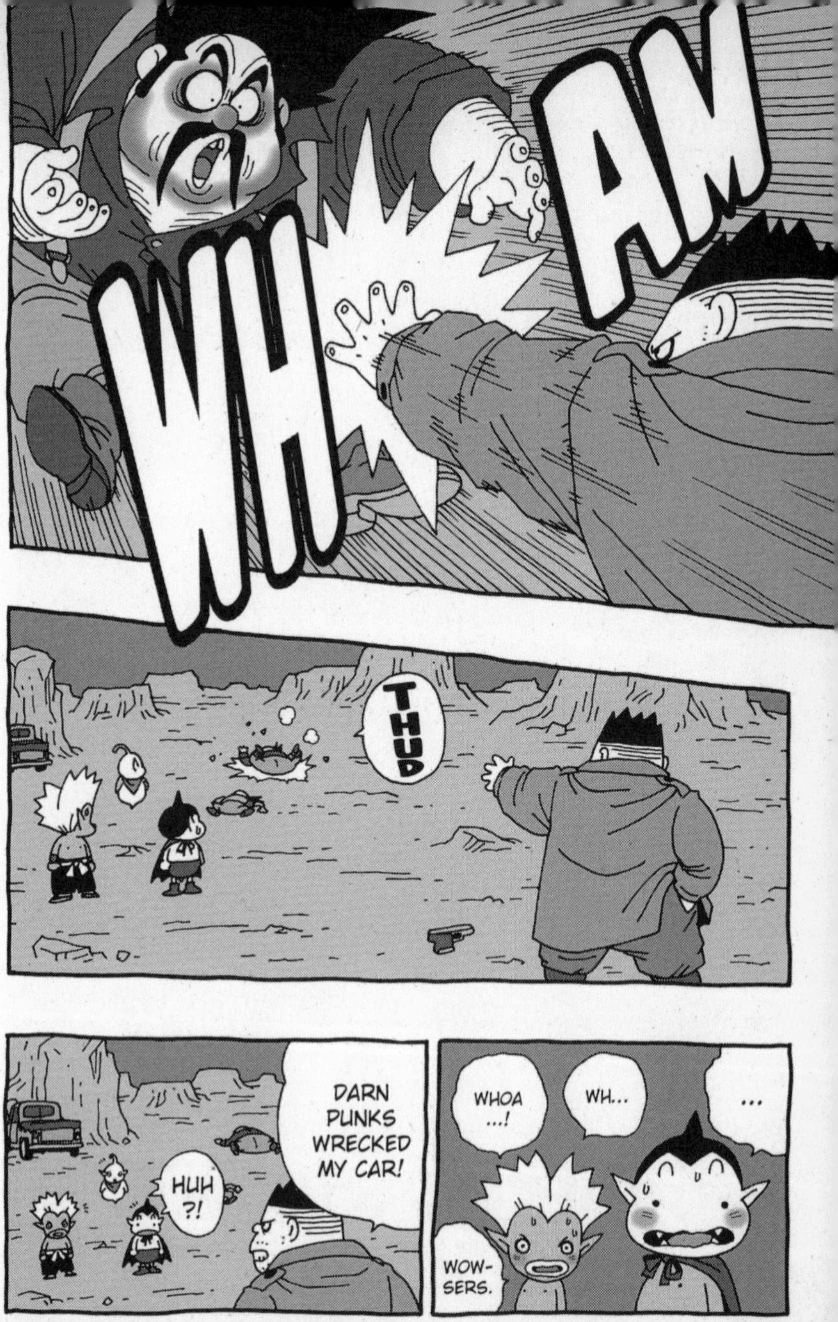
WH
AM
THUD
...
WH...
WHOA ...!
WOW-SERS.
DARN PUNKS WRECKED MY CAR!
HUH ?!

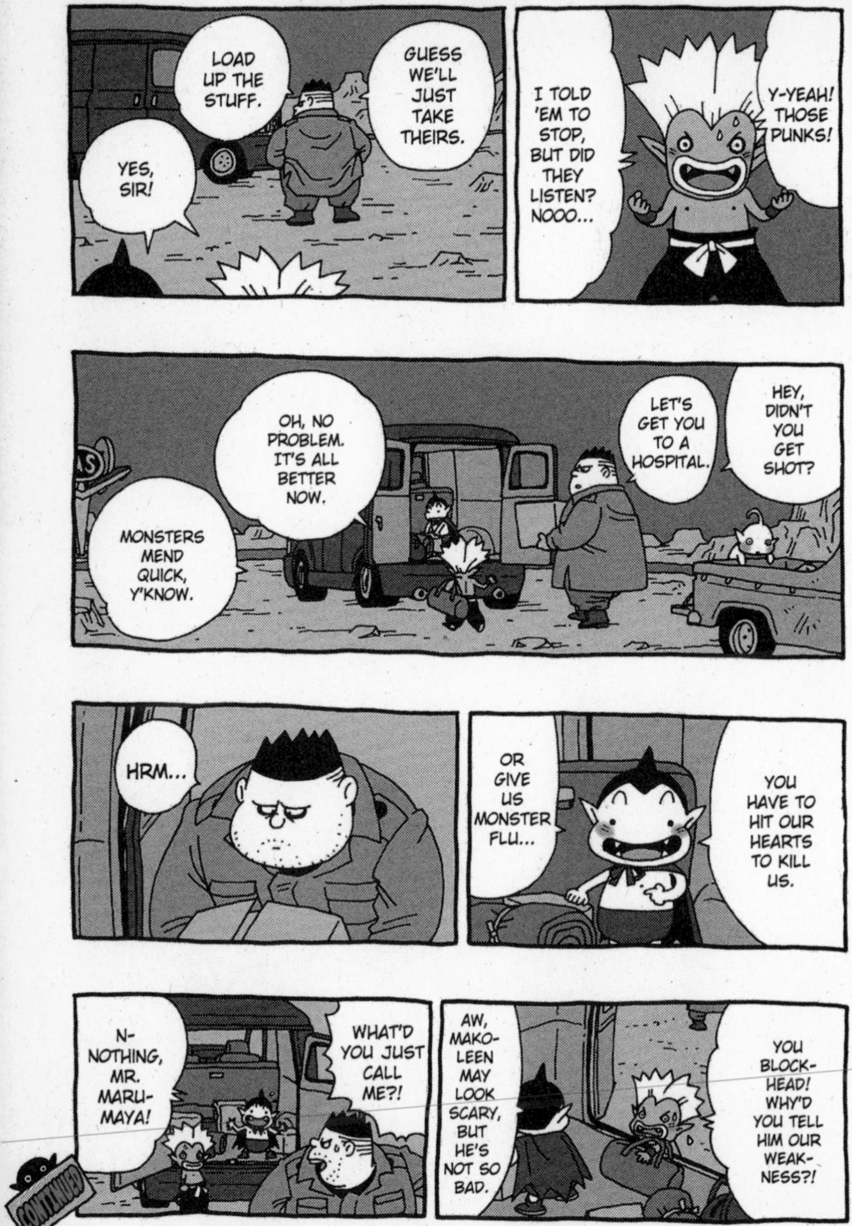
Y-YEAH! THOSE PUNKS!
I TOLD 'EM TO STOP, BUT DID THEY LISTEN? NOOO...
GUESS WE'LL JUST TAKE THEIRS.
LOAD UP THE STUFF.
YES, SIR!
HEY, DIDN'T YOU GET SHOT?
LET'S GET YOU TO A HOSPITAL.
OH, NO PROBLEM. IT'S ALL BETTER NOW.
MONSTERS MEND QUICK, Y'KNOW.
YOU HAVE TO HIT OUR HEARTS TO KILL US.
OR GIVE US MONSTER FLU...
HRM...
YOU BLOCKHEAD! WHY'D YOU TELL HIM OUR WEAKNESS?!
AW, MAKOLEEN MAY LOOK SCARY, BUT HE'S NOT SO BAD.
WHAT'D YOU JUST CALL ME?!
N-NOTHING, MR. MARUMAYA!
CONTINUED

COWA!

FRIGHT 7

The Road Goes On

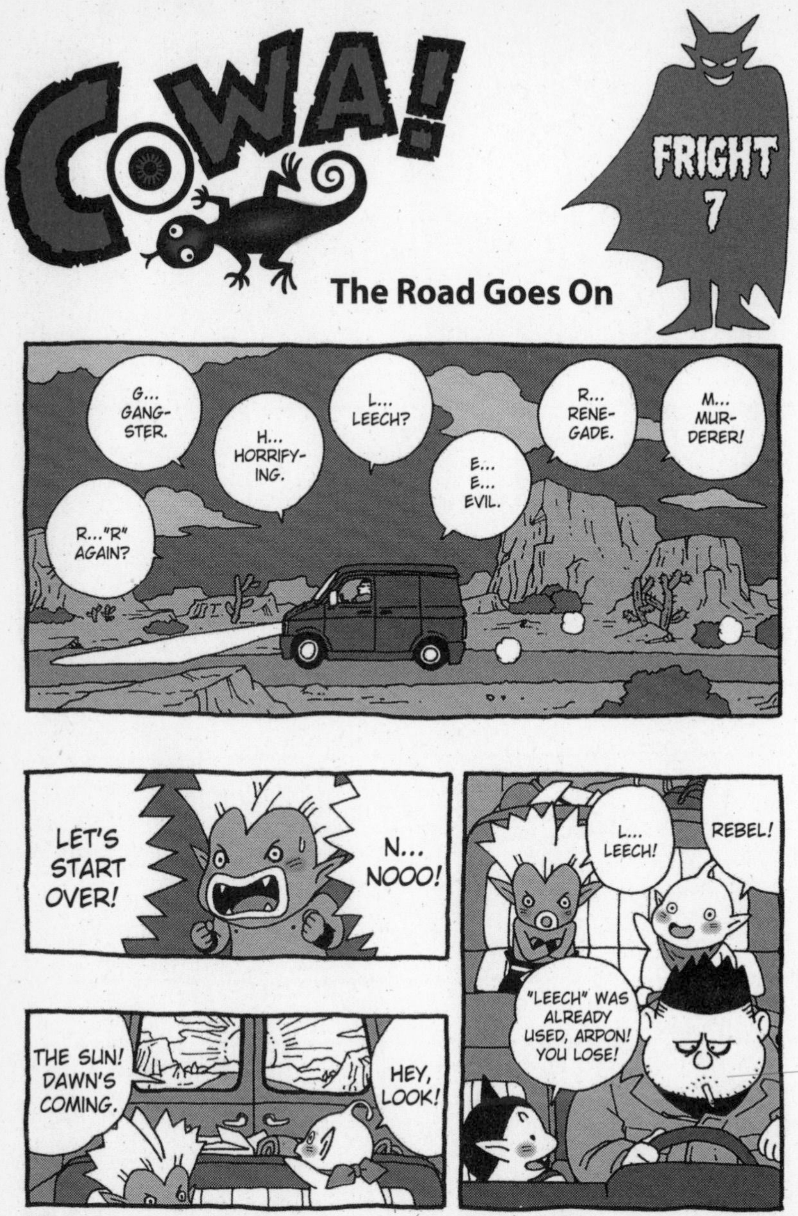
M... MURDERER!
R... RENEGADE.
E... E... EVIL.
L... LEECH?
H... HORRIFYING.
G... GANGSTER.
R..."R" AGAIN?
REBEL!
L... LEECH!
"LEECH" WAS ALREADY USED, ARPON! YOU LOSE!
N... NOOO!
LET'S START OVER!
HEY, LOOK!
THE SUN! DAWN'S COMING.

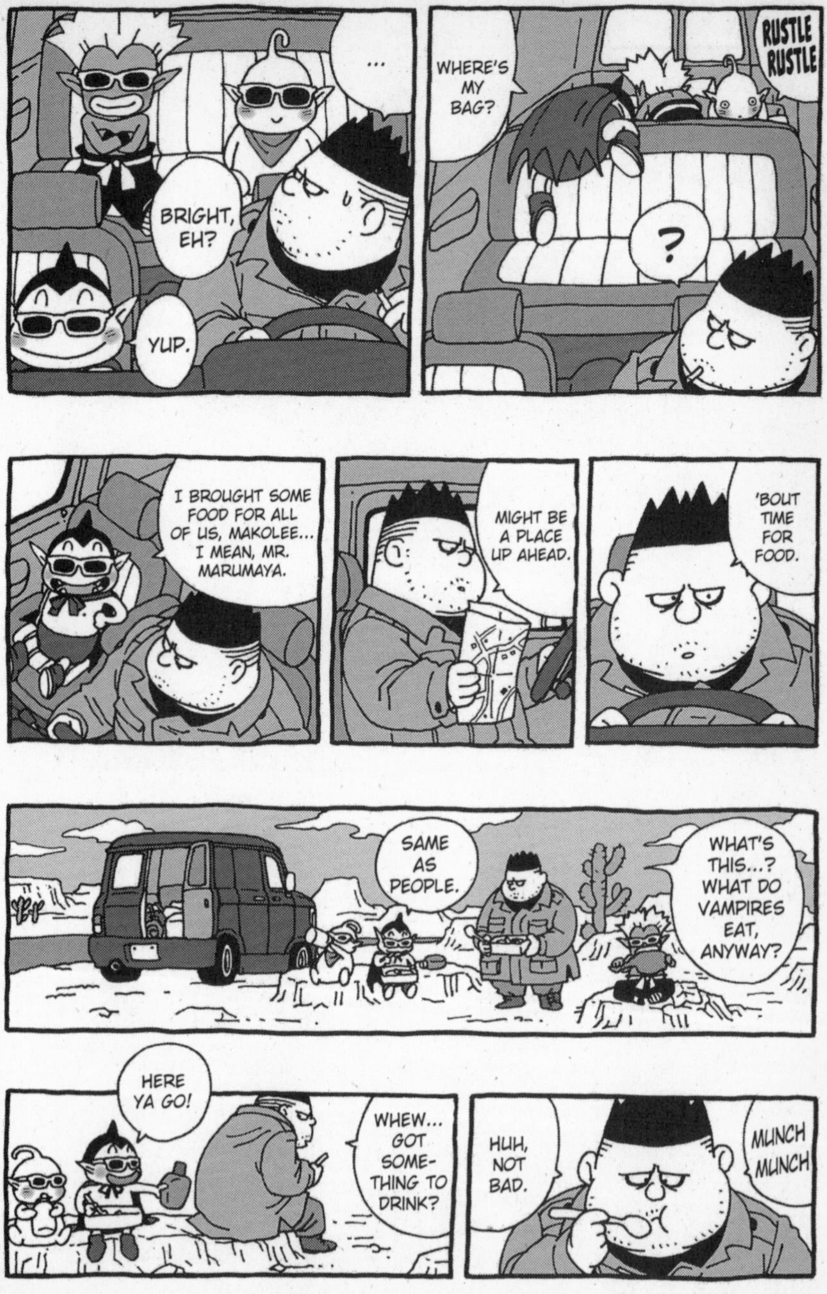
RUSTLE RUSTLE
WHERE'S MY BAG?
?
...
BRIGHT, EH?
YUP.
'BOUT TIME FOR FOOD.
MIGHT BE A PLACE UP AHEAD.
I BROUGHT SOME FOOD FOR ALL OF US, MAKOLEE... I MEAN, MR. MARUMAYA.
WHAT'S THIS...? WHAT DO VAMPIRES EAT, ANYWAY?
SAME AS PEOPLE.
MUNCH MUNCH
HUH, NOT BAD.
WHEW... GOT SOME-THING TO DRINK?
HERE YA GO!

READ THIS WAY

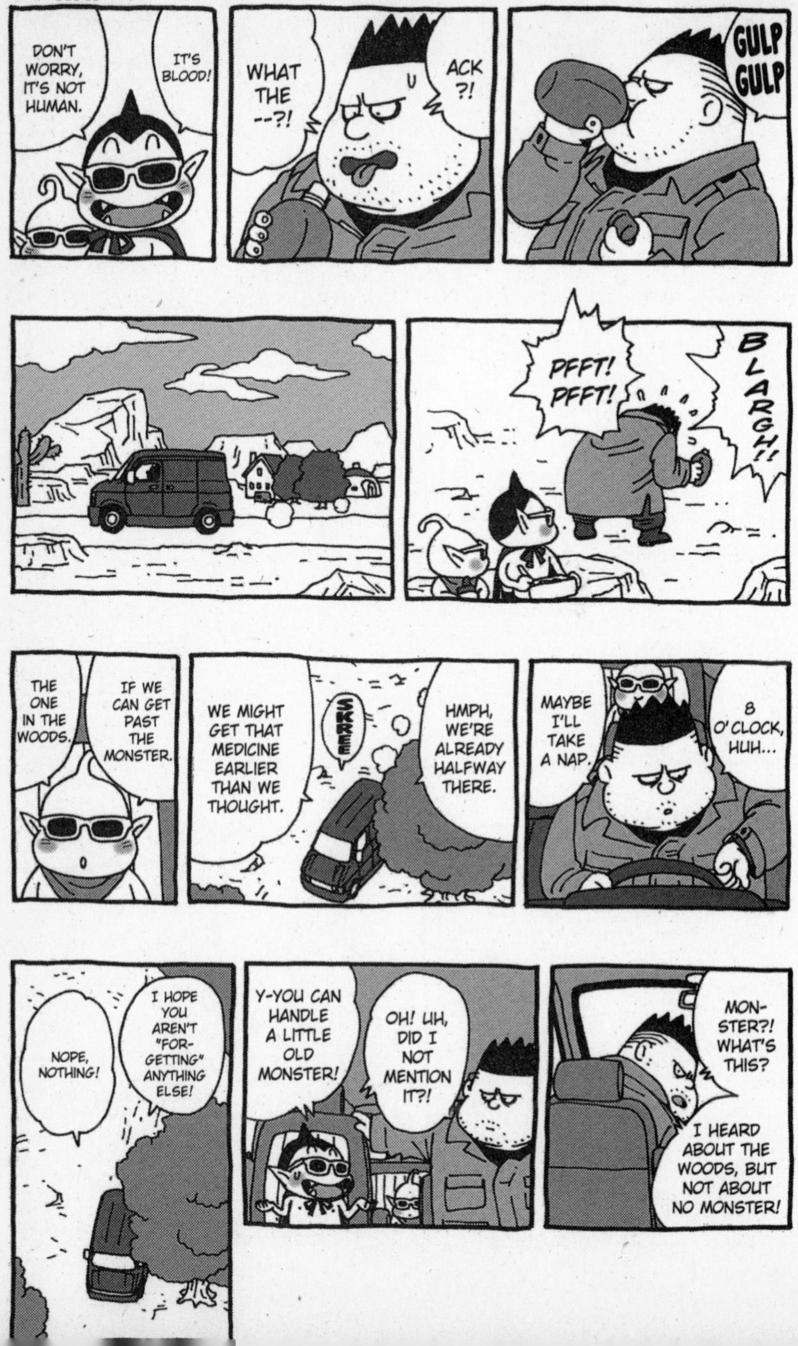
GULP GULP
ACK ?!
WHAT THE --?!
IT'S BLOOD!
DON'T WORRY, IT'S NOT HUMAN.
BLARGH!!
PFFT! PFFT!
8 O'CLOCK, HUH...
MAYBE I'LL TAKE A NAP.
HMPH, WE'RE ALREADY HALFWAY THERE.
SKREE
WE MIGHT GET THAT MEDICINE EARLIER THAN WE THOUGHT.
IF WE CAN GET PAST THE MONSTER.
THE ONE IN THE WOODS.
MON-STER?! WHAT'S THIS?
I HEARD ABOUT THE WOODS, BUT NOT ABOUT NO MONSTER!
OH! UH, DID I NOT MENTION IT?!
Y-YOU CAN HANDLE A LITTLE OLD MONSTER!
I HOPE YOU AREN'T "FOR-GETTING" ANYTHING ELSE!
NOPE, NOTHING!

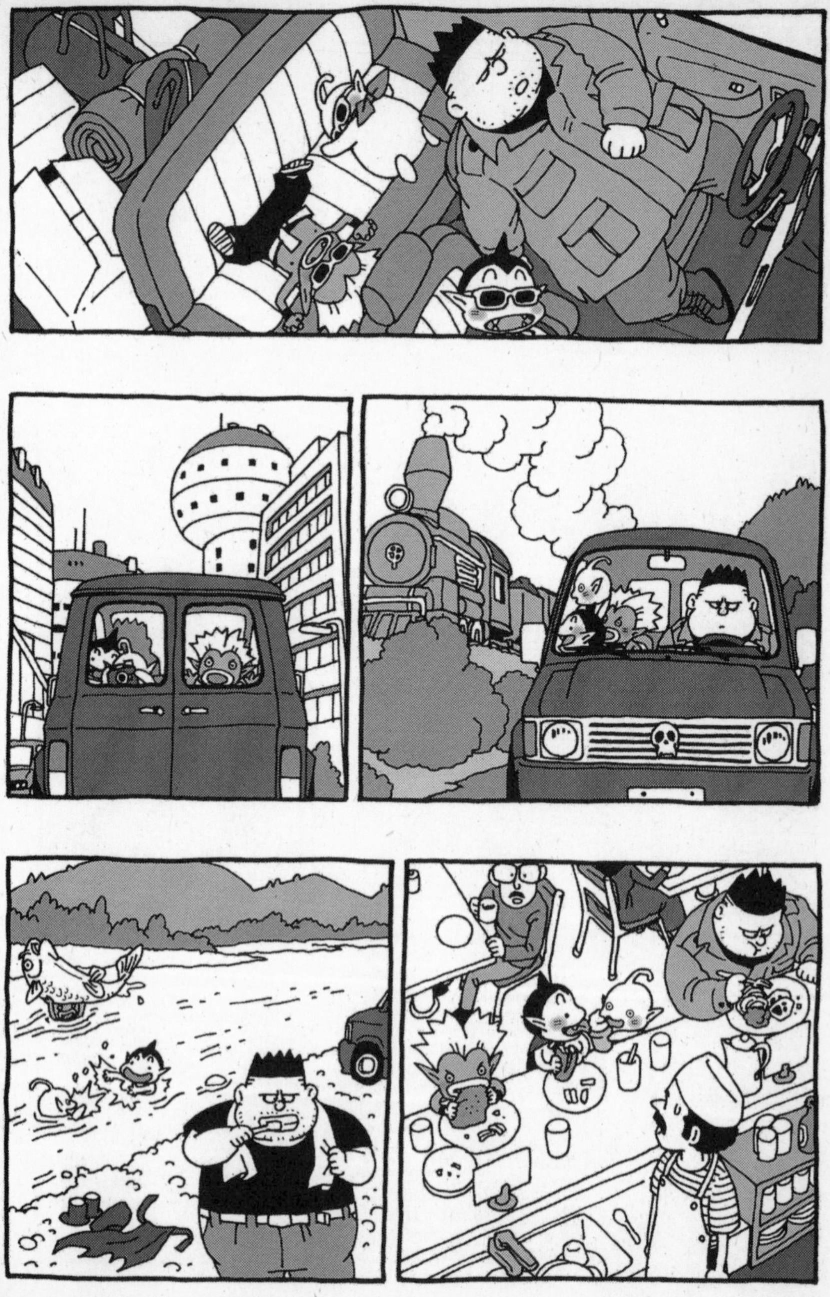

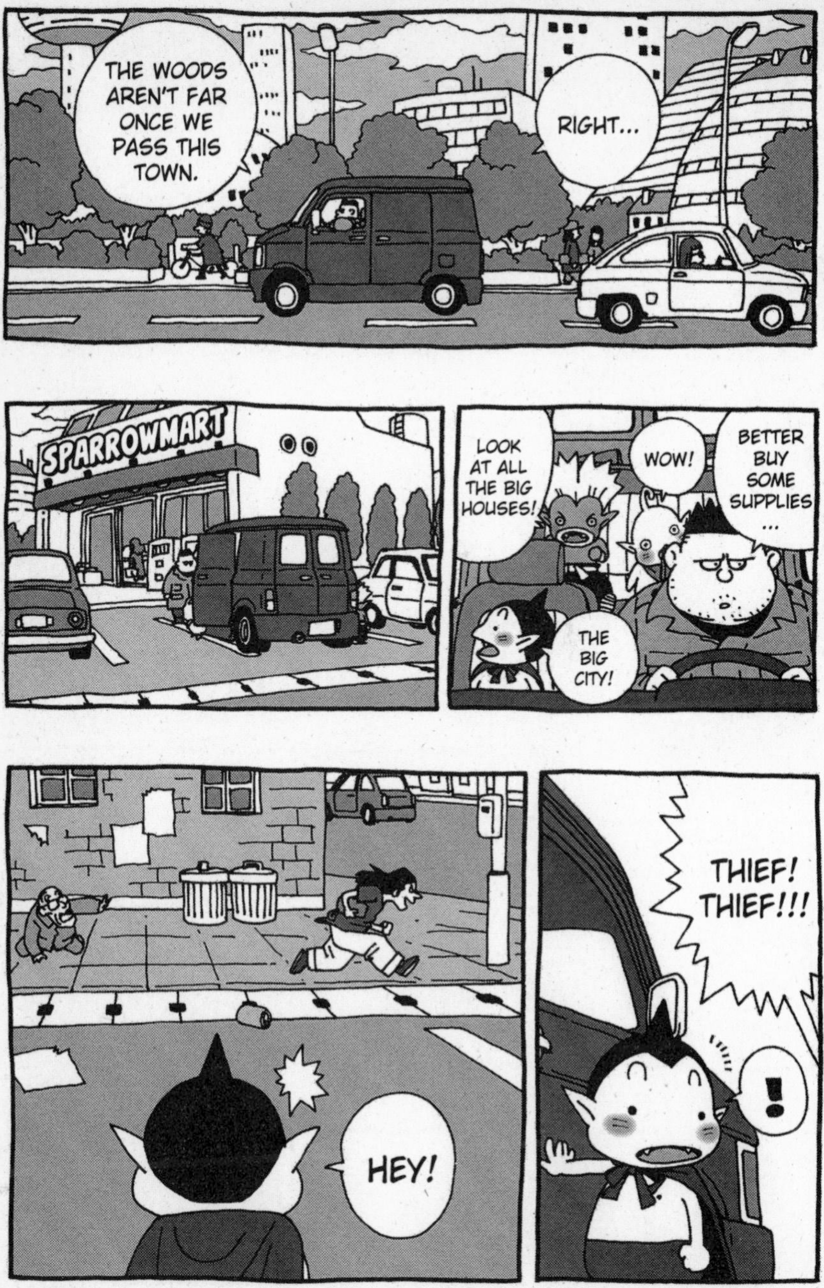
THE WOODS AREN'T FAR ONCE WE PASS THIS TOWN.
RIGHT...
BETTER BUY SOME SUPPLIES ...
WOW!
LOOK AT ALL THE BIG HOUSES!
THE BIG CITY!
SPARROWMART
THIEF! THIEF!!!
!
HEY!

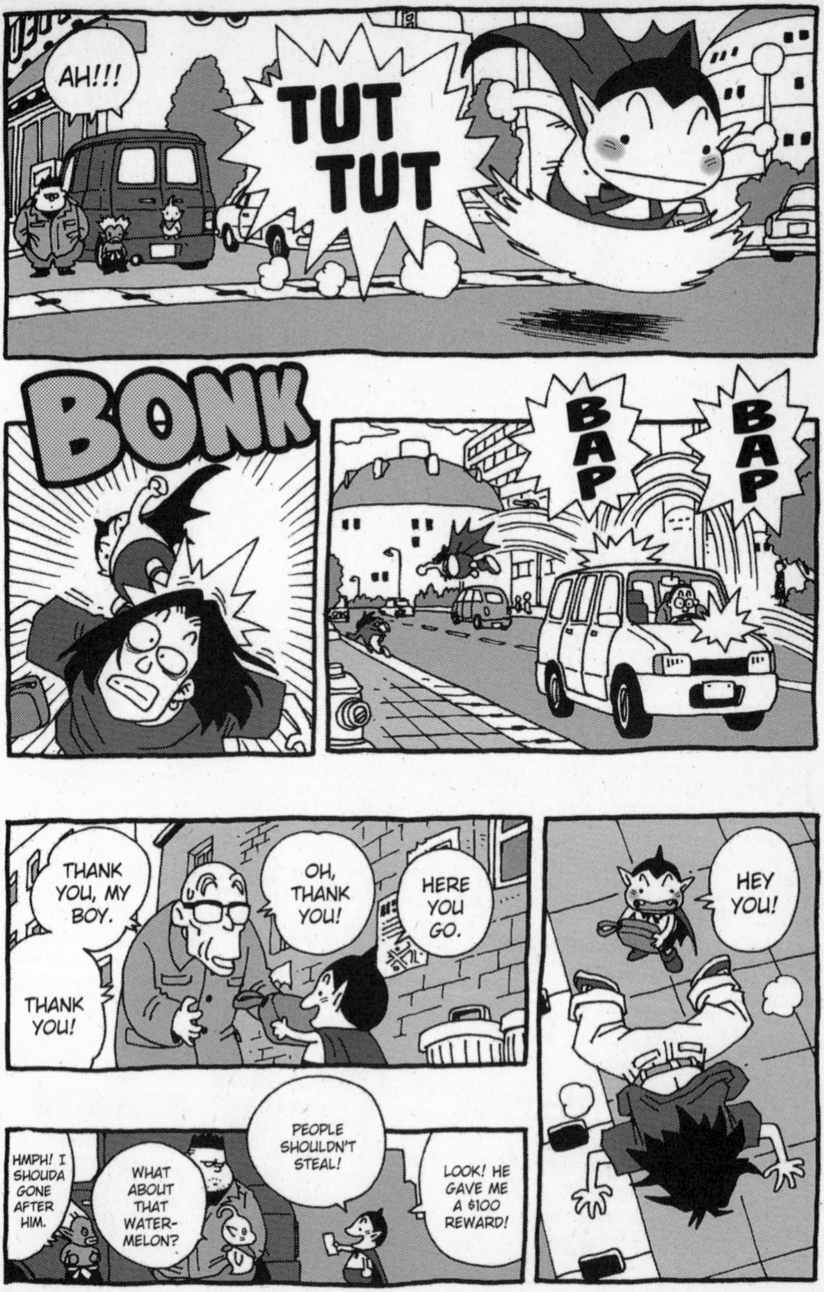
TUT TUT
AH!!!
BAP BAP
BONK
HEY YOU!
HERE YOU GO.
OH, THANK YOU!
THANK YOU, MY BOY.
THANK YOU!
LOOK! HE GAVE ME A $100 REWARD!
PEOPLE SHOULDN'T STEAL!
WHAT ABOUT THAT WATER-MELON?
HMPH! I SHOUDA GONE AFTER HIM.

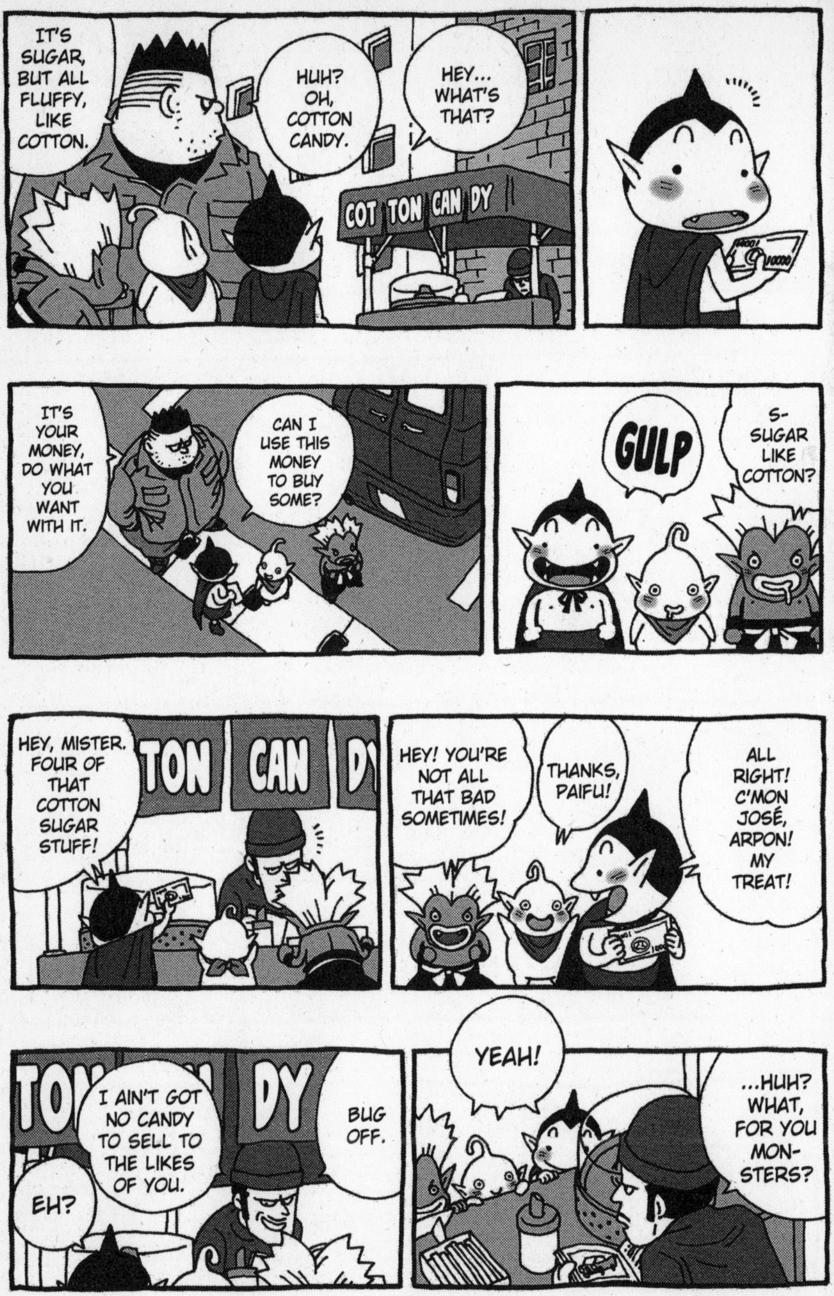
HEY... WHAT'S THAT?
HUH? OH, COTTON CANDY.
IT'S SUGAR, BUT ALL FLUFFY, LIKE COTTON.
COT TON CAN DY
S- SUGAR LIKE COTTON?
GULP
CAN I USE THIS MONEY TO BUY SOME?
IT'S YOUR MONEY, DO WHAT YOU WANT WITH IT.
ALL RIGHT! C'MON JOSÉ, ARPON! MY TREAT!
THANKS, PAIFU!
HEY! YOU'RE NOT ALL THAT BAD SOMETIMES!
HEY, MISTER. FOUR OF THAT COTTON SUGAR STUFF!
YEAH!
...HUH? WHAT, FOR YOU MON- STERS?
I AIN'T GOT NO CANDY TO SELL TO THE LIKES OF YOU.
BUG OFF.
EH?

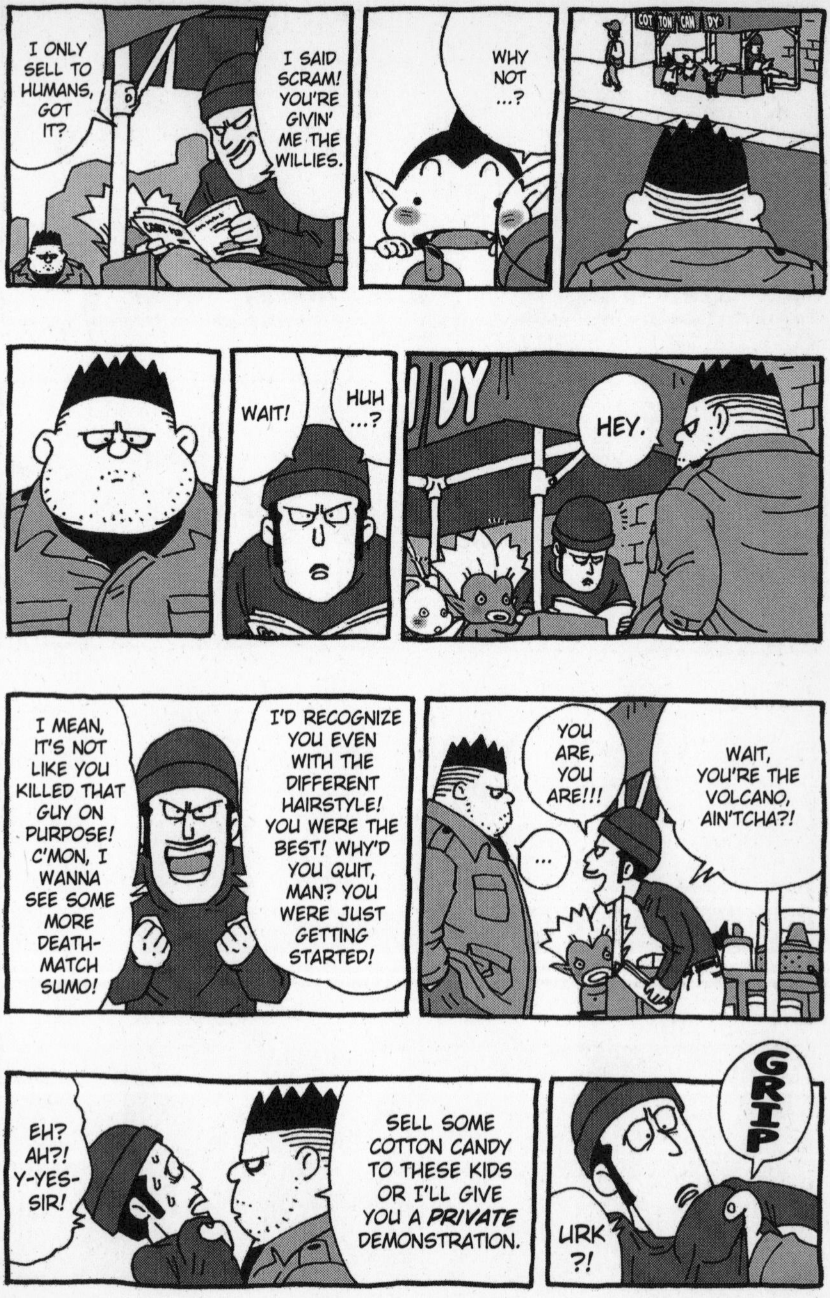
COT TON CAN DY
WHY NOT ...?
I SAID SCRAM! YOU'RE GIVIN' ME THE WILLIES.
I ONLY SELL TO HUMANS, GOT IT?
HEY.
HUH ...?
WAIT!
WAIT, YOU'RE THE VOLCANO, AIN'TCHA?!
YOU ARE, YOU ARE!!!
...
I'D RECOGNIZE YOU EVEN WITH THE DIFFERENT HAIRSTYLE! YOU WERE THE BEST! WHY'D YOU QUIT, MAN? YOU WERE JUST GETTING STARTED!
I MEAN, IT'S NOT LIKE YOU KILLED THAT GUY ON PURPOSE! C'MON, I WANNA SEE SOME MORE DEATH-MATCH SUMO!
GRIP
URK ?!
SELL SOME COTTON CANDY TO THESE KIDS OR I'LL GIVE YOU A *PRIVATE* DEMONSTRATION.
EH? AH?! Y-YES-SIR!

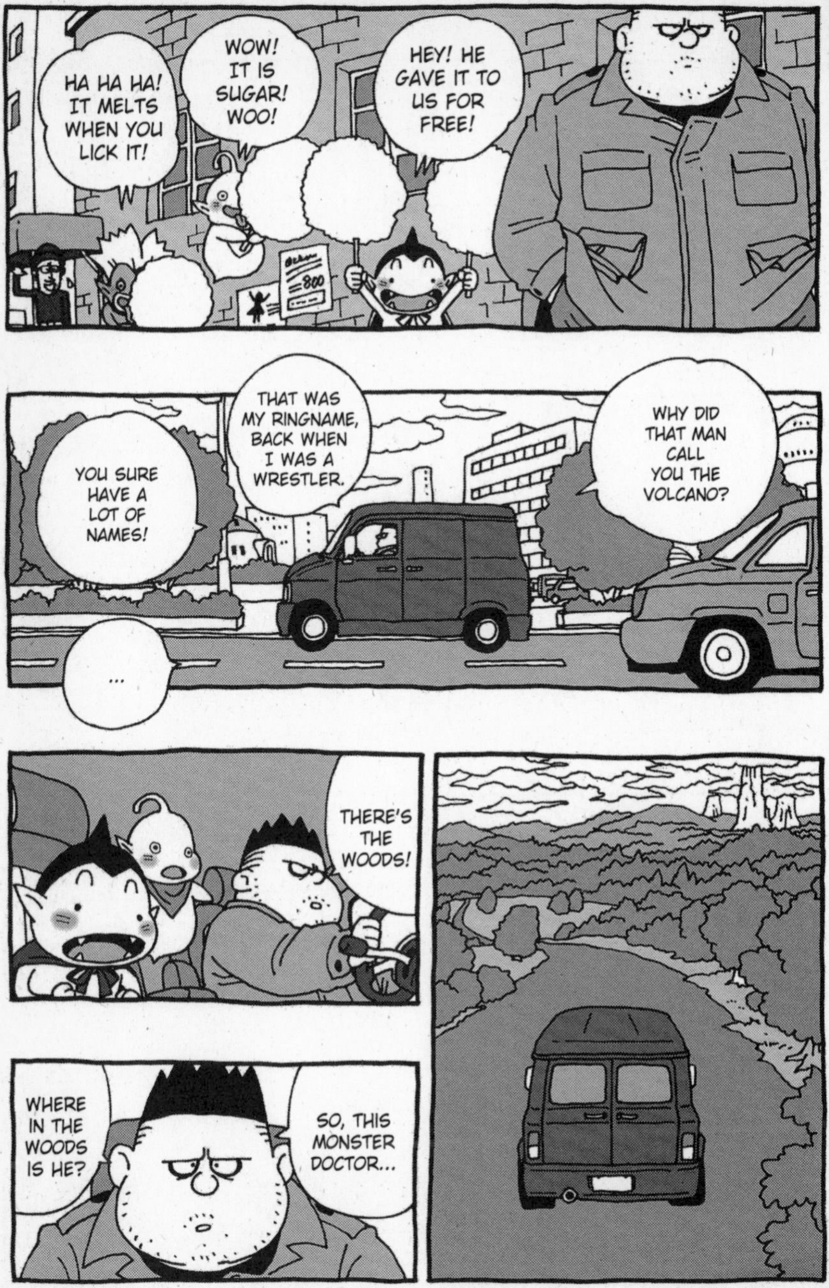
HEY! HE GAVE IT TO US FOR FREE!
WOW! IT IS SUGAR! WOO!
HA HA HA! IT MELTS WHEN YOU LICK IT!
WHY DID THAT MAN CALL YOU THE VOLCANO?
THAT WAS MY RINGNAME, BACK WHEN I WAS A WRESTLER.
YOU SURE HAVE A LOT OF NAMES!
...
THERE'S THE WOODS!
SO, THIS MONSTER DOCTOR...
WHERE IN THE WOODS IS HE?

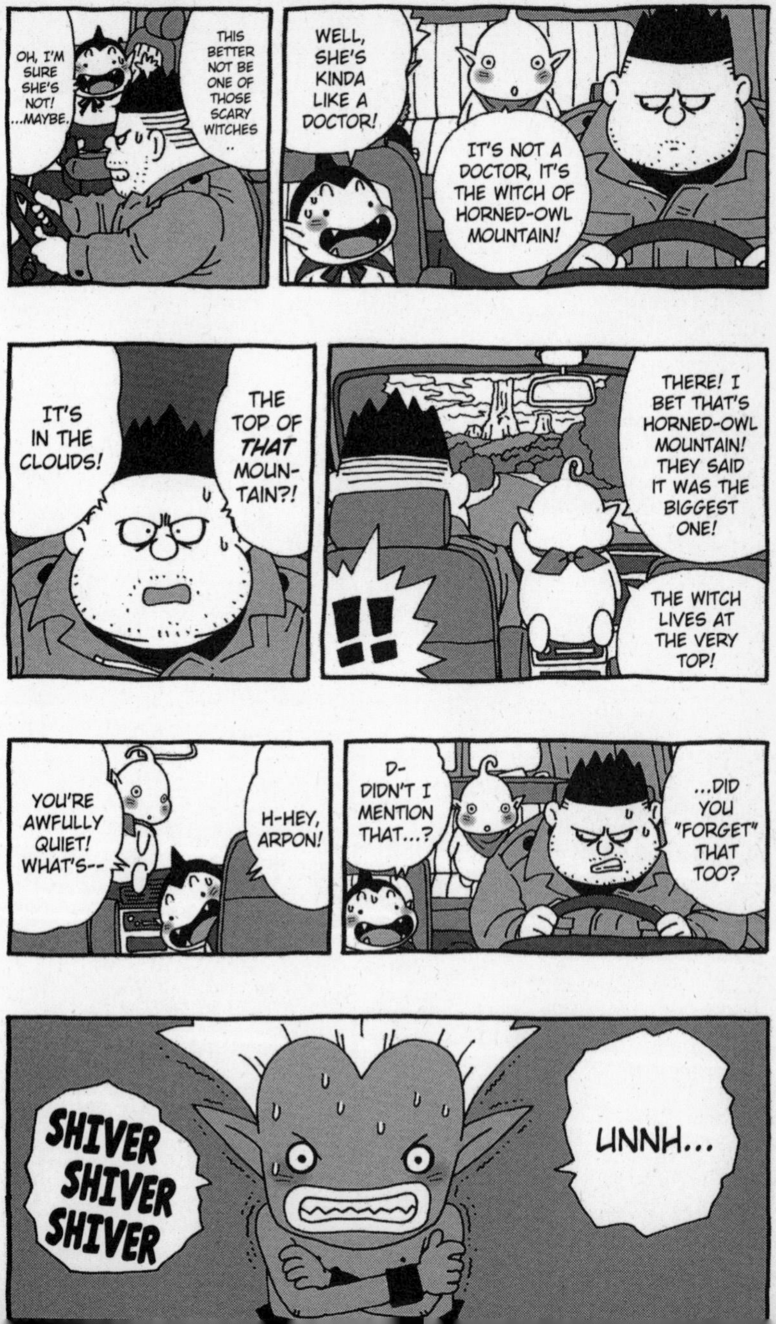
WELL, SHE'S KINDA LIKE A DOCTOR!
IT'S NOT A DOCTOR, IT'S THE WITCH OF HORNED-OWL MOUNTAIN!
THIS BETTER NOT BE ONE OF THOSE SCARY WITCHES..
OH, I'M SURE SHE'S NOT! ...MAYBE.
THERE! I BET THAT'S HORNED-OWL MOUNTAIN! THEY SAID IT WAS THE BIGGEST ONE!
THE WITCH LIVES AT THE VERY TOP!
!!
THE TOP OF THAT MOUN-TAIN?!
IT'S IN THE CLOUDS!
...DID YOU "FORGET" THAT TOO?
D-DIDN'T I MENTION THAT...?
H-HEY, ARPON!
YOU'RE AWFULLY QUIET! WHAT'S--
UNNH...
SHIVER SHIVER SHIVER

READ THIS WAY

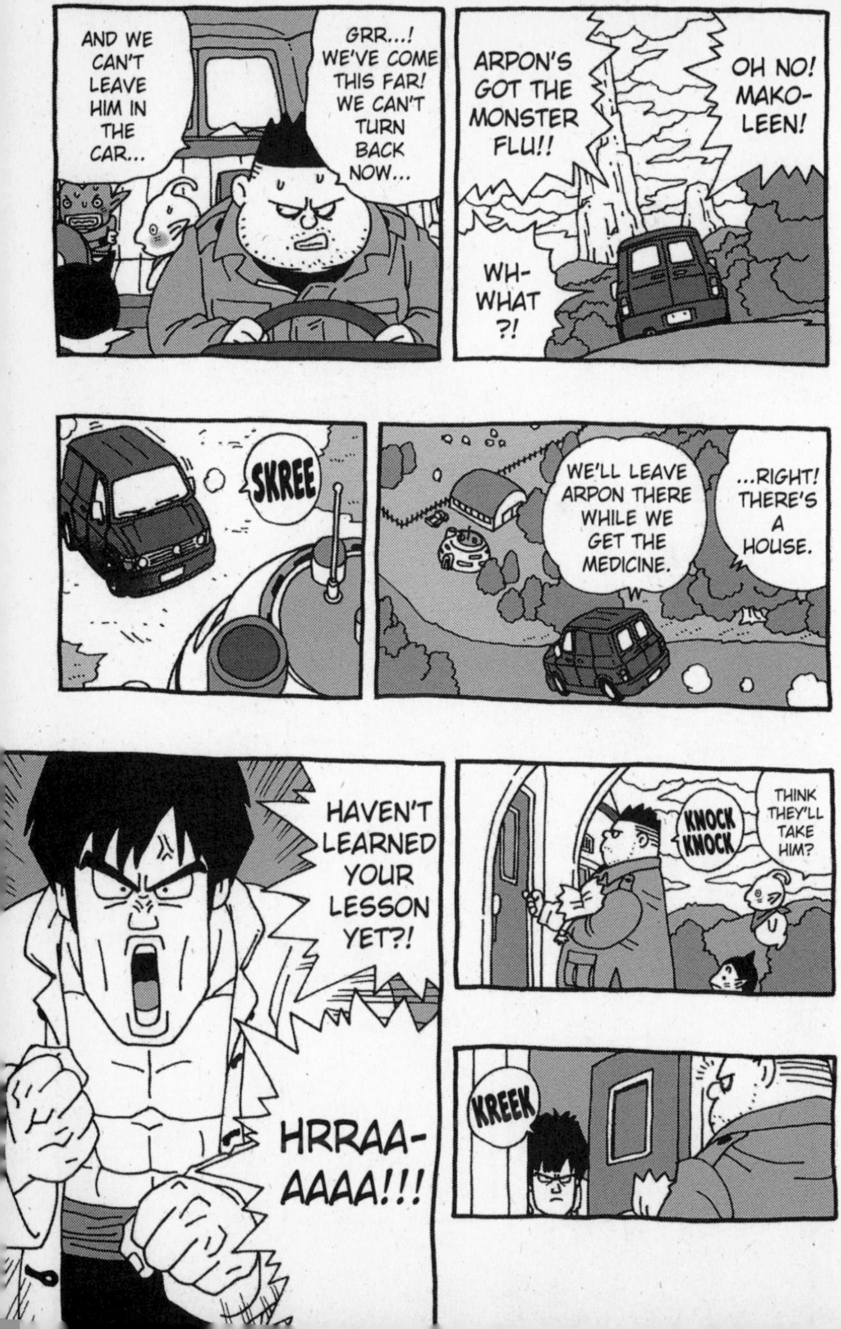
OH NO! MAKO-LEEN!
ARPON'S GOT THE MONSTER FLU!!
WH-WHAT?!
GRR...! WE'VE COME THIS FAR! WE CAN'T TURN BACK NOW...
AND WE CAN'T LEAVE HIM IN THE CAR...
...RIGHT! THERE'S A HOUSE.
WE'LL LEAVE ARPON THERE WHILE WE GET THE MEDICINE.
SKREE
THINK THEY'LL TAKE HIM?
KNOCK KNOCK
KREEK
HAVEN'T LEARNED YOUR LESSON YET?!
HRRAA-AAAA!!!

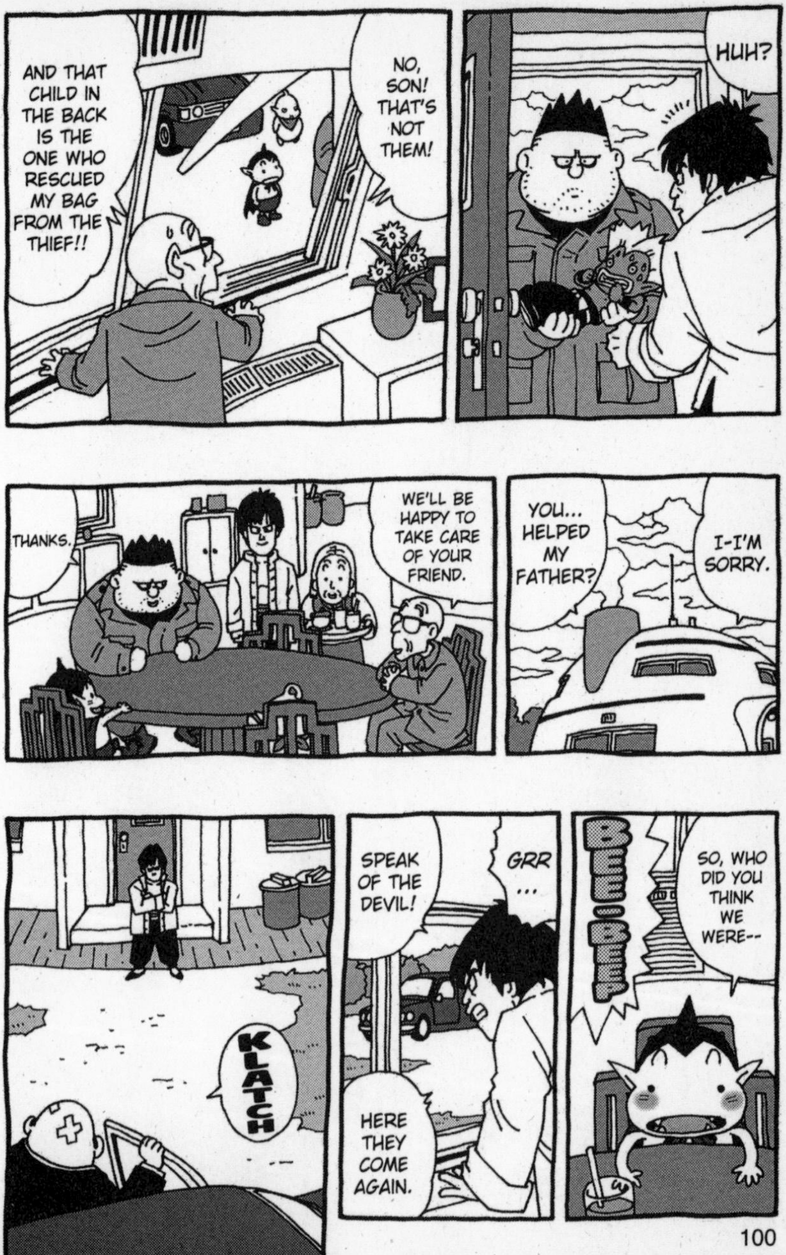
HUH?
NO, SON! THAT'S NOT THEM!
AND THAT CHILD IN THE BACK IS THE ONE WHO RESCUED MY BAG FROM THE THIEF!!
I-I'M SORRY.
YOU... HELPED MY FATHER?
WE'LL BE HAPPY TO TAKE CARE OF YOUR FRIEND.
THANKS.
SO, WHO DID YOU THINK WE WERE--
BEE-BEEP
GRR...
SPEAK OF THE DEVIL!
HERE THEY COME AGAIN.
KLATCH

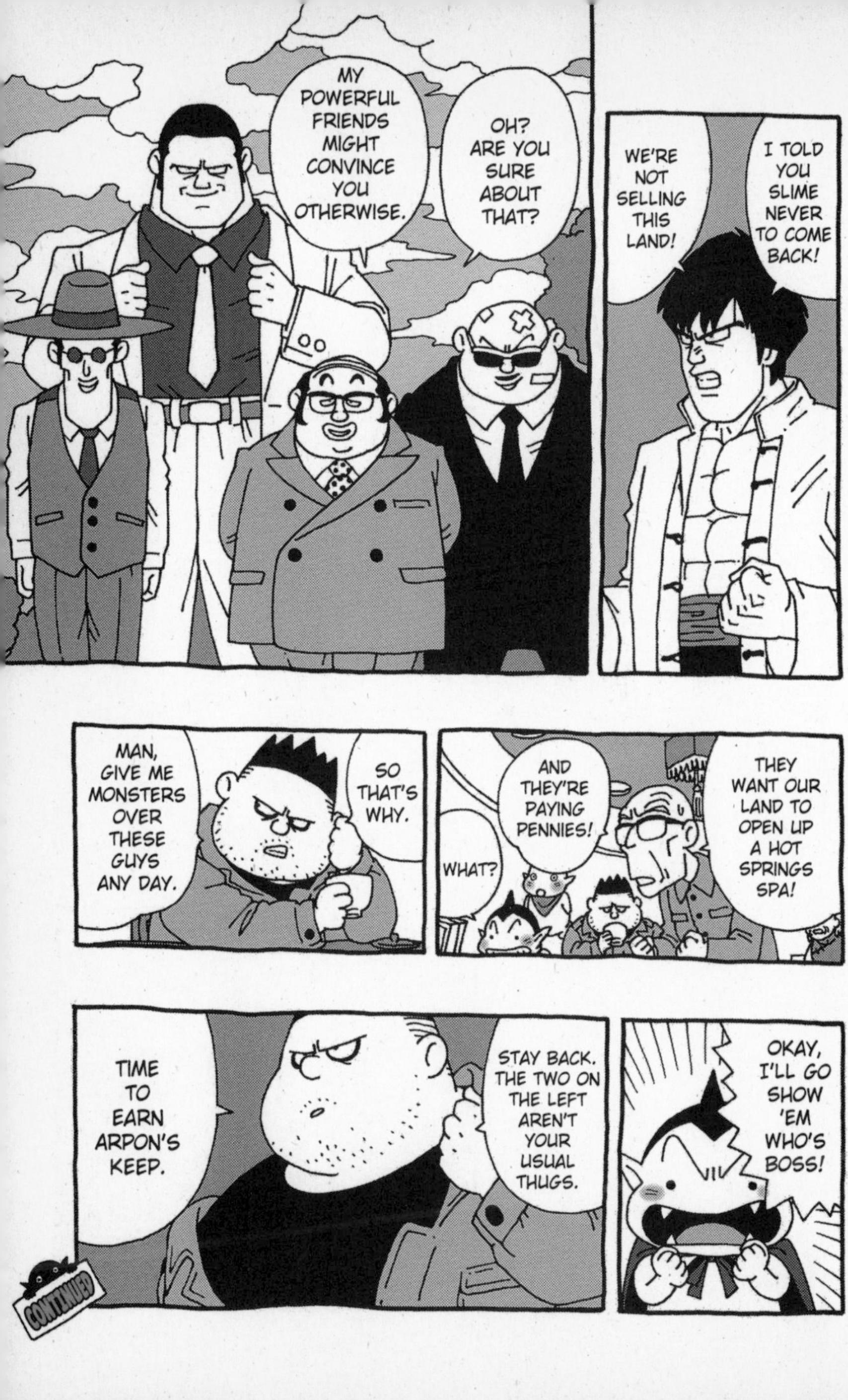
I TOLD YOU SLIME NEVER TO COME BACK!
WE'RE NOT SELLING THIS LAND!
OH? ARE YOU SURE ABOUT THAT?
MY POWERFUL FRIENDS MIGHT CONVINCE YOU OTHERWISE.
THEY WANT OUR LAND TO OPEN UP A HOT SPRINGS SPA!
AND THEY'RE PAYING PENNIES!
WHAT?
SO THAT'S WHY.
MAN, GIVE ME MONSTERS OVER THESE GUYS ANY DAY.
OKAY, I'LL GO SHOW 'EM WHO'S BOSS!
STAY BACK. THE TWO ON THE LEFT AREN'T YOUR USUAL THUGS.
TIME TO EARN ARPON'S KEEP.
CONTINUED

COWA!

FRIGHT 8

The Volcano Awakens

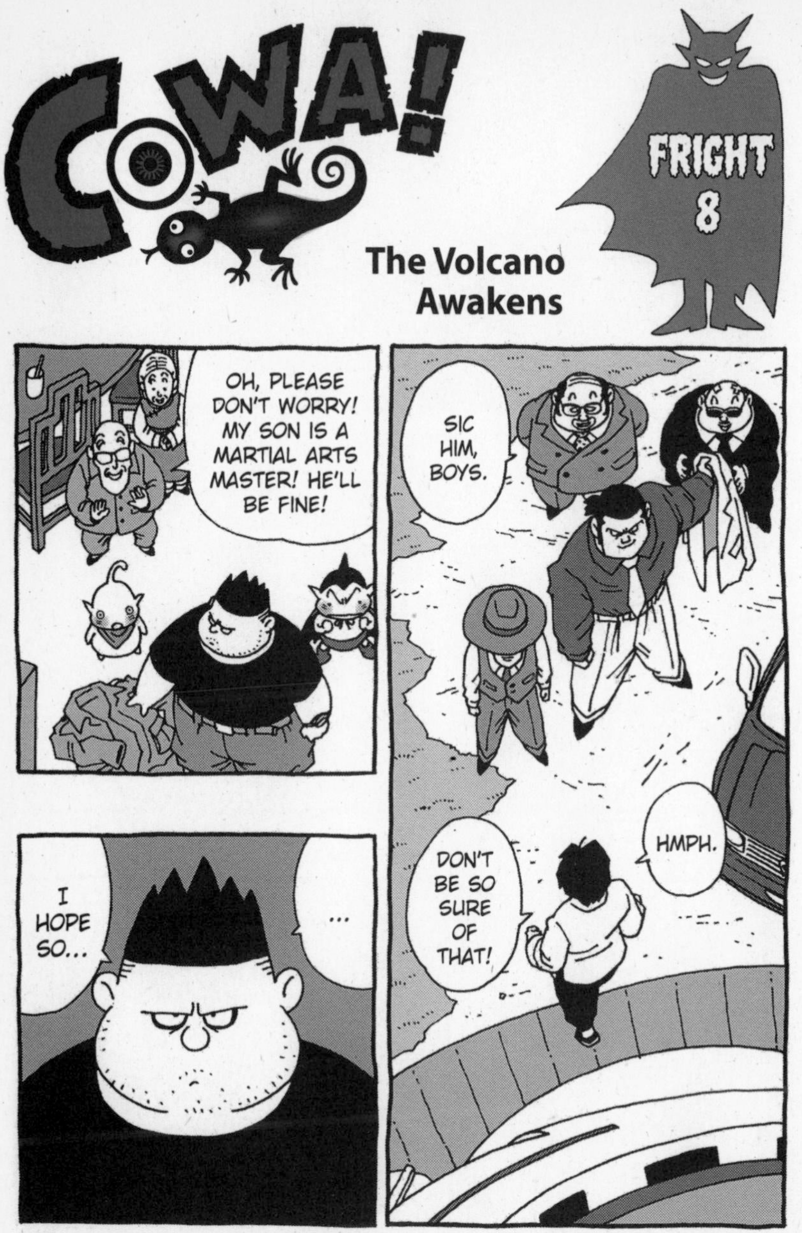
SIC HIM, BOYS.
HMPH.
DON'T BE SO SURE OF THAT!
OH, PLEASE DON'T WORRY! MY SON IS A MARTIAL ARTS MASTER! HE'LL BE FINE!
...
I HOPE SO...

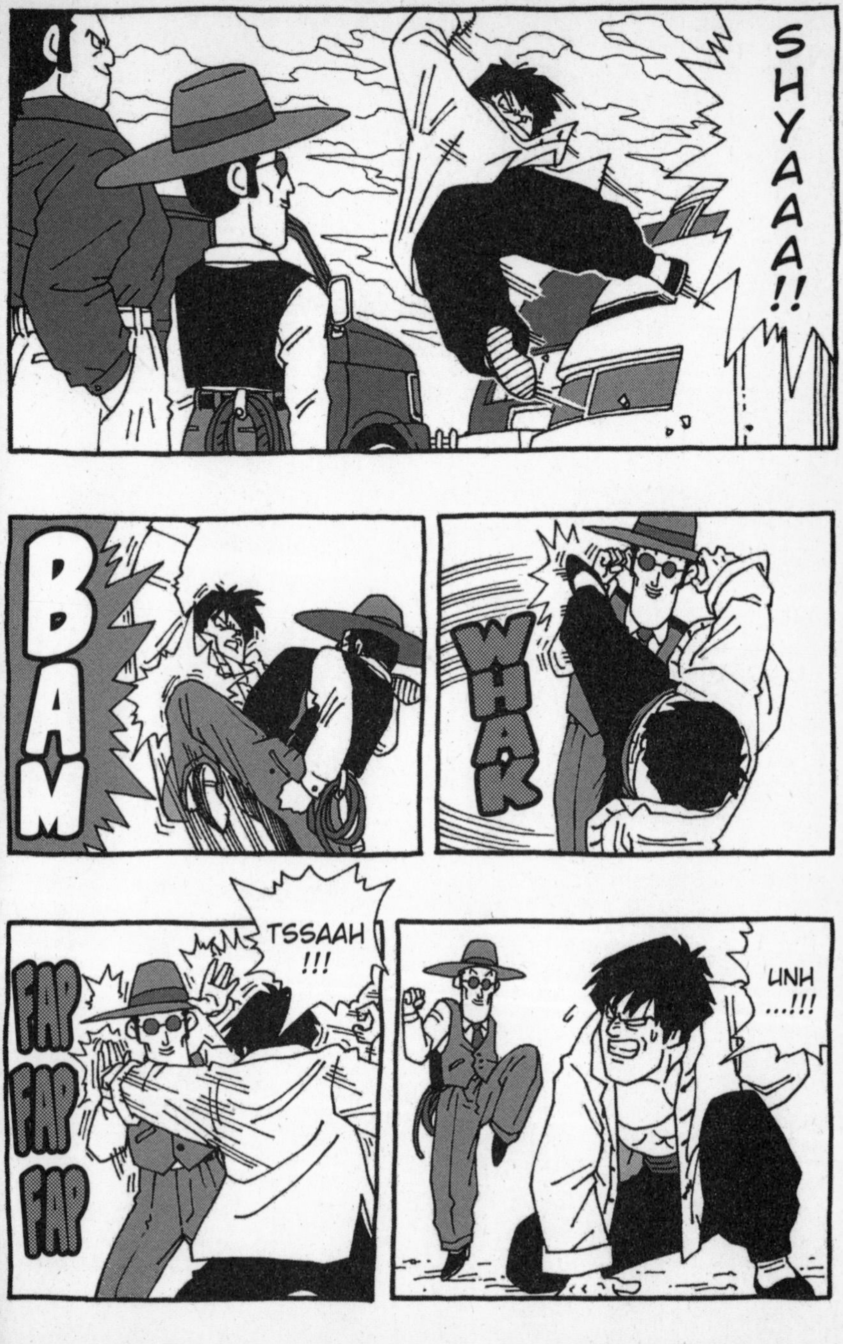
SHYAAAA!!
WHAK
BAM
UNH ...!!!
TSSAAH !!!
FAP FAP FAP

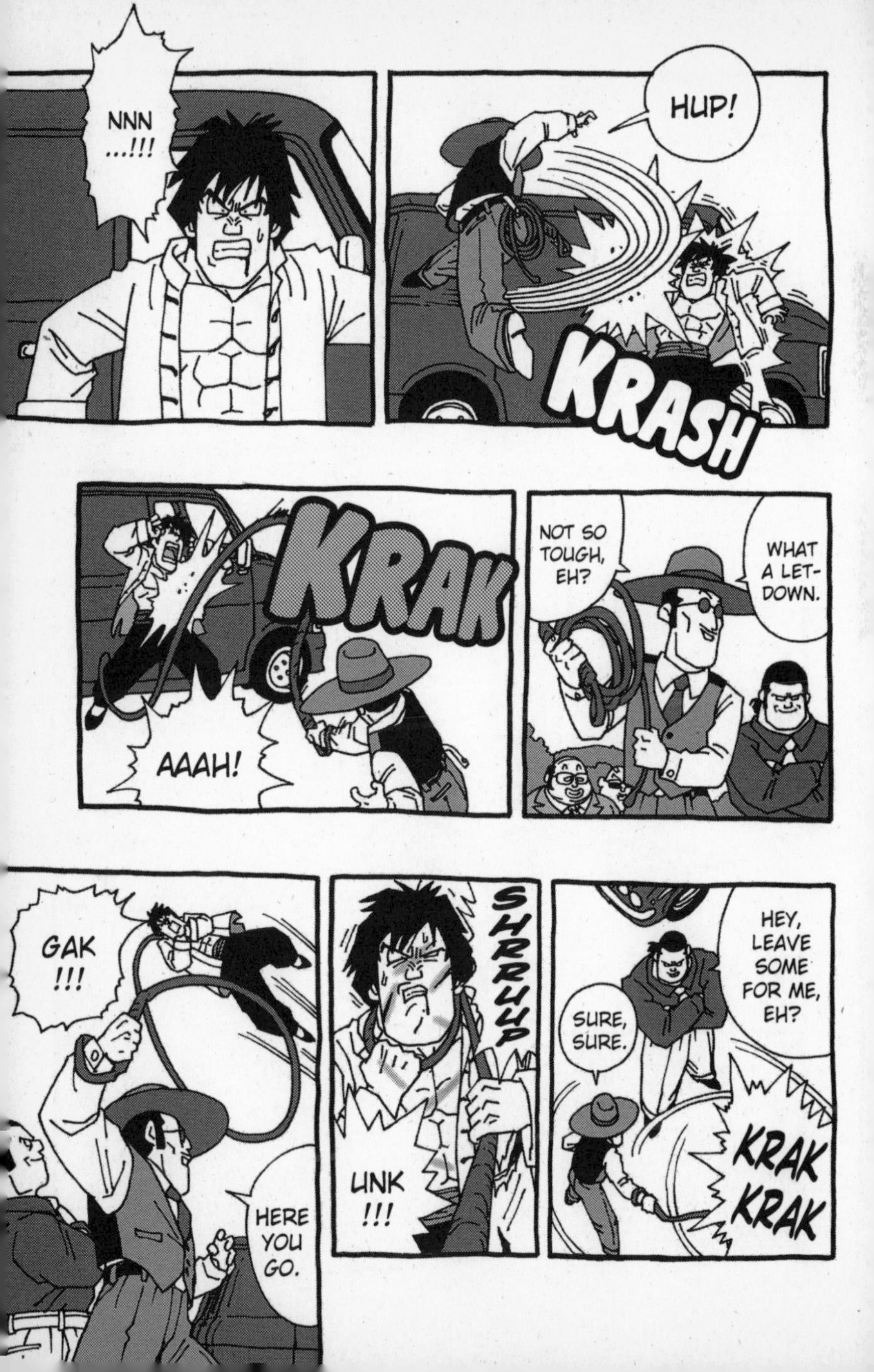
HUP!
KRASH
NNN ...!!!
WHAT A LET-DOWN.
NOT SO TOUGH, EH?
KRAK
AAAH!
HEY, LEAVE SOME FOR ME, EH?
SURE, SURE.
KRAK KRAK
SHRRUUP
UNK !!!
GAK !!!
HERE YOU GO.

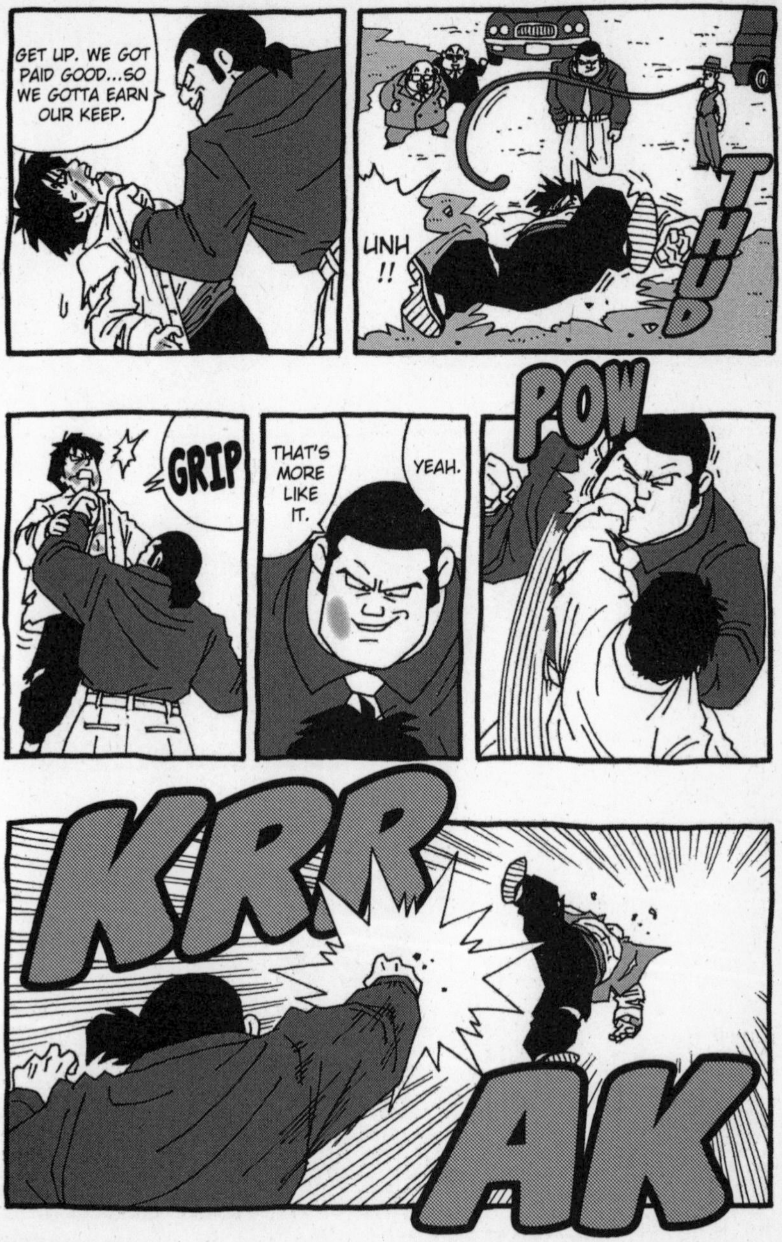
THUD
UNH !!
GET UP. WE GOT PAID GOOD...SO WE GOTTA EARN OUR KEEP.
POW
YEAH.
THAT'S MORE LIKE IT.
GRIP
KRRAK

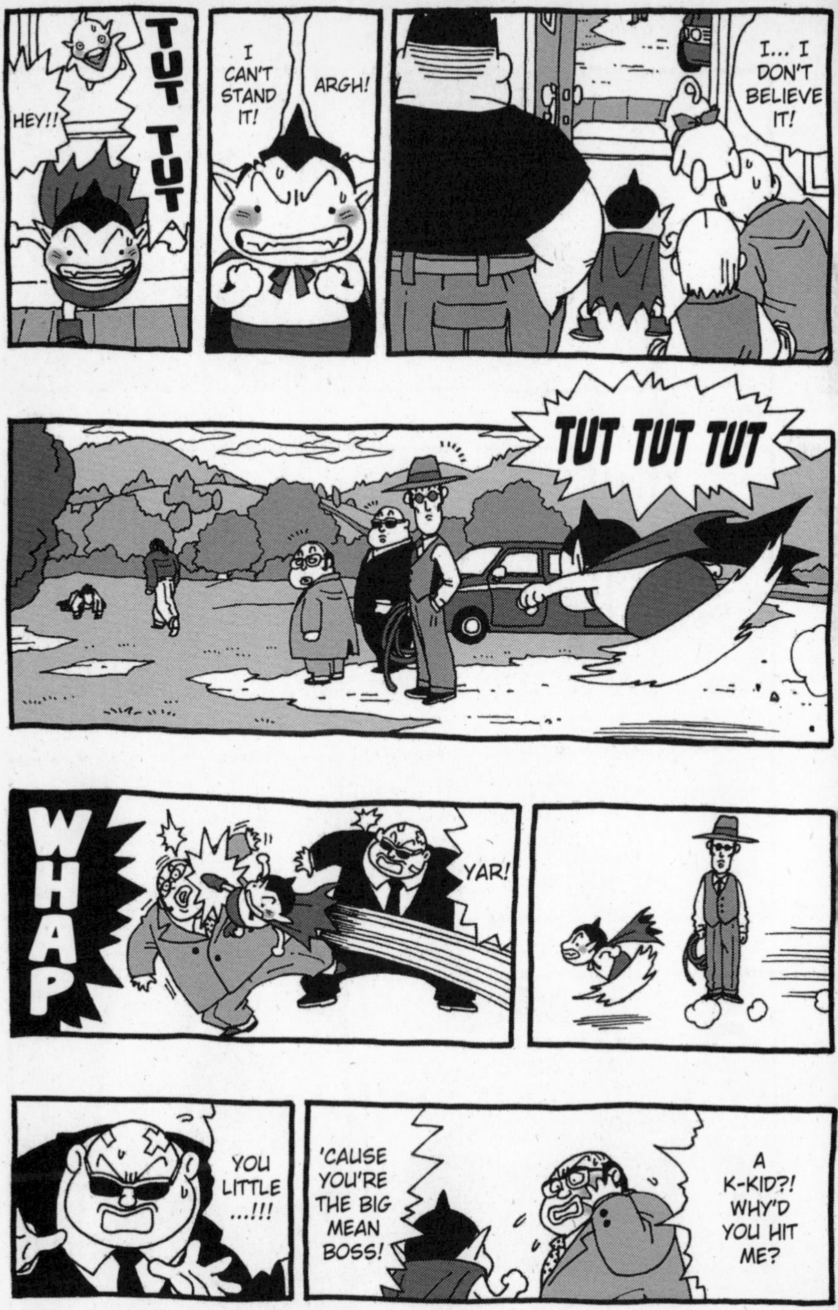
I... I DON'T BELIEVE IT!
ARGH!
I CAN'T STAND IT!
TUT TUT TUT
HEY!!
TUT TUT TUT
YAR!
WHAP
A K-KID?! WHY'D YOU HIT ME?
'CAUSE YOU'RE THE BIG MEAN BOSS!
YOU LITTLE ...!!!

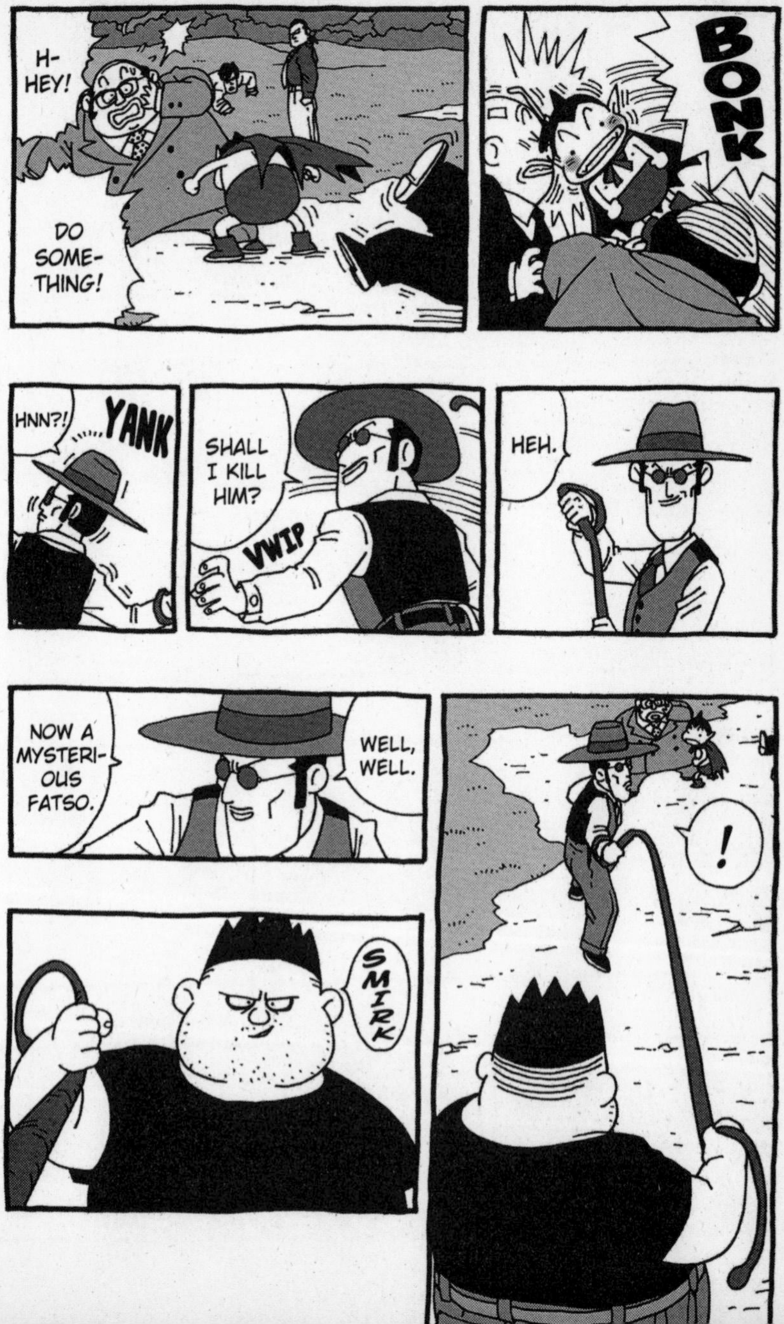
BONK
H-HEY!
DO SOME-THING!
HEH.
SHALL I KILL HIM?
VWIP
HNN?!
YANK
!
WELL, WELL.
NOW A MYSTERI-OUS FATSO.
SMIRK

READ THIS WAY

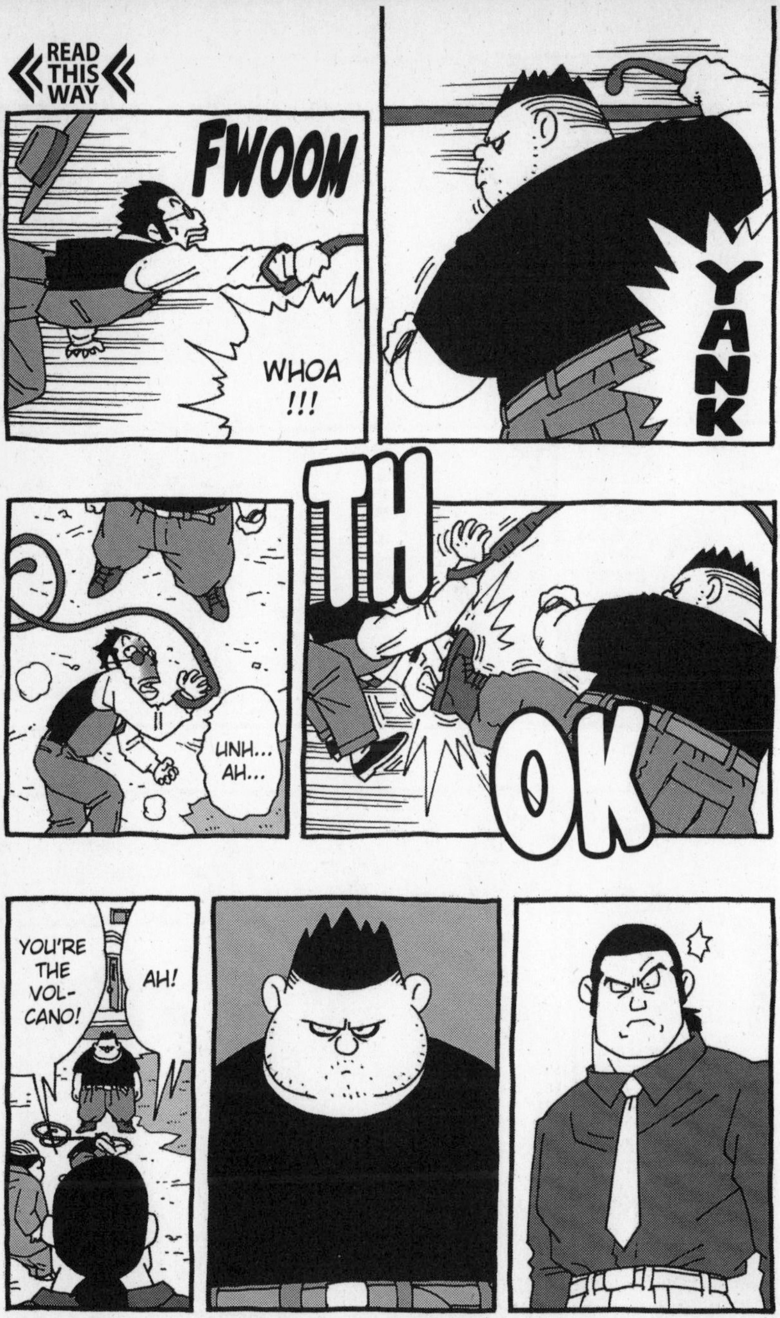
YANK
FWOOM
WHOA !!!
TH
OK
UNH... AH...
AH!
YOU'RE THE VOL- CANO!

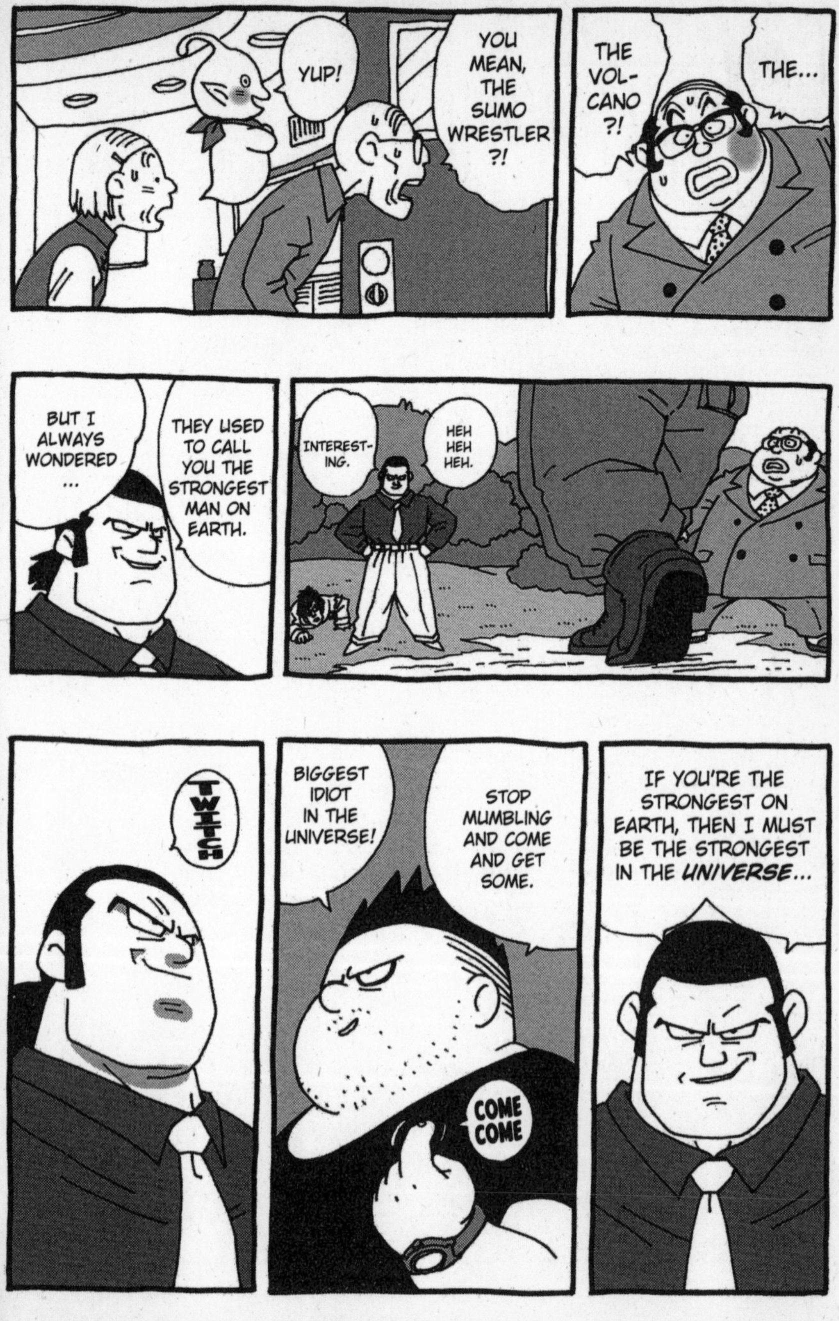
THE...
THE VOL-CANO ?!
YOU MEAN, THE SUMO WRESTLER ?!
YUP!
HEH HEH HEH.
INTEREST-ING.
THEY USED TO CALL YOU THE STRONGEST MAN ON EARTH.
BUT I ALWAYS WONDERED ...
IF YOU'RE THE STRONGEST ON EARTH, THEN I MUST BE THE STRONGEST IN THE *UNIVERSE*...
STOP MUMBLING AND COME AND GET SOME.
BIGGEST IDIOT IN THE UNIVERSE!
COME COME
TWITCH

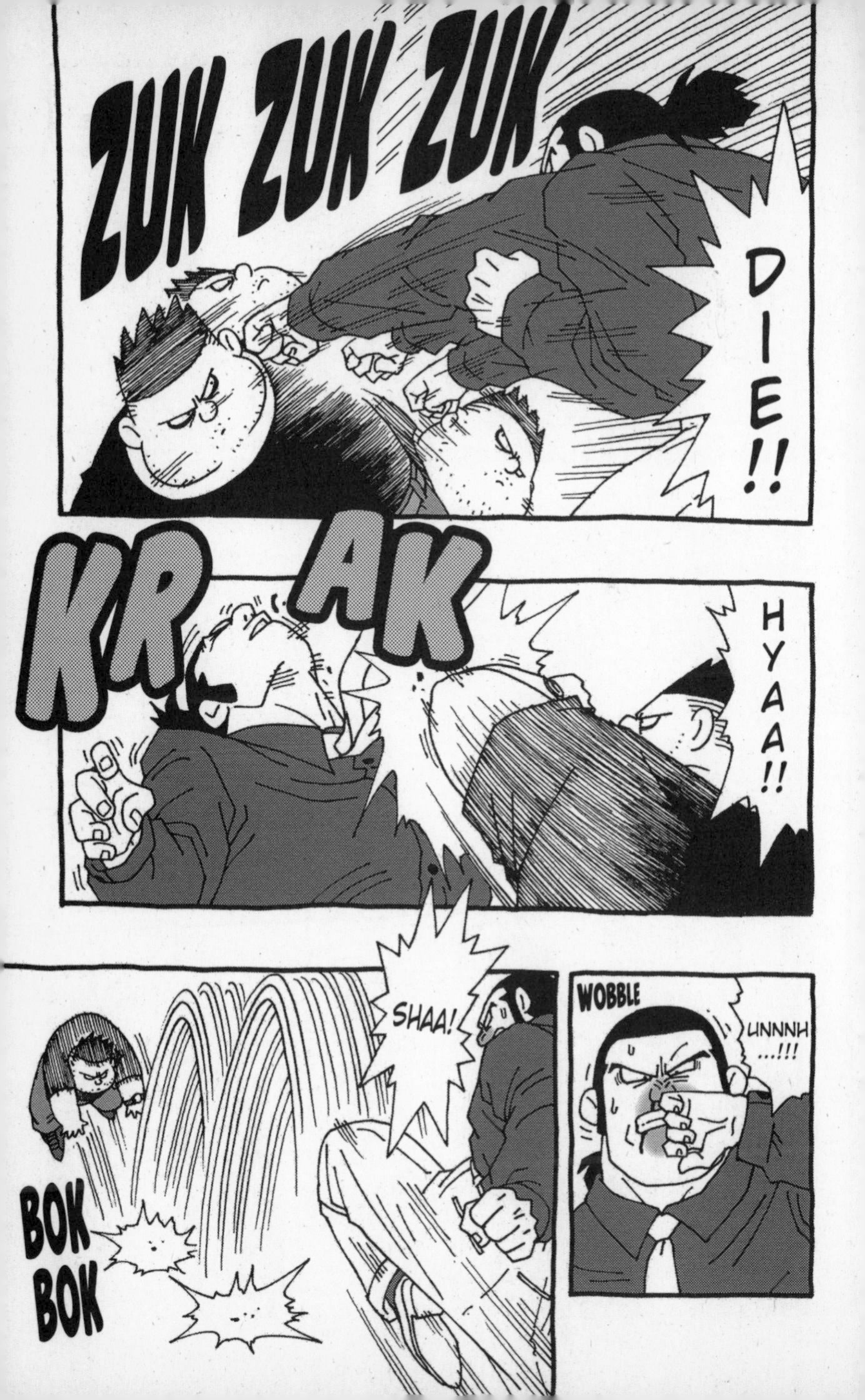
DIE!!
ZUK ZUK ZUK
HYAA!!
KRAK
UNNNH ...!!!
WOBBLE
SHAA!
BOK BOK

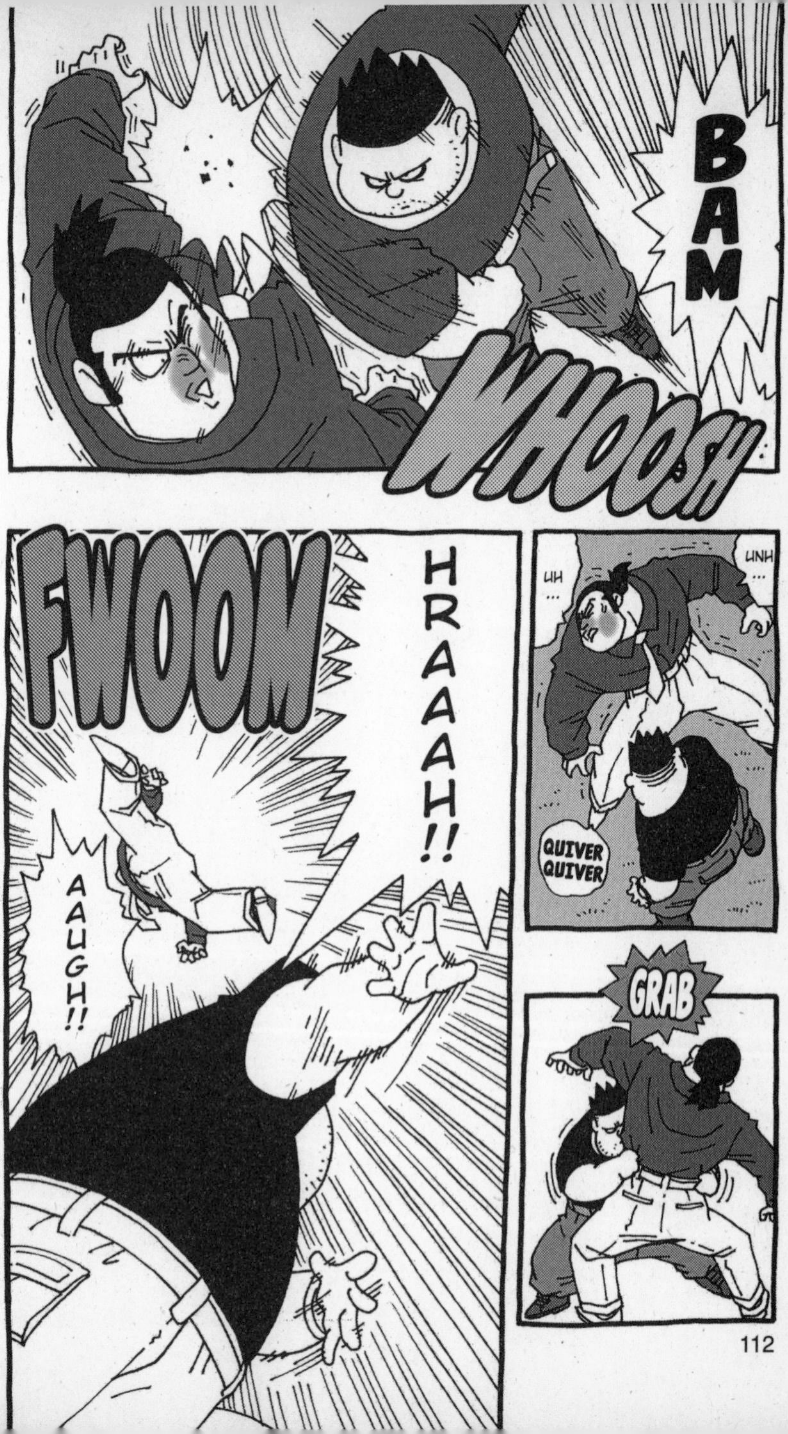

BAM
WHOOSH
UNH...
UH...
QUIVER QUIVER
GRAB
FWOOM
HRAAAAH!!
AAUGH!!

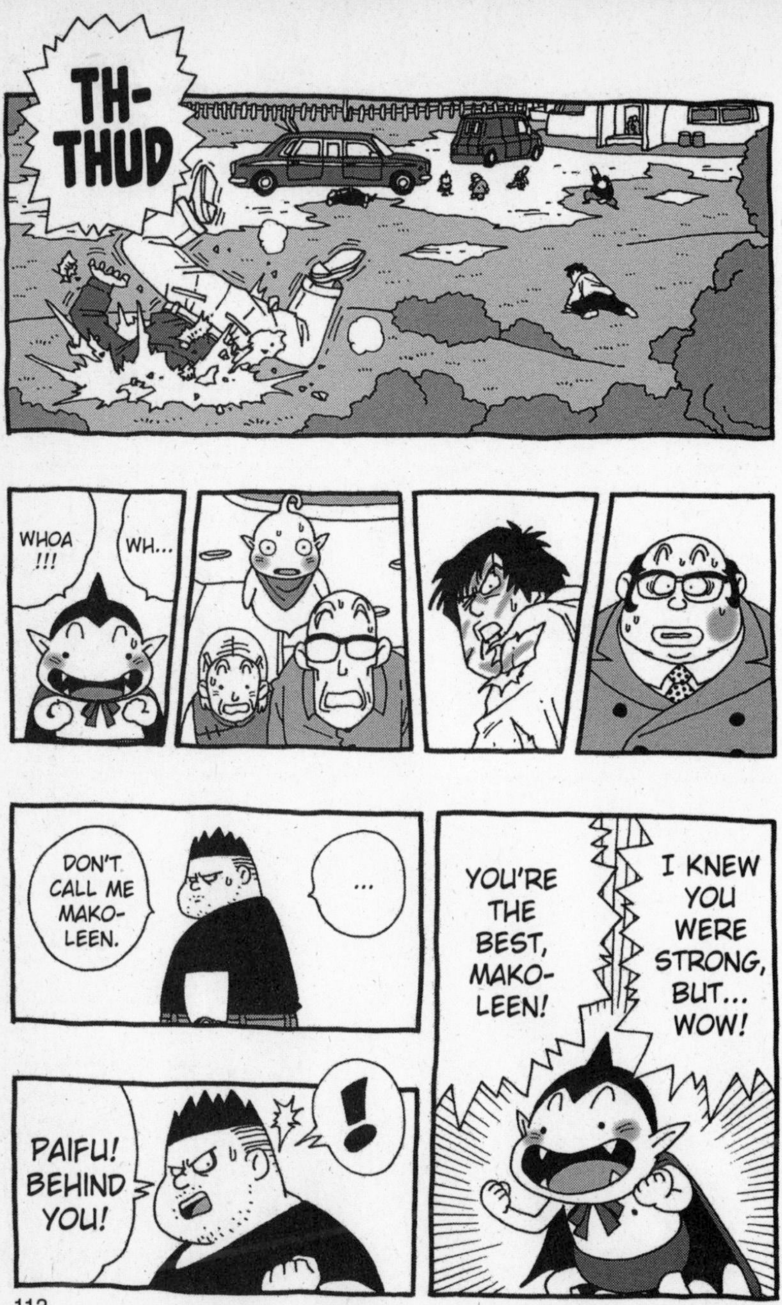
TH-THUD
WH...
WHOA!!!
I KNEW YOU WERE STRONG, BUT... WOW!
YOU'RE THE BEST, MAKO-LEEN!
...
DON'T CALL ME MAKO-LEEN.
!
PAIFU! BEHIND YOU!

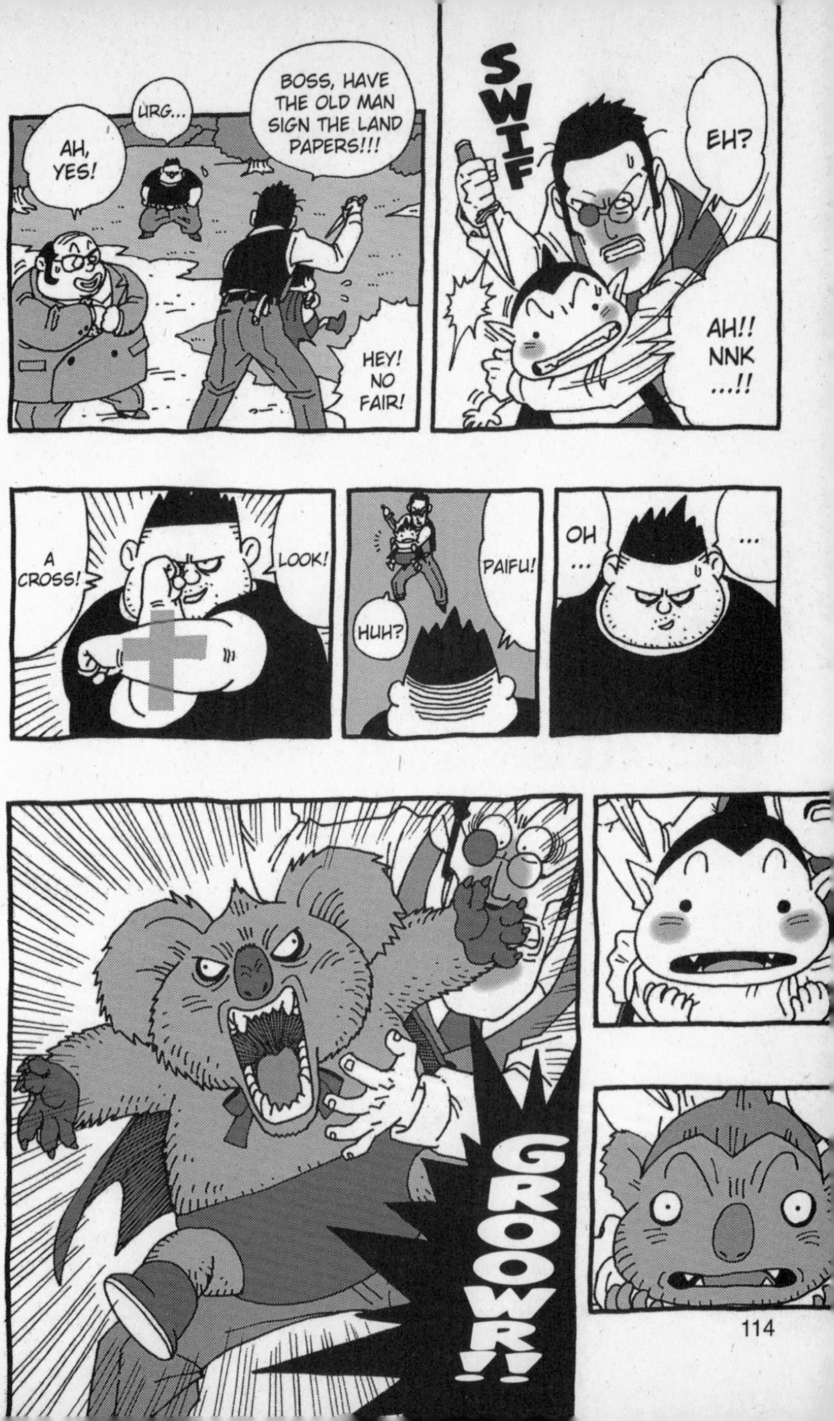
SWIF
EH?
AH!! NNK ...!!
BOSS, HAVE THE OLD MAN SIGN THE LAND PAPERS!!!
URG...
AH, YES!
HEY! NO FAIR!
...
OH ...
PAIFU!
HUH?
LOOK!
A CROSS!
GROOWR!!

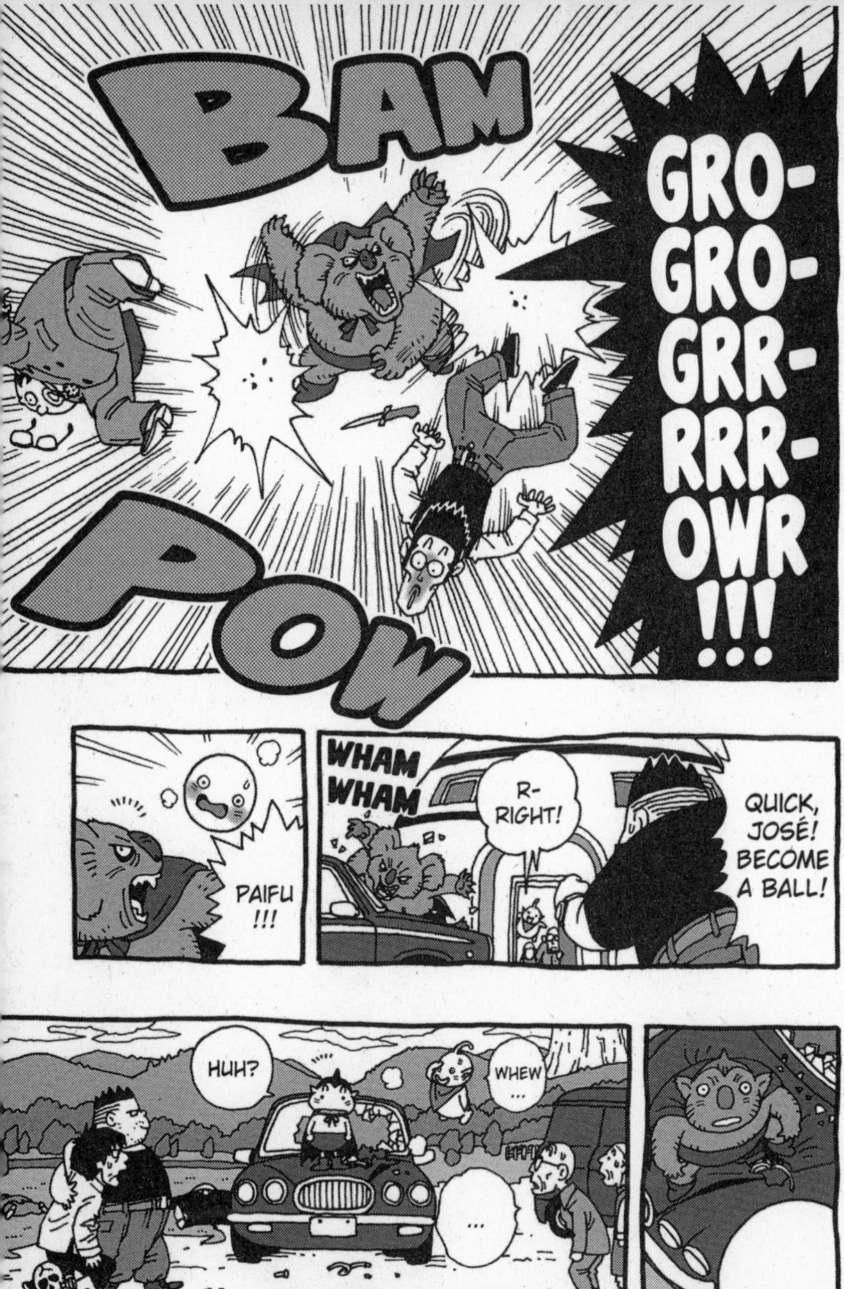
GRO-
GRO-
GRR-
RRR-
OWR
!!!
BAM
POW
QUICK, JOSÉ! BECOME A BALL!
R-RIGHT!
WHAM
WHAM
PAIFU !!!
WHEW ...
HUH?
...
CONTINUED

COWA!

FRIGHT 9

The Scary Monster in the Woods

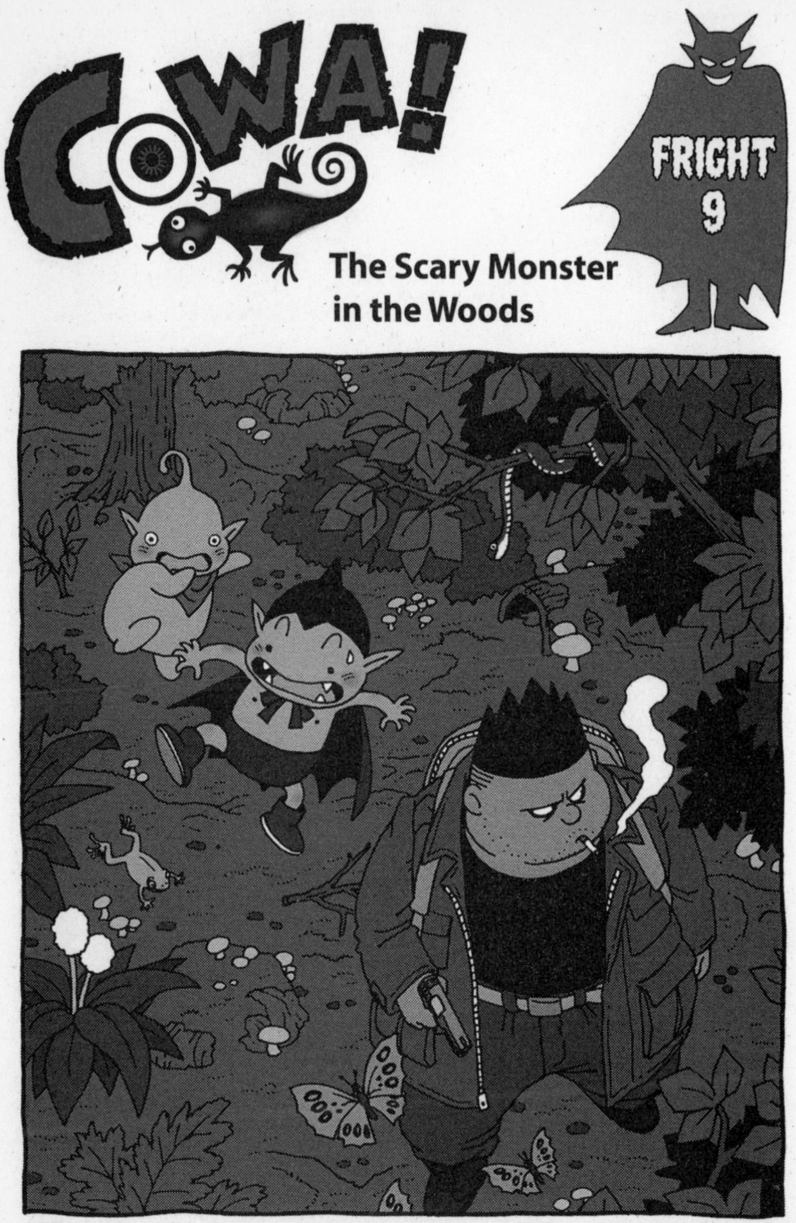

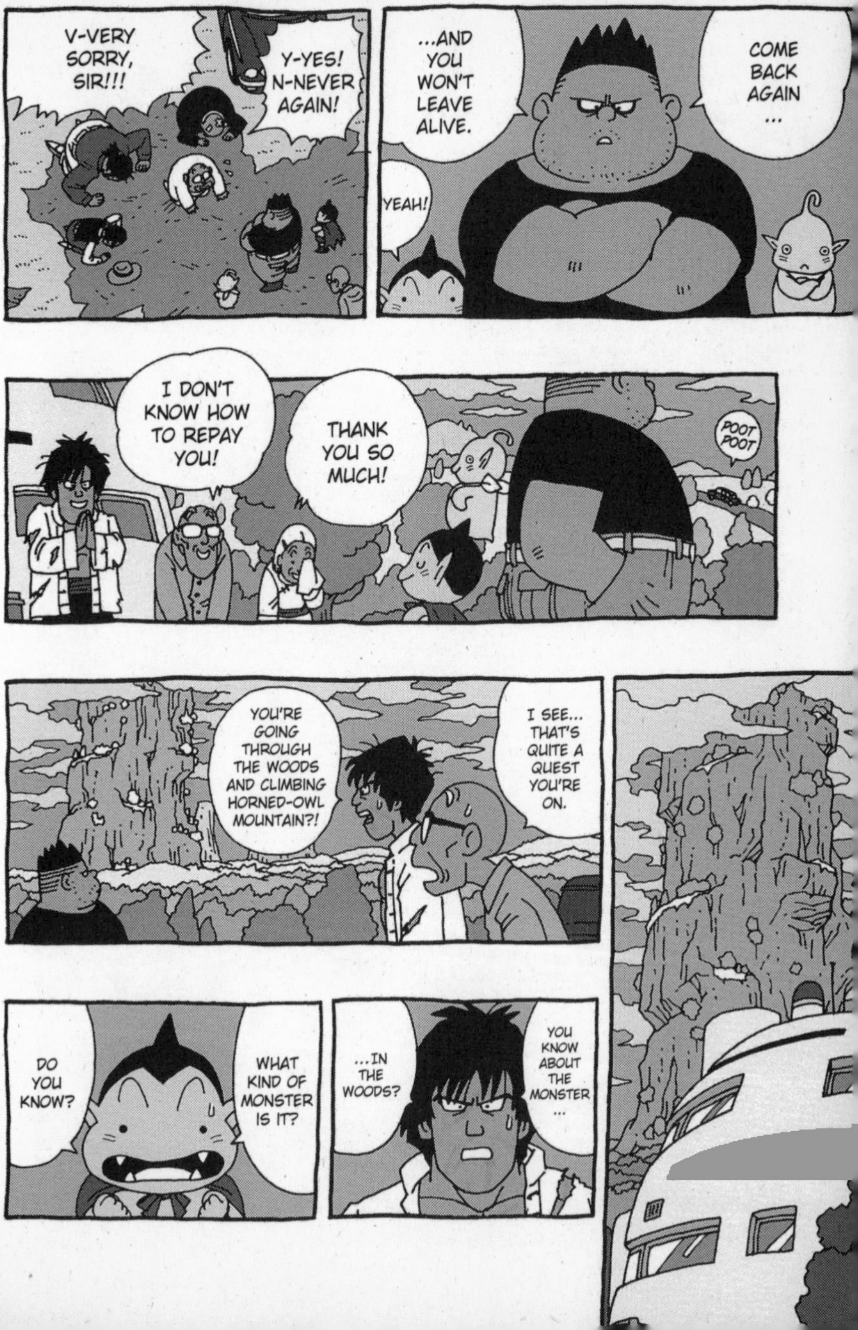
COME BACK AGAIN ...
...AND YOU WON'T LEAVE ALIVE.
YEAH!
Y-YES! N-NEVER AGAIN!
V-VERY SORRY, SIR!!!
POOT POOT
THANK YOU SO MUCH!
I DON'T KNOW HOW TO REPAY YOU!
I SEE... THAT'S QUITE A QUEST YOU'RE ON.
YOU'RE GOING THROUGH THE WOODS AND CLIMBING HORNED-OWL MOUNTAIN?!
YOU KNOW ABOUT THE MONSTER ...
...IN THE WOODS?
WHAT KIND OF MONSTER IS IT?
DO YOU KNOW?

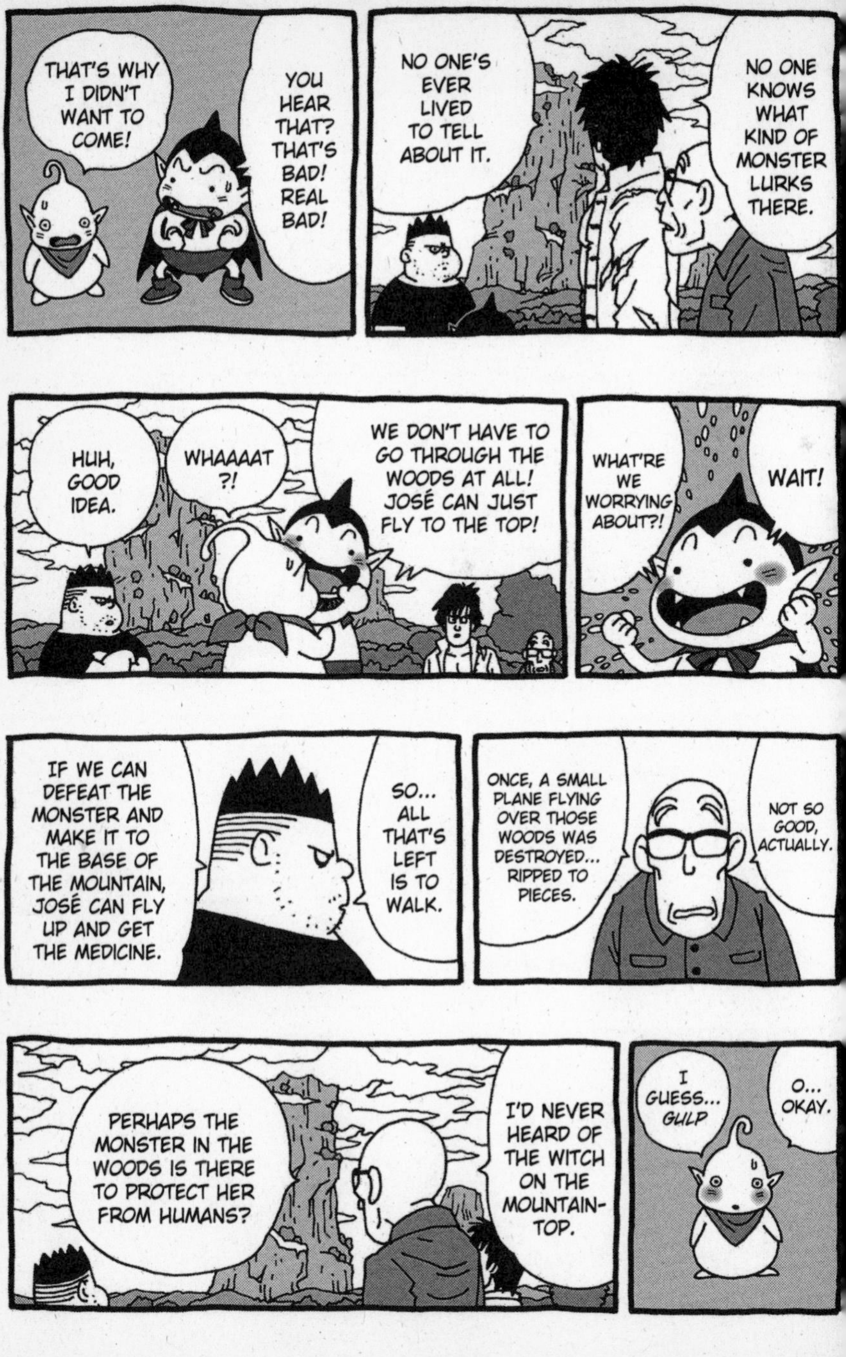
NO ONE KNOWS WHAT KIND OF MONSTER LURKS THERE.
NO ONE'S EVER LIVED TO TELL ABOUT IT.
YOU HEAR THAT? THAT'S BAD! REAL BAD!
THAT'S WHY I DIDN'T WANT TO COME!
WAIT!
WHAT'RE WE WORRYING ABOUT?!
WE DON'T HAVE TO GO THROUGH THE WOODS AT ALL! JOSÉ CAN JUST FLY TO THE TOP!
WHAAAAT?!
HUH, GOOD IDEA.
NOT SO GOOD, ACTUALLY.
ONCE, A SMALL PLANE FLYING OVER THOSE WOODS WAS DESTROYED... RIPPED TO PIECES.
SO... ALL THAT'S LEFT IS TO WALK.
IF WE CAN DEFEAT THE MONSTER AND MAKE IT TO THE BASE OF THE MOUNTAIN, JOSÉ CAN FLY UP AND GET THE MEDICINE.
O... OKAY.
I GUESS... *GULP*
I'D NEVER HEARD OF THE WITCH ON THE MOUNTAIN-TOP.
PERHAPS THE MONSTER IN THE WOODS IS THERE TO PROTECT HER FROM HUMANS?

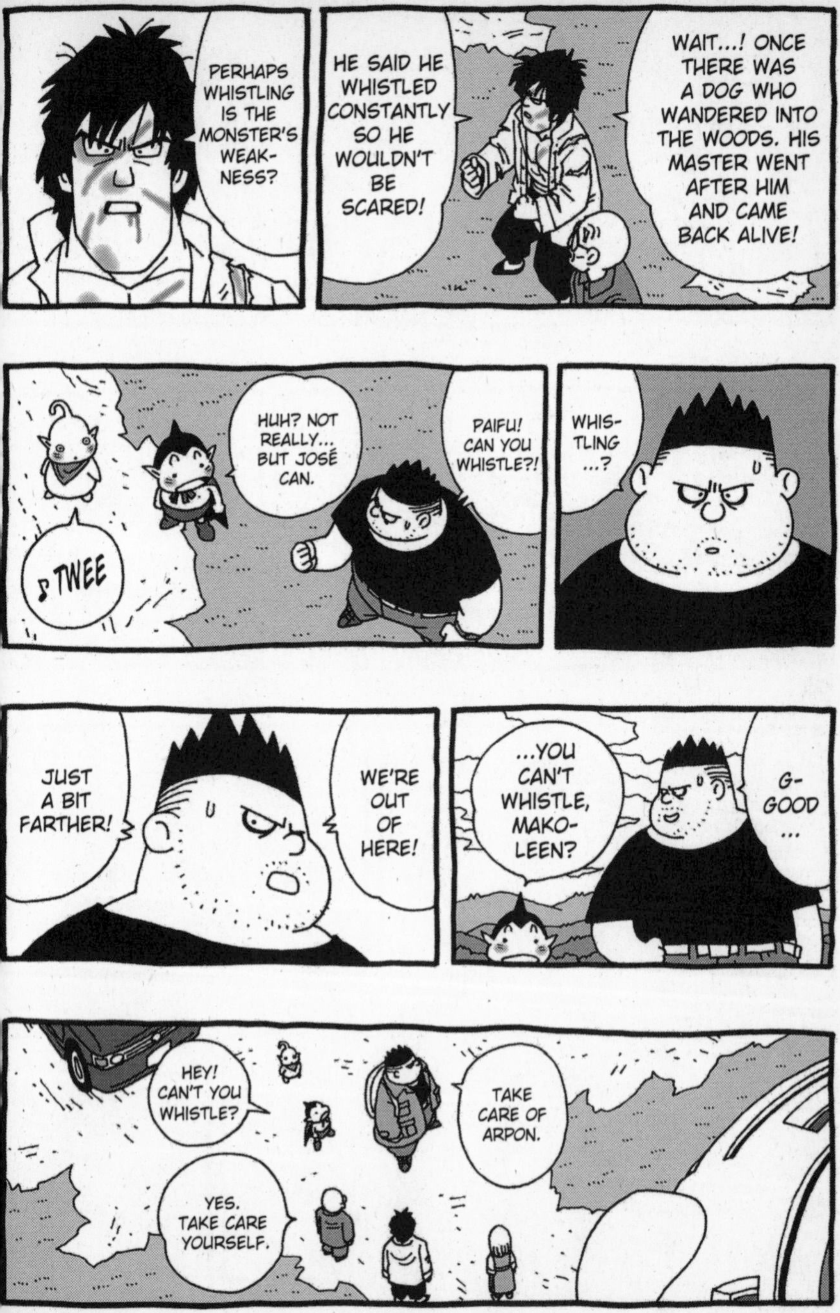
WAIT...! ONCE THERE WAS A DOG WHO WANDERED INTO THE WOODS. HIS MASTER WENT AFTER HIM AND CAME BACK ALIVE!
HE SAID HE WHISTLED CONSTANTLY SO HE WOULDN'T BE SCARED!
PERHAPS WHISTLING IS THE MONSTER'S WEAK-NESS?
WHIS-TLING ...?
PAIFU! CAN YOU WHISTLE?!
HUH? NOT REALLY... BUT JOSÉ CAN.
♪ TWEE
G-GOOD ...
...YOU CAN'T WHISTLE, MAKO-LEEN?
WE'RE OUT OF HERE!
JUST A BIT FARTHER!
TAKE CARE OF ARPON.
HEY! CAN'T YOU WHISTLE?
YES. TAKE CARE YOURSELF.

READ THIS WAY

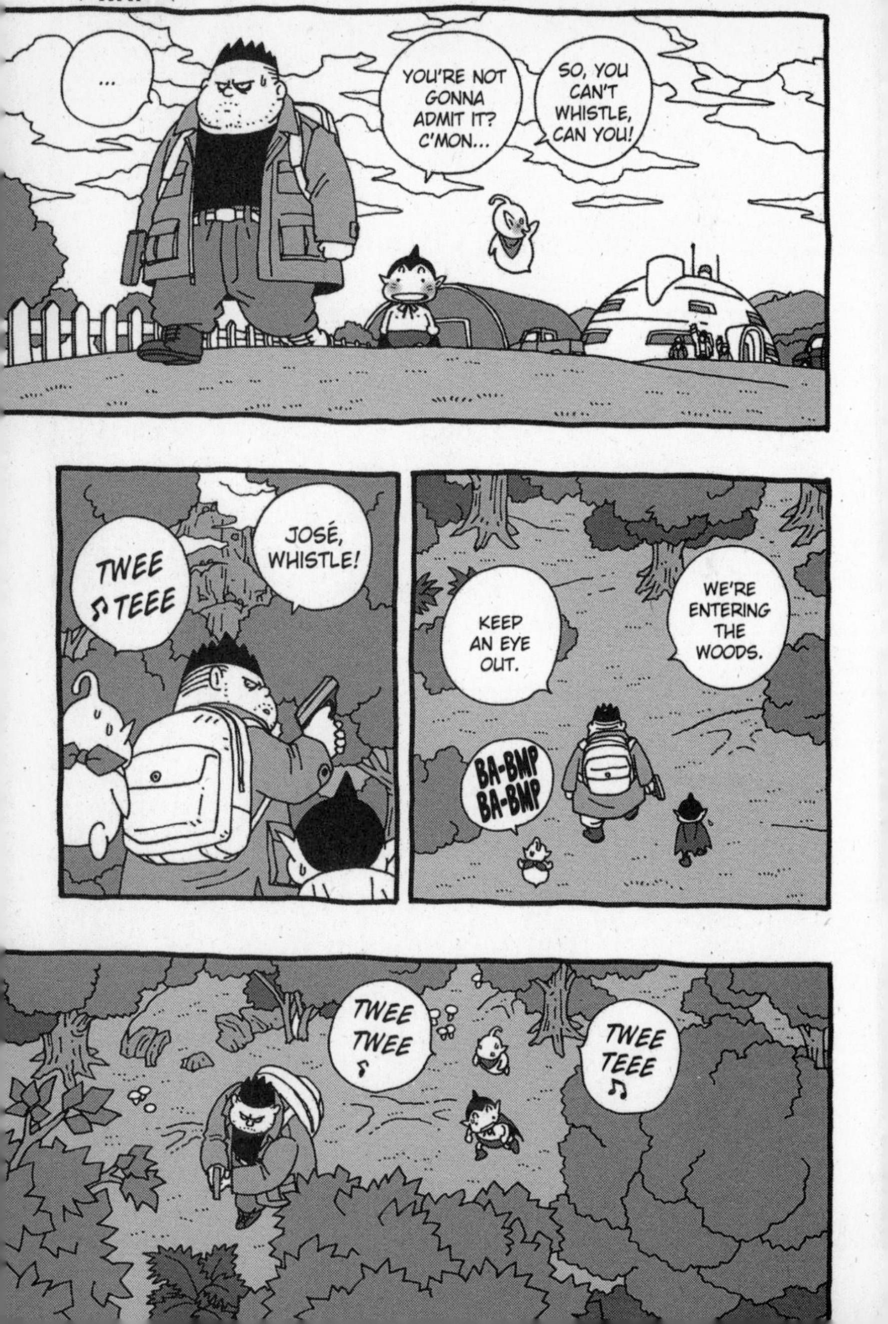

SO, YOU CAN'T WHISTLE, CAN YOU!
YOU'RE NOT GONNA ADMIT IT? C'MON...
...
WE'RE ENTERING THE WOODS.
KEEP AN EYE OUT.
BA-BMP BA-BMP
JOSÉ, WHISTLE!
TWEE ♪ TEEE
TWEE TEEE ♪
TWEE TWEE ♪

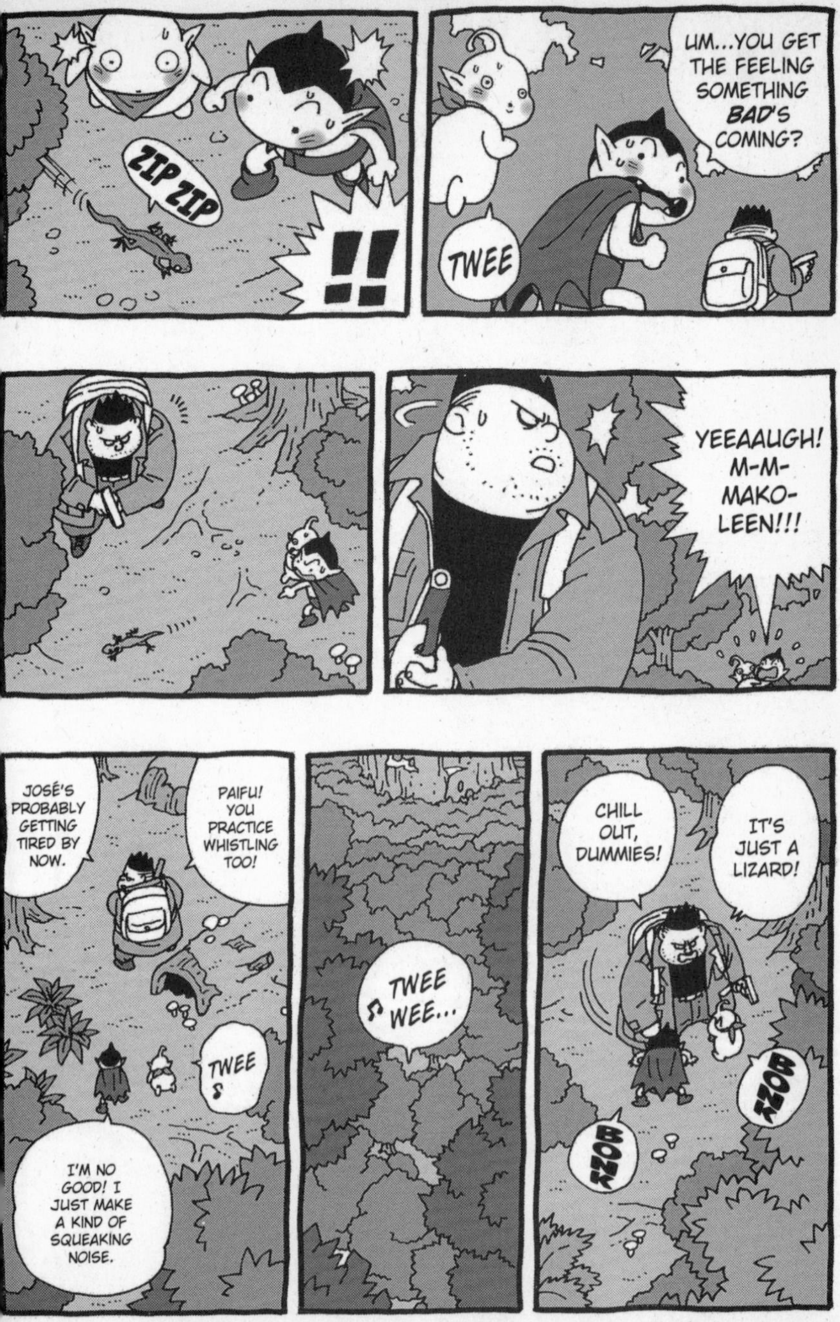
UM...YOU GET THE FEELING SOMETHING *BAD'S* COMING?
TWEE
ZIP ZIP
!!
YEEAAUGH! M-M-MAKO-LEEN!!!
IT'S JUST A LIZARD!
CHILL OUT, DUMMIES!
BONK
BONK
TWEE WEE...
PAIFU! YOU PRACTICE WHISTLING TOO!
JOSÉ'S PROBABLY GETTING TIRED BY NOW.
TWEE
I'M NO GOOD! I JUST MAKE A KIND OF SQUEAKING NOISE.

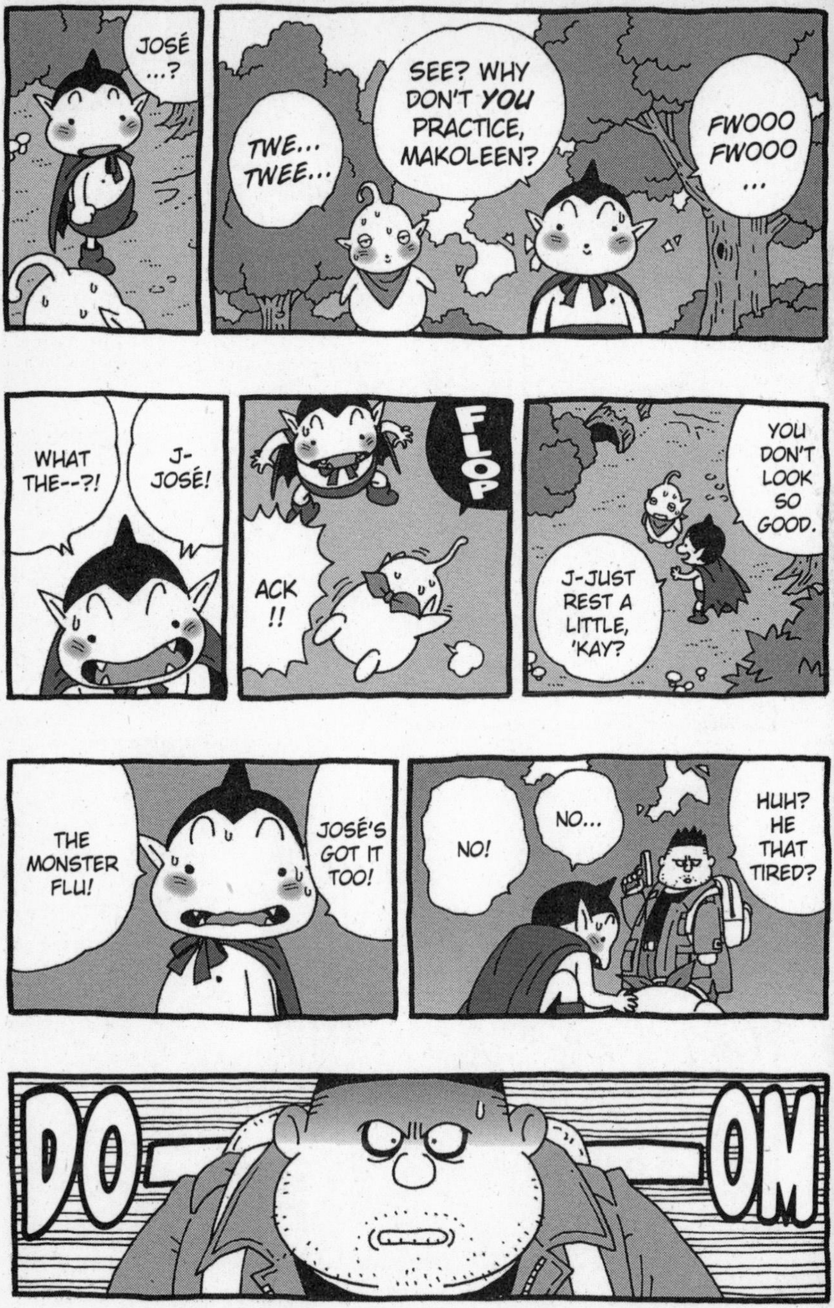
FWOOO FWOOO ...
SEE? WHY DON'T YOU PRACTICE, MAKOLEEN?
TWE... TWEE...
JOSÉ ...?
YOU DON'T LOOK SO GOOD.
J-JUST REST A LITTLE, 'KAY?
FLOP
ACK !!
J- JOSÉ!
WHAT THE--?!
HUH? HE THAT TIRED?
NO...
NO!
JOSÉ'S GOT IT TOO!
THE MONSTER FLU!
DO— OM

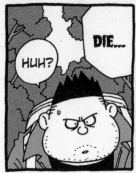

WHAT'RE WE GOING TO DO NOW?! WE WERE COUNTING ON HIM!
IT WAS FINALLY JOSÉ'S TURN TO SHINE!
DIE...
HUH?
DEATH TO ALL WHO ENTER MY WOODS!
TH-THE MONSTER!
WH--?!
WHERE IS IT?!
PAIFU! WHISTLE! QUICK!
FWOO FOO

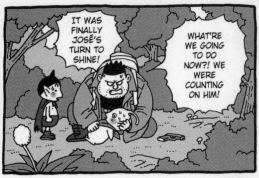

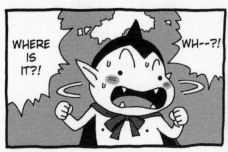

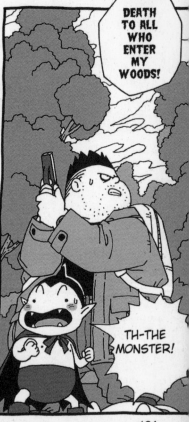

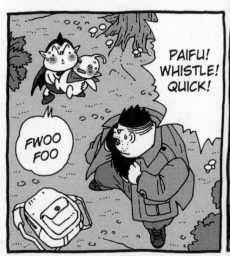

READ THIS WAY

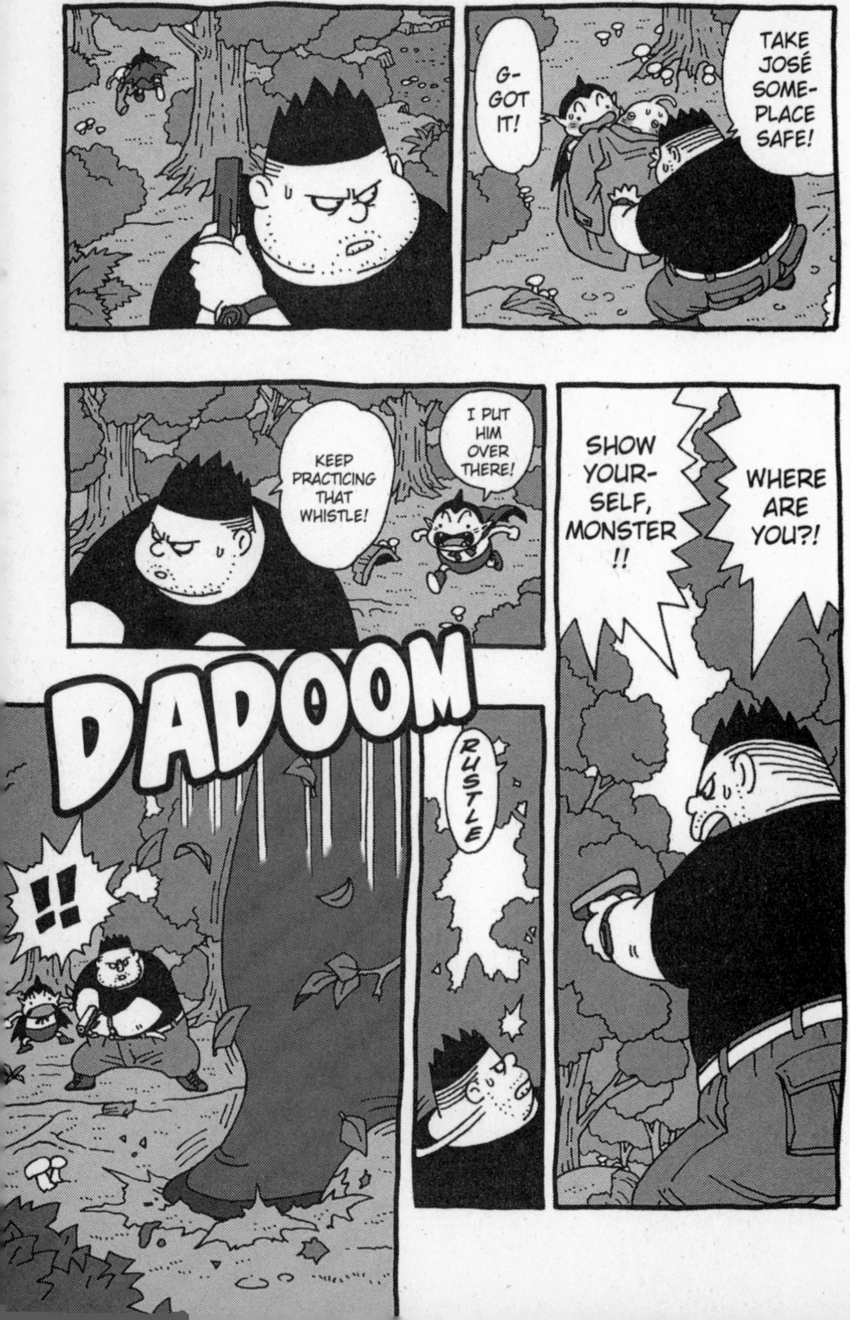
TAKE JOSÉ SOME-PLACE SAFE!
G-GOT IT!
WHERE ARE YOU?!
SHOW YOUR-SELF, MONSTER!!
I PUT HIM OVER THERE!
KEEP PRACTICING THAT WHISTLE!
RUSTLE
DADOOM
!!

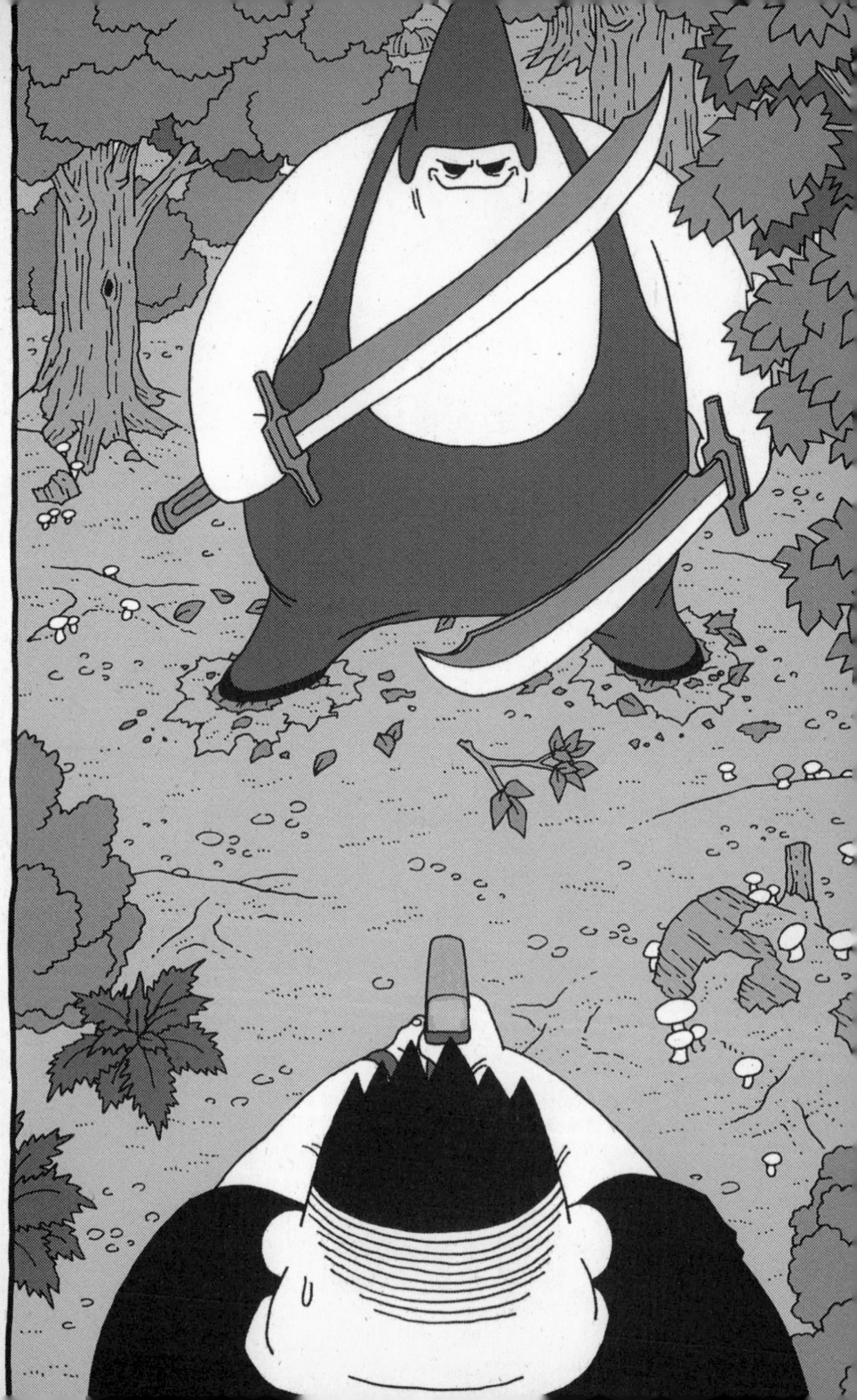

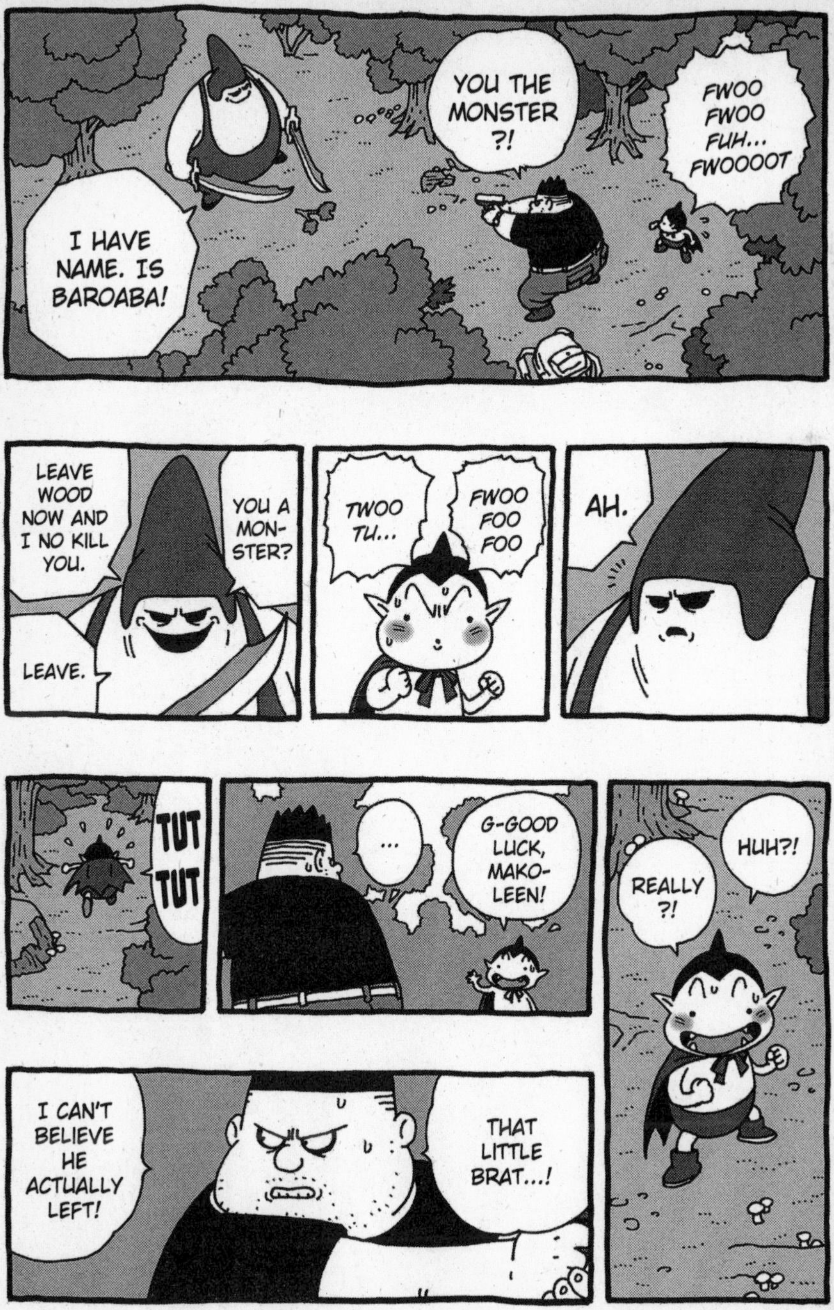
FWOO FWOO FUH... FWOOOOT
YOU THE MONSTER ?!
I HAVE NAME. IS BAROABA!
AH.
FWOO FOO FOO
TWOO TU...
YOU A MON-STER?
LEAVE WOOD NOW AND I NO KILL YOU.
LEAVE.
HUH?!
REALLY ?!
G-GOOD LUCK, MAKO-LEEN!
...
TUT TUT
THAT LITTLE BRAT...!
I CAN'T BELIEVE HE ACTUALLY LEFT!

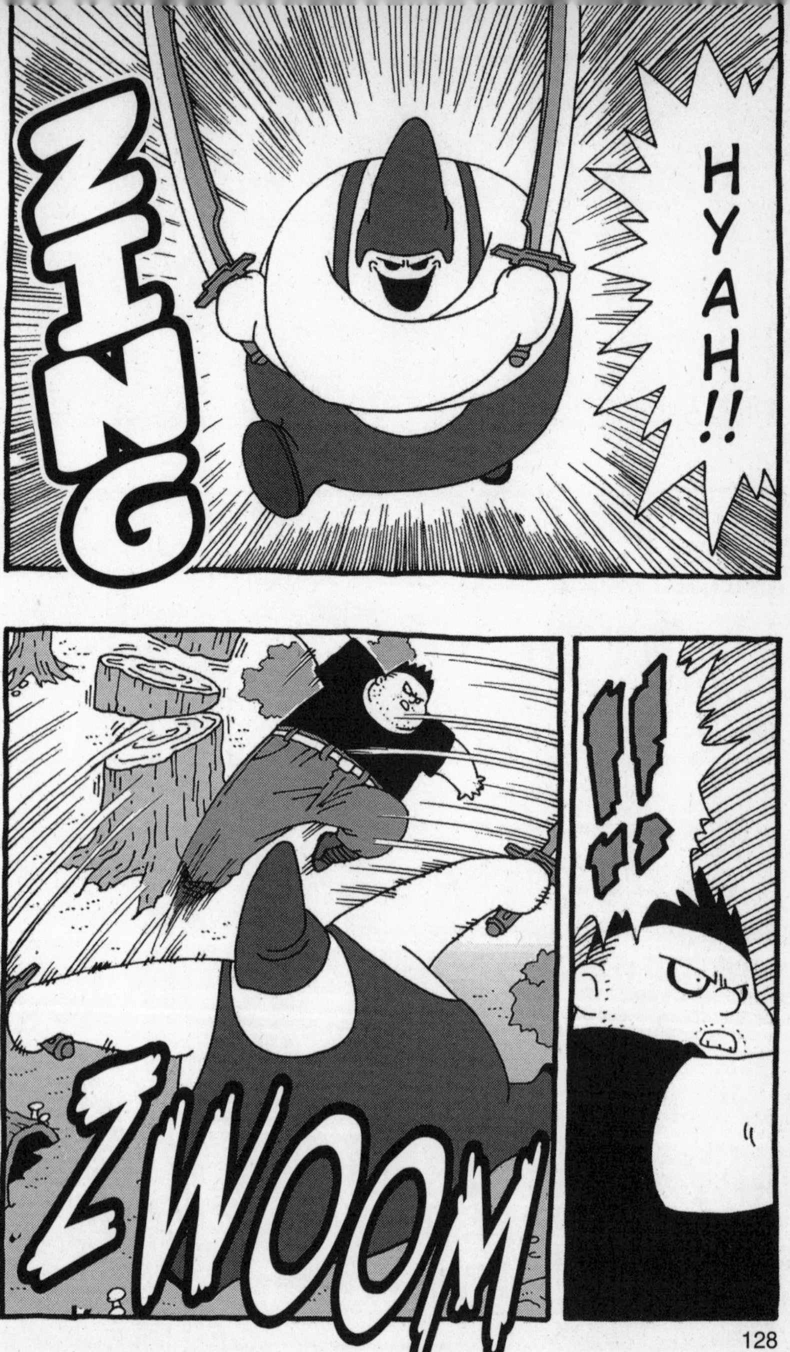
HYAH!!
ZING
!!
ZWOOM

READ THIS WAY

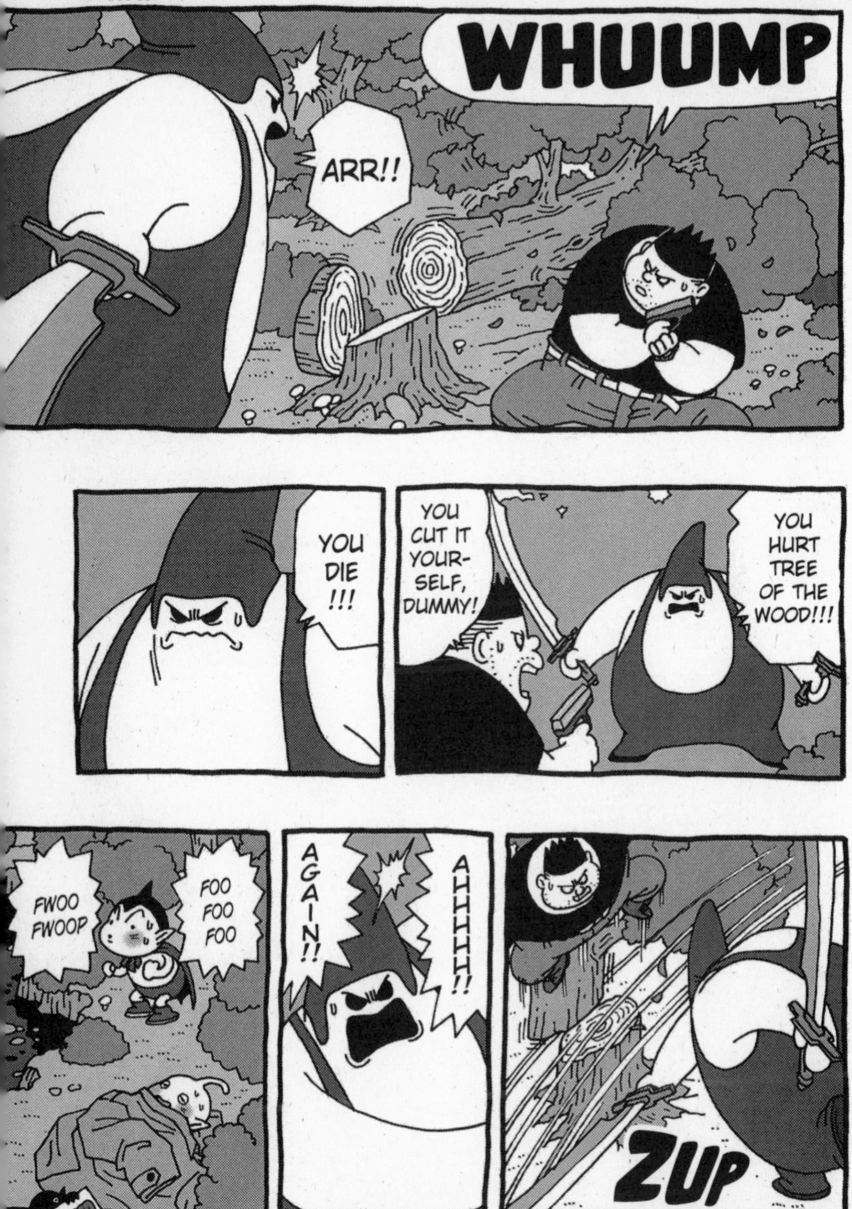
WHUUMP
ARR!!
YOU HURT TREE OF THE WOOD!!!
YOU CUT IT YOURSELF, DUMMY!
YOU DIE!!!
ZUP
AHHHHH!!
AGAIN!!
FOO FOO FOO
FWOO FWOOP
CONTINUED

COWA!

FRIGHT 10

Makoleen, the Strongest Man in the World, Struggles

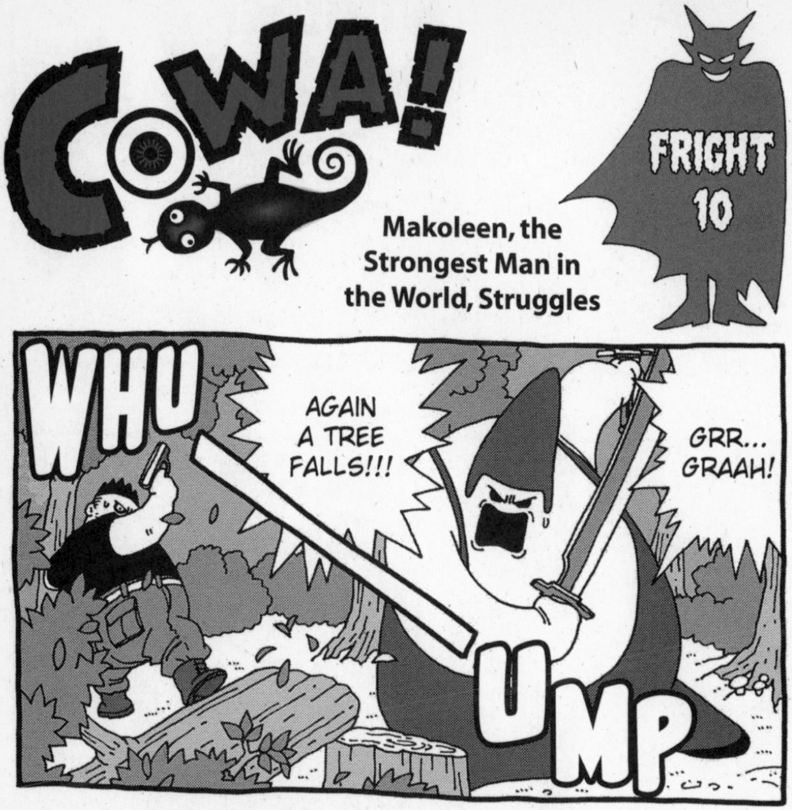
WHU
AGAIN A TREE FALLS!!!
GRR... GRAAH!
UMP

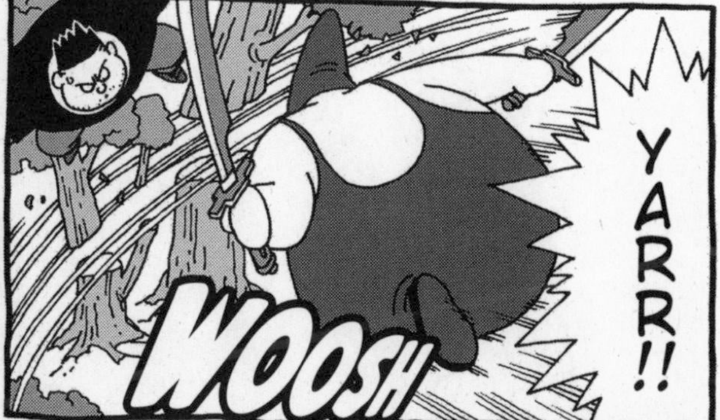
YARR!!
WOOSH

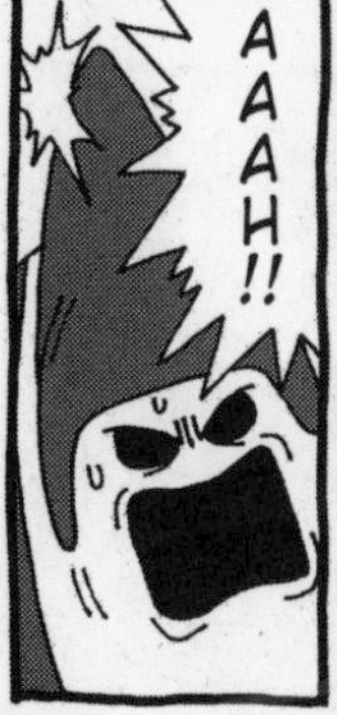
AAAH!!

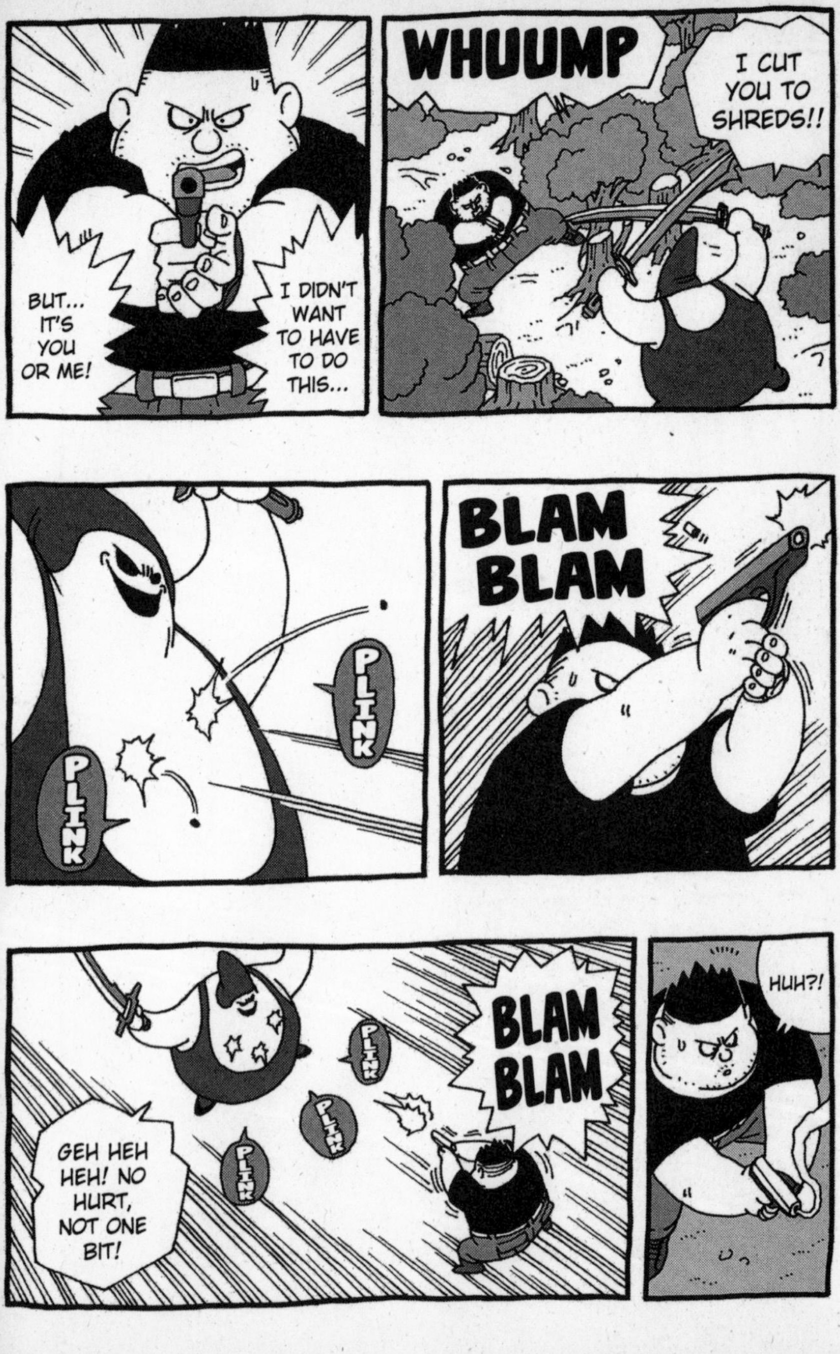
WHUUMP
I CUT YOU TO SHREDS!!
I DIDN'T WANT TO HAVE TO DO THIS...
BUT... IT'S YOU OR ME!
BLAM BLAM
PLINK
PLINK
HUH?!
BLAM BLAM
PLINK
PLINK
PLINK
GEH HEH HEH! NO HURT, NOT ONE BIT!

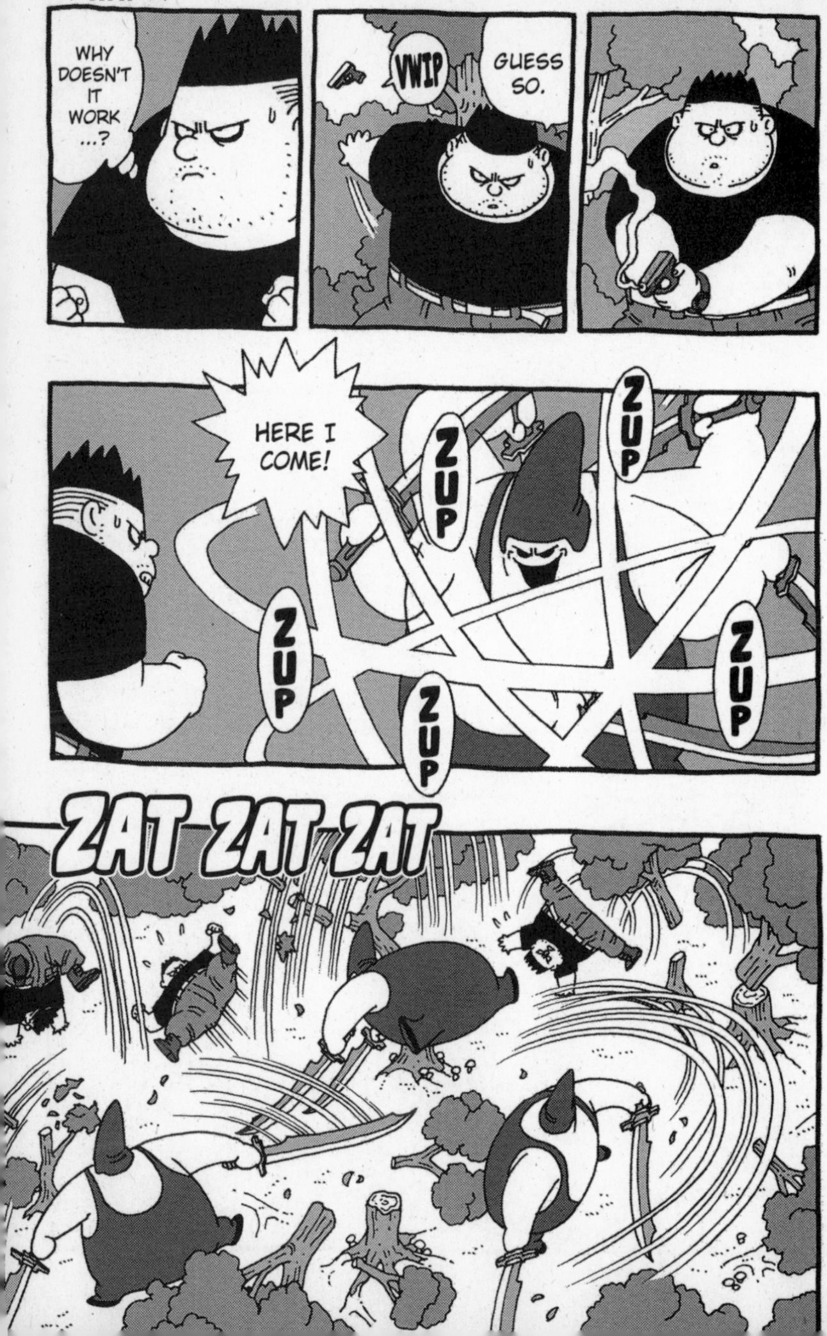
READ THIS WAY
GUESS SO.
VWIP
WHY DOESN'T IT WORK ...?
ZUP
ZUP
HERE I COME!
ZUP
ZUP
ZUP
ZUP
ZAT ZAT ZAT

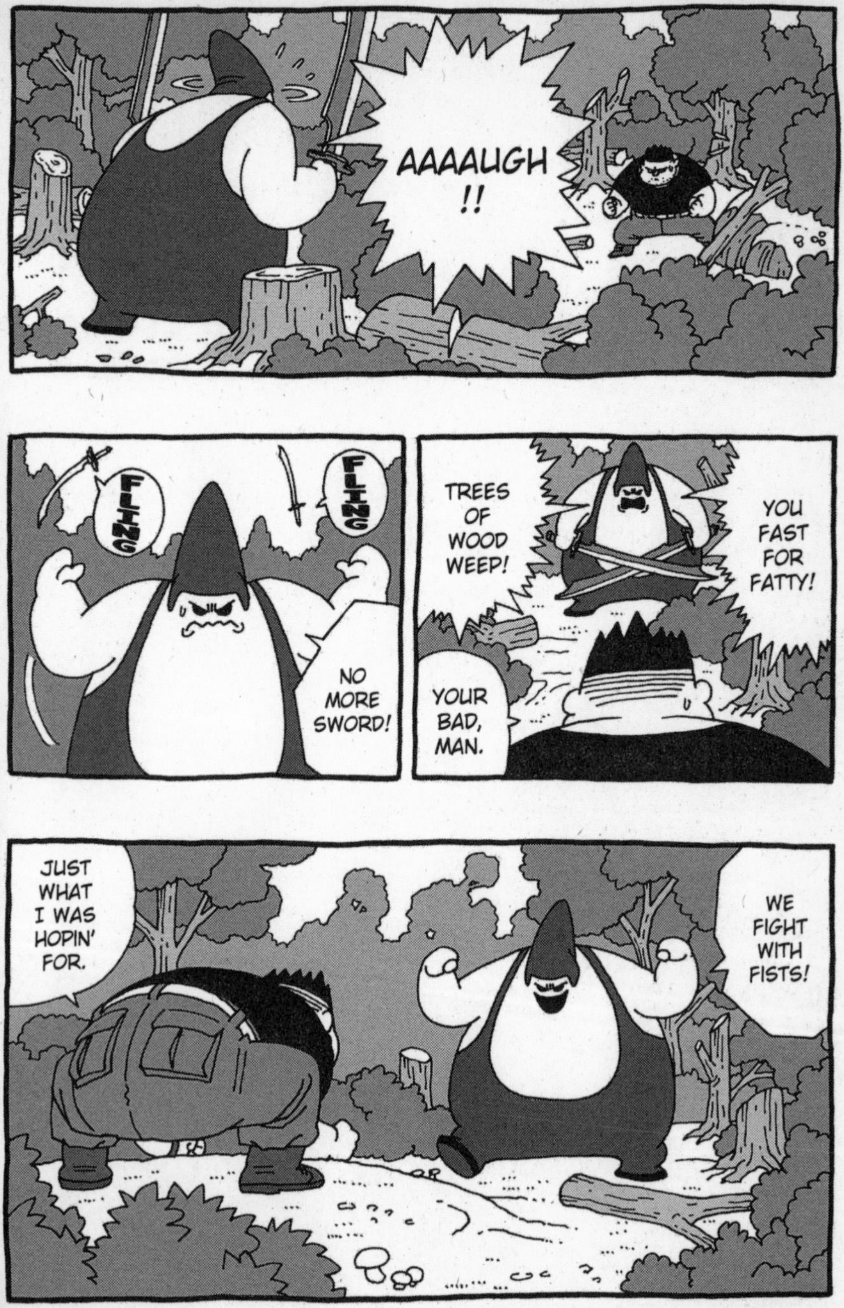
AAAAUGH!!
YOU FAST FOR FATTY!
TREES OF WOOD WEEP!
YOUR BAD, MAN.
FLING
FLING
NO MORE SWORD!
WE FIGHT WITH FISTS!
JUST WHAT I WAS HOPIN' FOR.

READ THIS WAY

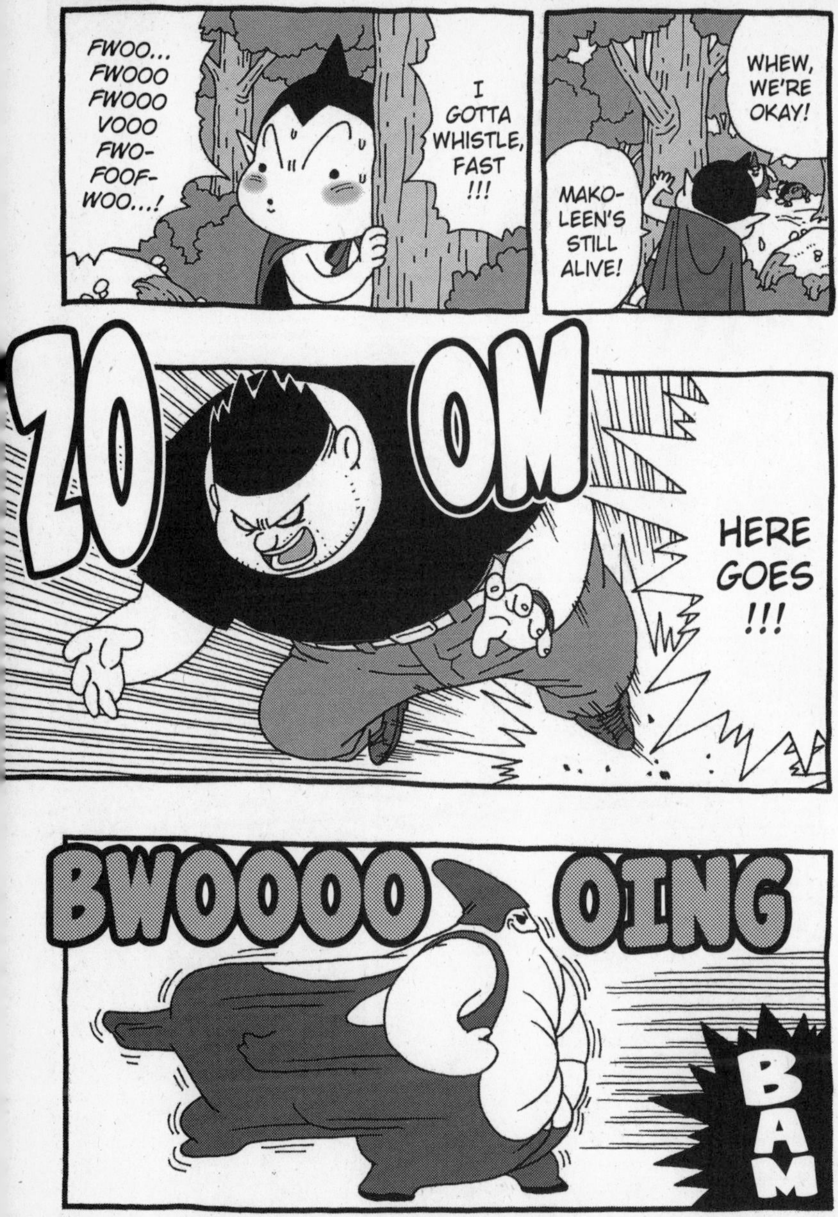
WHEW, WE'RE OKAY!
MAKO-LEEN'S STILL ALIVE!
I GOTTA WHISTLE, FAST!!!
FWOO... FWOOO FWOOO VOOO FWO-FOOF-WOO...!
ZOOM
HERE GOES!!!
BWOOOO OING
BAM

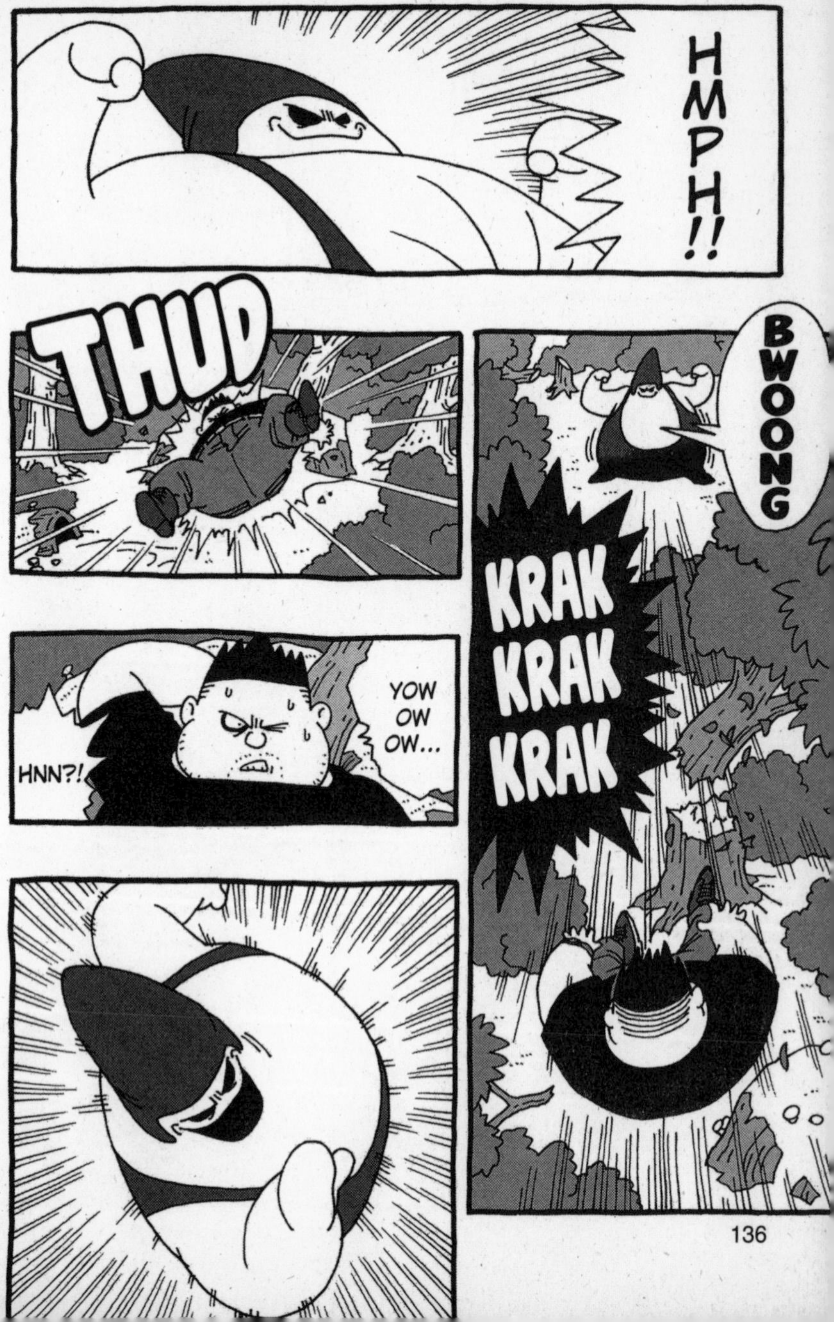
HMPH!!
BWOONG
KRAK
KRAK
KRAK
THUD
YOW OW OW...
HNN?!

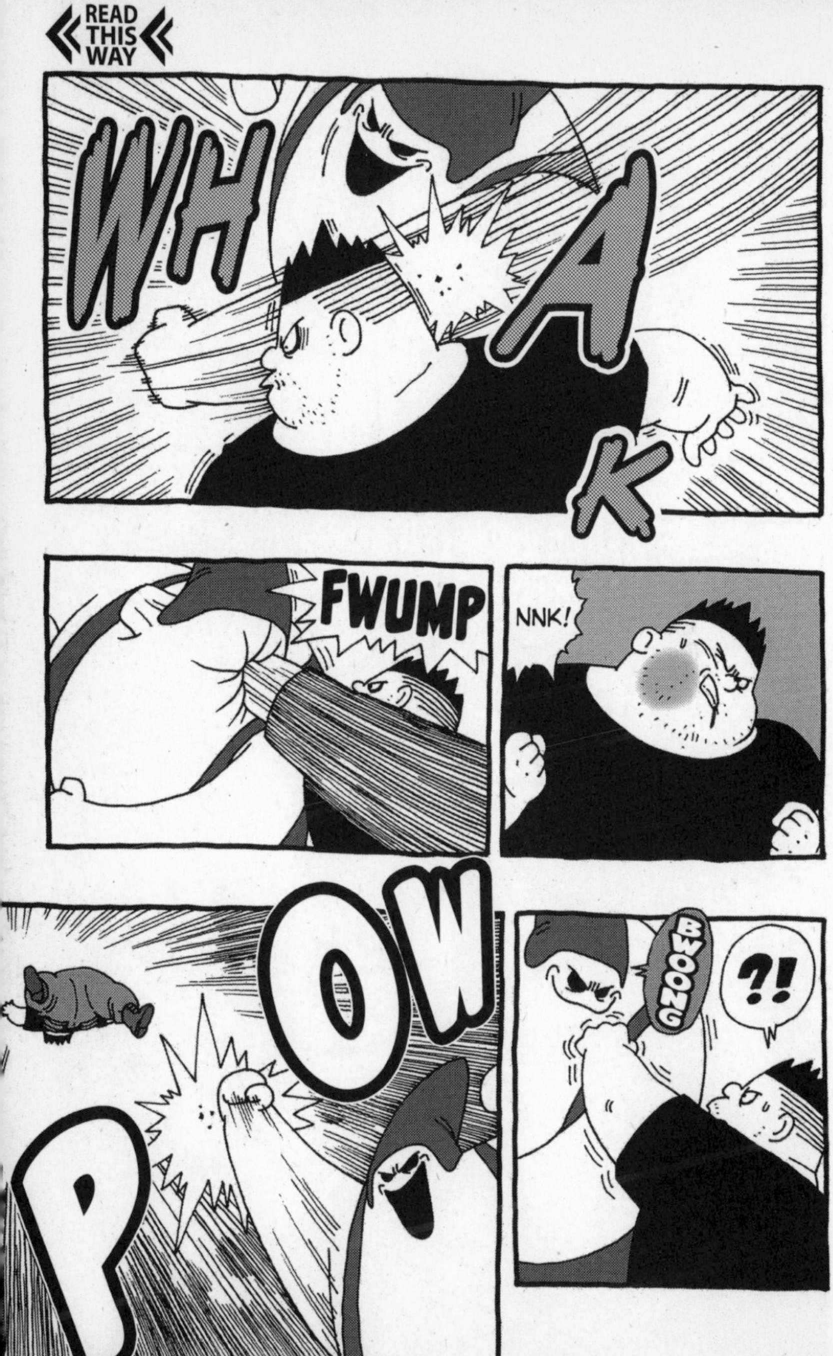
READ THIS WAY
WHACK
NNK!
FWUMP
BWOONG
?!
POW

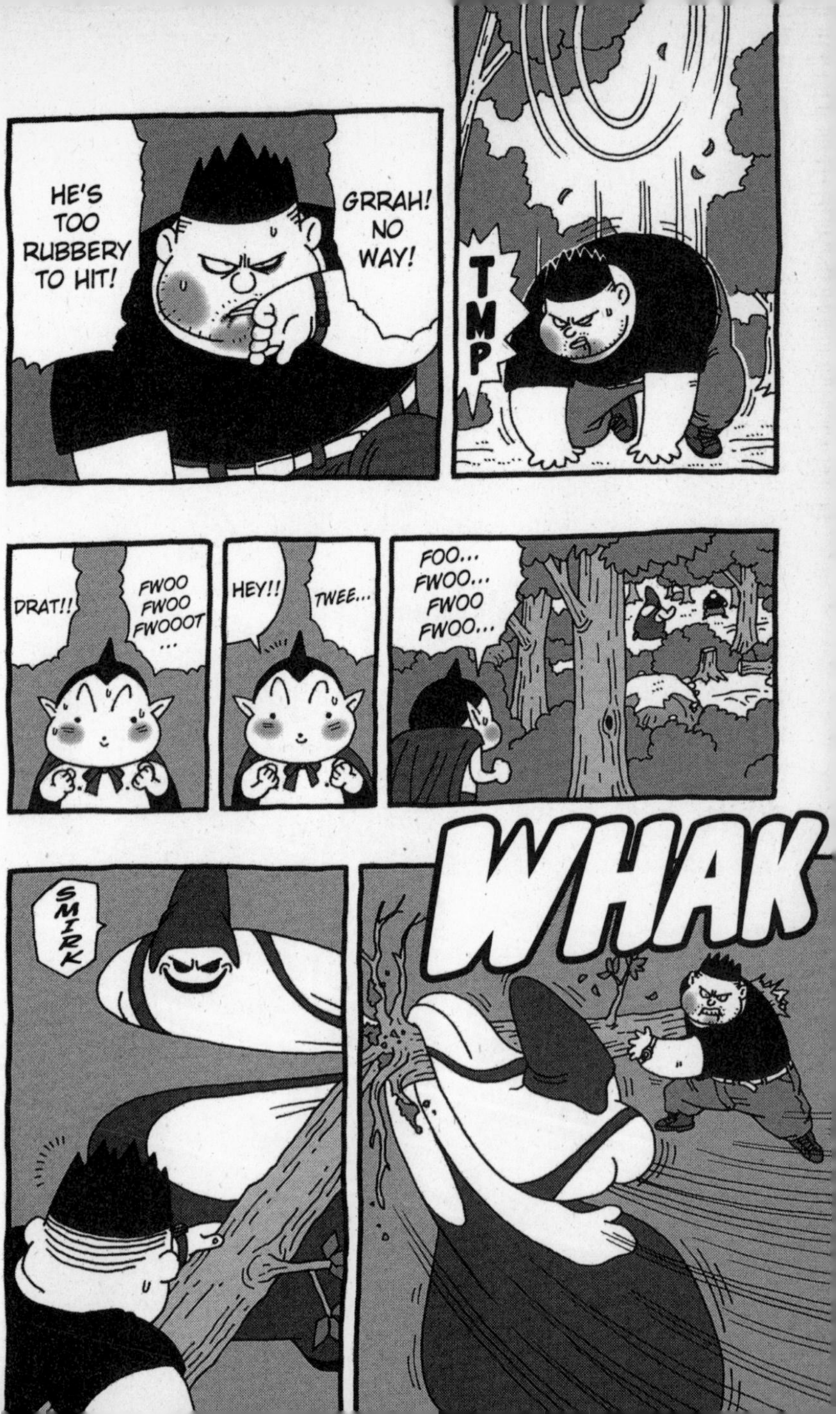
TMP
GRRAH! NO WAY!
HE'S TOO RUBBERY TO HIT!
FOO... FWOO... FWOO FWOO...
TWEE...
HEY!!
FWOO FWOO FWOOOT ...
DRAT!!
WHAK
SMIRK

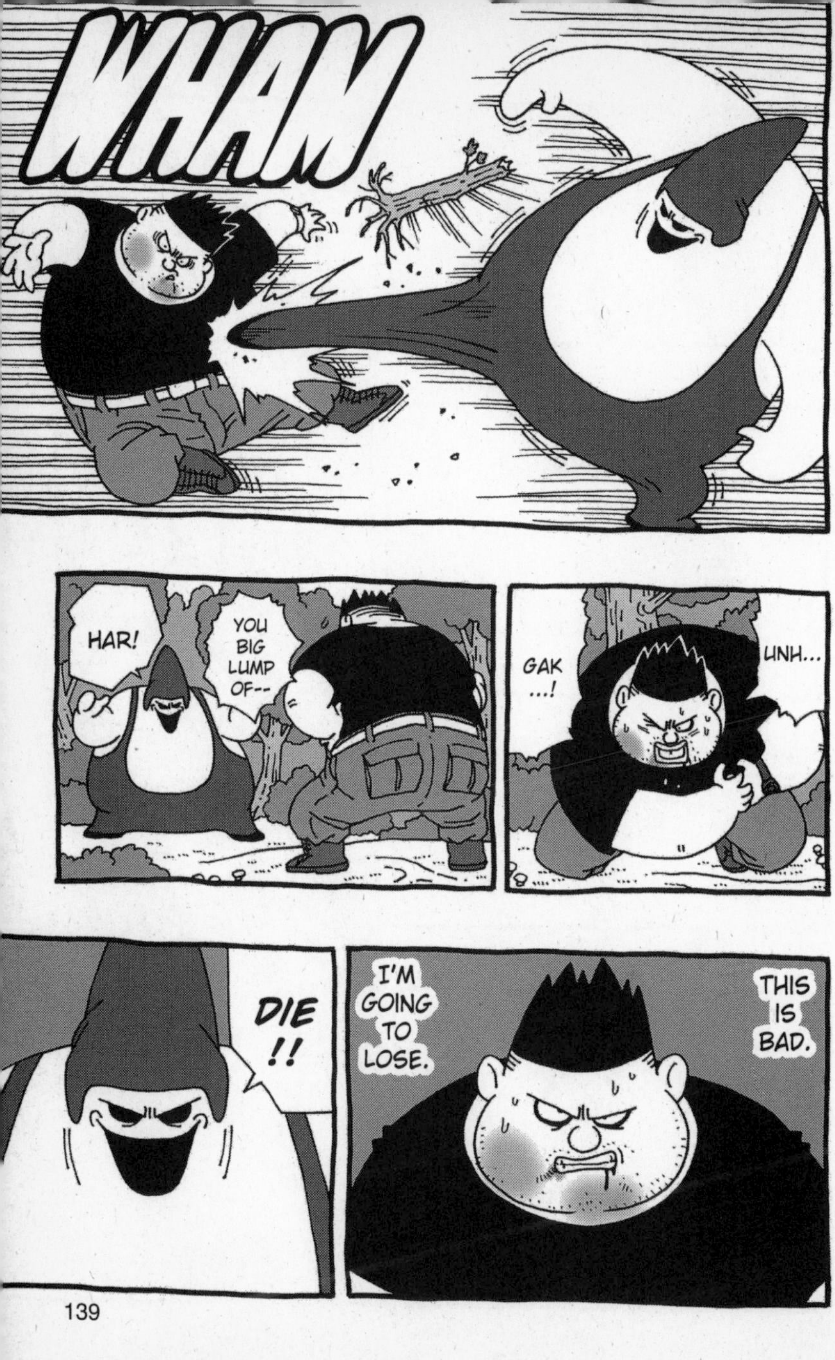
WHAM
UNH...
GAK ...!
YOU BIG LUMP OF--
HAR!
THIS IS BAD.
I'M GOING TO LOSE.
DIE!!

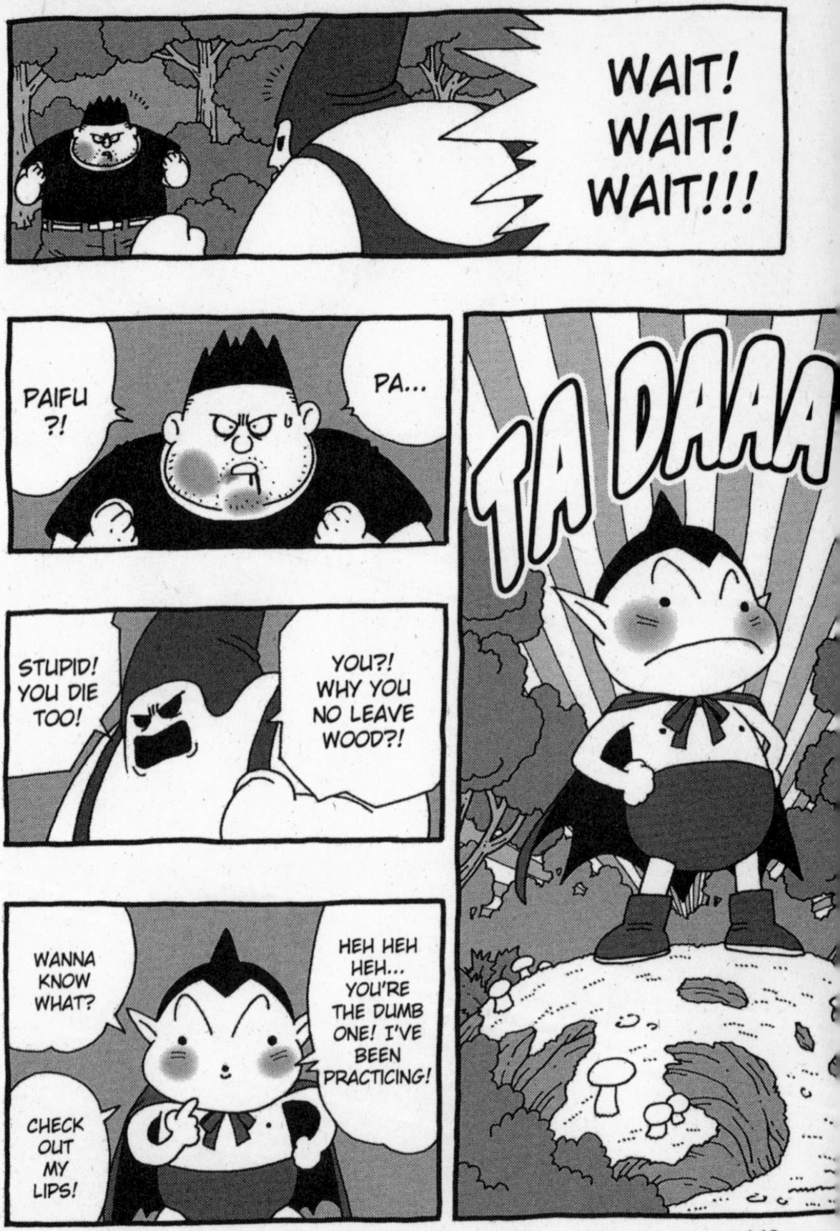
WAIT! WAIT! WAIT!!!
TA DAAA
PA...
PAIFU ?!
YOU?! WHY YOU NO LEAVE WOOD?!
STUPID! YOU DIE TOO!
HEH HEH HEH... YOU'RE THE DUMB ONE! I'VE BEEN PRACTICING!
WANNA KNOW WHAT?
CHECK OUT MY LIPS!

READ THIS WAY

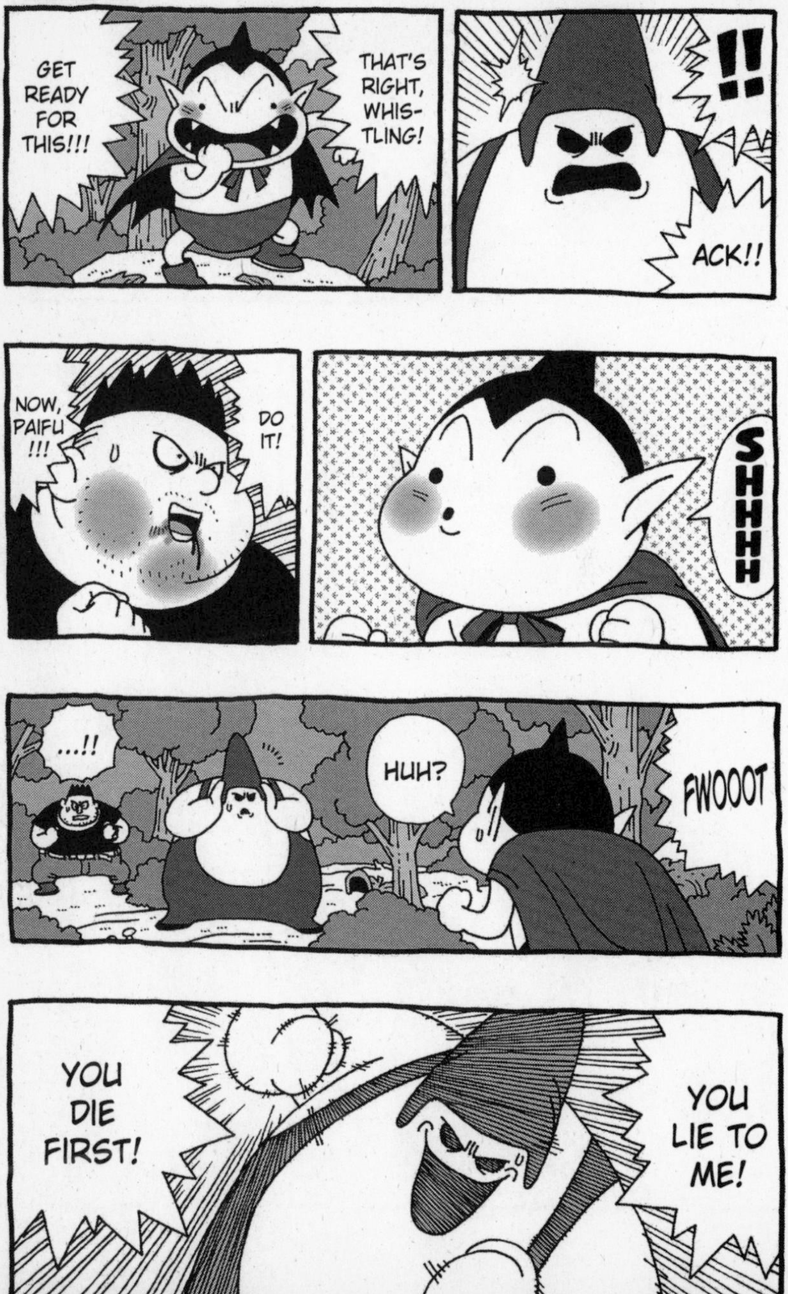
!!
ACK!!
THAT'S RIGHT, WHISTLING!
GET READY FOR THIS!!!
SHHHH
NOW, PAIFU!!!
DO IT!
FWOOOT
HUH?
...!!
YOU LIE TO ME!
YOU DIE FIRST!

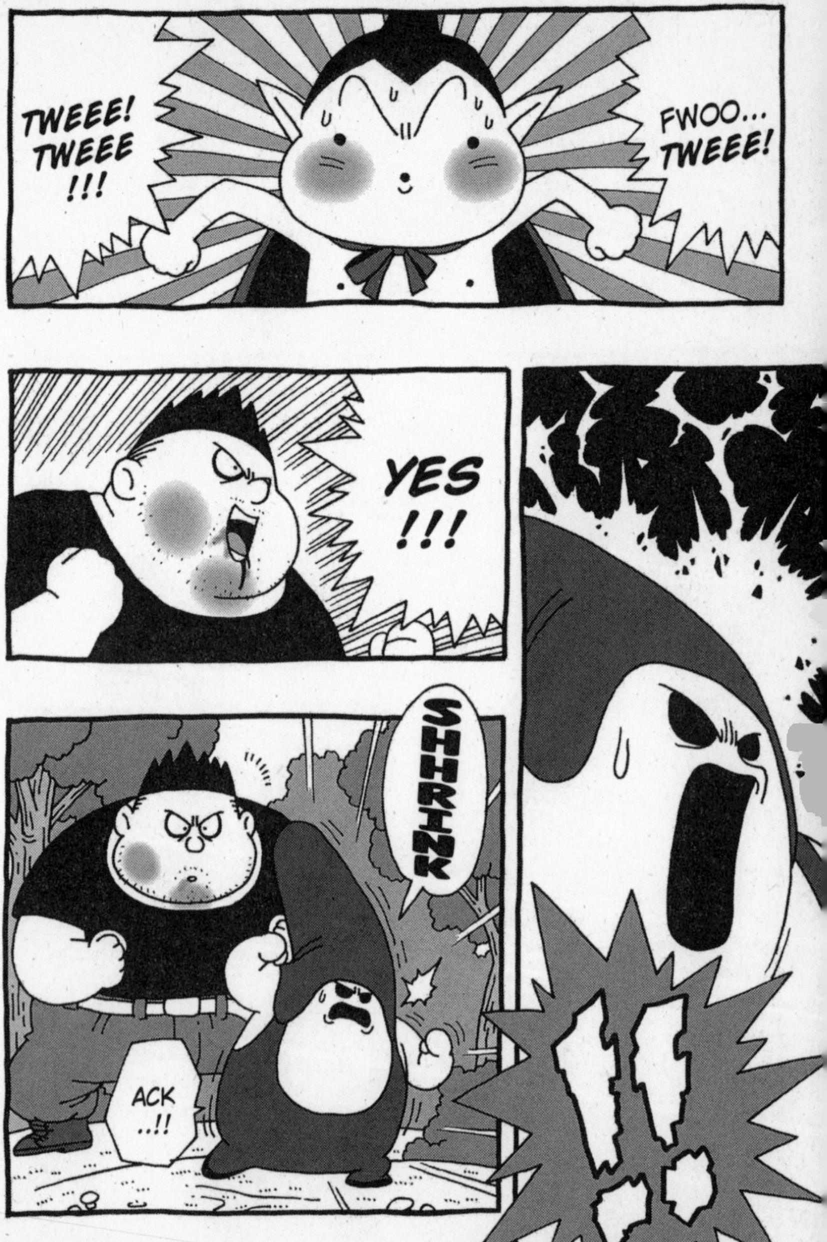
FWOO... TWEEE!
TWEEE! TWEEE !!!
!!
YES !!!
SHRINK
ACK ..!!

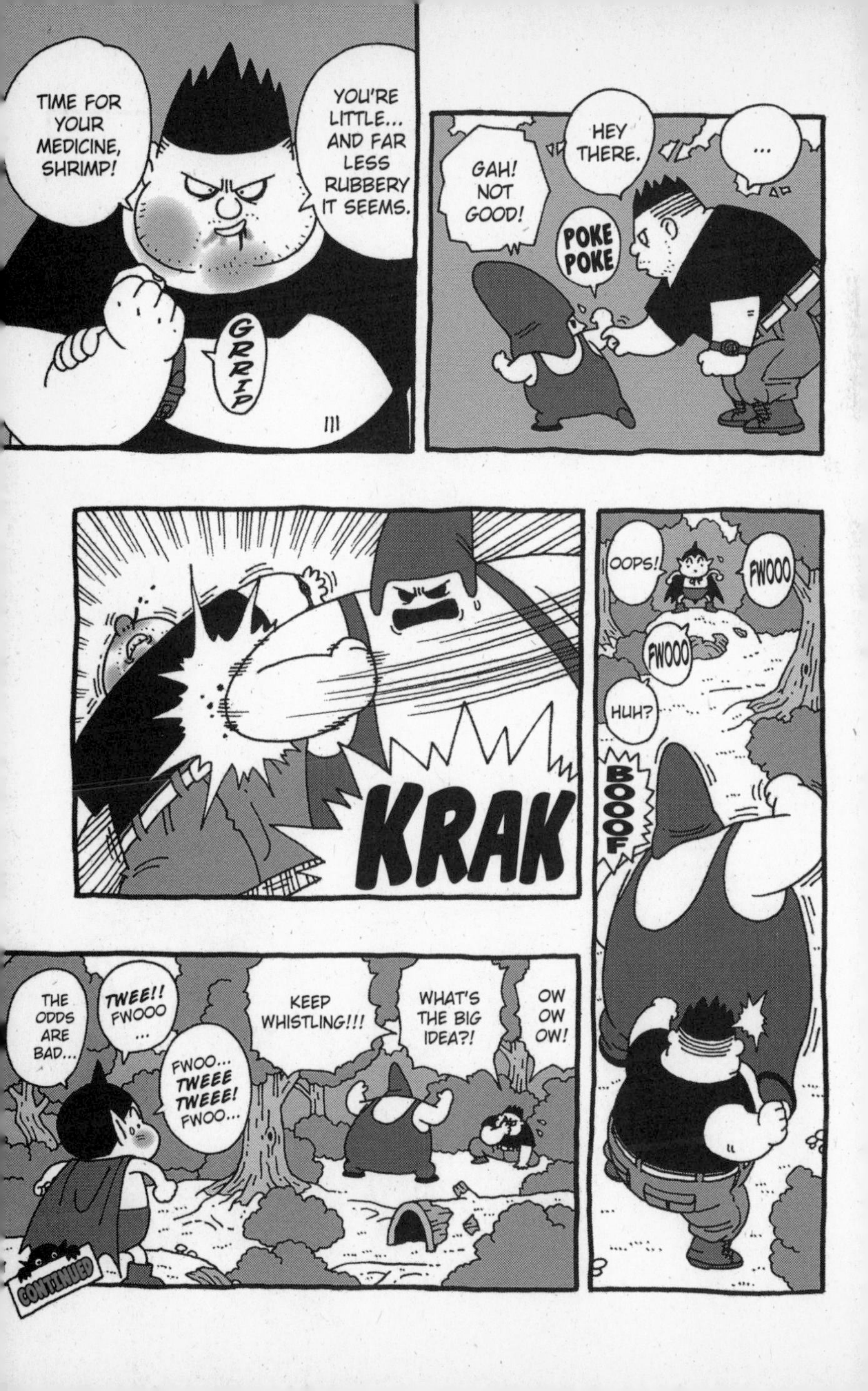
...
HEY THERE.
GAH! NOT GOOD!
POKE POKE
YOU'RE LITTLE... AND FAR LESS RUBBERY IT SEEMS.
TIME FOR YOUR MEDICINE, SHRIMP!
GRRIP
FWOOO
OOPS!
FWOOO
HUH?
BOOOF
KRAK
OW OW OW!
WHAT'S THE BIG IDEA?!
KEEP WHISTLING!!!
TWEE!! FWOOO ...
THE ODDS ARE BAD...
FWOO... TWEEE TWEEE! FWOO...
CONTINUED

COWA!

FRIGHT 11

At the Witch's House

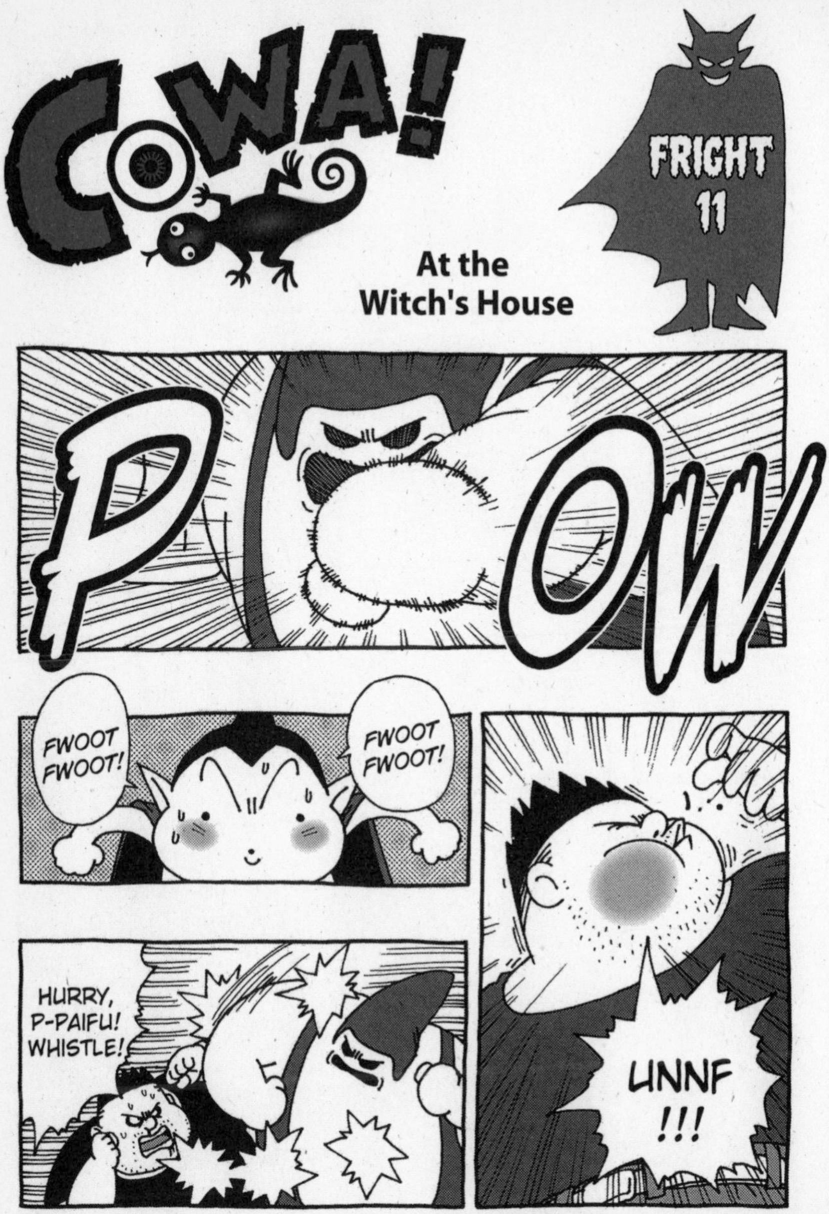
POW
UNNF !!!
FWOOT FWOOT!
FWOOT FWOOT!
HURRY, P-PAIFU! WHISTLE!

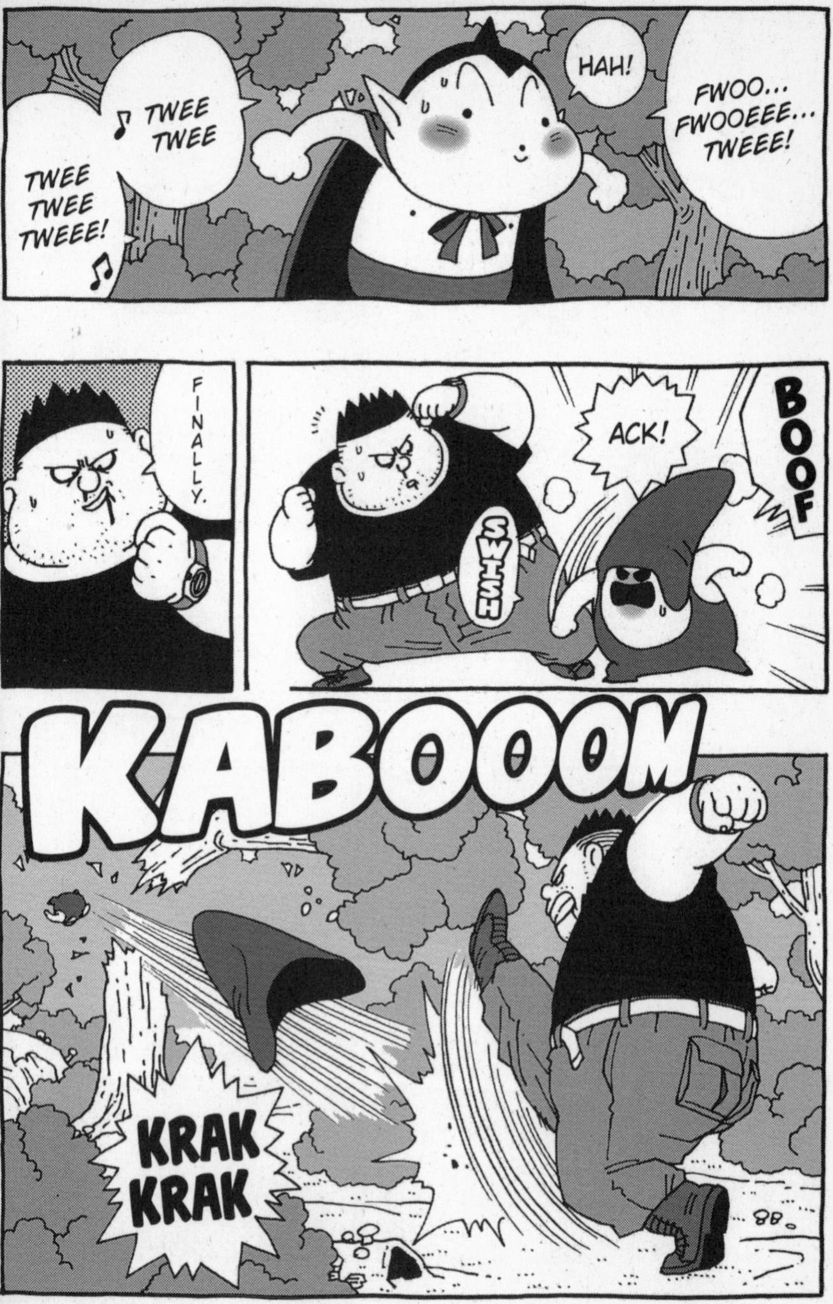

FWOO... FWOOEEE... TWEEE!
HAH!
TWEE TWEE
TWEE TWEE TWEEE!
BOOF
ACK!
SWISH
FINALLY.
KABOOOM
KRAK KRAK

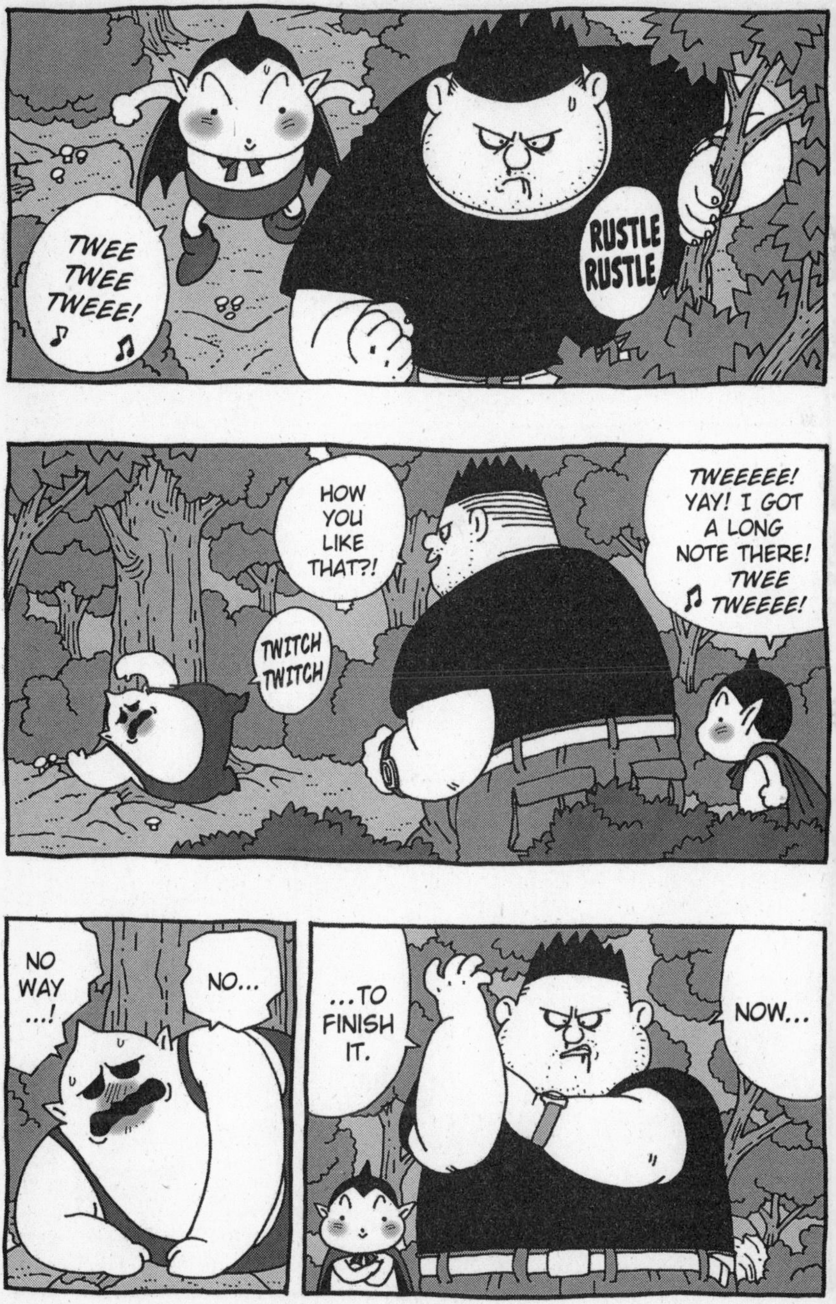
RUSTLE RUSTLE
TWEE TWEE TWEEE!
TWEEEEE! YAY! I GOT A LONG NOTE THERE! TWEE TWEEEE!
HOW YOU LIKE THAT?!
TWITCH TWITCH
NOW...
...TO FINISH IT.
NO...
NO WAY ...!

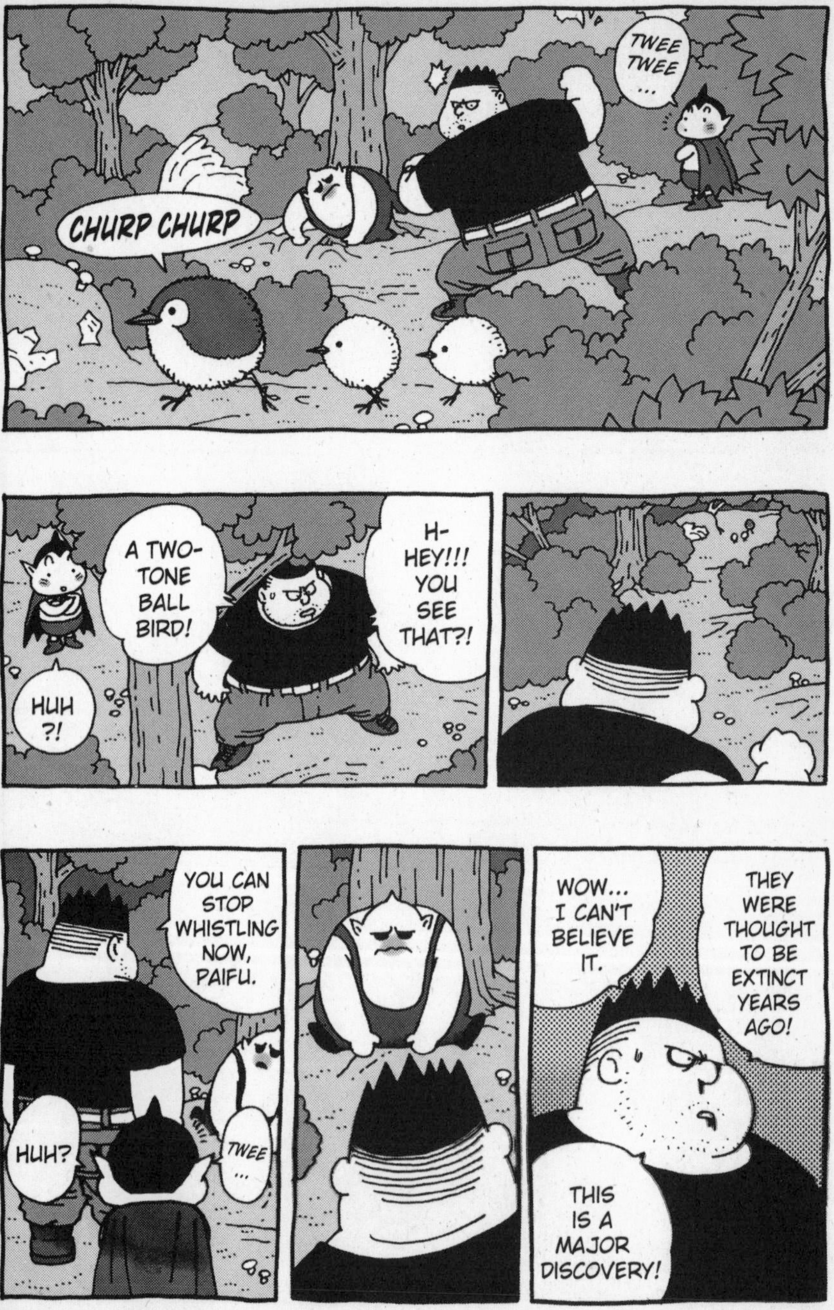
TWEE TWEE ...
CHURP CHURP
H- HEY!!! YOU SEE THAT?!
A TWO-TONE BALL BIRD!
HUH ?!
THEY WERE THOUGHT TO BE EXTINCT YEARS AGO!
WOW... I CAN'T BELIEVE IT.
THIS IS A MAJOR DISCOVERY!
YOU CAN STOP WHISTLING NOW, PAIFU.
TWEE ...
HUH?

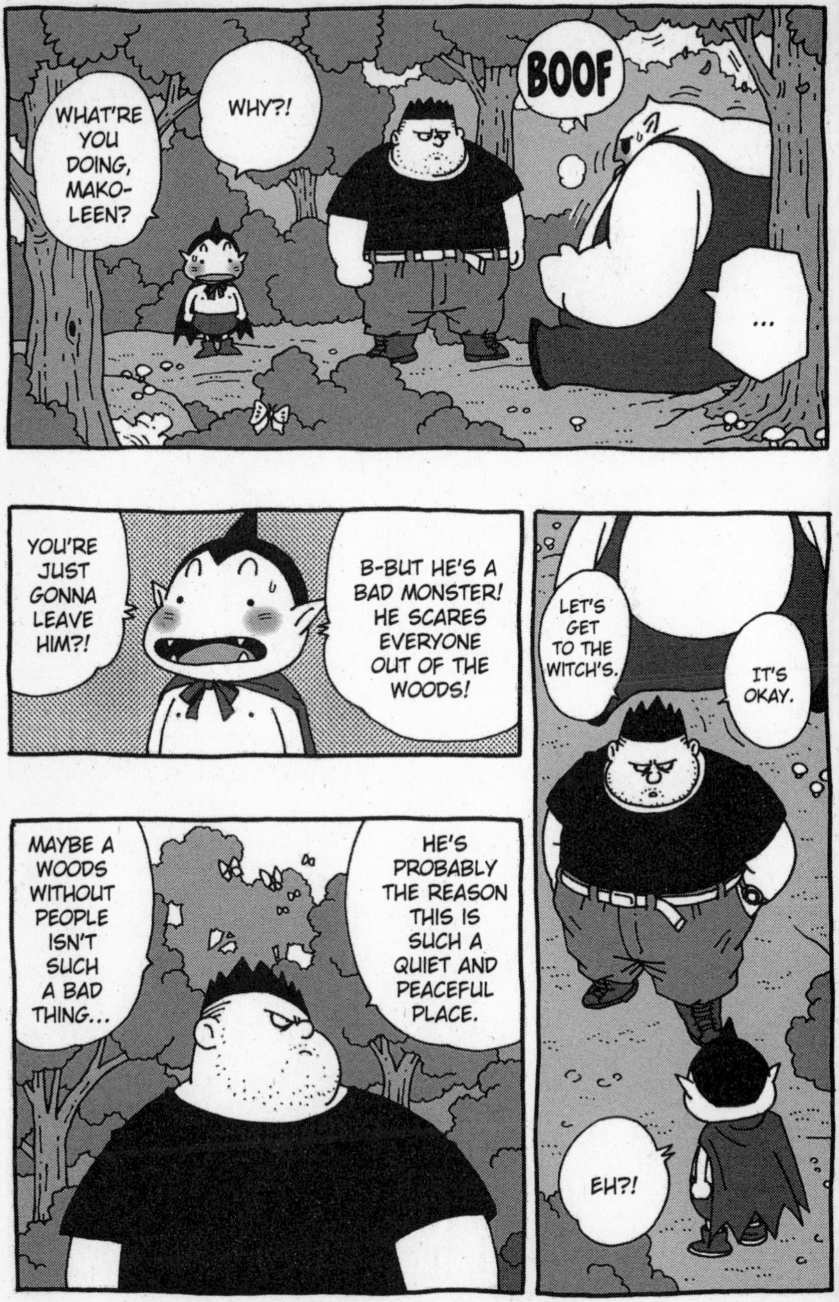
BOOF
...
WHY?!
WHAT'RE YOU DOING, MAKO-LEEN?
IT'S OKAY.
LET'S GET TO THE WITCH'S.
EH?!
B-BUT HE'S A BAD MONSTER! HE SCARES EVERYONE OUT OF THE WOODS!
YOU'RE JUST GONNA LEAVE HIM?!
HE'S PROBABLY THE REASON THIS IS SUCH A QUIET AND PEACEFUL PLACE.
MAYBE A WOODS WITHOUT PEOPLE ISN'T SUCH A BAD THING...

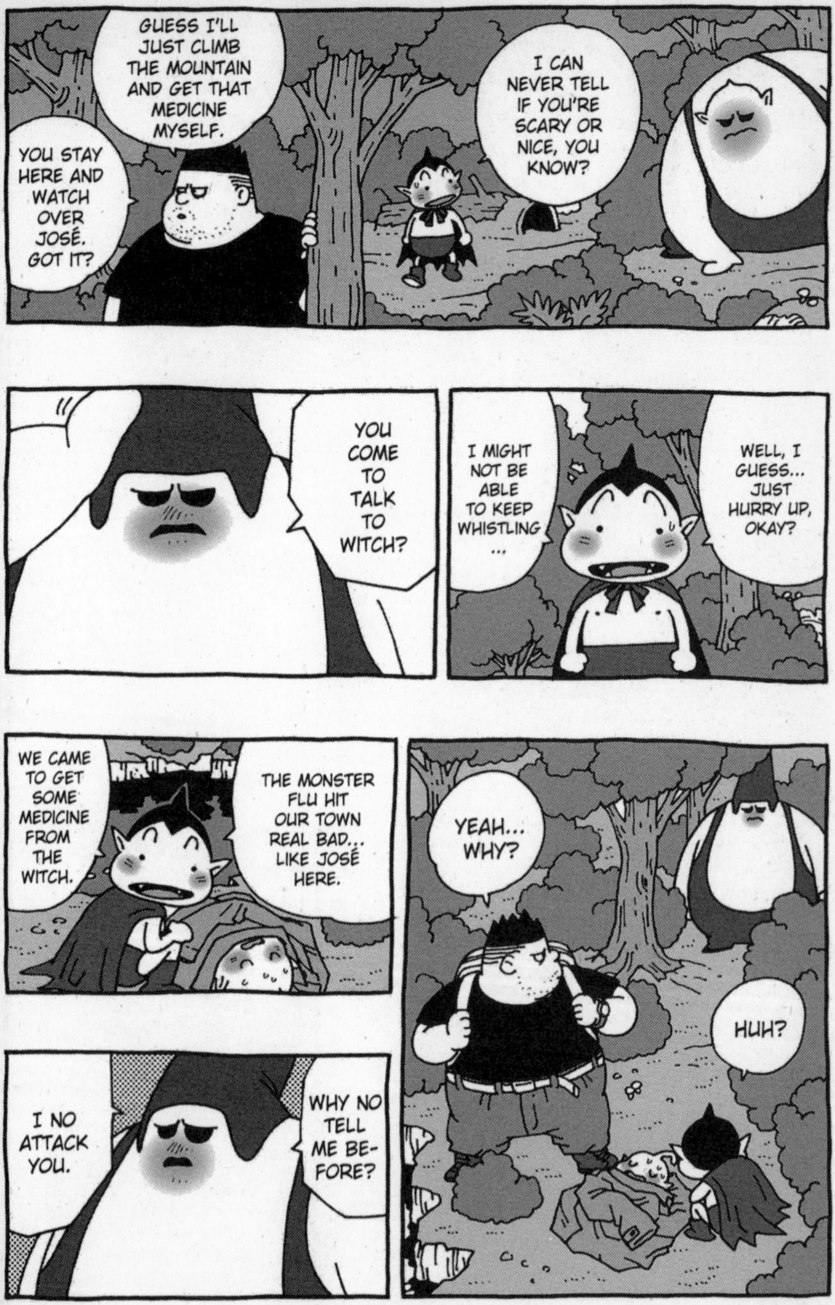
I CAN NEVER TELL IF YOU'RE SCARY OR NICE, YOU KNOW?
GUESS I'LL JUST CLIMB THE MOUNTAIN AND GET THAT MEDICINE MYSELF.
YOU STAY HERE AND WATCH OVER JOSÉ. GOT IT?
WELL, I GUESS... JUST HURRY UP, OKAY?
I MIGHT NOT BE ABLE TO KEEP WHISTLING ...
YOU COME TO TALK TO WITCH?
YEAH... WHY?
HUH?
THE MONSTER FLU HIT OUR TOWN REAL BAD... LIKE JOSÉ HERE.
WE CAME TO GET SOME MEDICINE FROM THE WITCH.
WHY NO TELL ME BE-FORE?
I NO ATTACK YOU.

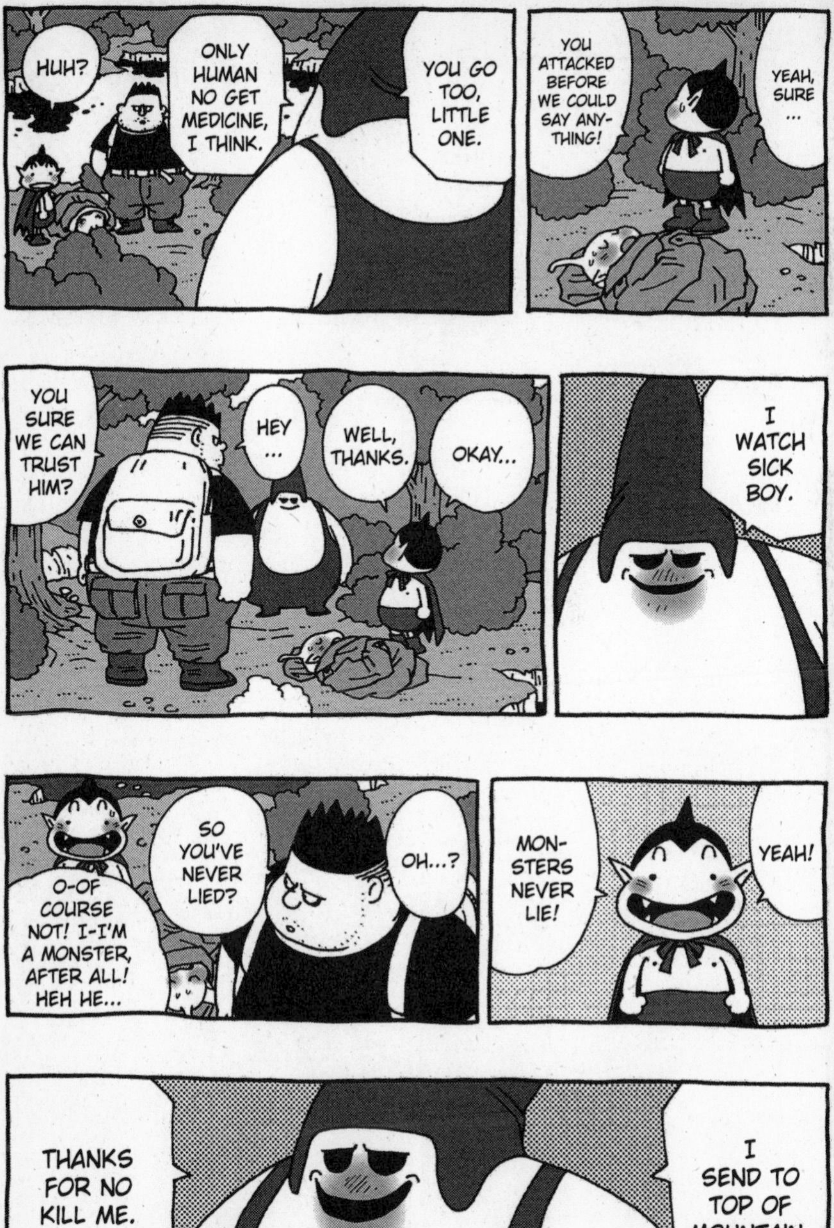
YEAH, SURE ...
YOU ATTACKED BEFORE WE COULD SAY ANY-THING!
YOU GO TOO, LITTLE ONE.
ONLY HUMAN NO GET MEDICINE, I THINK.
HUH?
I WATCH SICK BOY.
OKAY...
WELL, THANKS.
HEY ...
YOU SURE WE CAN TRUST HIM?
YEAH!
MON-STERS NEVER LIE!
OH...?
SO YOU'VE NEVER LIED?
O-OF COURSE NOT! I-I'M A MONSTER, AFTER ALL! HEH HE...
I SEND TO TOP OF MOUNTAIN.
THANKS FOR NO KILL ME.

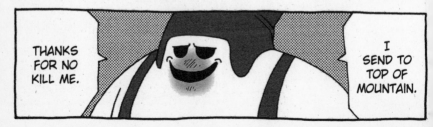

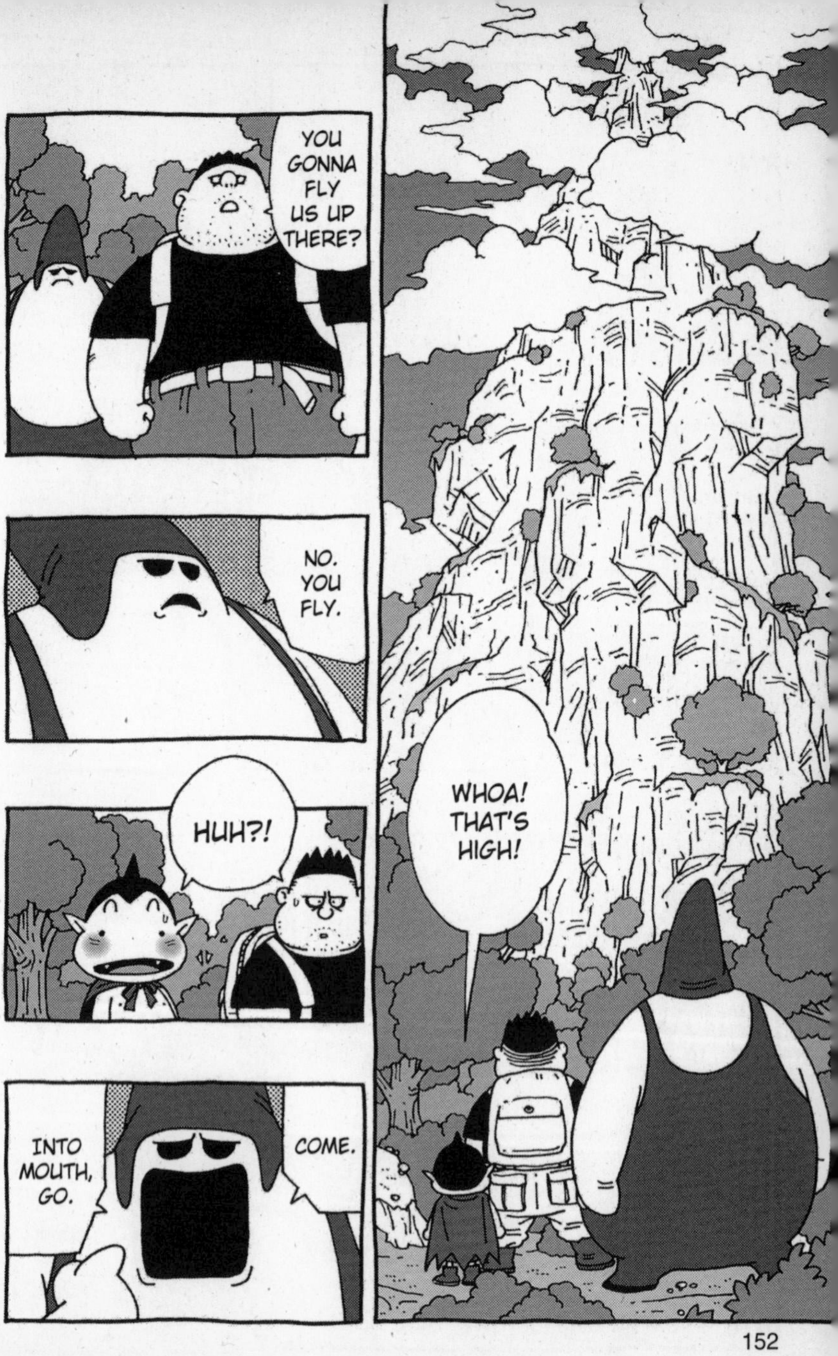
WHOA! THAT'S HIGH!
YOU GONNA FLY US UP THERE?
NO. YOU FLY.
HUH?!
COME.
INTO MOUTH, GO.

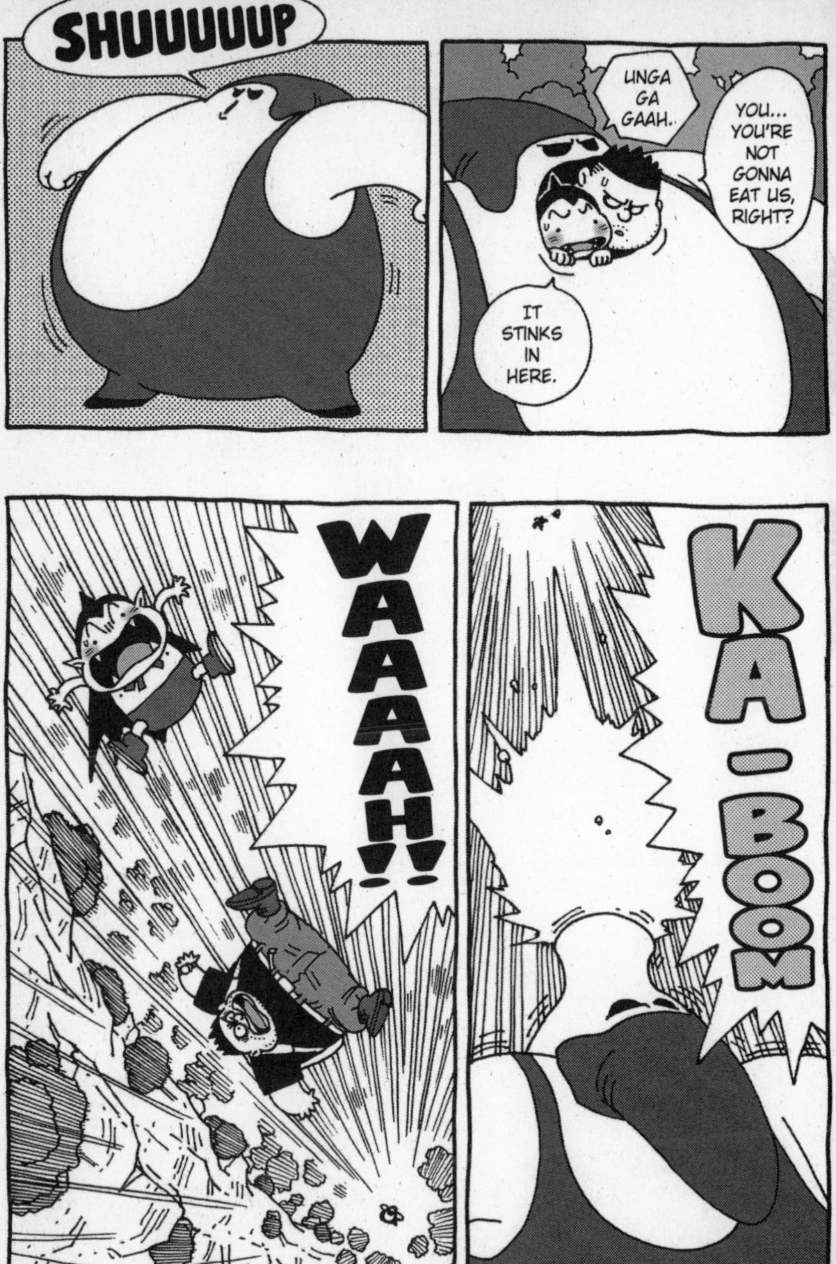
YOU... YOU'RE NOT GONNA EAT US, RIGHT?
UNGA GA GAAH..
IT STINKS IN HERE.
SHUUUUUP
KA-BOOM
WAAAAH!!

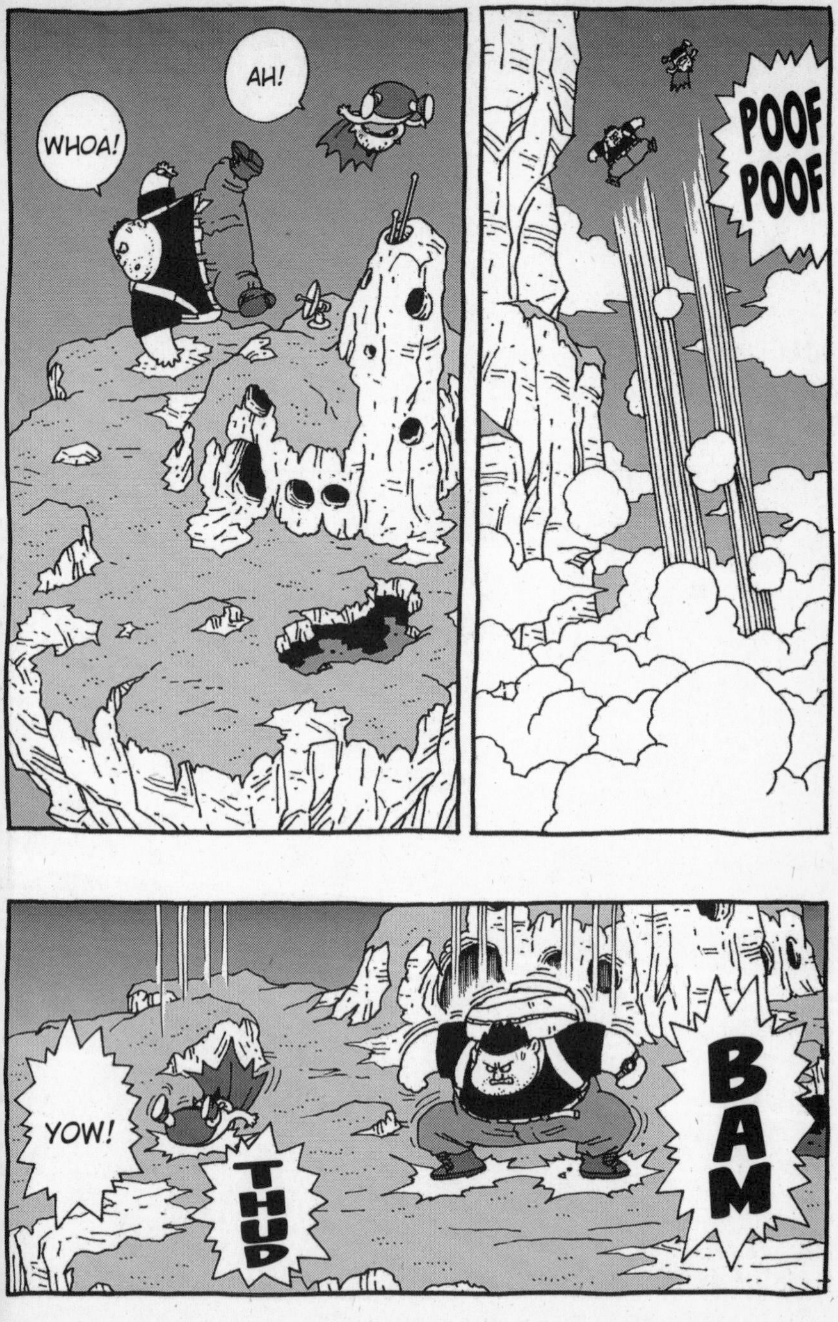
POOF POOF
AH!
WHOA!
BAM
THUD
YOW!

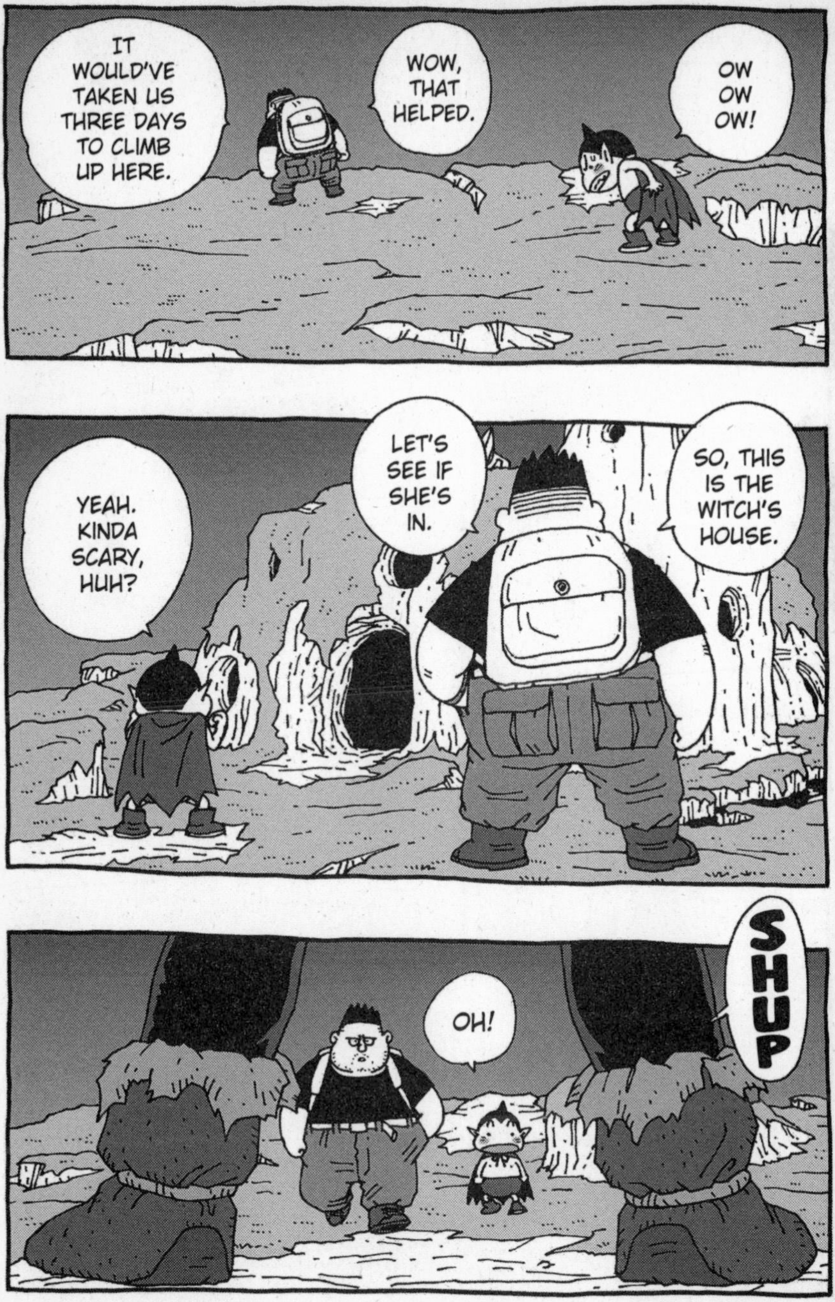
OW OW OW!
WOW, THAT HELPED.
IT WOULD'VE TAKEN US THREE DAYS TO CLIMB UP HERE.
SO, THIS IS THE WITCH'S HOUSE.
YEAH. KINDA SCARY, HUH?
LET'S SEE IF SHE'S IN.
SHUP
OH!

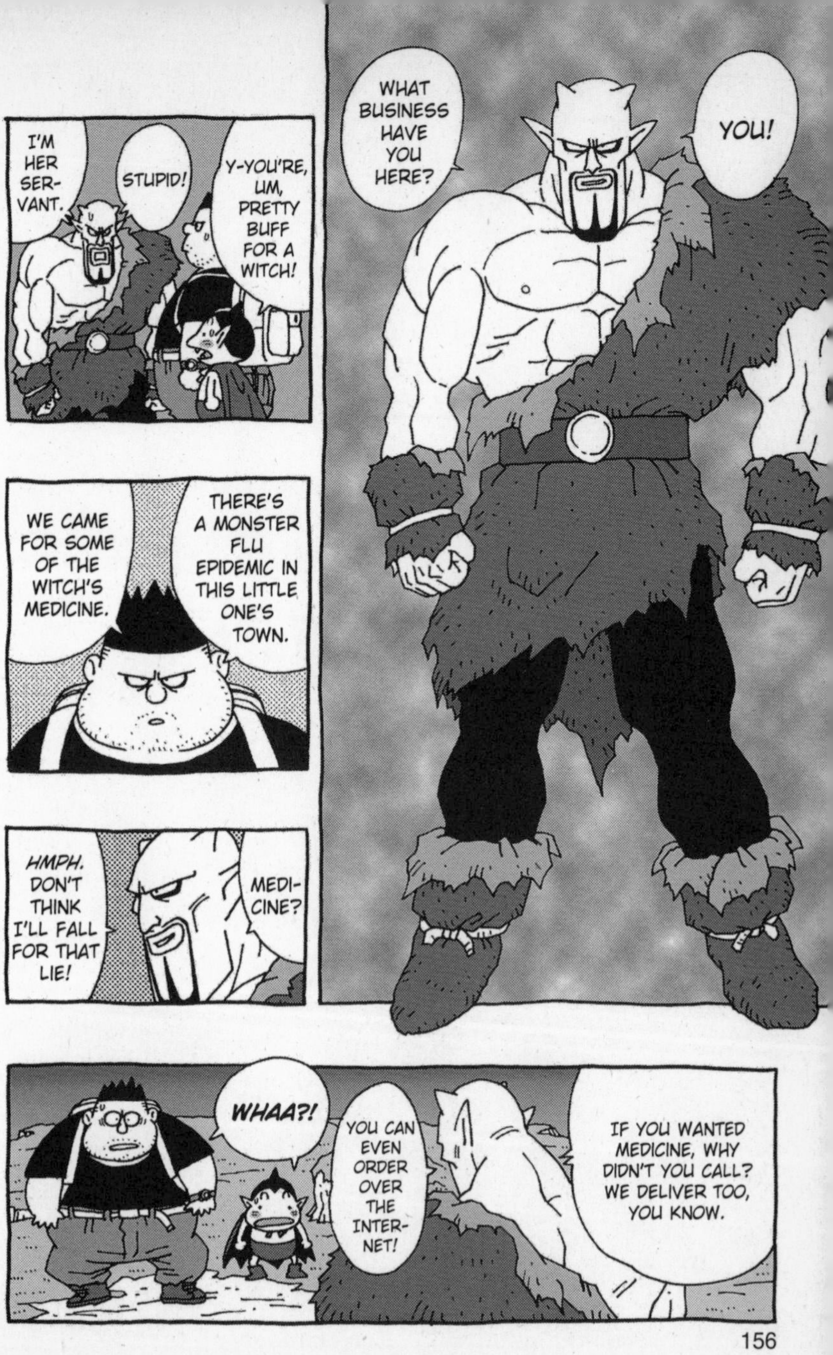
YOU!
WHAT BUSINESS HAVE YOU HERE?
Y-YOU'RE, UM, PRETTY BUFF FOR A WITCH!
STUPID!
I'M HER SERVANT.
THERE'S A MONSTER FLU EPIDEMIC IN THIS LITTLE ONE'S TOWN.
WE CAME FOR SOME OF THE WITCH'S MEDICINE.
MEDICINE?
HMPH. DON'T THINK I'LL FALL FOR THAT LIE!
IF YOU WANTED MEDICINE, WHY DIDN'T YOU CALL? WE DELIVER TOO, YOU KNOW.
YOU CAN EVEN ORDER OVER THE INTERNET!
WHAA?!

READ THIS WAY

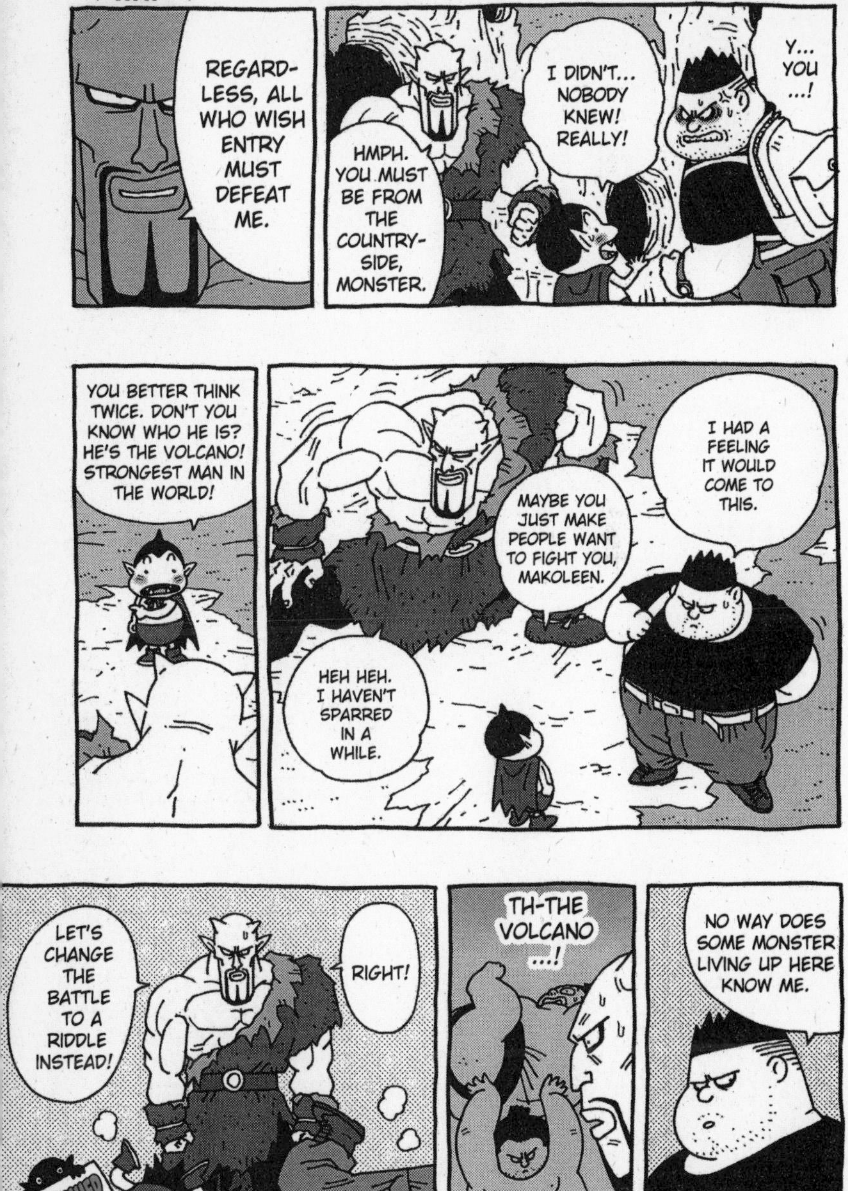
Y... YOU ...!
I DIDN'T... NOBODY KNEW! REALLY!
HMPH. YOU MUST BE FROM THE COUNTRY-SIDE, MONSTER.
REGARD-LESS, ALL WHO WISH ENTRY MUST DEFEAT ME.
I HAD A FEELING IT WOULD COME TO THIS.
MAYBE YOU JUST MAKE PEOPLE WANT TO FIGHT YOU, MAKOLEEN.
HEH HEH. I HAVEN'T SPARRED IN A WHILE.
YOU BETTER THINK TWICE. DON'T YOU KNOW WHO HE IS? HE'S THE VOLCANO! STRONGEST MAN IN THE WORLD!
NO WAY DOES SOME MONSTER LIVING UP HERE KNOW ME.
TH-THE VOLCANO ...!
RIGHT!
LET'S CHANGE THE BATTLE TO A RIDDLE INSTEAD!
CONTINUED

FRIGHT 12

The Medicine Is Ours!

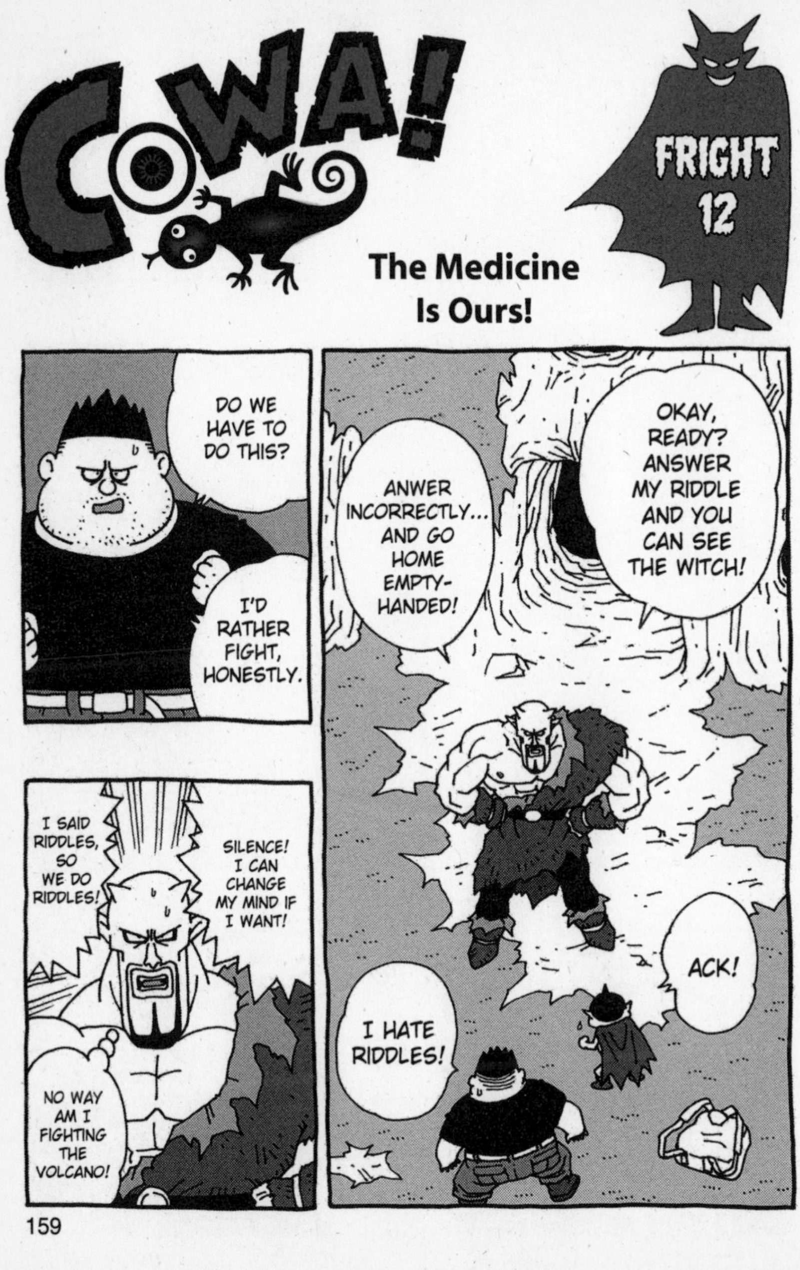
OKAY, READY? ANSWER MY RIDDLE AND YOU CAN SEE THE WITCH!
ANWER INCORRECTLY... AND GO HOME EMPTY-HANDED!
ACK!
I HATE RIDDLES!
DO WE HAVE TO DO THIS?
I'D RATHER FIGHT, HONESTLY.
SILENCE! I CAN CHANGE MY MIND IF I WANT!
I SAID RIDDLES, SO WE DO RIDDLES!
NO WAY AM I FIGHTING THE VOLCANO!

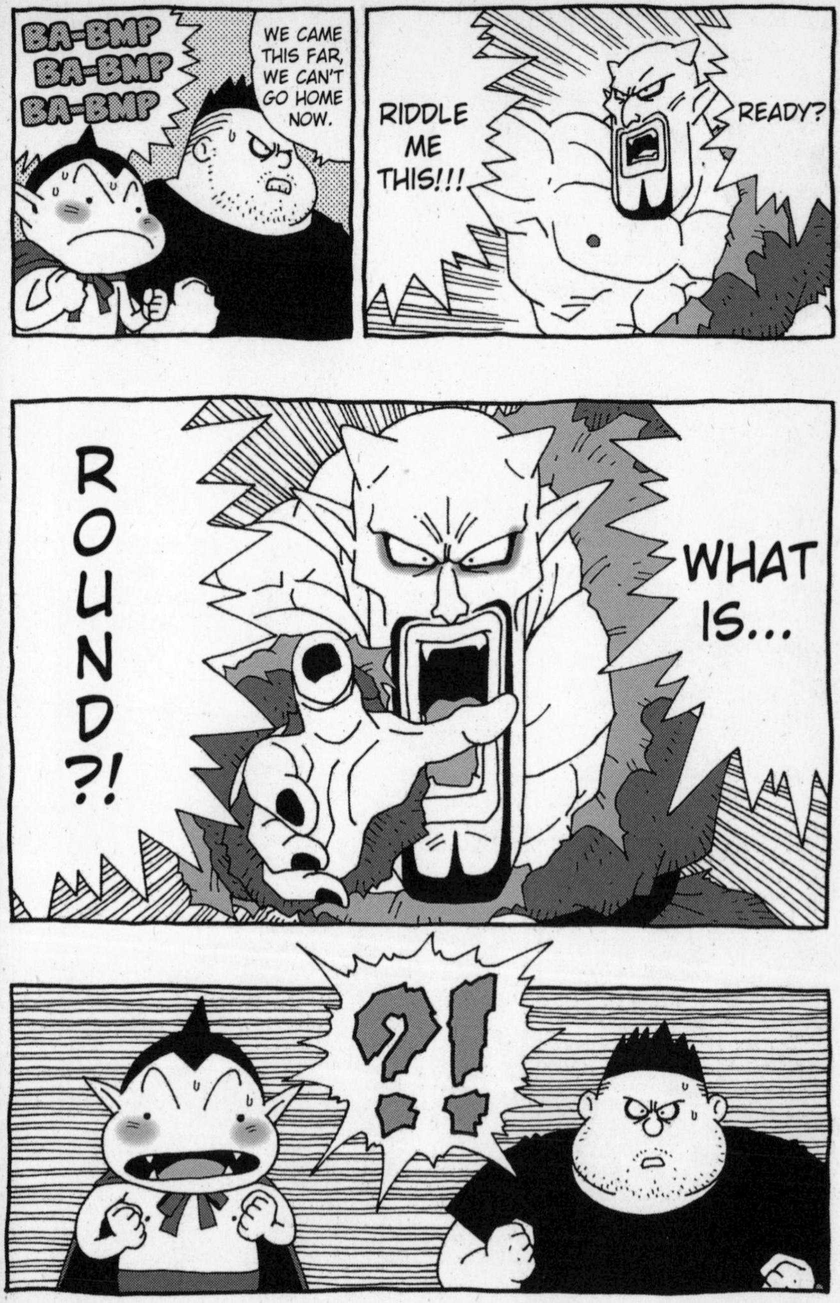
READY?
RIDDLE ME THIS!!!
WE CAME THIS FAR, WE CAN'T GO HOME NOW.
BA-BMP BA-BMP BA-BMP
WHAT IS...
ROUND?!
?!

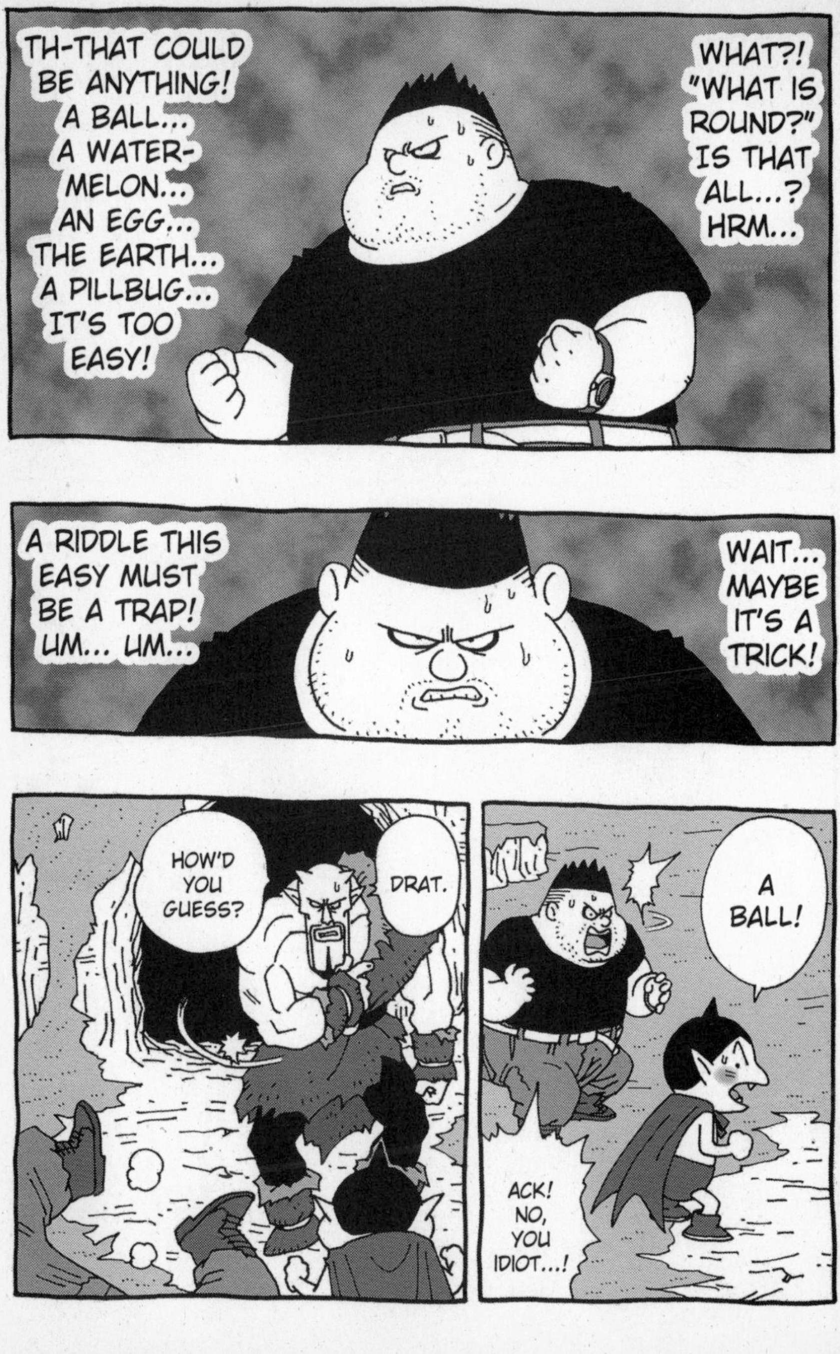
WHAT?! "WHAT IS ROUND?" IS THAT ALL...? HRM...
TH-THAT COULD BE ANYTHING! A BALL... A WATER-MELON... AN EGG... THE EARTH... A PILLBUG... IT'S TOO EASY!
WAIT... MAYBE IT'S A TRICK!
A RIDDLE THIS EASY MUST BE A TRAP! UM... UM...
A BALL!
ACK! NO, YOU IDIOT...!
DRAT.
HOW'D YOU GUESS?

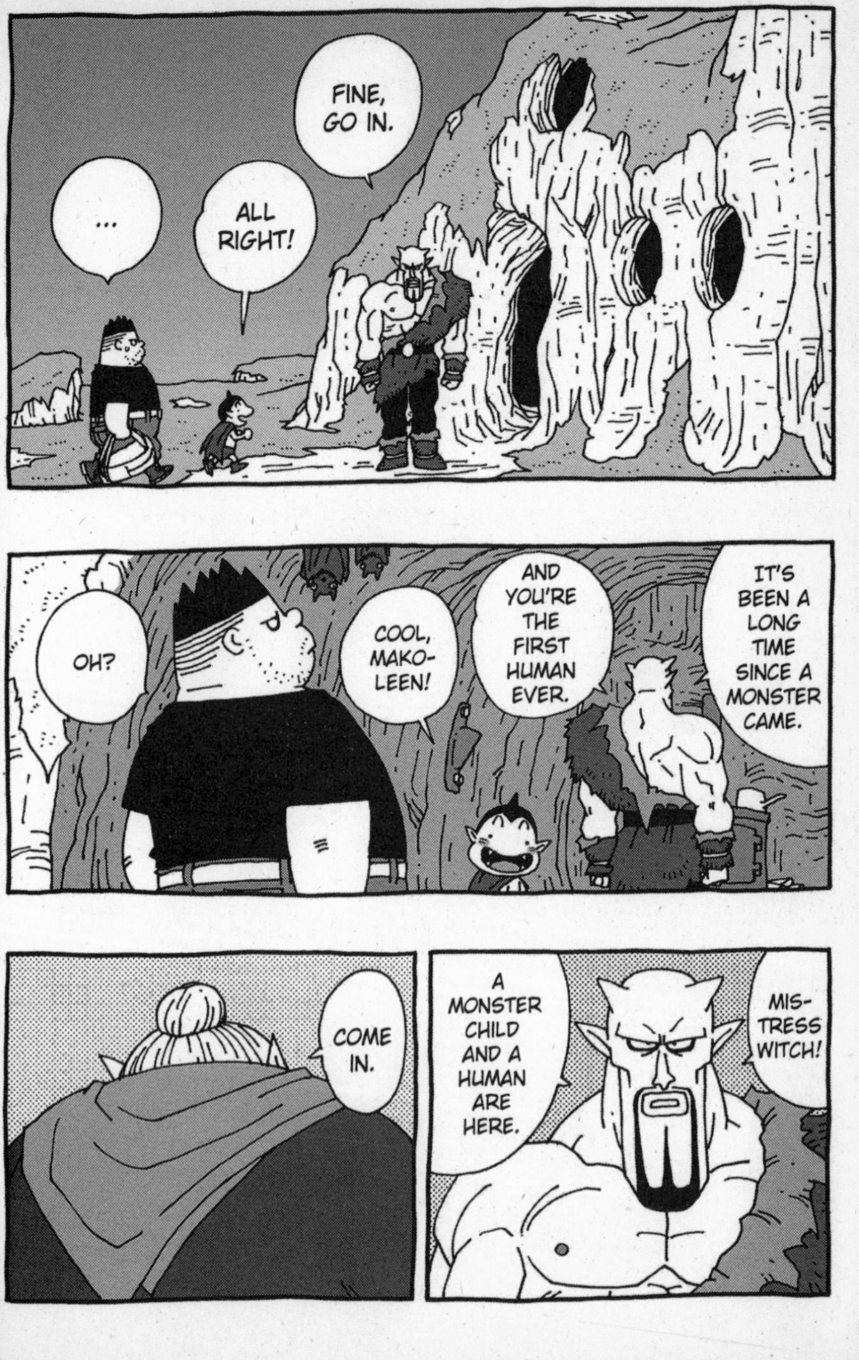
FINE, GO IN.
ALL RIGHT!
...
IT'S BEEN A LONG TIME SINCE A MONSTER CAME.
AND YOU'RE THE FIRST HUMAN EVER.
COOL, MAKO-LEEN!
OH?
MIS-TRESS WITCH!
A MONSTER CHILD AND A HUMAN ARE HERE.
COME IN.

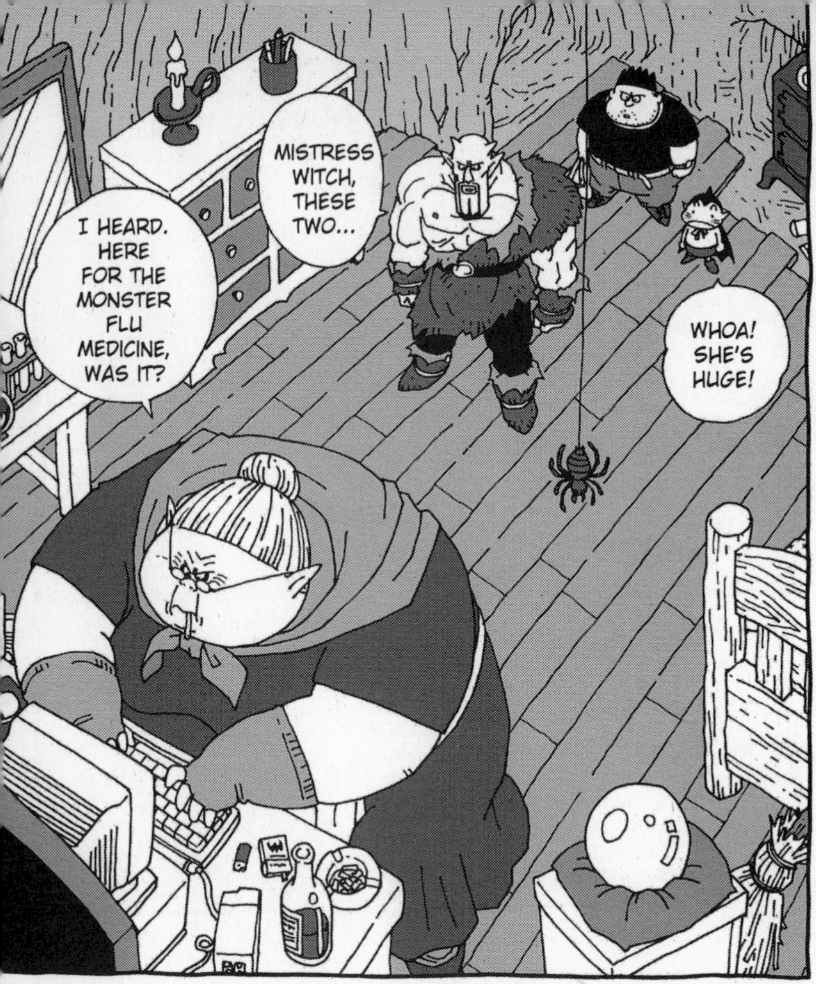
MISTRESS WITCH, THESE TWO...
WHOA! SHE'S HUGE!
I HEARD. HERE FOR THE MONSTER FLU MEDICINE, WAS IT?

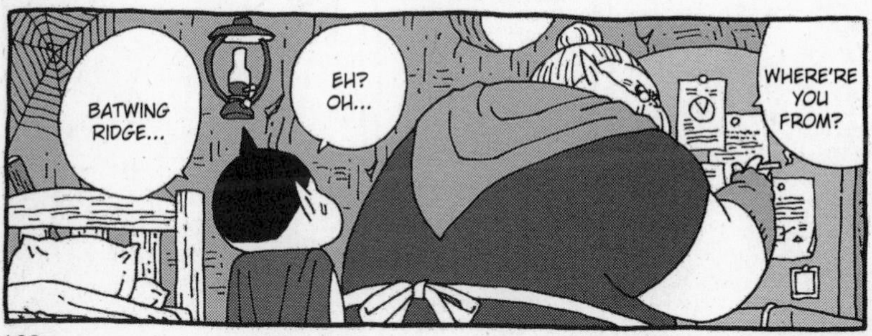
WHERE'RE YOU FROM?
EH? OH...
BATWING RIDGE...

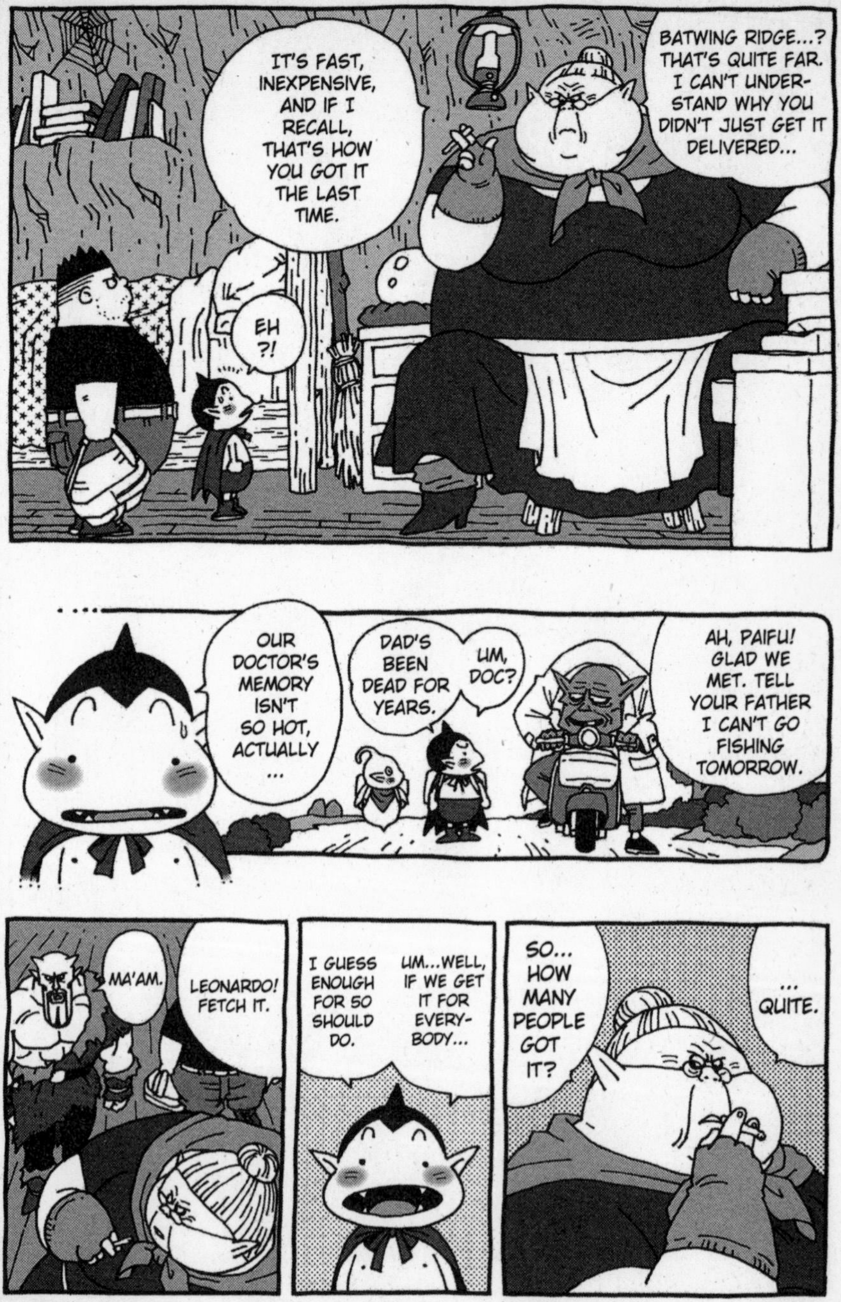
BATWING RIDGE...? THAT'S QUITE FAR. I CAN'T UNDER-STAND WHY YOU DIDN'T JUST GET IT DELIVERED...
IT'S FAST, INEXPENSIVE, AND IF I RECALL, THAT'S HOW YOU GOT IT THE LAST TIME.
EH ?!
AH, PAIFU! GLAD WE MET. TELL YOUR FATHER I CAN'T GO FISHING TOMORROW.
UM, DOC?
DAD'S BEEN DEAD FOR YEARS.
.....
OUR DOCTOR'S MEMORY ISN'T SO HOT, ACTUALLY ...
... QUITE.
SO... HOW MANY PEOPLE GOT IT?
UM...WELL, IF WE GET IT FOR EVERY-BODY...
I GUESS ENOUGH FOR 50 SHOULD DO.
LEONARDO! FETCH IT.
MA'AM.

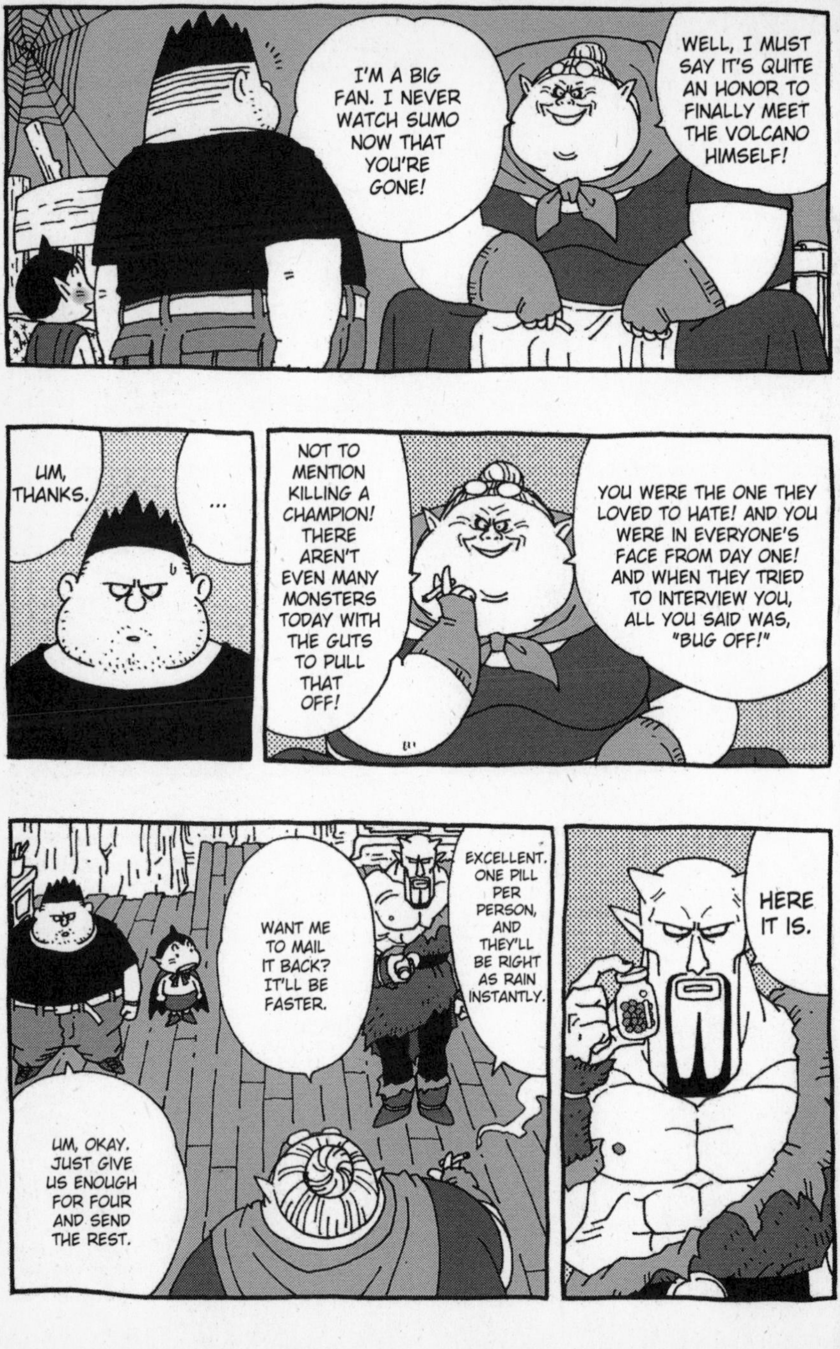
WELL, I MUST SAY IT'S QUITE AN HONOR TO FINALLY MEET THE VOLCANO HIMSELF!
I'M A BIG FAN. I NEVER WATCH SUMO NOW THAT YOU'RE GONE!
YOU WERE THE ONE THEY LOVED TO HATE! AND YOU WERE IN EVERYONE'S FACE FROM DAY ONE! AND WHEN THEY TRIED TO INTERVIEW YOU, ALL YOU SAID WAS, "BUG OFF!"
NOT TO MENTION KILLING A CHAMPION! THERE AREN'T EVEN MANY MONSTERS TODAY WITH THE GUTS TO PULL THAT OFF!
...
UM, THANKS.
HERE IT IS.
EXCELLENT. ONE PILL PER PERSON, AND THEY'LL BE RIGHT AS RAIN INSTANTLY.
WANT ME TO MAIL IT BACK? IT'LL BE FASTER.
UM, OKAY. JUST GIVE US ENOUGH FOR FOUR AND SEND THE REST.

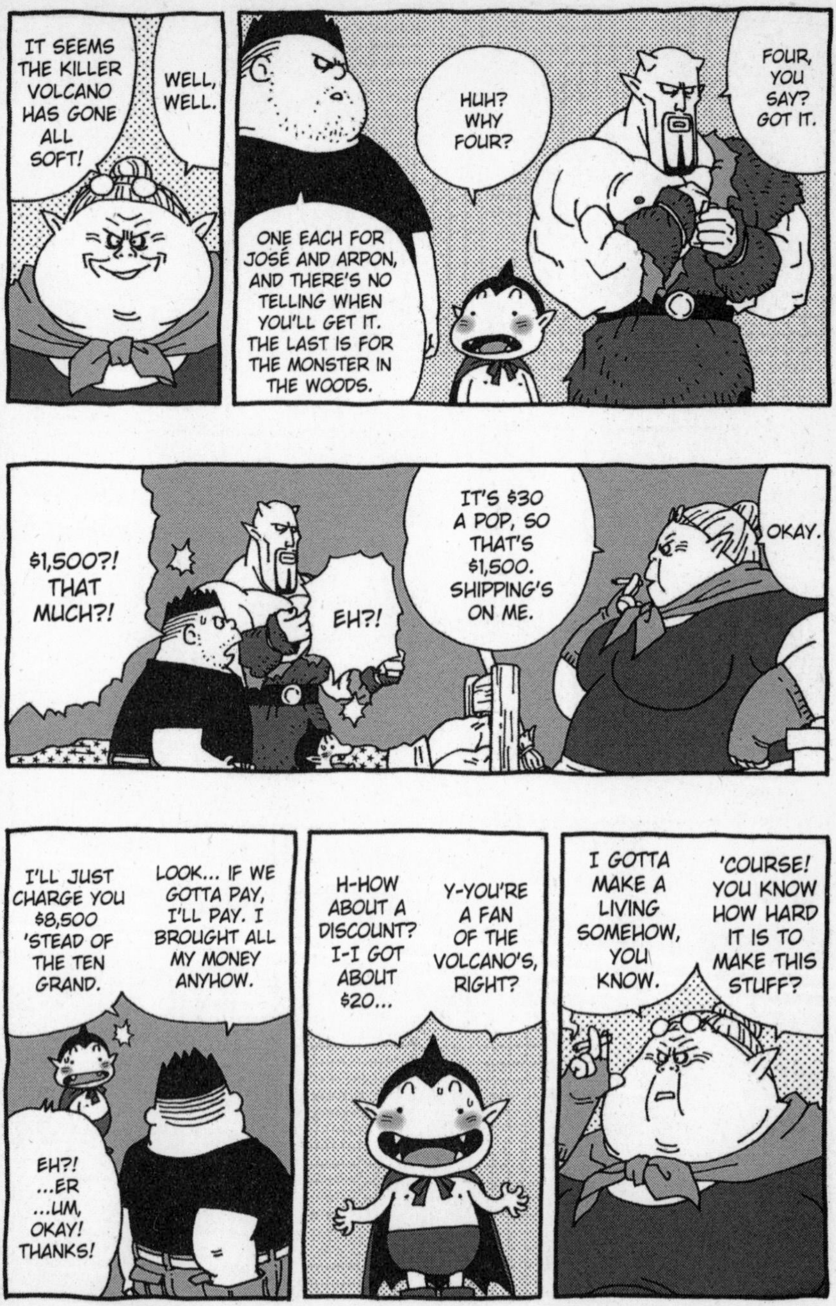
FOUR, YOU SAY? GOT IT.
HUH? WHY FOUR?
ONE EACH FOR JOSÉ AND ARPON, AND THERE'S NO TELLING WHEN YOU'LL GET IT. THE LAST IS FOR THE MONSTER IN THE WOODS.
WELL, WELL.
IT SEEMS THE KILLER VOLCANO HAS GONE ALL SOFT!
OKAY.
IT'S $30 A POP, SO THAT'S $1,500. SHIPPING'S ON ME.
EH?!
$1,500?! THAT MUCH?!
'COURSE! YOU KNOW HOW HARD IT IS TO MAKE THIS STUFF?
I GOTTA MAKE A LIVING SOMEHOW, YOU KNOW.
Y-YOU'RE A FAN OF THE VOLCANO'S, RIGHT?
H-HOW ABOUT A DISCOUNT? I-I GOT ABOUT $20...
LOOK... IF WE GOTTA PAY, I'LL PAY. I BROUGHT ALL MY MONEY ANYHOW.
I'LL JUST CHARGE YOU $8,500 'STEAD OF THE TEN GRAND.
EH?! ...ER ...UM, OKAY! THANKS!

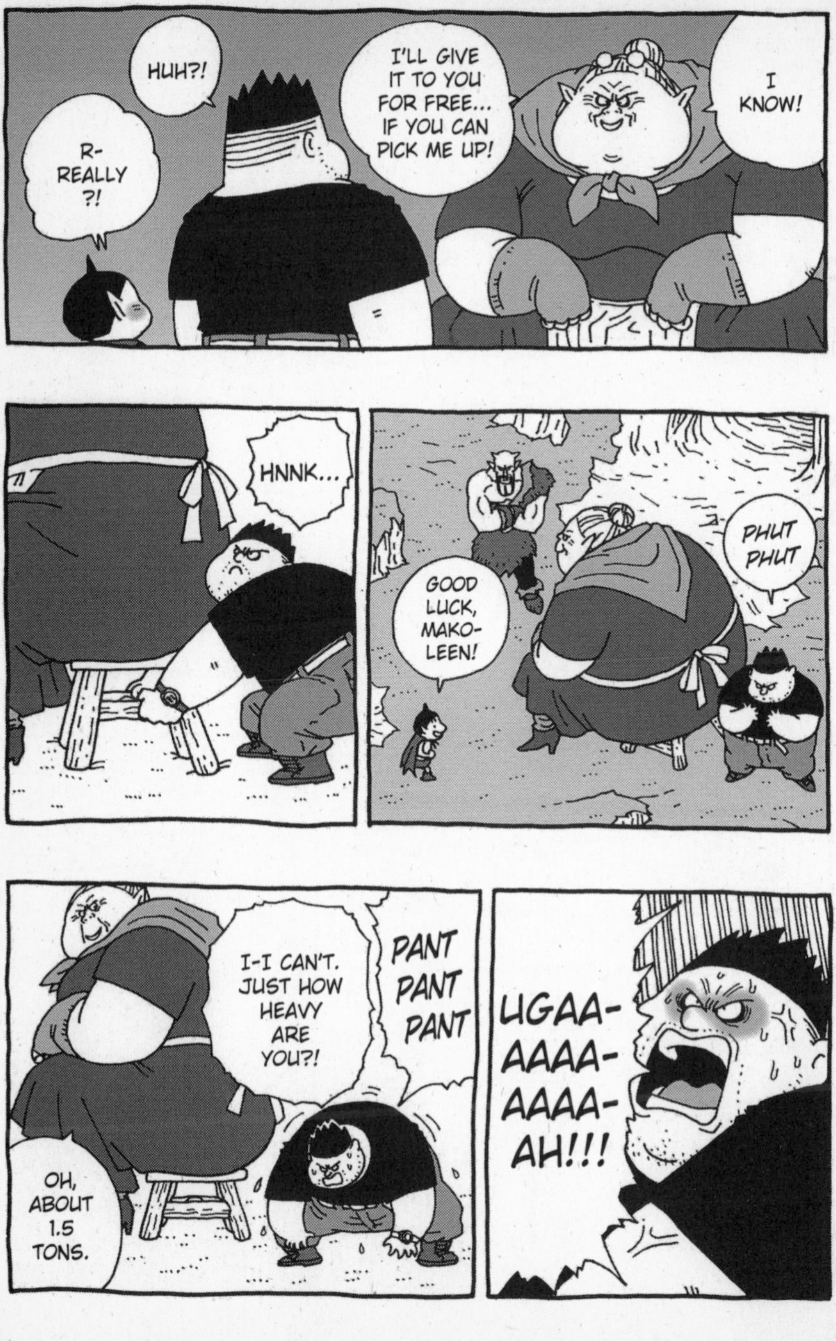
I KNOW!
I'LL GIVE IT TO YOU FOR FREE... IF YOU CAN PICK ME UP!
HUH?!
R-REALLY ?!
PHUT PHUT
GOOD LUCK, MAKO-LEEN!
HNNK...
UGAA-AAAA-AAAA-AH!!!
PANT PANT PANT
I-I CAN'T. JUST HOW HEAVY ARE YOU?!
OH, ABOUT 1.5 TONS.

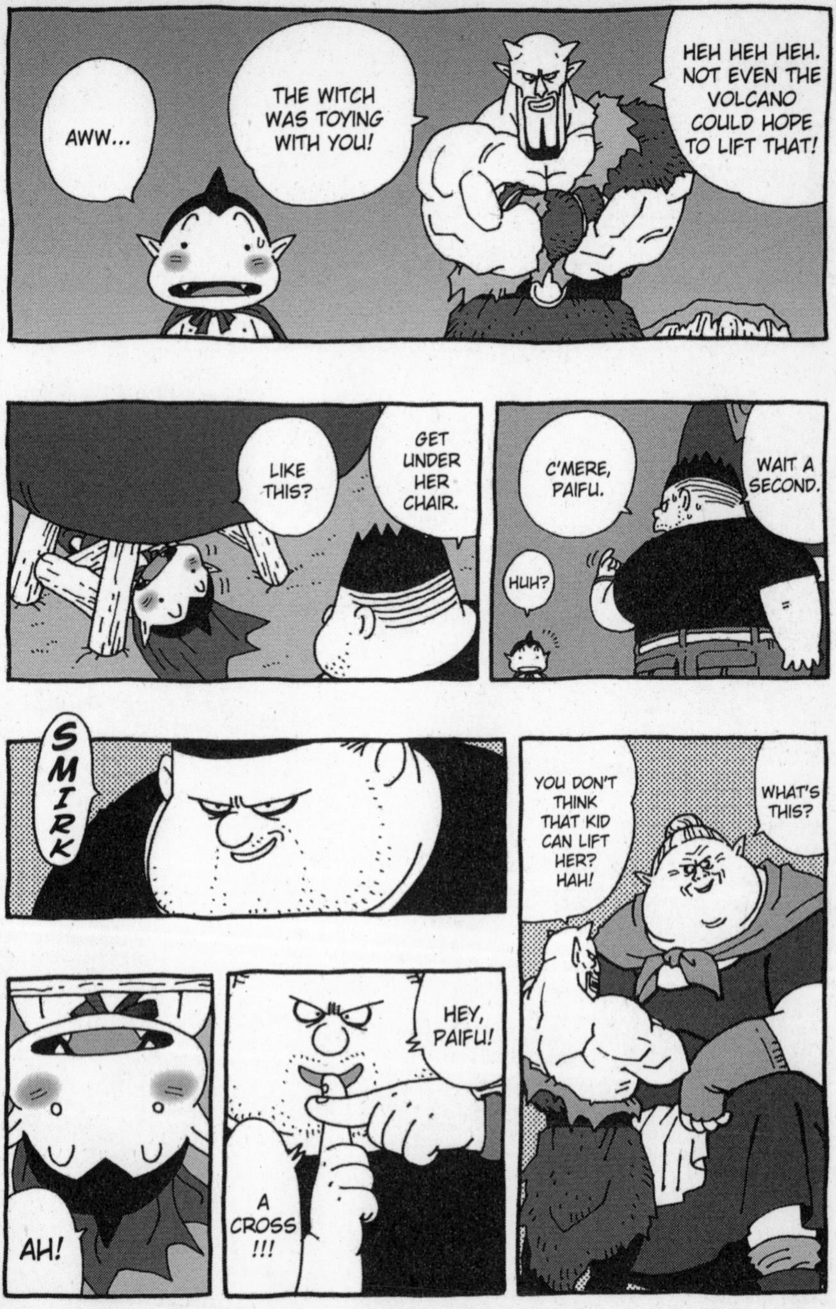
HEH HEH HEH. NOT EVEN THE VOLCANO COULD HOPE TO LIFT THAT!
THE WITCH WAS TOYING WITH YOU!
AWW...
WAIT A SECOND.
C'MERE, PAIFU.
HUH?
GET UNDER HER CHAIR.
LIKE THIS?
WHAT'S THIS?
YOU DON'T THINK THAT KID CAN LIFT HER? HAH!
SMIRK
HEY, PAIFU!
A CROSS!!!
AH!

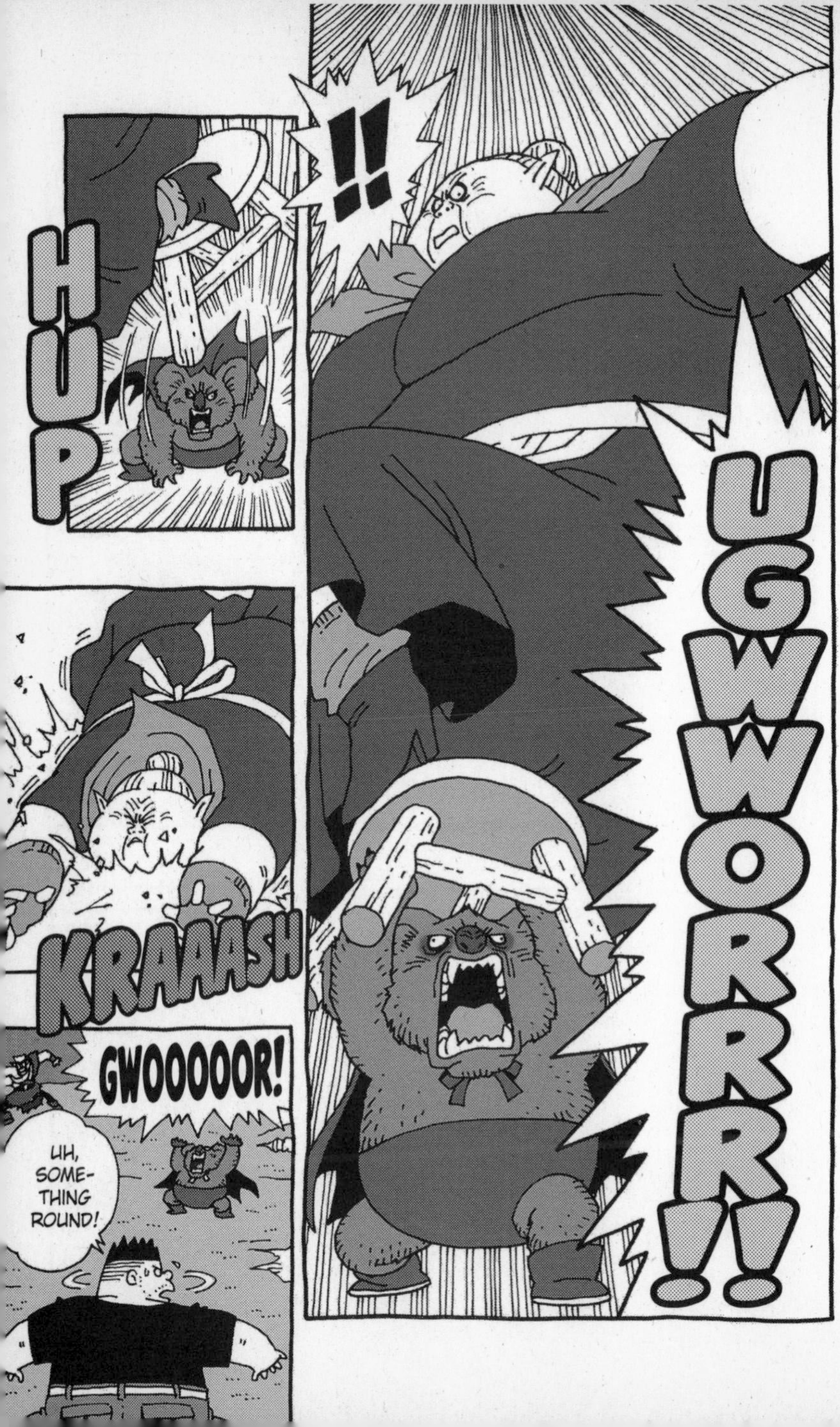
!!
UGWWORRR!!
HUP
KRAAASH
GWOOOOOR!
UH, SOME-THING ROUND!

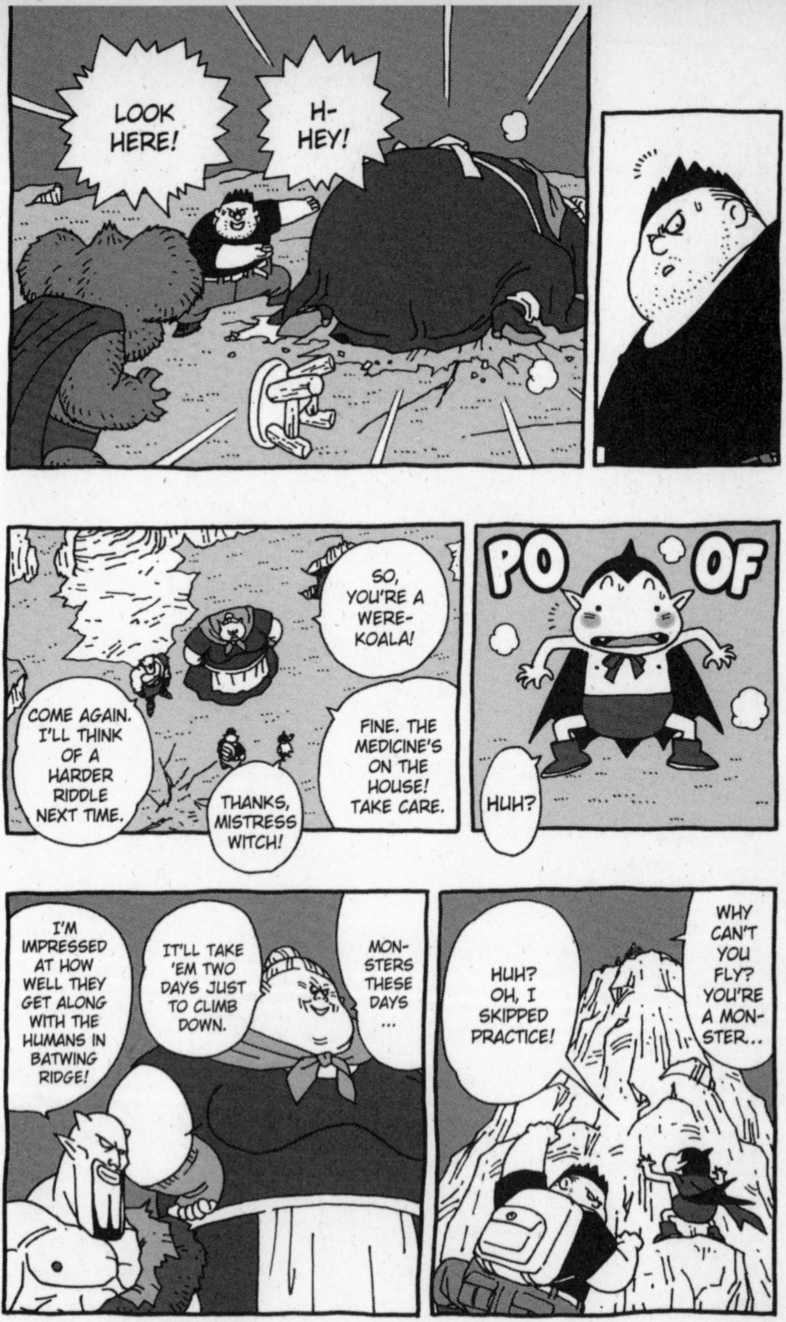
H-HEY!
LOOK HERE!
POOF
HUH?
SO, YOU'RE A WERE-KOALA!
FINE. THE MEDICINE'S ON THE HOUSE! TAKE CARE.
THANKS, MISTRESS WITCH!
COME AGAIN. I'LL THINK OF A HARDER RIDDLE NEXT TIME.
WHY CAN'T YOU FLY? YOU'RE A MONSTER...
HUH? OH, I SKIPPED PRACTICE!
MONSTERS THESE DAYS...
IT'LL TAKE 'EM TWO DAYS JUST TO CLIMB DOWN.
I'M IMPRESSED AT HOW WELL THEY GET ALONG WITH THE HUMANS IN BATWING RIDGE!

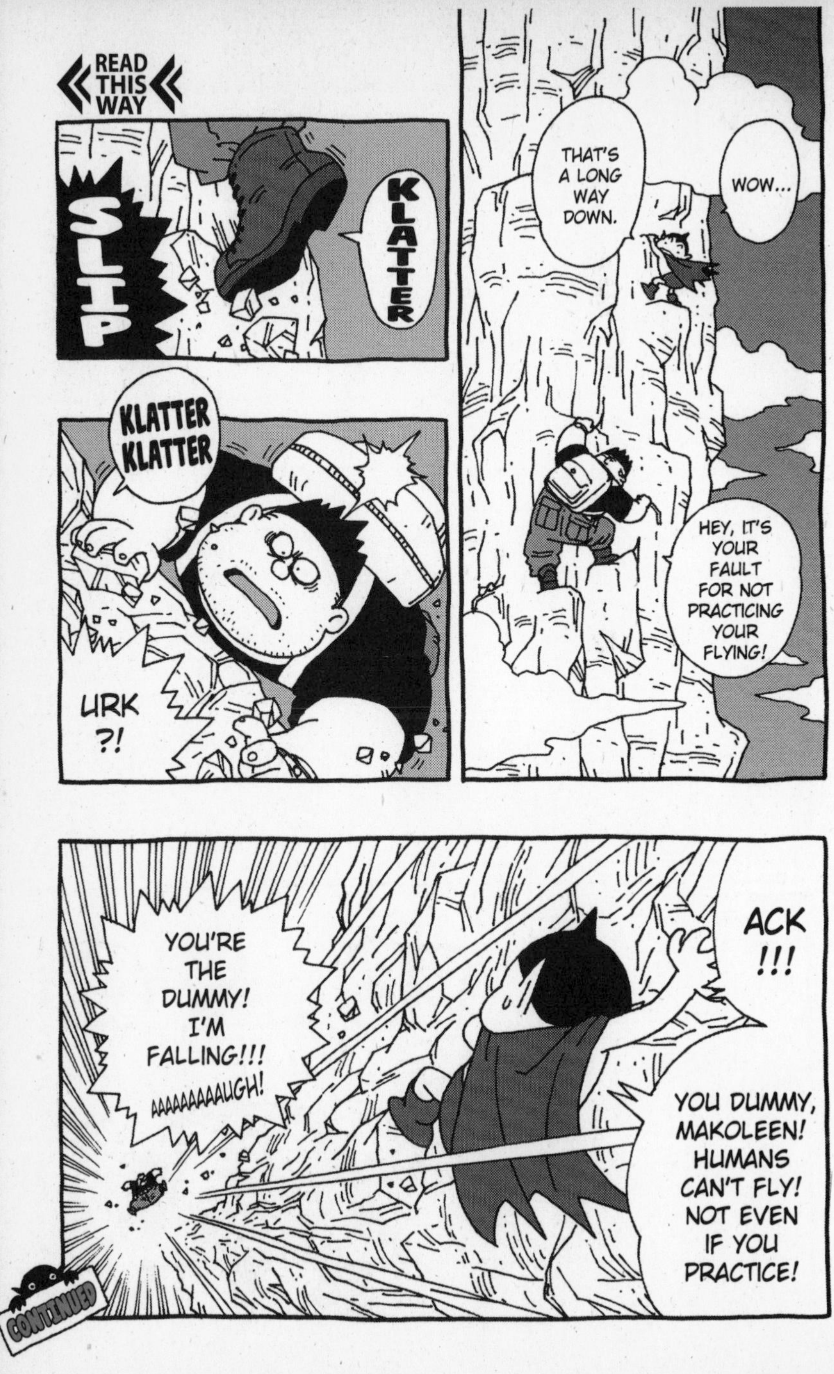
READ THIS WAY
WOW...
THAT'S A LONG WAY DOWN.
HEY, IT'S YOUR FAULT FOR NOT PRACTICING YOUR FLYING!
SLIP
KLATTER
KLATTER KLATTER
URK ?!
ACK !!!
YOU DUMMY, MAKOLEEN! HUMANS CAN'T FLY! NOT EVEN IF YOU PRACTICE!
YOU'RE THE DUMMY! I'M FALLING!!!
AAAAAAAAAUGH!
CONTINUED

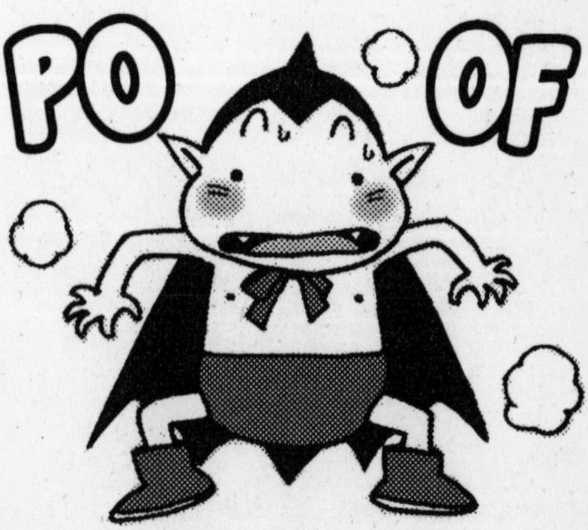
POOF

COWA!

FRIGHT 13

Go, Go, Paifu!

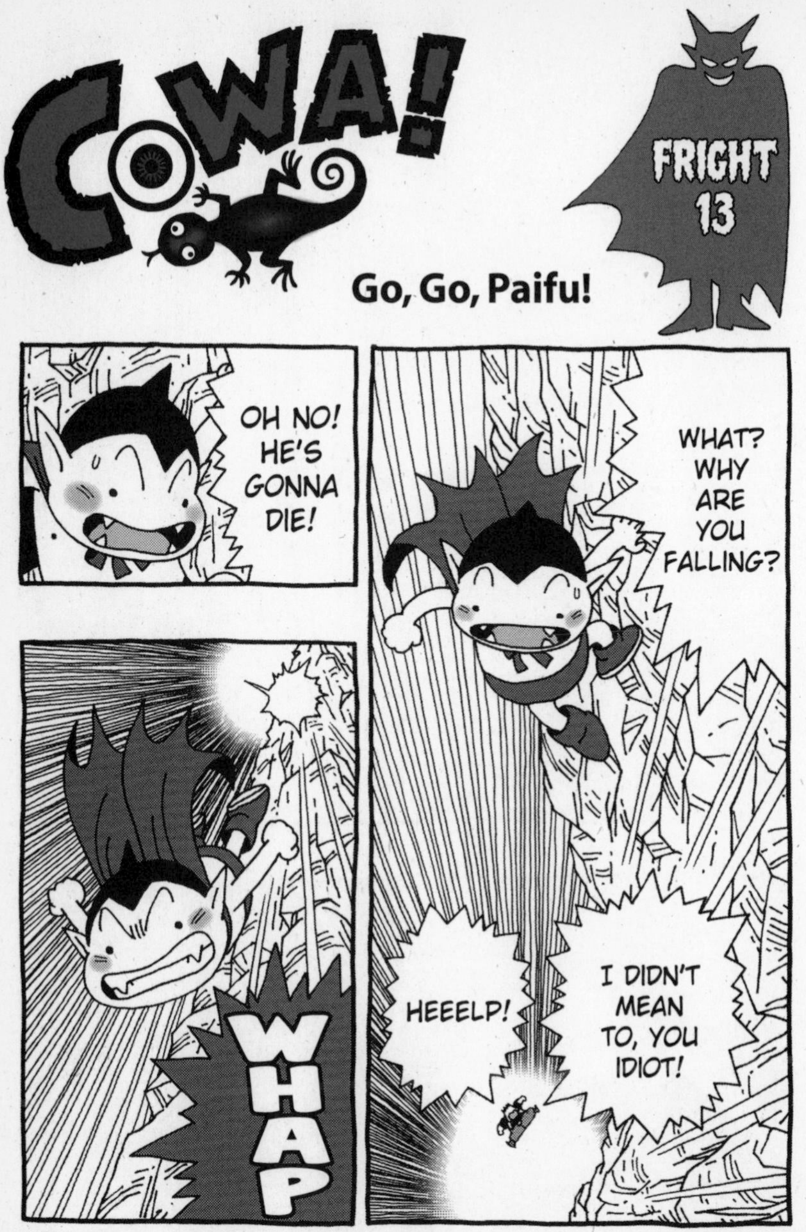

WHAT? WHY ARE YOU FALLING?
I DIDN'T MEAN TO, YOU IDIOT!
HEEELP!
OH NO! HE'S GONNA DIE!
WHAP

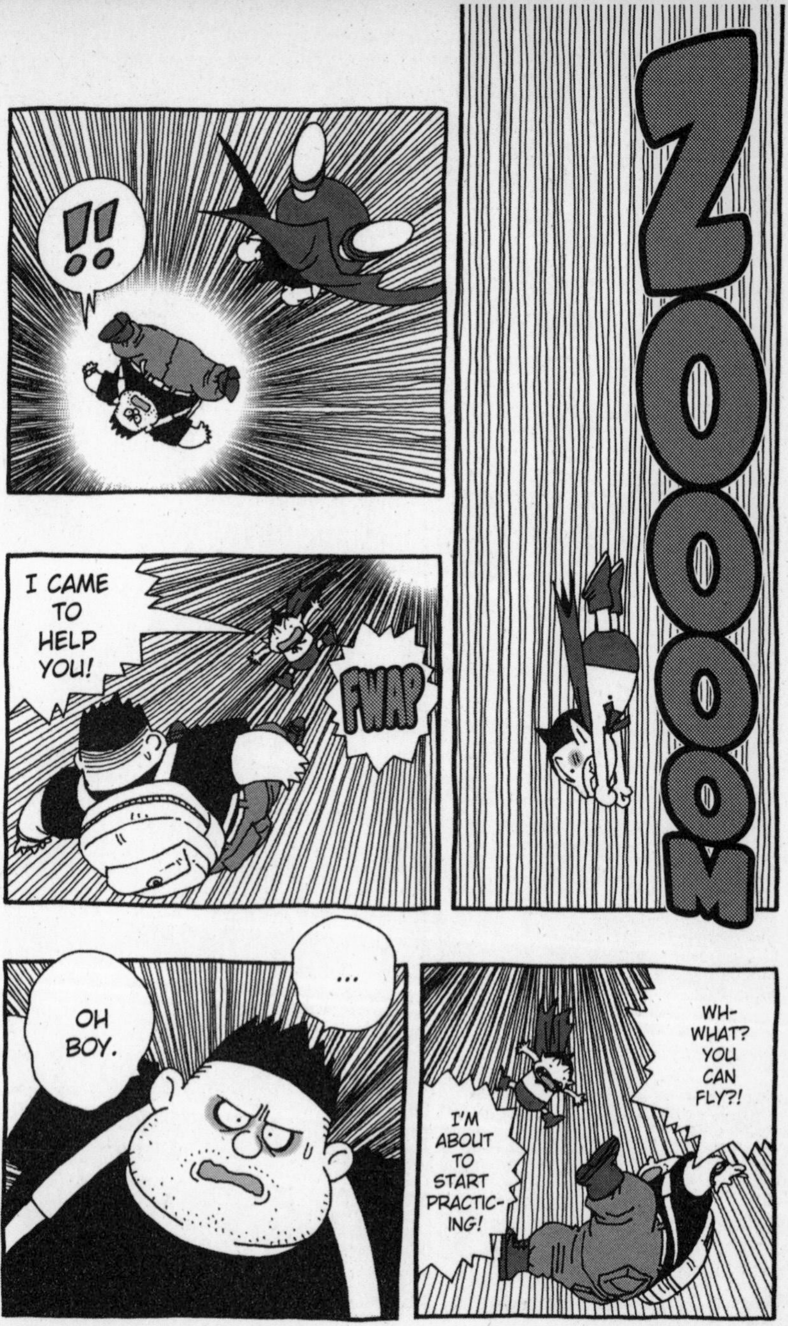
ZOOOOM
!!
I CAME TO HELP YOU!
FWAP
WH-WHAT? YOU CAN FLY?!
I'M ABOUT TO START PRACTIC-ING!
...
OH BOY.

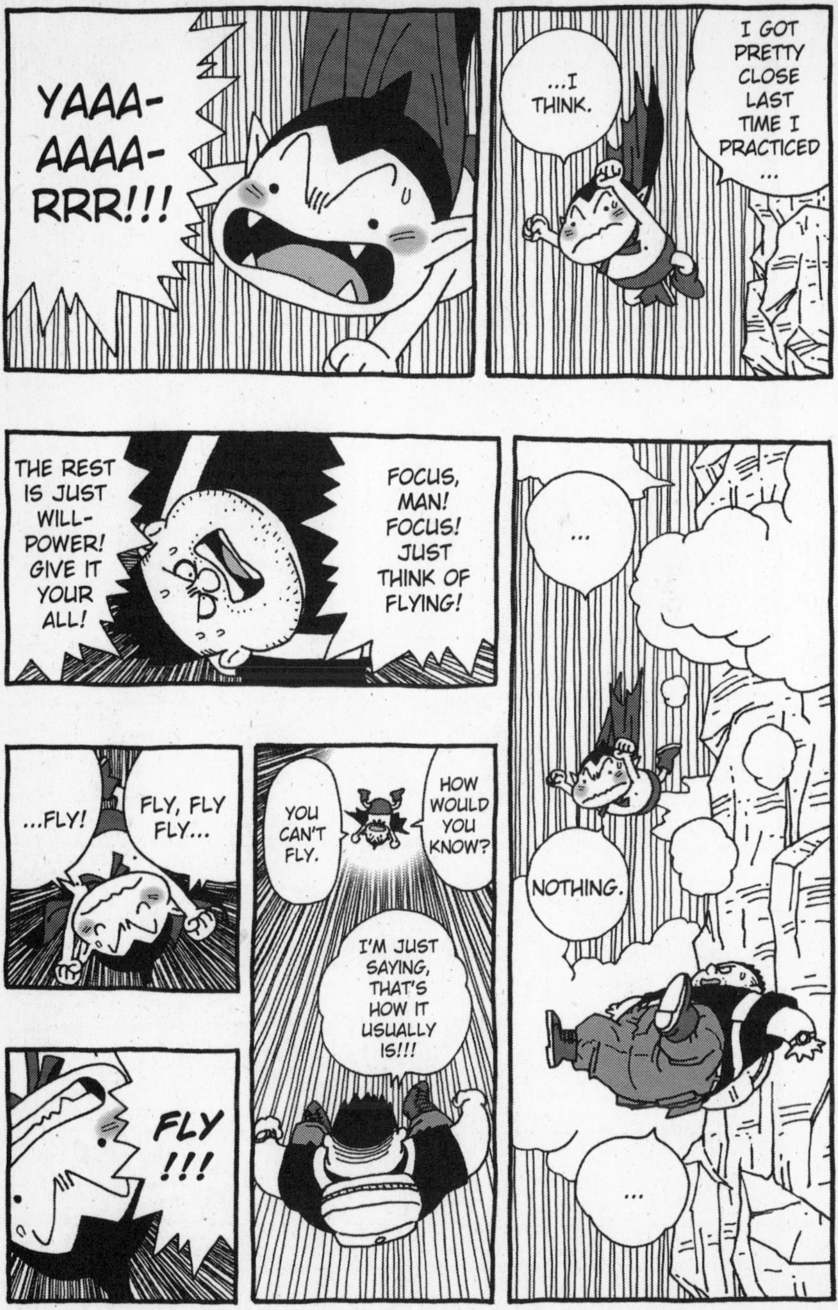
I GOT PRETTY CLOSE LAST TIME I PRACTICED ...
...I THINK.
YAAAA-AAAA-RRR!!!
...
NOTHING.
...
FOCUS, MAN! FOCUS! JUST THINK OF FLYING!
THE REST IS JUST WILL-POWER! GIVE IT YOUR ALL!
HOW WOULD YOU KNOW?
YOU CAN'T FLY.
I'M JUST SAYING, THAT'S HOW IT USUALLY IS!!!
FLY, FLY FLY...
...FLY!
FLY !!!

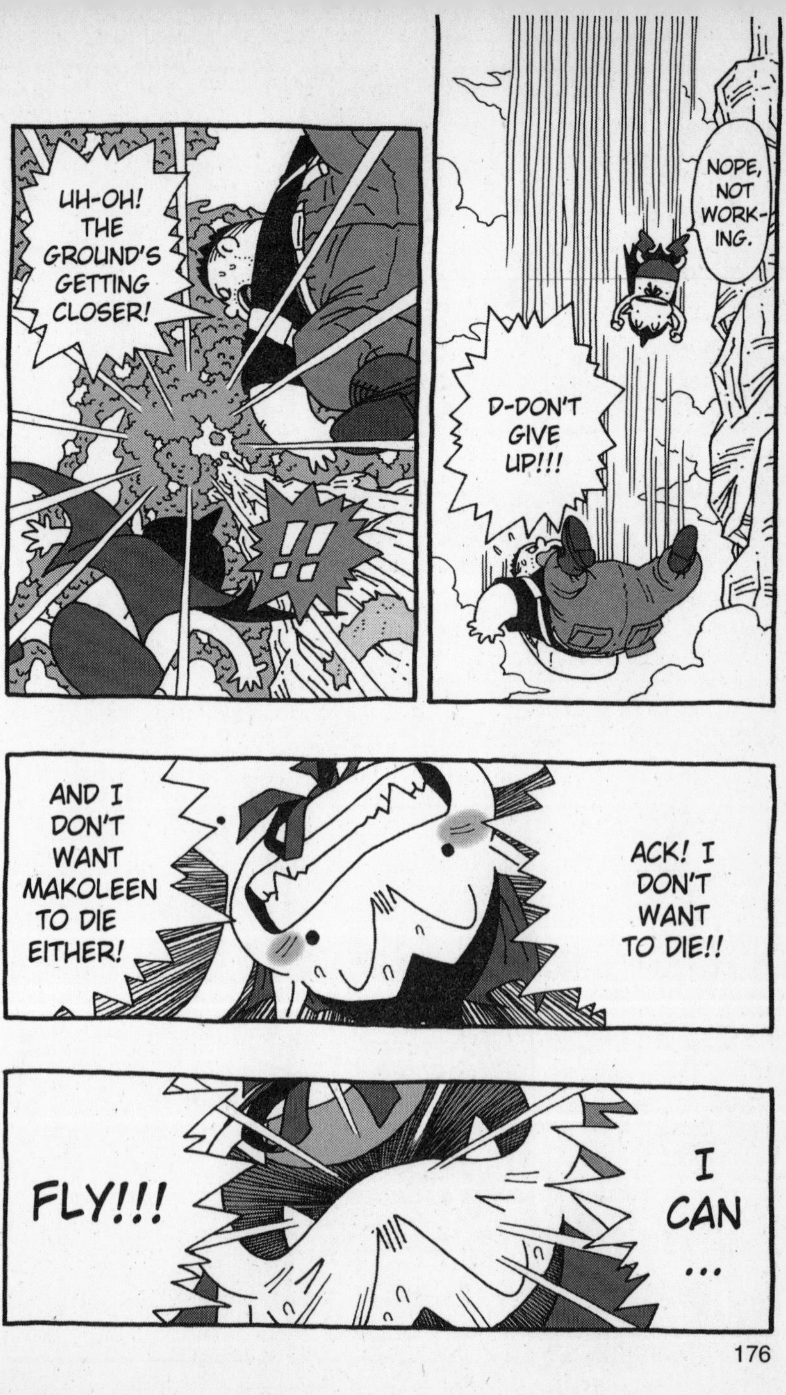
NOPE, NOT WORK-ING.
D-DON'T GIVE UP!!!
UH-OH! THE GROUND'S GETTING CLOSER!
!!
ACK! I DON'T WANT TO DIE!!
AND I DON'T WANT MAKOLEEN TO DIE EITHER!
I CAN ...
FLY!!!

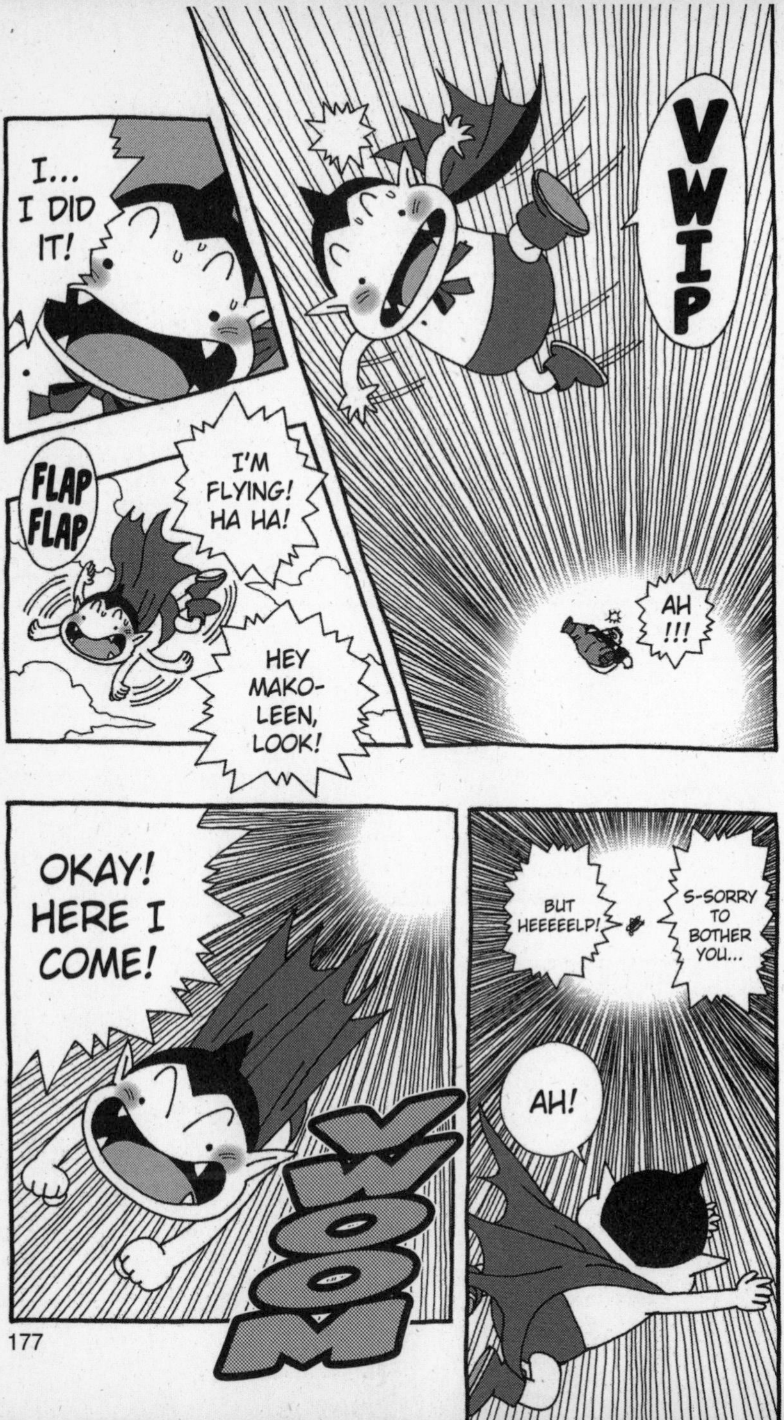

VWIP
AH !!!
I... I DID IT!
FLAP FLAP
I'M FLYING! HA HA!
HEY MAKO-LEEN, LOOK!
S-SORRY TO BOTHER YOU...
BUT HEEEEELP!
AH!
OKAY! HERE I COME!
VWOOM

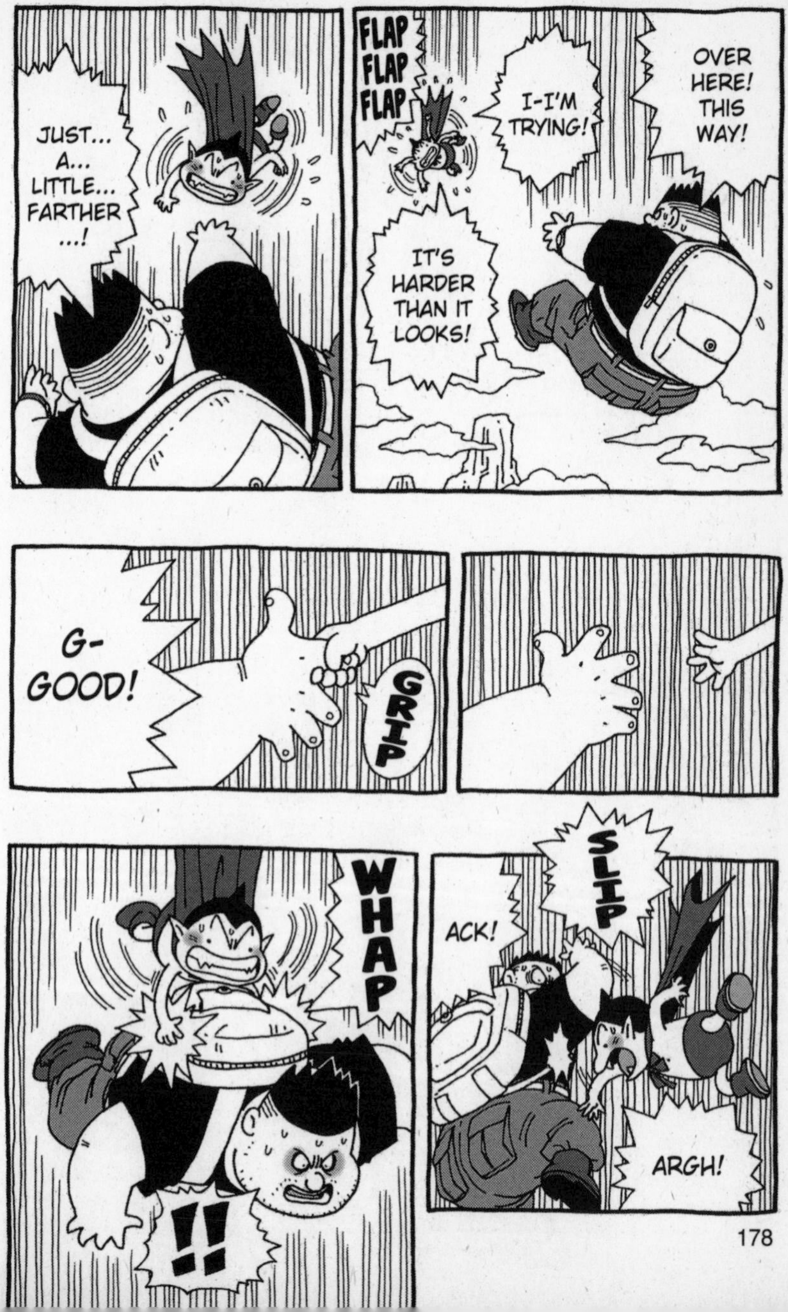
OVER HERE! THIS WAY!
I-I'M TRYING!
FLAP FLAP FLAP
IT'S HARDER THAN IT LOOKS!
JUST... A... LITTLE... FARTHER ...!
GRIP
G- GOOD!
SLIP
ACK!
ARGH!
WHAP
!!

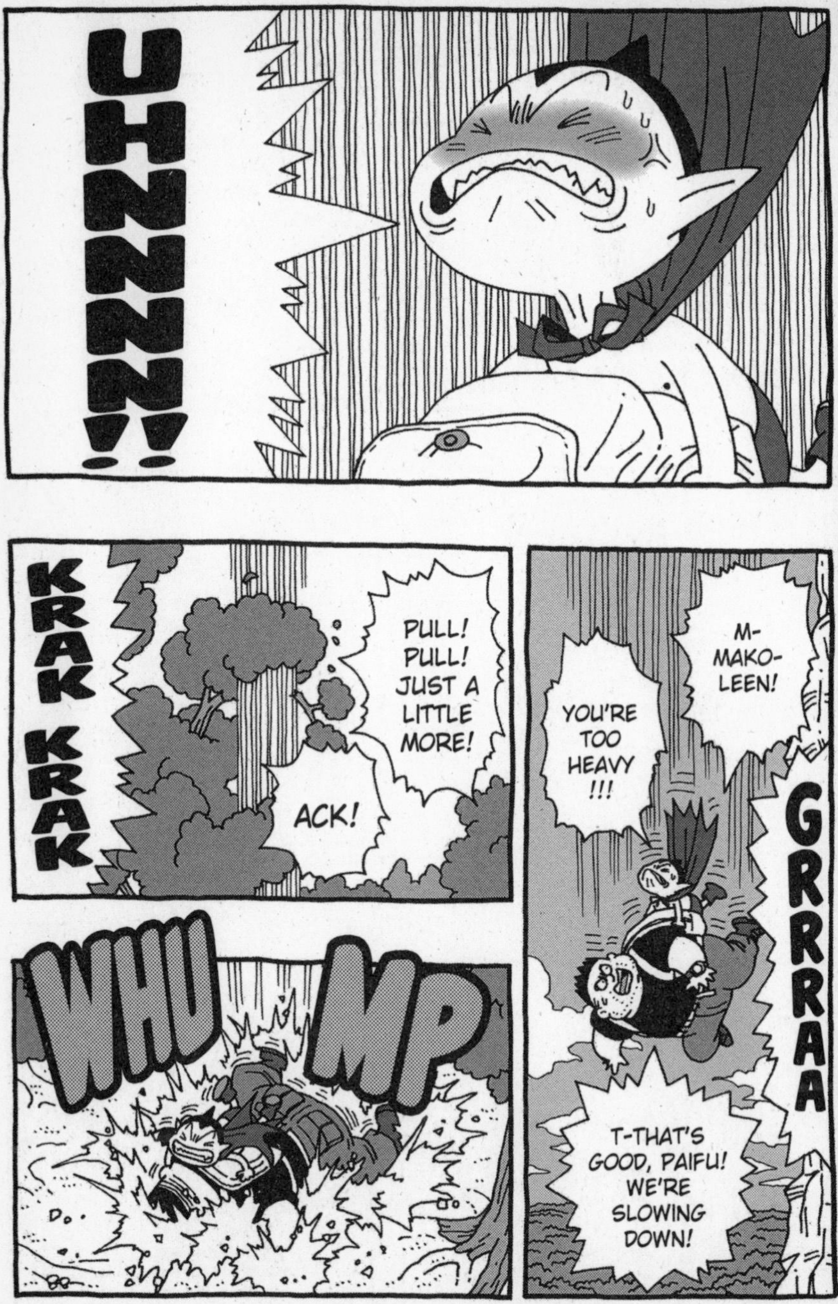
UHNNNN!!
M-MAKO-LEEN!
YOU'RE TOO HEAVY!!!
GRRRAA
T-THAT'S GOOD, PAIFU! WE'RE SLOWING DOWN!
KRAK KRAK
PULL! PULL! JUST A LITTLE MORE!
ACK!
WHUMP

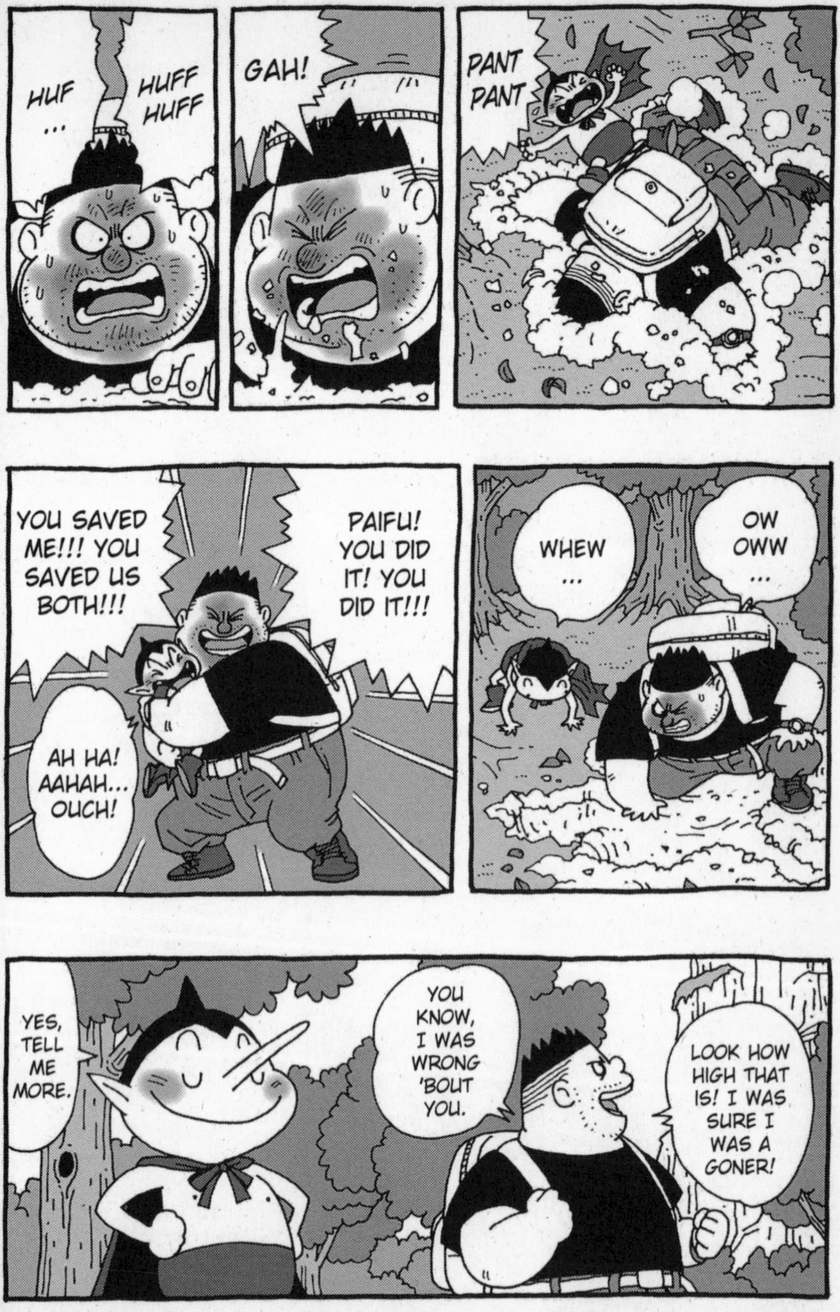
PANT PANT
GAH!
HUFF HUFF
HUF ...
OW OWW ...
WHEW ...
PAIFU! YOU DID IT! YOU DID IT!!!
YOU SAVED ME!!! YOU SAVED US BOTH!!!
AH HA! AAHAH... OUCH!
LOOK HOW HIGH THAT IS! I WAS SURE I WAS A GONER!
YOU KNOW, I WAS WRONG 'BOUT YOU.
YES, TELL ME MORE.

READ THIS WAY

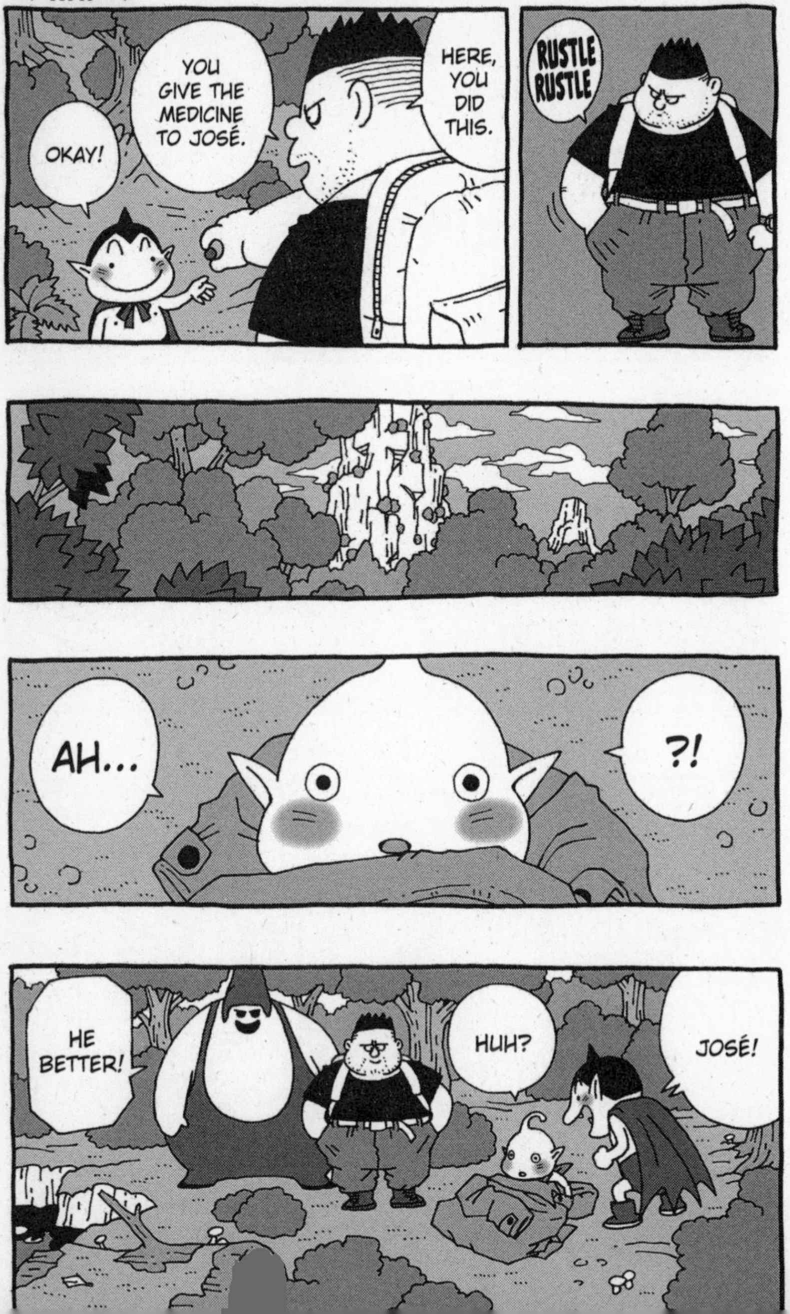
RUSTLE RUSTLE
HERE, YOU DID THIS.
YOU GIVE THE MEDICINE TO JOSÉ.
OKAY!
?!
AH...
JOSÉ!
HUH?
HE BETTER!

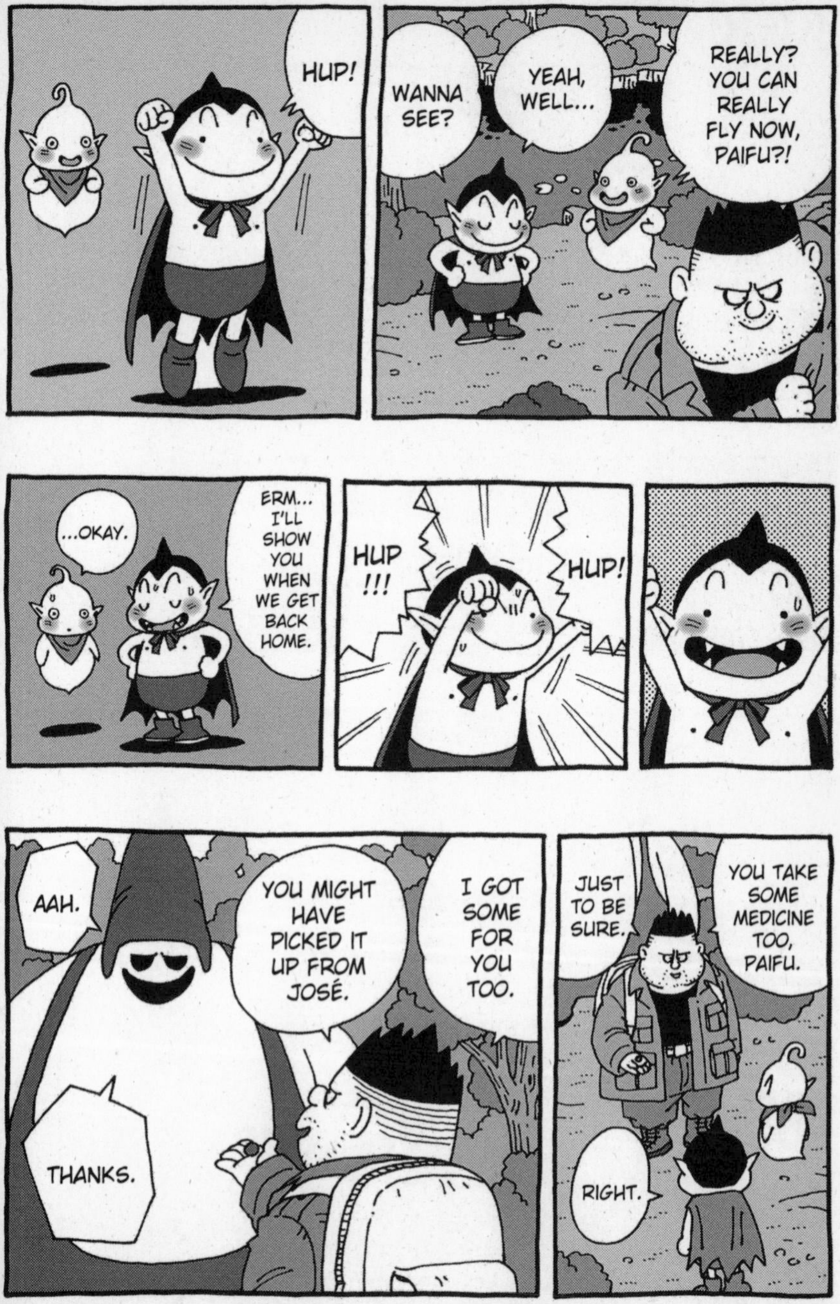
REALLY? YOU CAN REALLY FLY NOW, PAIFU?!
YEAH, WELL...
WANNA SEE?
HUP!
HUP!
HUP !!!
ERM... I'LL SHOW YOU WHEN WE GET BACK HOME.
...OKAY.
YOU TAKE SOME MEDICINE TOO, PAIFU.
JUST TO BE SURE.
RIGHT.
I GOT SOME FOR YOU TOO.
YOU MIGHT HAVE PICKED IT UP FROM JOSÉ.
AAH.
THANKS.

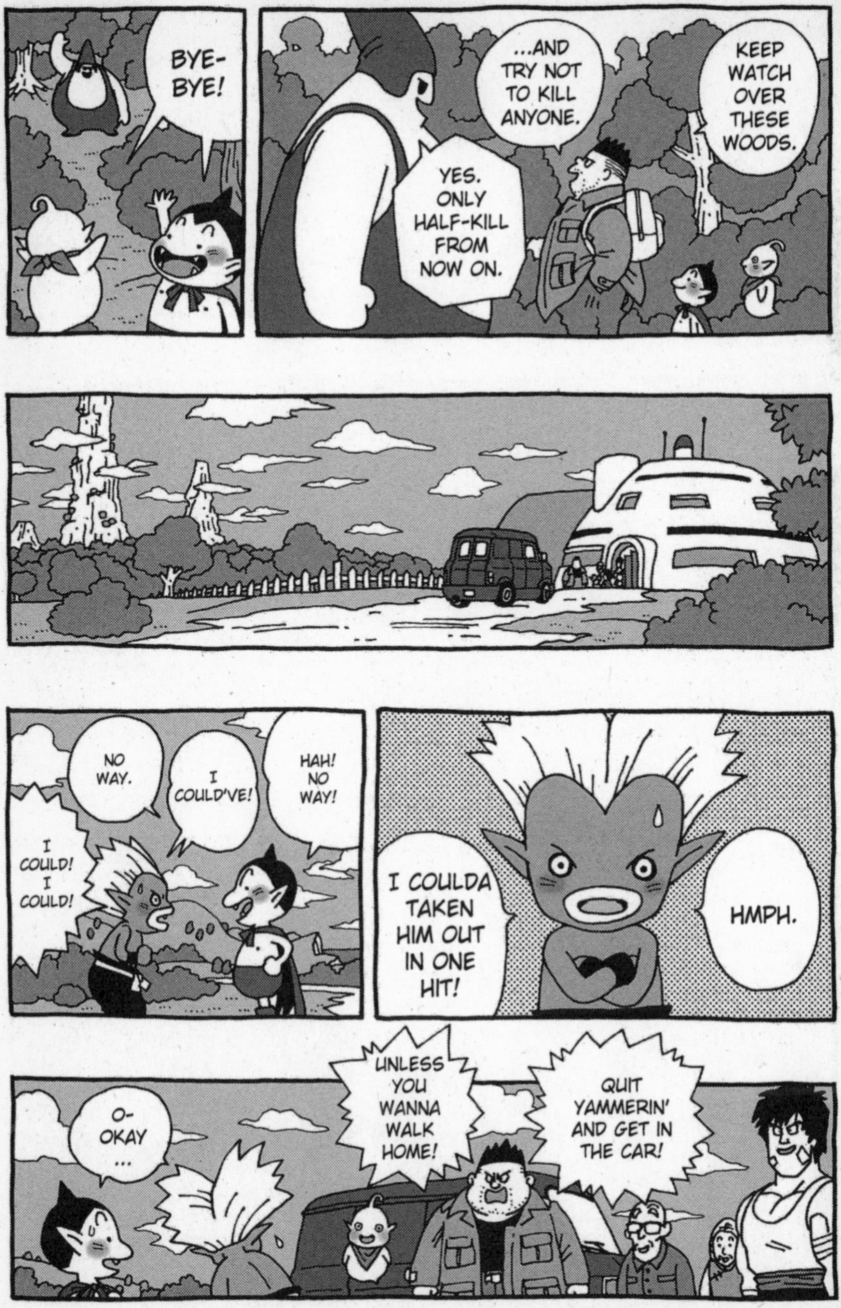
KEEP WATCH OVER THESE WOODS.
...AND TRY NOT TO KILL ANYONE.
YES. ONLY HALF-KILL FROM NOW ON.
BYE-BYE!
HMPH.
I COULDA TAKEN HIM OUT IN ONE HIT!
HAH! NO WAY!
I COULD'VE!
NO WAY.
I COULD! I COULD!
QUIT YAMMERIN' AND GET IN THE CAR!
UNLESS YOU WANNA WALK HOME!
O-OKAY ...

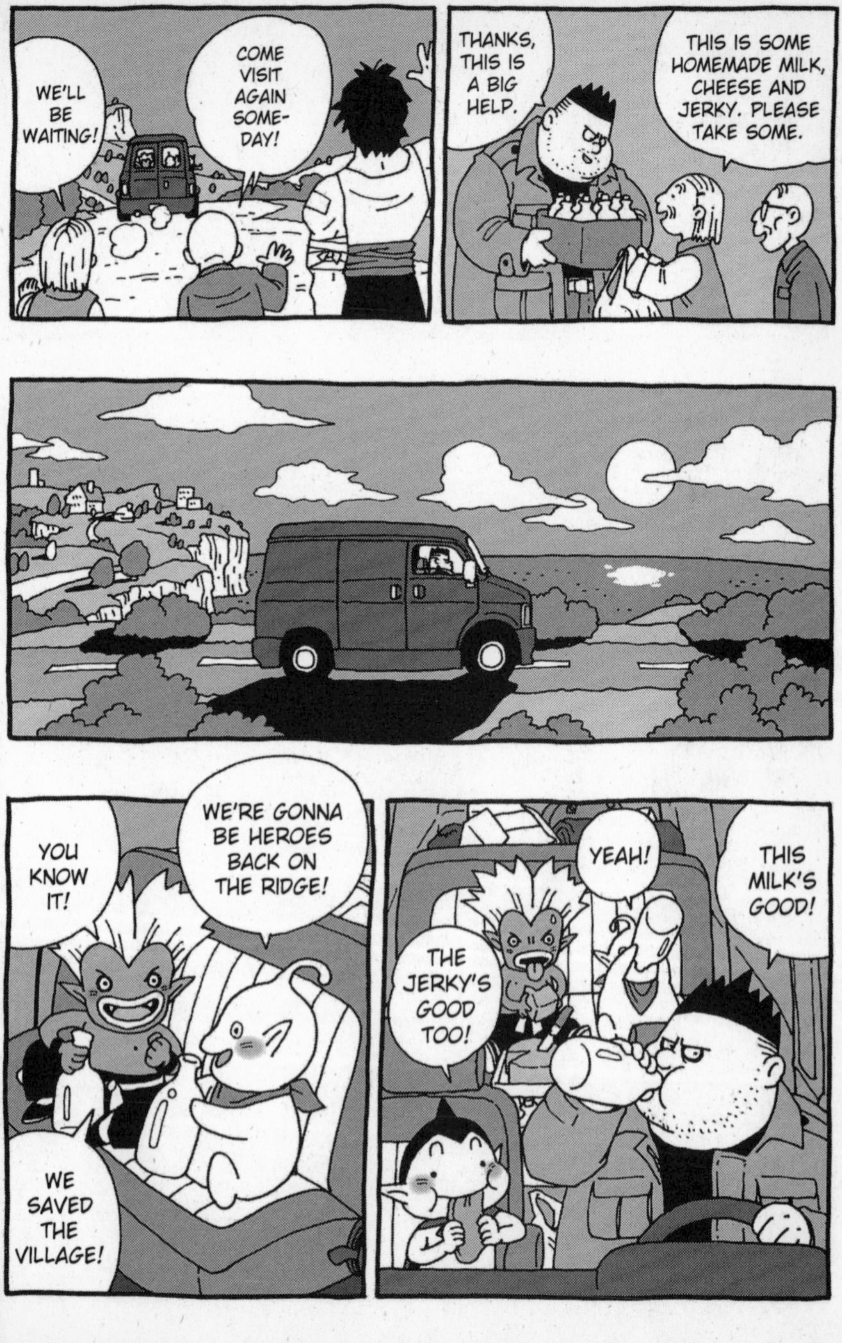
THIS IS SOME HOMEMADE MILK, CHEESE AND JERKY. PLEASE TAKE SOME.
THANKS, THIS IS A BIG HELP.
COME VISIT AGAIN SOME-DAY!
WE'LL BE WAITING!
THIS MILK'S GOOD!
YEAH!
THE JERKY'S GOOD TOO!
WE'RE GONNA BE HEROES BACK ON THE RIDGE!
YOU KNOW IT!
WE SAVED THE VILLAGE!

READ THIS WAY

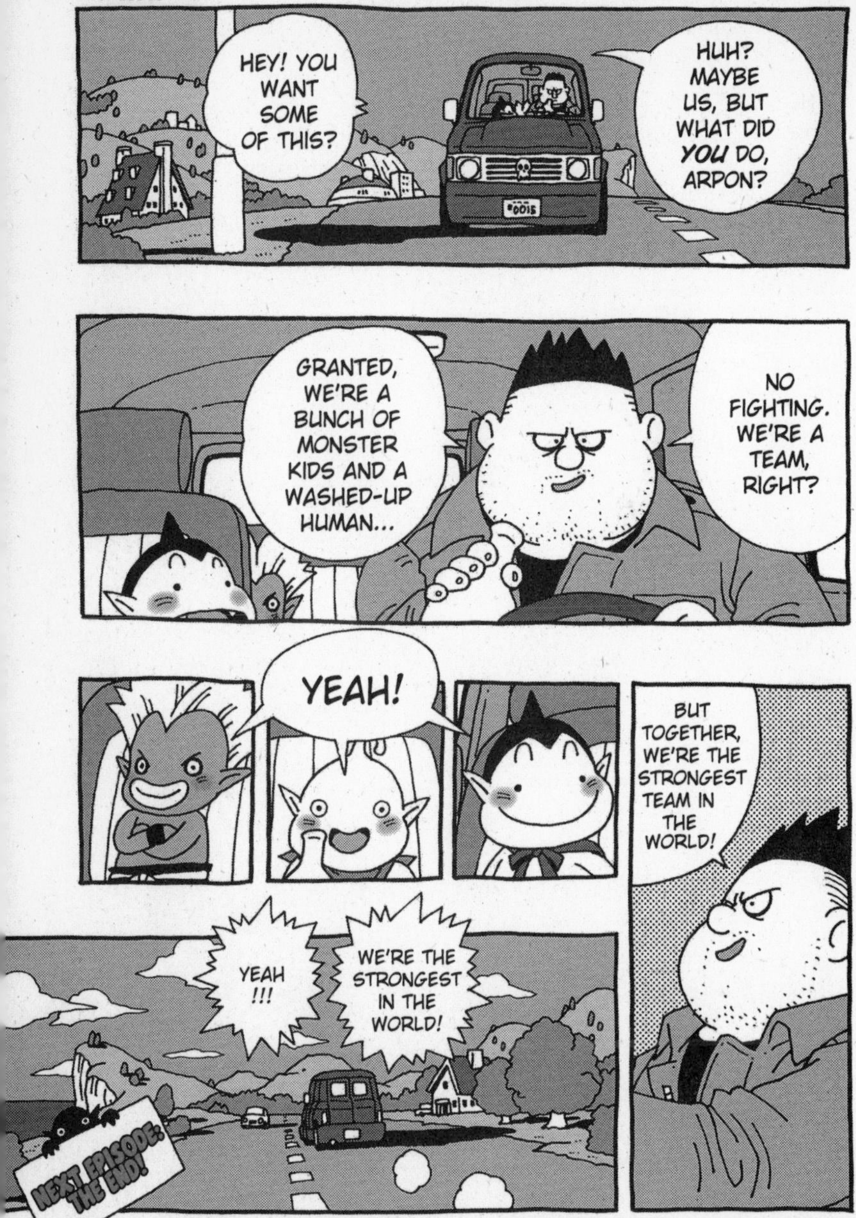
HUH? MAYBE US, BUT WHAT DID *YOU* DO, ARPON?
HEY! YOU WANT SOME OF THIS?
NO FIGHTING. WE'RE A TEAM, RIGHT?
GRANTED, WE'RE A BUNCH OF MONSTER KIDS AND A WASHED-UP HUMAN...
BUT TOGETHER, WE'RE THE STRONGEST TEAM IN THE WORLD!
YEAH!
WE'RE THE STRONGEST IN THE WORLD!
YEAH !!!
NEXT EPISODE: THE END!

COWA!

FRIGHT 14

Makoleen's Boat

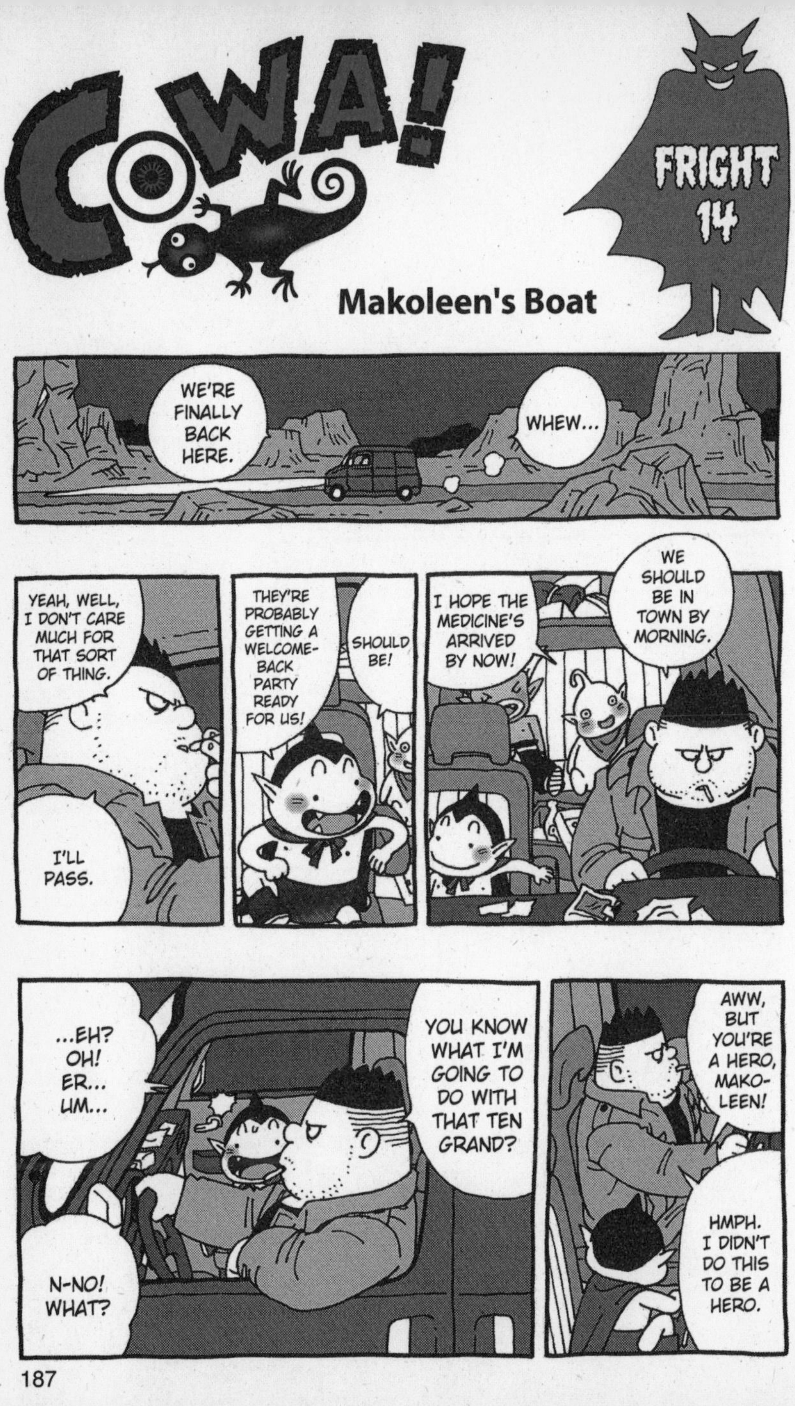

WHEW...
WE'RE FINALLY BACK HERE.
WE SHOULD BE IN TOWN BY MORNING.
I HOPE THE MEDICINE'S ARRIVED BY NOW!
SHOULD BE!
THEY'RE PROBABLY GETTING A WELCOME-BACK PARTY READY FOR US!
YEAH, WELL, I DON'T CARE MUCH FOR THAT SORT OF THING.
I'LL PASS.
AWW, BUT YOU'RE A HERO, MAKO-LEEN!
HMPH. I DIDN'T DO THIS TO BE A HERO.
YOU KNOW WHAT I'M GOING TO DO WITH THAT TEN GRAND?
...EH? OH! ER... UM...
N-NO! WHAT?

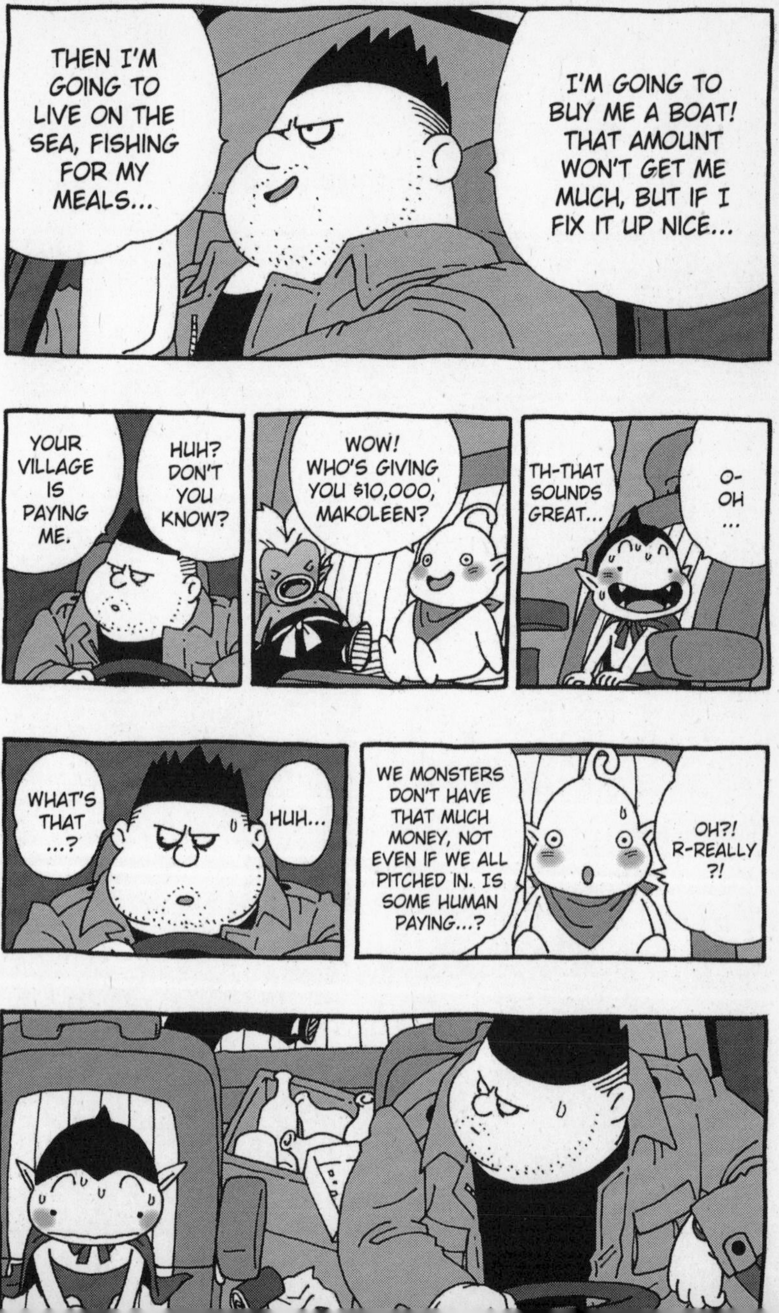
I'M GOING TO BUY ME A BOAT! THAT AMOUNT WON'T GET ME MUCH, BUT IF I FIX IT UP NICE...
THEN I'M GOING TO LIVE ON THE SEA, FISHING FOR MY MEALS...
O-OH ...
TH-THAT SOUNDS GREAT...
WOW! WHO'S GIVING YOU $10,000, MAKOLEEN?
HUH? DON'T YOU KNOW?
YOUR VILLAGE IS PAYING ME.
OH?! R-REALLY ?!
WE MONSTERS DON'T HAVE THAT MUCH MONEY, NOT EVEN IF WE ALL PITCHED IN. IS SOME HUMAN PAYING...?
HUH...
WHAT'S THAT ...?

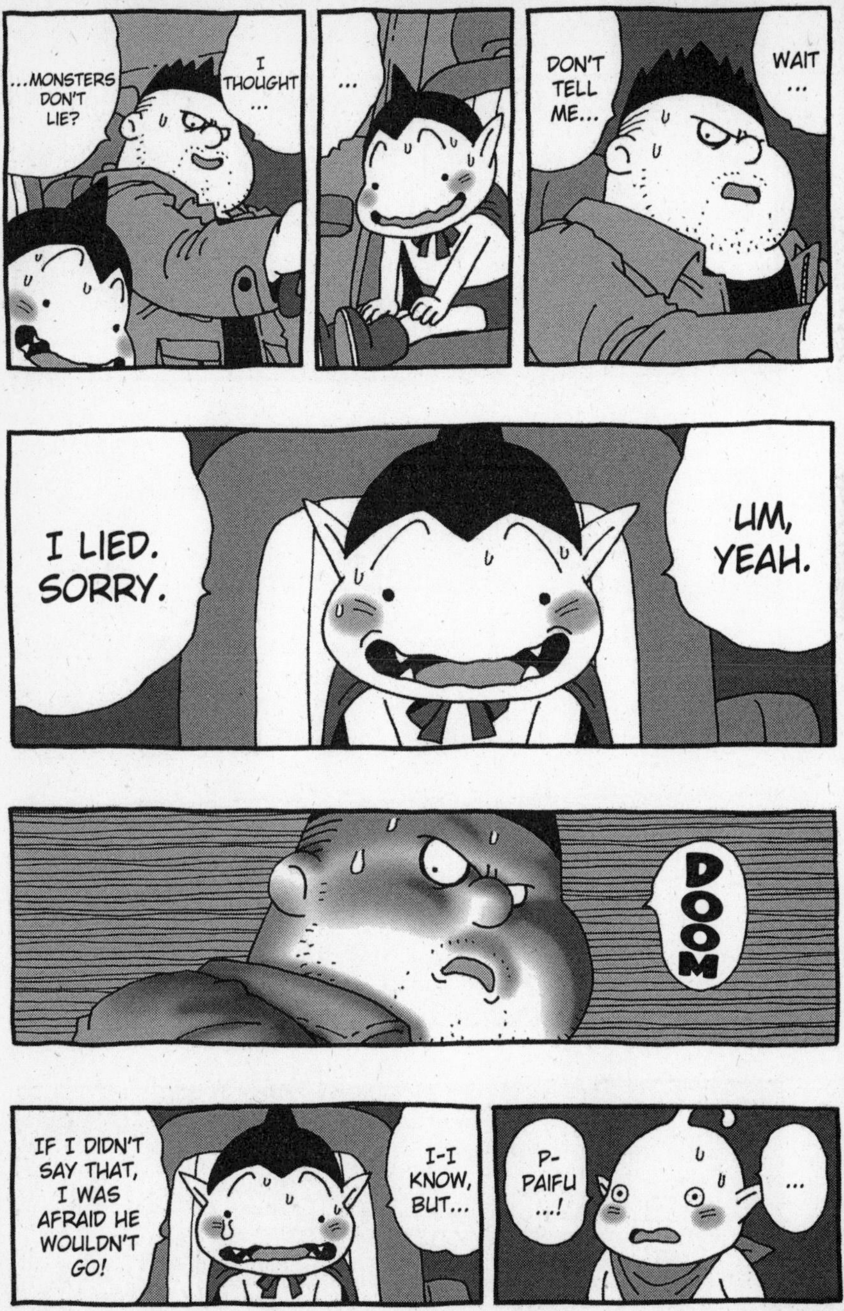
WAIT ...
DON'T TELL ME...
...
I THOUGHT ...
...MONSTERS DON'T LIE?
UM, YEAH.
I LIED. SORRY.
DOOM
...
P-PAIFU ...!
I-I KNOW, BUT...
IF I DIDN'T SAY THAT, I WAS AFRAID HE WOULDN'T GO!

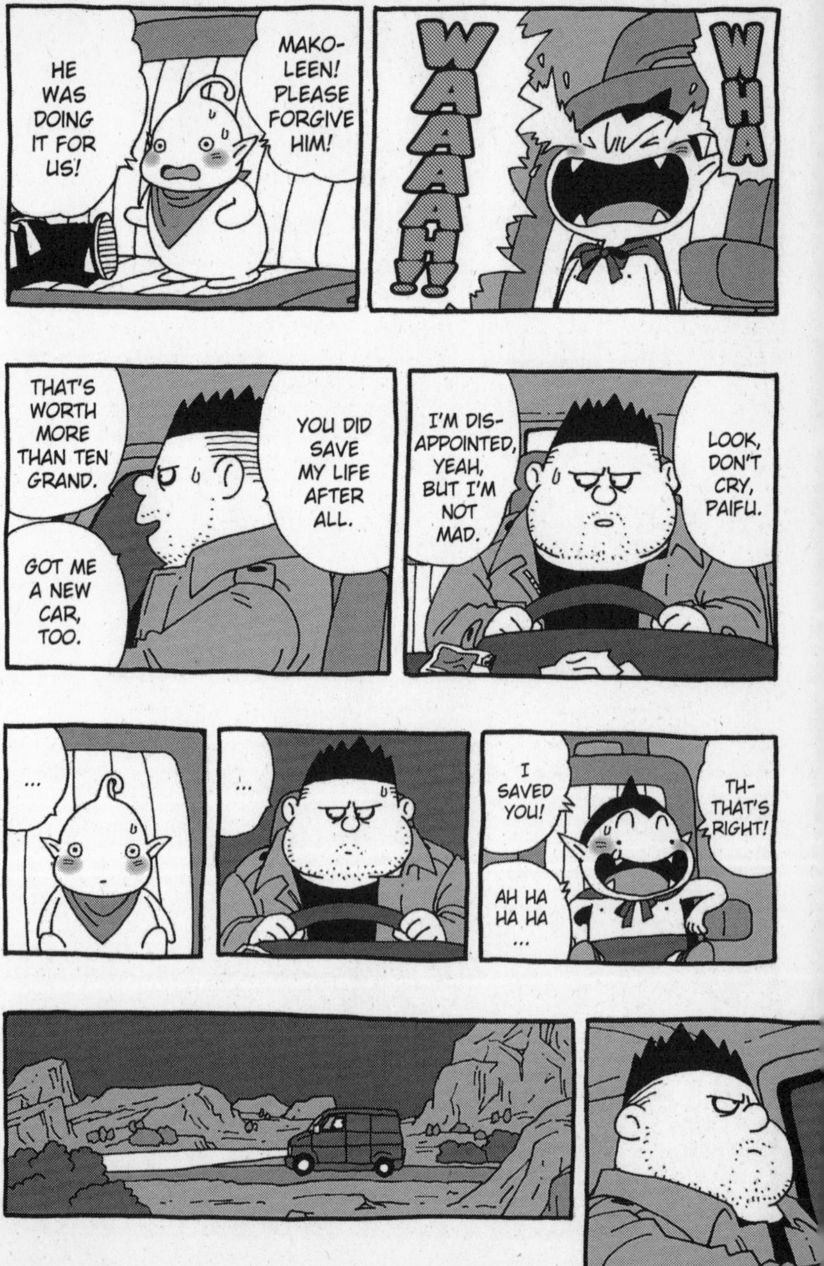
WHA
WAAAAH
MAKO-LEEN! PLEASE FORGIVE HIM!
HE WAS DOING IT FOR US!
LOOK, DON'T CRY, PAIFU.
I'M DIS-APPOINTED, YEAH, BUT I'M NOT MAD.
YOU DID SAVE MY LIFE AFTER ALL.
THAT'S WORTH MORE THAN TEN GRAND.
GOT ME A NEW CAR, TOO.
TH- THAT'S RIGHT!
I SAVED YOU!
AH HA HA HA ...
...
...

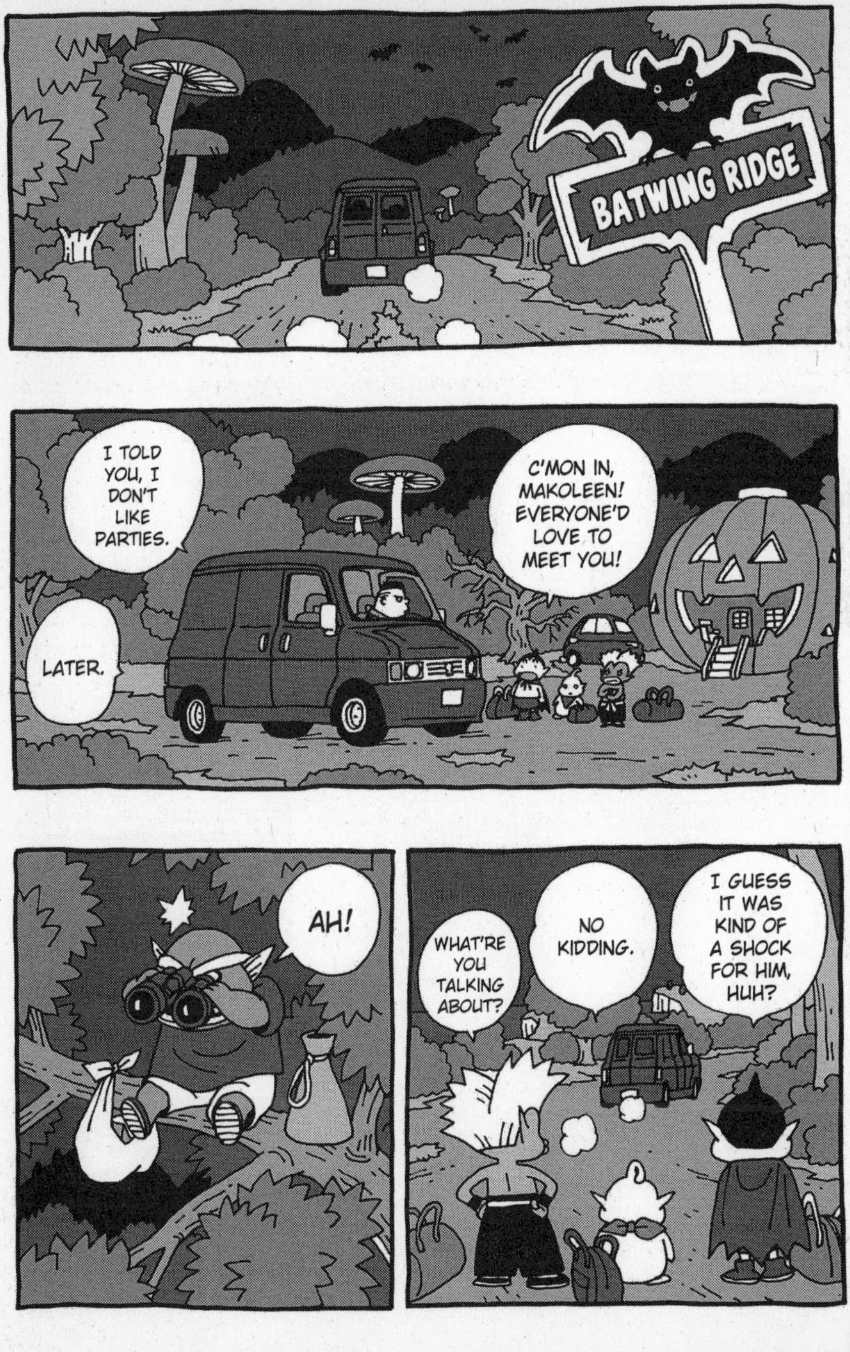
BATWING RIDGE
C'MON IN, MAKOLEEN! EVERYONE'D LOVE TO MEET YOU!
I TOLD YOU, I DON'T LIKE PARTIES.
LATER.
I GUESS IT WAS KIND OF A SHOCK FOR HIM, HUH?
NO KIDDING.
WHAT'RE YOU TALKING ABOUT?
AH!

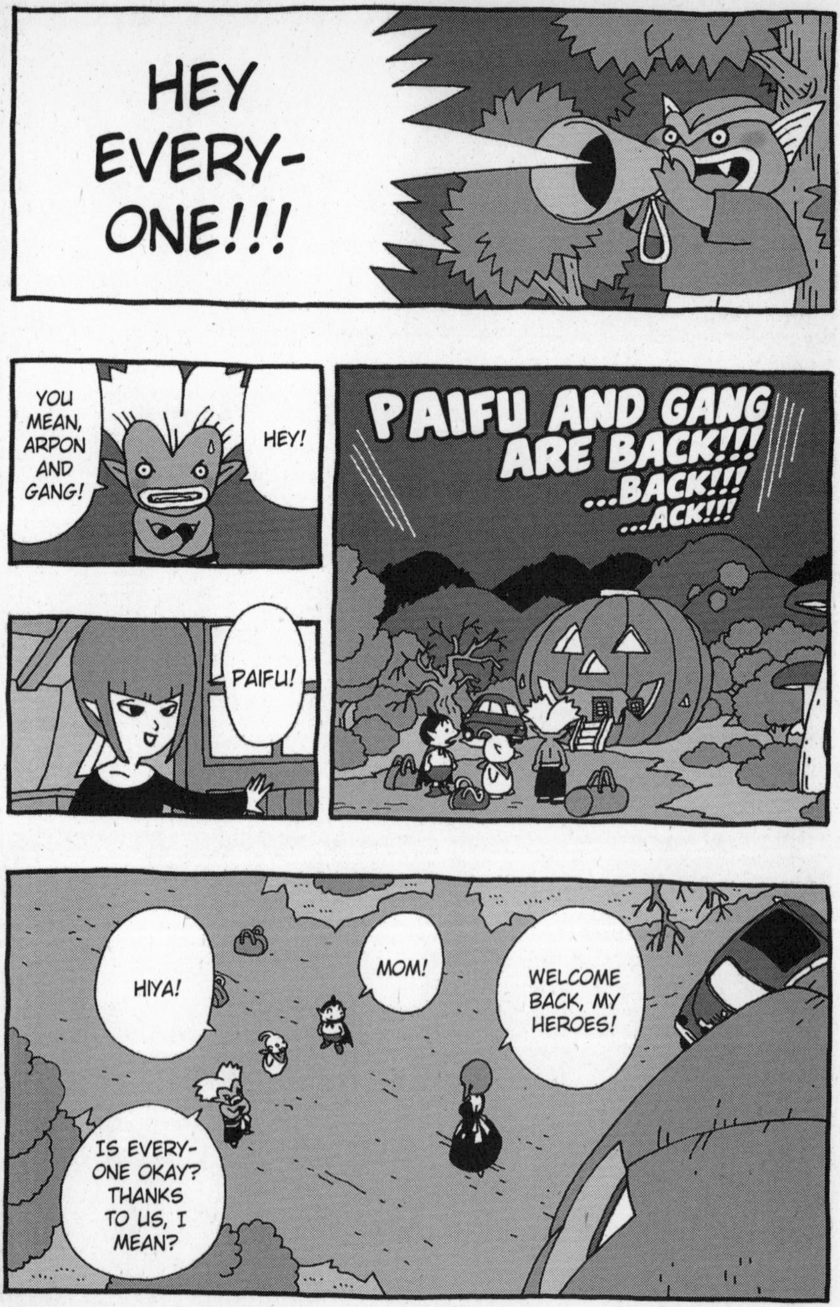
HEY EVERY-ONE!!!
PAIFU AND GANG ARE BACK!!! ...BACK!!! ...ACK!!!
HEY!
YOU MEAN, ARPON AND GANG!
PAIFU!
WELCOME BACK, MY HEROES!
MOM!
HIYA!
IS EVERY-ONE OKAY? THANKS TO US, I MEAN?

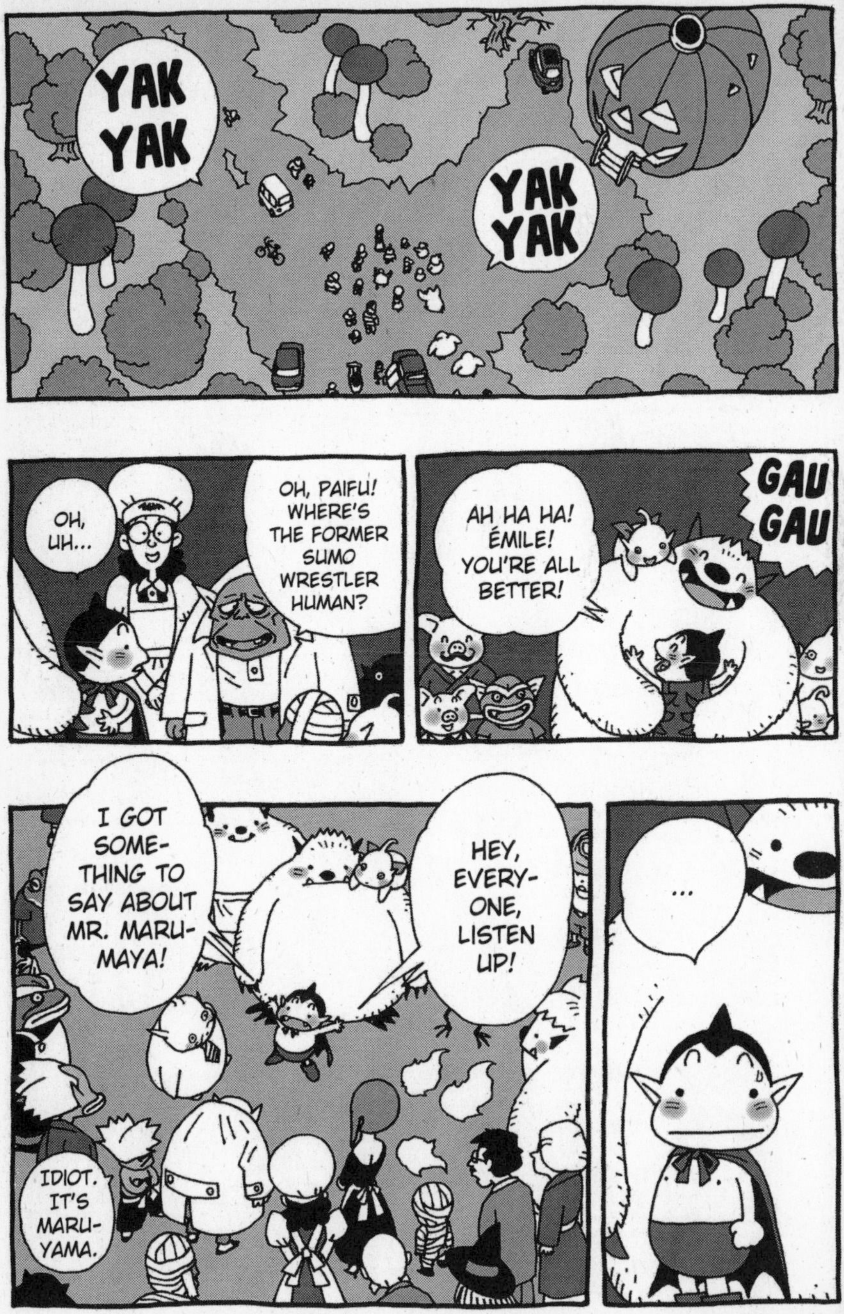
YAK YAK
YAK YAK
GAU GAU
AH HA HA! ÉMILE! YOU'RE ALL BETTER!
OH, PAIFU! WHERE'S THE FORMER SUMO WRESTLER HUMAN?
OH, UH...
...
HEY, EVERY-ONE, LISTEN UP!
I GOT SOME-THING TO SAY ABOUT MR. MARU-MAYA!
IDIOT. IT'S MARU-YAMA.

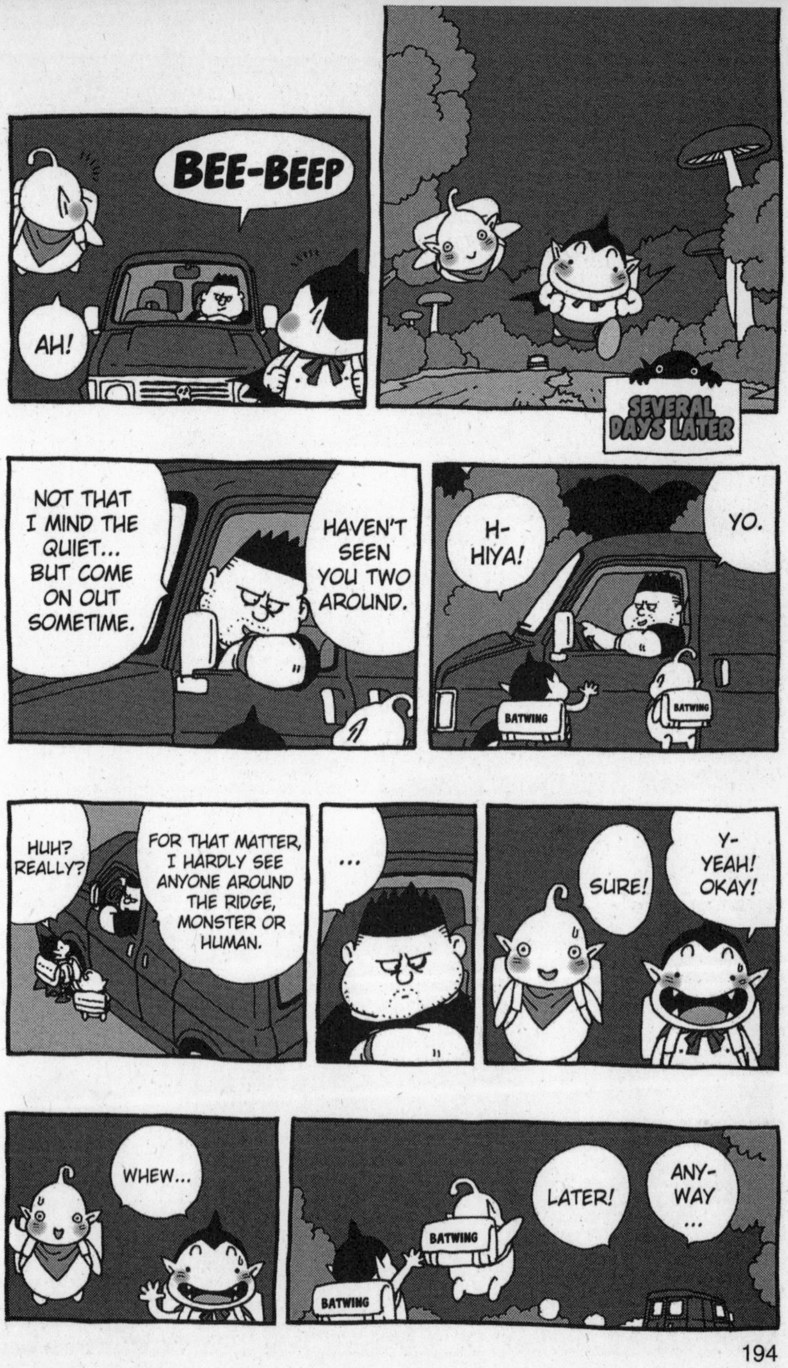
SEVERAL DAYS LATER
BEE-BEEP
AH!
YO.
H-HIYA!
BATWING
BATWING
HAVEN'T SEEN YOU TWO AROUND.
NOT THAT I MIND THE QUIET... BUT COME ON OUT SOMETIME.
Y-YEAH! OKAY!
SURE!
...
FOR THAT MATTER, I HARDLY SEE ANYONE AROUND THE RIDGE, MONSTER OR HUMAN.
HUH? REALLY?
ANY-WAY ...
LATER!
BATWING
BATWING
WHEW...

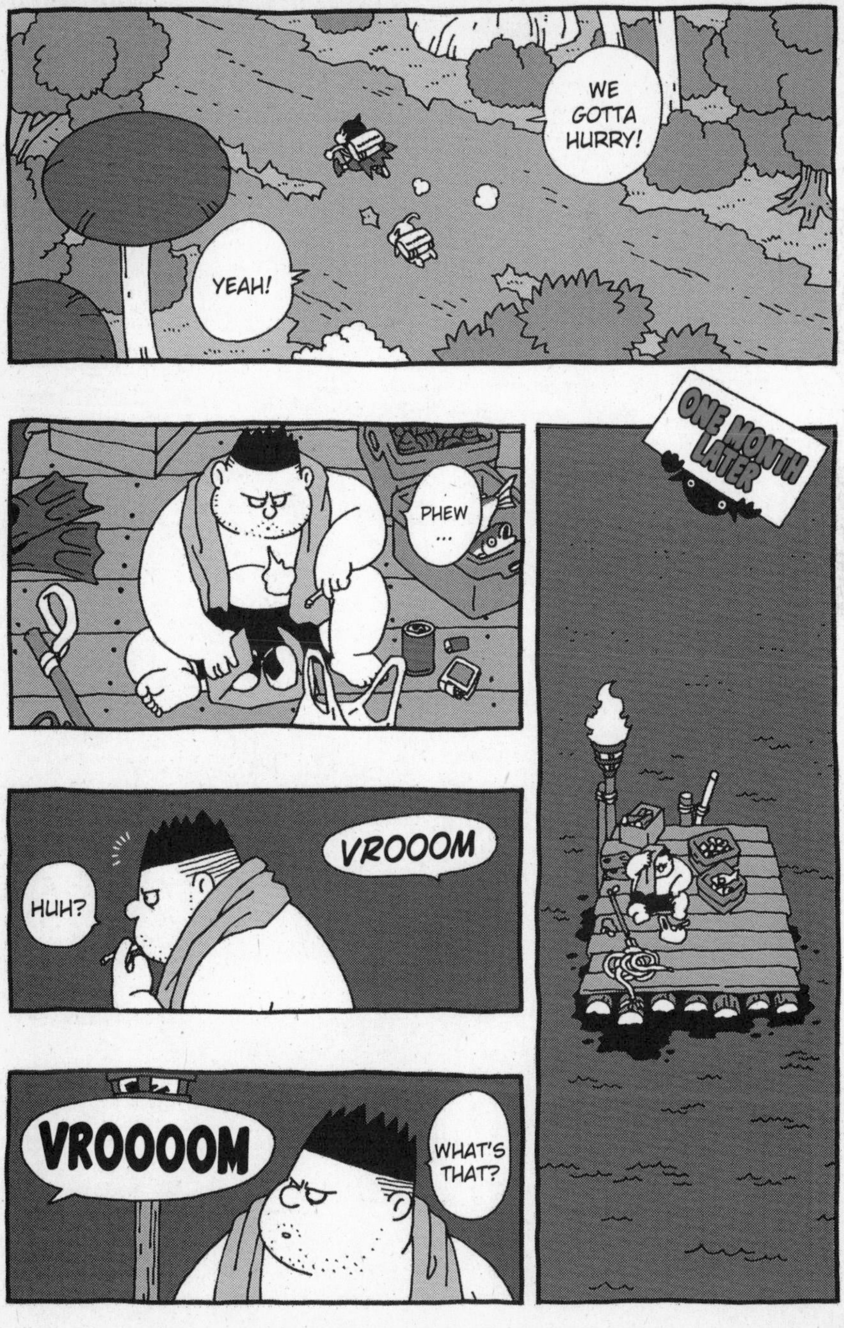
WE GOTTA HURRY!
YEAH!
ONE MONTH LATER
PHEW ...
VROOOM
HUH?
WHAT'S THAT?
VROOOOM

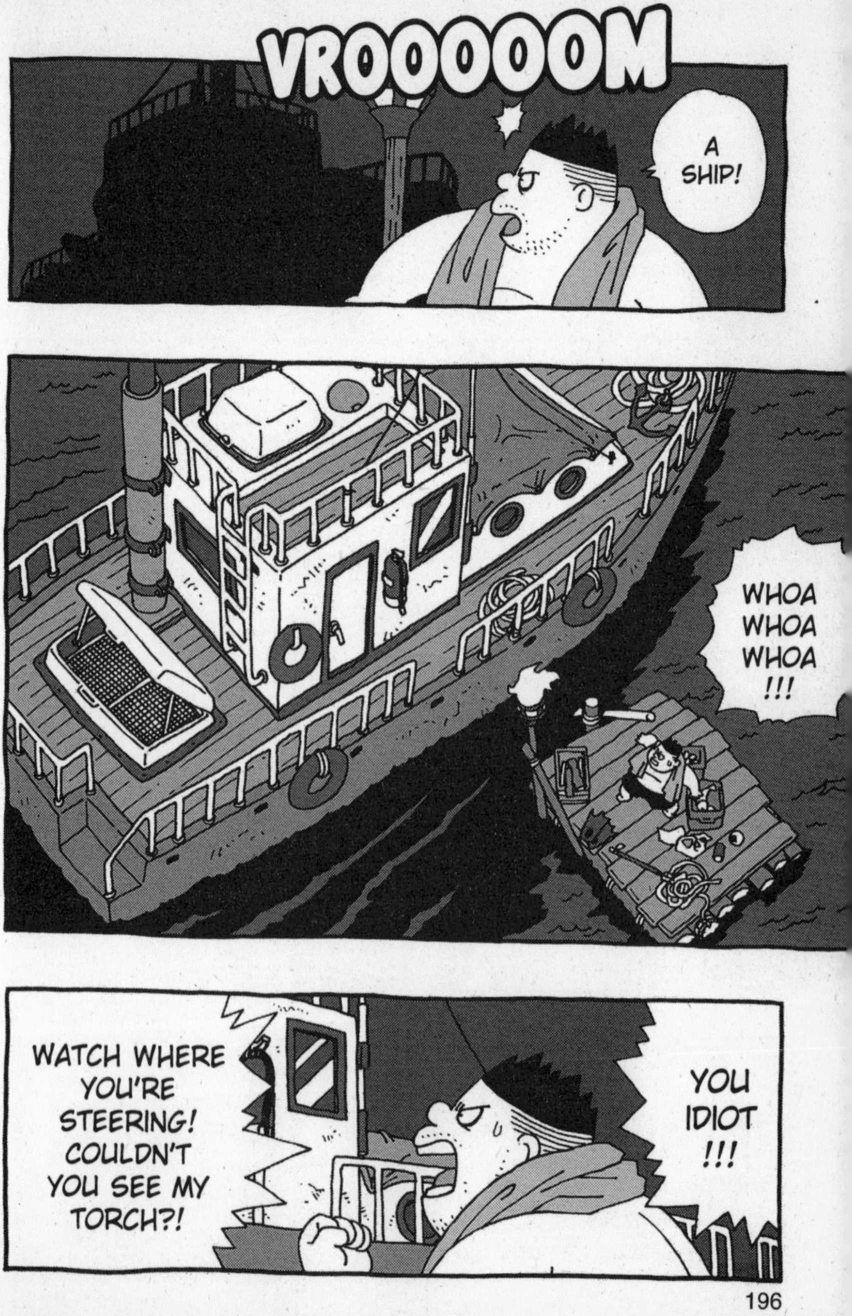
VROOOOOM
A SHIP!
WHOA WHOA WHOA !!!
YOU IDIOT !!!
WATCH WHERE YOU'RE STEERING! COULDN'T YOU SEE MY TORCH?!

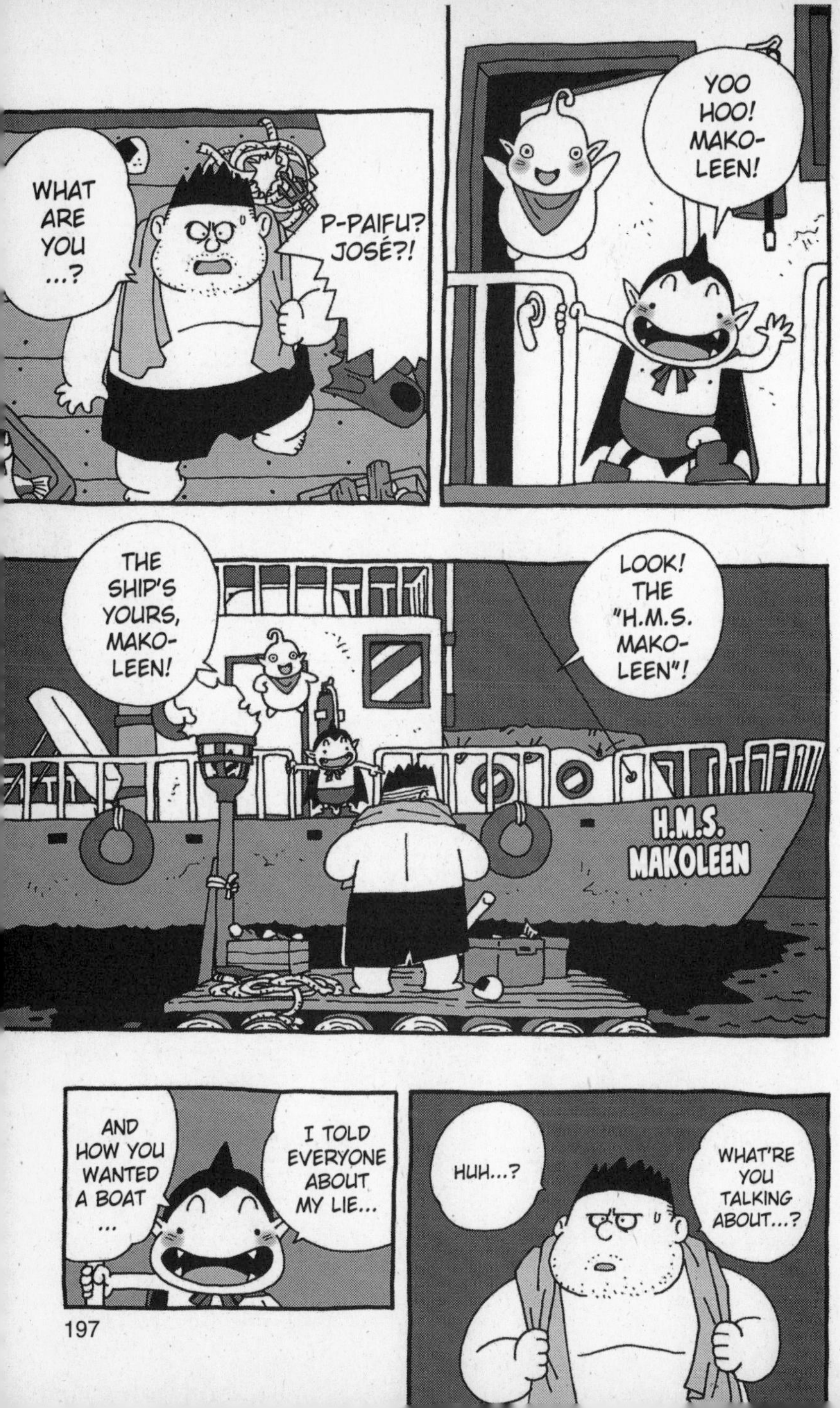
YOO HOO! MAKO-LEEN!
P-PAIFU? JOSÉ?!
WHAT ARE YOU ...?
LOOK! THE "H.M.S. MAKO-LEEN"!
THE SHIP'S YOURS, MAKO-LEEN!
H.M.S. MAKOLEEN
WHAT'RE YOU TALKING ABOUT...?
HUH...?
I TOLD EVERYONE ABOUT MY LIE...
AND HOW YOU WANTED A BOAT ...

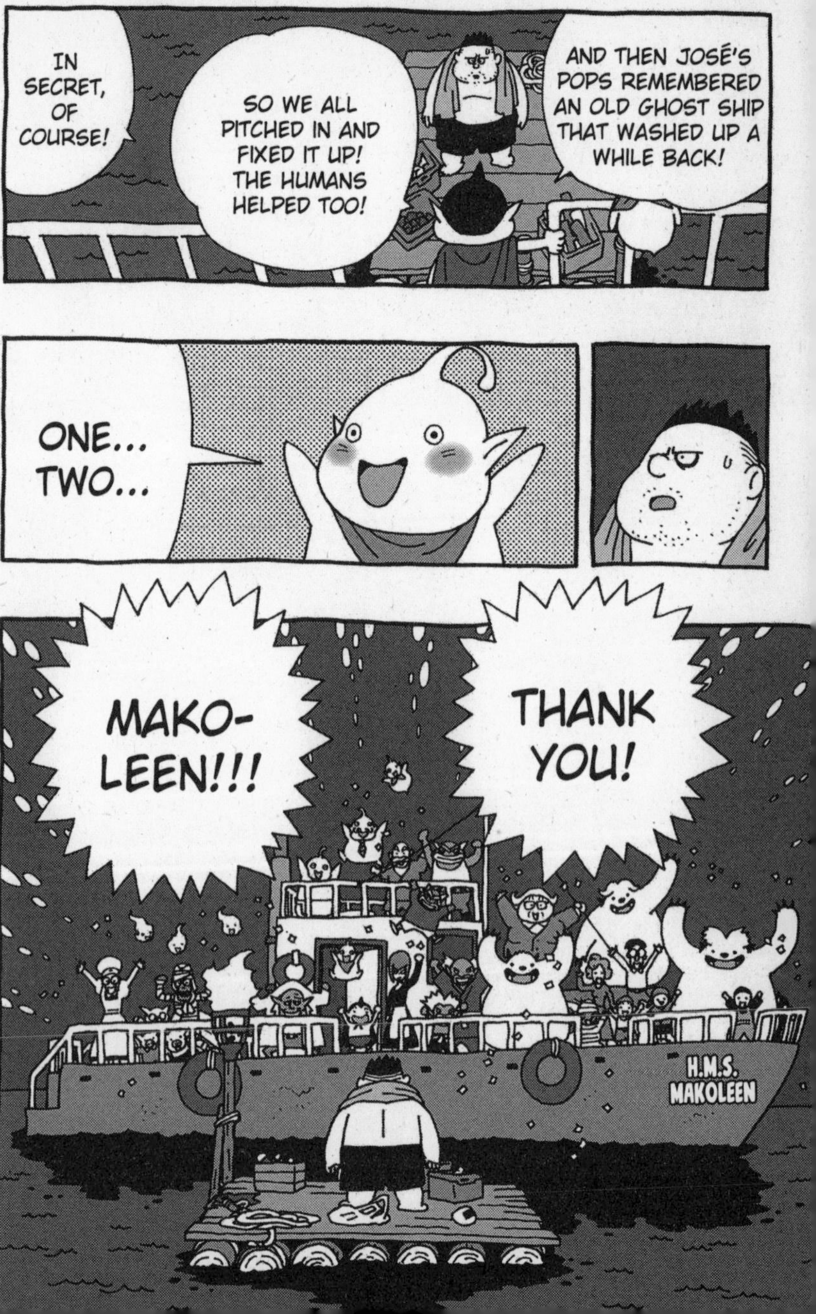
AND THEN JOSÉ'S POPS REMEMBERED AN OLD GHOST SHIP THAT WASHED UP A WHILE BACK!
SO WE ALL PITCHED IN AND FIXED IT UP! THE HUMANS HELPED TOO!
IN SECRET, OF COURSE!
ONE... TWO...
THANK YOU!
MAKO-LEEN!!!
H.M.S. MAKOLEEN

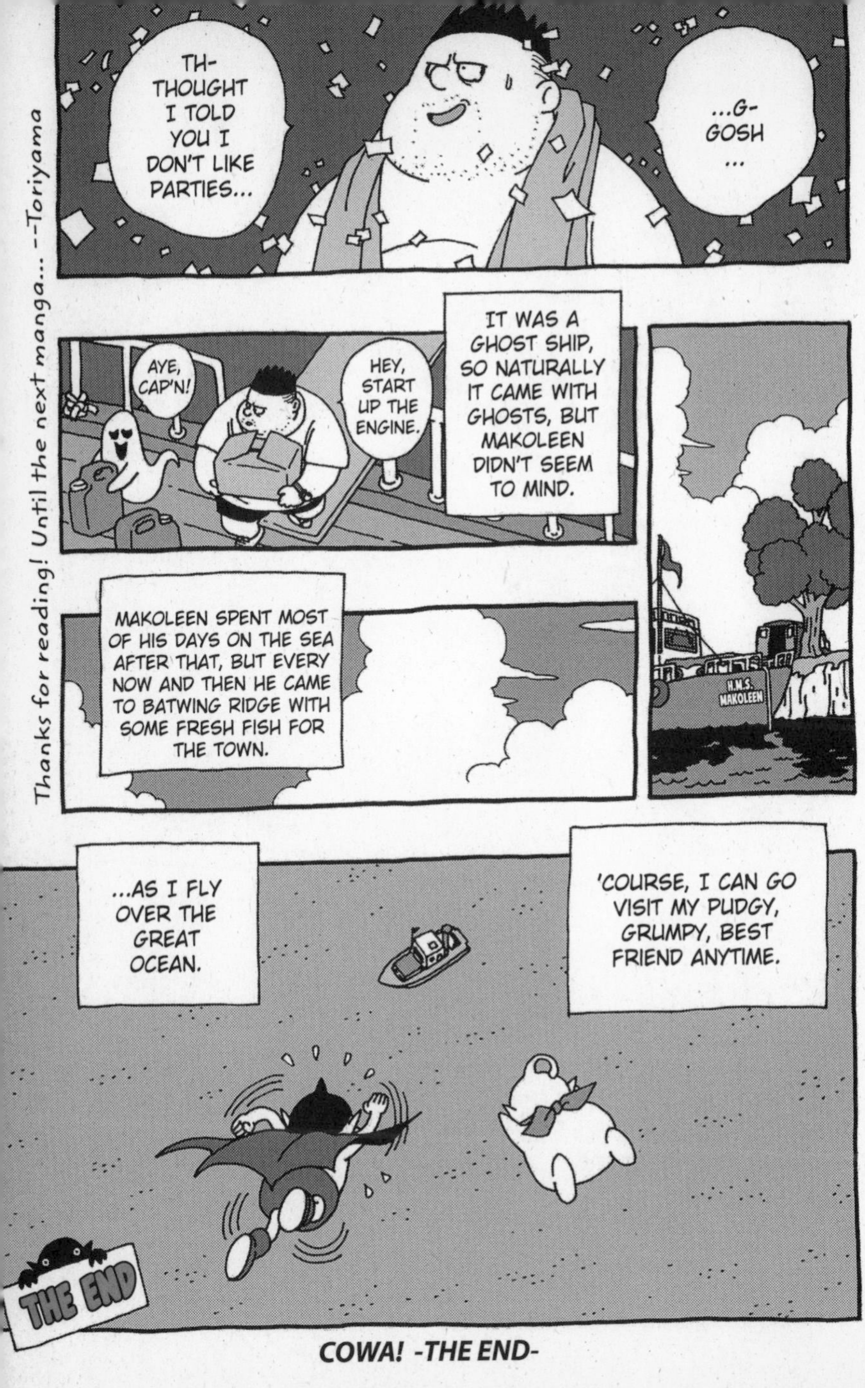
...G-GOSH...
TH-THOUGHT I TOLD YOU I DON'T LIKE PARTIES...
H.M.S. MAKOLEEN
IT WAS A GHOST SHIP, SO NATURALLY IT CAME WITH GHOSTS, BUT MAKOLEEN DIDN'T SEEM TO MIND.
HEY, START UP THE ENGINE.
AYE, CAP'N!
MAKOLEEN SPENT MOST OF HIS DAYS ON THE SEA AFTER THAT, BUT EVERY NOW AND THEN HE CAME TO BATWING RIDGE WITH SOME FRESH FISH FOR THE TOWN.
'COURSE, I CAN GO VISIT MY PUDGY, GRUMPY, BEST FRIEND ANYTIME.
...AS I FLY OVER THE GREAT OCEAN.
THE END

COWA! -THE END-

Thanks for reading! Until the next manga... --Toriyama

COWA!

AKIRA
TORIYAMA
BIRDSTUDIO

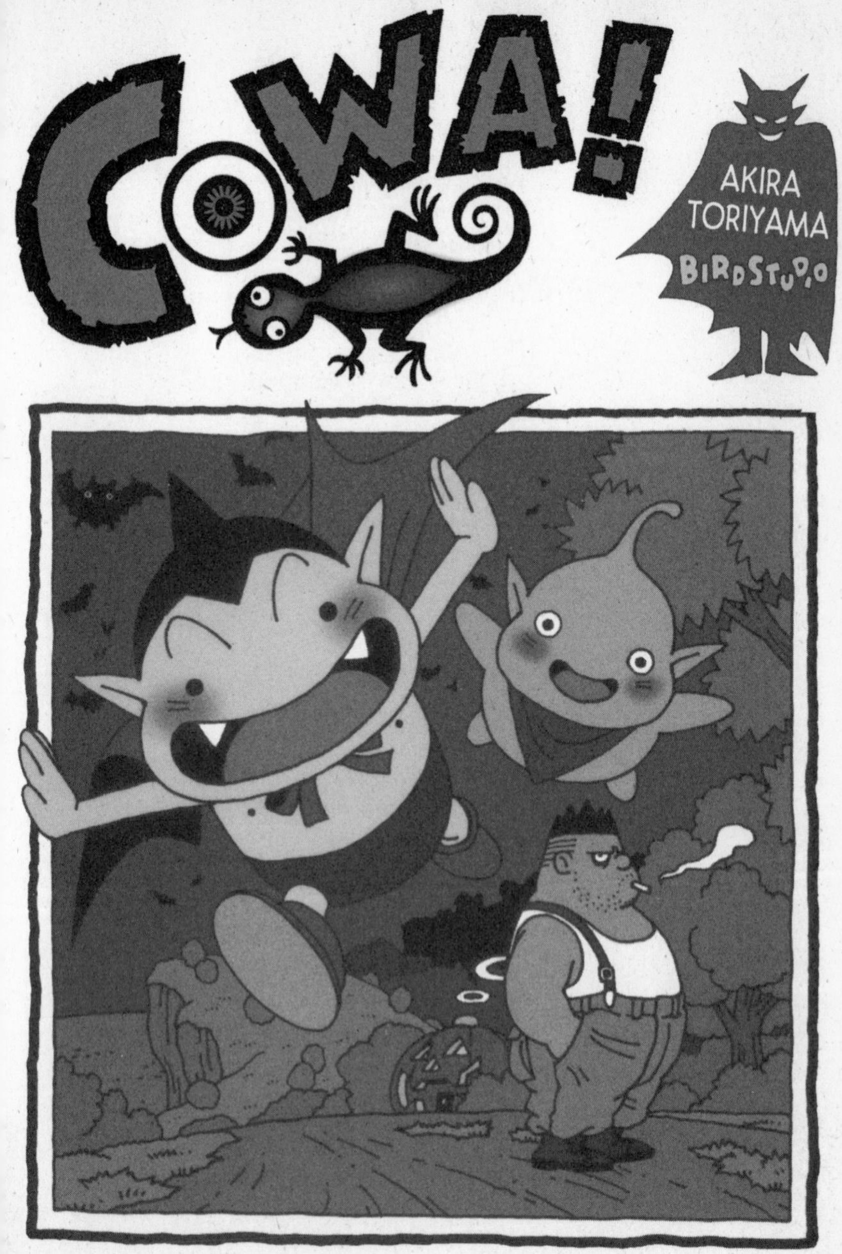

鳥 山 明

Maybe I'm just getting old, but lately my arm's been hurting, and I want to draw everything all by myself, so I decided I was done with weekly comics. But the editor for this was my first editor ever, and so, for a short time, here I am doing a weekly again... I figured if I'm going to do it, I might as well do it the way I want! I'd always wanted to try a more storybook approach and have my main character be a totally unlovable grumpy guy. So there!

-Akira Toriyama, 1998

Renowned worldwide for his playful, innovative storytelling and humorous, distinctive art style, Akira Toriyama burst onto the manga scene in 1980 with the wildly popular *Dr. Slump*. His hit series *Dragon Ball* (published in the U.S. as *Dragon Ball* and *Dragon Ball Z*) ran from 1984 to 1995 in Shueisha's *Weekly Shonen Jump* magazine. He is also known for his design work on video games such as *Dragon Quest, Chrono Trigger, Tobal No. 1* and, most recently, *Blue Dragon*. His recent manga works include *COWA!, Kajika, Sand Land, Neko Majin,* and a children's book, *Toccio the Angel.* He lives with his family in Japan.

COWA!

The SHONEN JUMP Manga Edition

STORY AND ART BY AKIRA TORIYAMA

Translation & English Adaptation/Alexander O. Smith
Touch-up Art & Lettering/Walden Wong
Design/Sean Lee
Editor/Yuki Murashige

Editor in Chief, Books/Alvin Lu
Editor in Chief, Magazines/Marc Weidenbaum
VP of Publishing Licensing/Rika Inouye
VP of Sales/Gonzalo Ferreyra
Sr. VP of Marketing/Liza Coppola
Publisher/Hyoe Narita

Printed in the U.S.A.

Published by VIZ Media, LLC
P.O. Box 77010
San Francisco, CA 94107

SHONEN JUMP Manga Edition
10 9 8 7 6 5 4 3 2 1
First printing, July 2008

PARENTAL ADVISORY
COWA! is rated A and is suitable
for readers of all ages.
ratings.viz.com

www.viz.com

store.viz.com

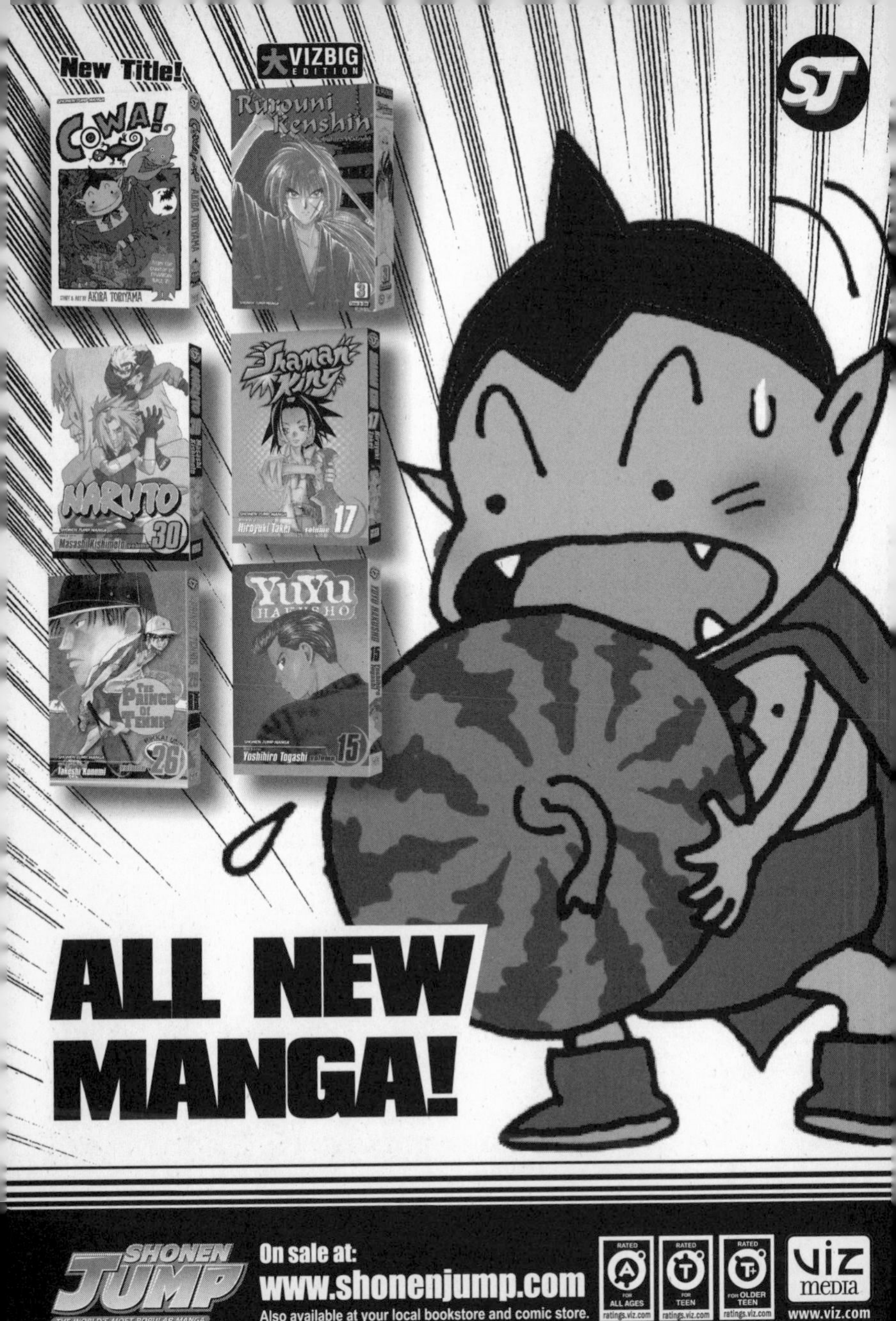
New Title!
COWA!
AKIRA TORIYAMA
VIZBIG EDITION
Rurouni Kenshin
NARUTO
30
Masashi Kishimoto
Shaman King
Hiroyuki Takei volume 17
THE PRINCE OF TENNIS
Takeshi Konomi
26
YuYu HAKUSHO
Yoshihiro Togashi volume 15
ALL NEW MANGA!
SHONEN JUMP
THE WORLD'S MOST POPULAR MANGA
On sale at:
www.shonenjump.com
Also available at your local bookstore and comic store.
RATED A FOR ALL AGES ratings.viz.com
RATED T FOR TEEN ratings.viz.com
RATED T+ FOR OLDER TEEN ratings.viz.com
VIZ MEDIA
www.viz.com

Akira Toriyama

One of the world's all-time best selling manga-kas

Born in Aichi Prefecture, Japan, Akira Toriyama grew from relative obscurity to become one of the most widely known creators of manga in the world. The early success of his *Dr. Slump* series led to the release of *Dragon Ball* (and later *Dragon Ball Z* in North America), which quickly became the most popular series of its time—with 42 volumes of graphic novels released in Japan, and a 12-year serialization in *Weekly Shonen Jump* magazine. Many of Toriyama's titles have since been made into anime, and he has provided character design direction on a number of role-playing and video games over the years. Commonly credited by many modern-day artists and authors as a major influence, chances are if you've ever read a manga, watched an anime, or picked up a joystick, you've been influenced by Toriyama as well.

GET THE COMPLETE AKIRA TORIYAMA MANGA COLLECTION TODAY!

Who can stop the spread of the Monster Flu?

The hit story of a goofy inventor and his robotic "daughter"

Dustup in the desert

Three volumes in one!

www.viz.com

COWA!

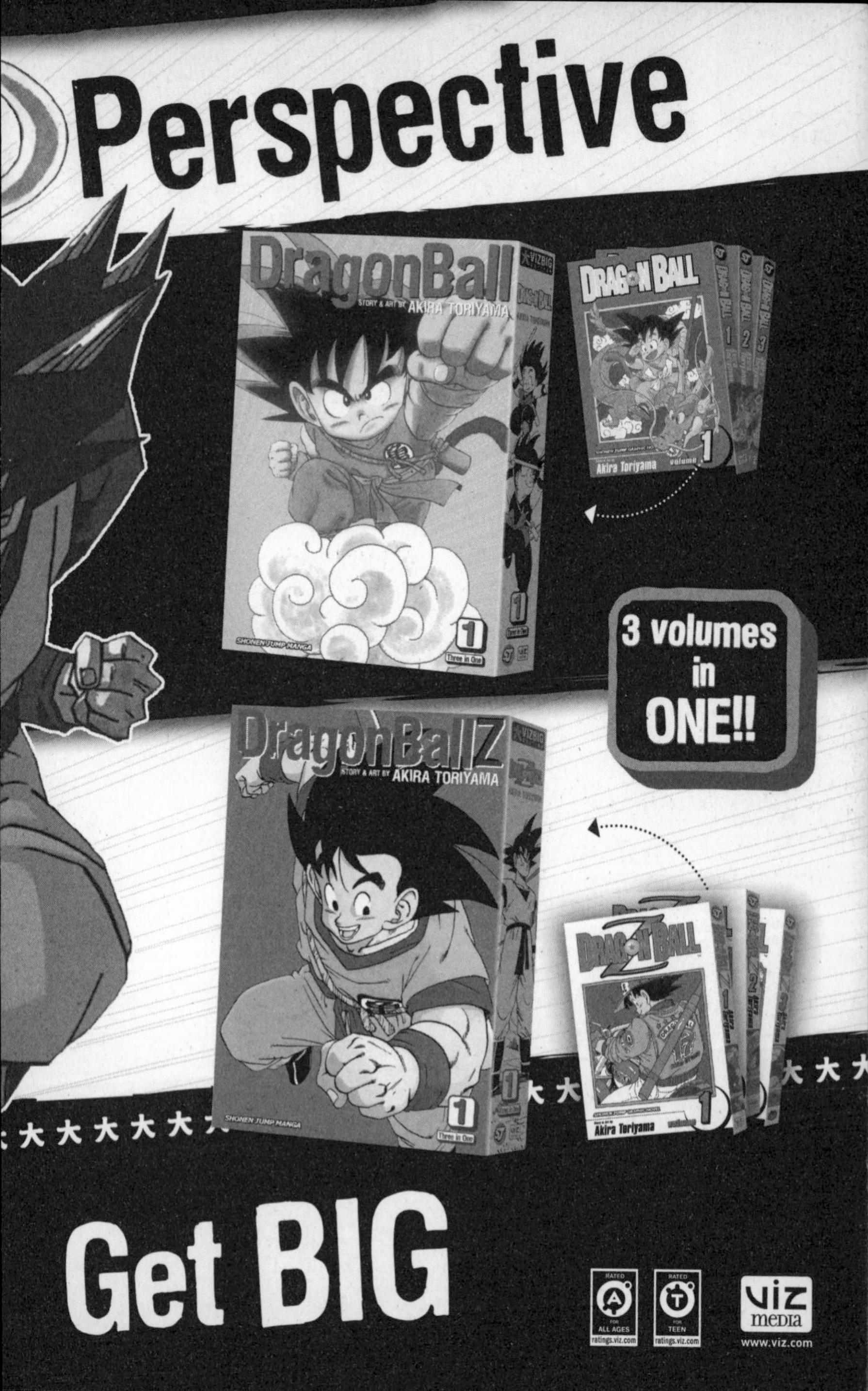
Perspective
DragonBall
STORY & ART BY AKIRA TORIYAMA
SHONEN JUMP MANGA
1
Three in One
DRAGON BALL
Akira Toriyama
volume 1
3 volumes in ONE!!
DragonBallZ
STORY & ART BY AKIRA TORIYAMA
SHONEN JUMP MANGA
1
Three in One
DRAGON BALL Z
Akira Toriyama
volume 1
Get BIG
RATED A FOR ALL AGES ratings.viz.com
RATED T FOR TEEN ratings.viz.com
viz media
www.viz.com